SMALL BUSINESS MANAGEMENT

A Planning Approach

SMALL BUSINESS MANAGEMENT

A Planning Approach

Joel Corman
Suffolk University

Robert N. Lussier
Springfield College

IRWIN

Chicago · Bogotá · Boston · Buenos Aires · Caracas
London · Madrid · Mexico City · Sydney · Toronto

IRWIN **Concerned about Our Environment**
In recognition of the fact that our company is a large end-user of fragile yet
replenishable resources, we at IRWIN can assure you that every effort is made to
meet or exceed Environmental Protection Agency (EPA) recommendations and requirements for a "greener" workplace.

To preserve these natural assets, a number of environmental policies, both companywide
and department-specific, have been implemented. From the use of 50% recycled paper in
our textbooks to the printing of promotional materials with recycled stock and soy inks to our
office paper recycling program, we are committed to reducing waste and replacing environ-
mentally unsafe products with safer alternatives.

Irwin Book Team
Sponsoring editor: *John E. Biernat*
Marketing manager: *Michael Campbell*
Project editor: *Karen J. Nelson*
Production supervisor: *Pat Frederickson*
Assistant manager, desktop services: *Jon Christopher*
Cover illustrator: *Tim Grajek*
Cover designer: *Jamie O'Neal*
Designer: *Crispin Prebys*
Compositor: *Better Graphics, Inc.*
Typeface: 10/12 Times Roman
Printer: *R. R. Donnelley & Sons Company*

Times Mirror
Higher Education Group

Library of Congress Cataloging-in-Publication Data
Corman, Joel,
    Small business management : a planning approach / Joel Corman,
  Robert N. Lussier.
      p.   cm.
    Includes index.
    ISBN 0-256-14517-2
    1. Small business—Management.   I. Lussier, Robert N.   II. Title.
  HD62.7.C673   1996
  658.02'2—dc20   95–21713

The primary reason for writing this book emanated from our goal of writing a text that would not teach about small business but would be used to teach students how to be small business managers. This book is our "how to" approach applied to a small business management textbook. Throughout this text, students learn "how to" develop a business plan; "how to" implement the business plan; and "how to" control and evaluate the implementation of the business plan. This is how the book is organized. We provide a means for students to leave the course with a small business plan in hand.

Some of the major features *Small Business Management: A Planning Approach* (SBM:APA) offers that most competitors do not are as follows:

SBM:APA is shorter, yet comprehensive. We find that the present best-selling textbooks are too long. They range from 700 to 900 pages with 20 to 27 chapters. We have written a concise book that can be completed in one semester without requiring the instructor to select chapters to omit. Our book has less than 600 pages with 15 chapters and an appendix. Yet we cover all the same major concepts in a more succinct manner.

SBM:APA focuses on planning. The organization of the text begins with an introductory section to small business, proceeds to the business planning components, goes on to explain how to implement each component of the business plan and then presents control techniques which may result in changing the business plan to ensure business plan implementation.

SBM:APA makes use of a systems approach to its content. A great number of textbooks present many topics or functions of the small business without explaining the interrelationship between the functions. Students learn about the various parts of a business (the trees) but do not become acquainted with business operations (the forest). In our text, Parts III and IV, the chapters begin with a section that explains the interrelationship between the business function of the chapter and the other functional planning components.

SBM:APA provides an integrated case. An integrated case which is presented after the textual material is used as the basis for questions in relevant chapters. Answering these questions students can develop the areas of the business plan that relate to that chapter. By the end of the book, they have developed a business plan for an actual small business. Students are now ready to develop their own small business plan.

Text Features
- Each chapter begins with an **Executive Summary** to provide an overview of the most important topics to be covered in the chapter.
- **Learning Objectives** state what the student should be able to do after completing the chapter.
- **Key Terms** are listed as the final learning objective.
- **Exhibits** are provided as a visual presentation of the material.
- Each chapter ends with a **Chapter Summary** which lists each of the major chapter headings and the important information presented in the chapter.
- The chapter summary also includes a **Glossary** of all the key terms by chapter heading.
- A list of **Questions** for review and discussion follow the chapter summary.
- **Application Exercises** present a series of exercises requiring the student to apply the concepts presented in the text to an actual business with which they are familiar.
- **Application Situations** provide two or three short cases which enable the student to apply the chapter concepts to a specific business.
- The **On-going Integrative Case** allows the student to develop a business plan for an actual small business.
- **Additional Readings** provide additional sources of information about owning and operating a small business.

Supplements to Learning
- A **Study Guide** to assist students in mastering the chapter concepts.
- **Computer Software** to use in developing a small business plan.
- **Videos** to learn about small business.
- An **Instructor's Manual** to aid the professor in developing and teaching the course.
- **Test Bank and Computer Test Bank** to aid professors in developing the contents of exams.
- **Transparency Masters** for presenting overhead projections of exhibits.

Acknowledgements

We would like to give special thanks to the reviewers of the manuscript for their recommendations: Dr. Burton Fletcher, Fletcher and Associates; Professor Lynn Hoffman, University of Northern Colorado; Professor Robert T. Justis, Louisiana State University; Professor George W. Rimler, Virginia Commonwealth University; Professor Nick Sarantakes, Austin Community College.

Thanks are also due Priscilla Sheridan without whose help this manuscript would not have been produced, to Chris Watson whose ideas produced important improvements in some of the chapters and to Lori Millett and Maria Fernandez for their invaluable assistance.

Joel Corman
Robert N. Lussier

C O N T E N T S   I N   B R I E F

C O N T E N T S

PART III

PLANNING AND IMPLEMENTATION

I   THE SMALL BUSINESS

1   SMALL BUSINESS MANAGEMENT: A PLANNING APPROACH

In this chapter, you will learn about the importance of small business to the economy and why many new businesses are being created. We will examine the advantages and disadvantages of founding or entering a small business, and we will look at some of the reasons why a business might fail. Finally we will consider what characteristics a small business owner must possess that will contribute to his or her success and entrepreneurship.

Chapter Learning Objectives

After completing this chapter, you should be able to:

- Define a small business by its size in various industries.
- Describe the advantages and disadvantages of owning a small business.
- List and discuss a business owner's personal characteristics that contribute to the success of a new business.
- Explain why so many small businesses fail and what factors lead to success.
- Define the following nine key terms in order of appearance:

  Small business
  Small Business Administration (SBA) guidelines
  Dun & Bradstreet
  Advantages of small business
  Disadvantages of small business
  Site planning
  Record keeping
  Undercapitalization
  Entrepreneur

Small Business: A New Perspective

With the downsizing of many companies and businesses during the last years of the 1980s and early 1990s, nearly everyone in the United States has had reason to reexamine their beliefs and perceptions about the nature of business. For example, following World War II, people believed that if you were lucky enough to get either a blue- or white-collar job in a large firm, you could reasonably expect lifetime security. If you were loyal and moderately hardworking, the organization would provide long-term security for you and your family. Despite the fact that you are aware that many small businesses exist—and, indeed, you probably are involved with a small business in either your professional or your private life—you probably believe that starting one, working in one, or owning or operating one is chancy. You may also believe that a small business will not pay you adequately and requires much more work than a comparable job in a large firm. When the economy was growing in the last decade, all of these ideas seemed to be true.

Today, however, the dominant theme of big business and large organizations is profitability through cost cutting and ever increasing efficiency. For firms to be competitive they have had to lay off many employees at all levels; factories have been closed or relocated. As cost cutting permeated the economy, many people began to reassess their thinking about small business and look at it differently.

With the progression to a more diverse economy, some of the assumptions about small business have changed. For example, it is commonly assumed that small business allows you to be independent and make lots of money. The harder you work, the greater will be your reward; furthermore, you will never be fired or laid off. Thus for the beginner, or those in mid-career, starting a small business is increasingly viewed as a viable option. This chapter will define and examine the myths and realities of small business, while the following chapters will examine in more detail how to operate and control your small business.

The Importance Of and Trends in Small Business

Research has shown and statistics have confirmed that small business is the chief job generator in the United States. In fact, even in the slow economy of the 1990s, the small business sector hires almost 9 out of 10 workers.[1] From 1980 through 1986, 31.8 million jobs were created by start-ups; from 1986 through 1988, the economy created 6.17 million new jobs, and small business contributed over 45 percent of these jobs.[2] "Most of these jobs, as David Birch would argue, are created by entrepreneurial growth-oriented companies."[3]

In 1990, an estimated 20.4 million tax returns for small business were filed; fewer than 7,000 of those businesses filing would be considered big business (more than 500 employees).[4] Important to the economy of small businesses is the U.S. Office of Advocacy's projection that from 1992 to 2005, 68 percent of future employment growth is likely to come from small firms. In this time frame 13.3 million jobs will be created; approximately 7.9 million of these jobs will be created by small business.[5] Exhibit 1.1 illustrates this trend. Small business job creation in 1993 appears to confirm this trend, as shown in Exhibit 1.2.[6]

Exhibit 1.1

Where the jobs will be: 1990–2005.

Job Creation by Small Business:

The historic trend of 1975 to 1990 . . .   . . . will continue from 1992 to 2005 . . .   . . . with services leading the way.

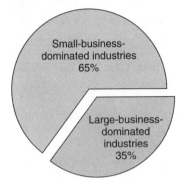

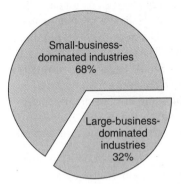

Small-business-dominated industries creating the most new jobs, 1992-2005

Eating and drinking places:
2.2 million jobs

Building material and gardening supply stores:
1.4 million jobs

Offices of physicians:
1.2 million jobs

Source: Adapted by U.S. Small Business Administration, Office of Advocacy, from projections published by the Bureau of Labor Statistics.

Exhibit 1.2

Job creation in 1993: What were the fastest-growing industries?

Small Business Job Creation in 1993

Small-business-dominated industries were the biggest job generators . . .   . . . with the following eight industries leading the way:

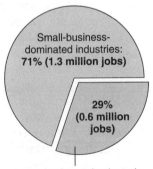

Large-business-dominated and "indeterminate" industries

- Personnel supply services*:
  296,100 jobs
- Eating and drinking places:
  281,400 jobs
- Special trade contractors:
  156,400 jobs
- Wholesale trade—durable goods:
  65,900 jobs

- Employment agencies:
  61,300 jobs
- Offices and clinics of medical doctors:
  56,100 jobs
- Miscellaneous retail stores:
  40,300 jobs
- Agricultural services:
  39,800 jobs

Source: Adapted by U.S. Small Business Administration, Office of Advocacy, from data published by the Bureau of Labor Statistics.
* A large-business-dominated industry; all others are small-business-dominated.

Small Business Defined

Before addressing the characteristics intrinsic to the success and failure of small businesses, it is important to define the term "small business." A **small business** is a firm that is *independently owned and operated and is too small to be dominant in its field.* While this serves as a generally satisfactory definition, we must be much more precise, since size is relative to a specific industry; that is, what might be considered a large business—one employing many people—is actually small for a specific industry. Therefore to establish a common basis for discussion, we use the United States **Small Business Administration's guidelines**, which are *those characteristics of a firm that define a small business,* in order to ensure that we are talking about the same kind of organizations.

According to the Small Business Administration, the following guidelines apply for small businesses within different fields:

1. Retail: annual sales receipts under $2 million.
2. Services: annual sales receipts under $2 million.
3. Wholesaling: annual sales receipts under $8.5 million.
4. Construction: annual receipts (average of preceding three fiscal years) under $5 million.
5. Manufacturing: fewer than 250 employees as general rule, but up to 1,500 employees for certain types based on industry standards.

Success or Failure

You should recognize that starting and/or operating a small business includes the possibility of success as well as the risk of failure. When forming a new business, an aspiring entrepreneur must take into account those factors that influence the success or failure of the venture. This chapter will analyze why so many small businesses fail every year and the factors inherent in those that succeed. The factors inherent in business failures are those characteristics or operating methodologies that are defined as causing business failures. Many experts cite lack of planning, improper financing, and poor management as the main causes of business failure. According to **Dun & Bradstreet,** *a financial services organization that collects, maintains, and analyses information concerning business activities,* the overall new business failure rates are summarized in Exhibit 1.3. With the odds stacked

EXHIBIT 1.3   Small business failure rates

By the end of	Percent that fail
1st year	24.1
5th year	40.1
10th year	91.7

Source: Dun & Bradstreet, *Business Failure Records,* p. 17.

heavily against success, it is surprising that so many new businesses are formed each year.

There appears to be a direct link between start-up dynamics and the size of the enterprise. The odds of survival and future expansion of a new firm can be directly related to the number of employees that the firm needs and can afford to hire. In other words, "The survival rates of new jobs increase sharply with employer size."[7] From the data it seems that

> There appears to be a minimum threshold size of at least 5 to 10 employees—and 20 is even better—and of sales of $500,000 to $6 million. . . . Based on a cross-section of all new firms one-year survival rates jump from approximately 78 percent for firms having up to 19 employees to approximately 95 percent for firms with between 20 and 99 employees."[8]

Exhibit 1.4 illustrates these survival rates.

Advantages of a Small Business

What, then, are the advantages of a small business—that is, an enterprise that falls within the definition of size in terms of sales or number of employees? The **advantages of a small business** are *the benefits derived from being in or owning a small business.* One important advantage is that a small business can maintain a closer relationship with its customers, employees, and its suppliers than a larger business. Since a small business has a smaller base, it can provide more individual attention to its customers such as manufacturing custom-made products or offering personal service.

Because of lower overhead, smaller firms can perform more efficiently than larger firms. Small firms have greater flexibility because their size allows them to adopt new processes, services, materials, and products. Larger firms, on the other hand, tend to be less flexible, since they are usually committed to large-scale production and operations based on economies of scale.[9] Small companies encourage competition in design and efficiency and therefore help prevent larger firms from forming monopolies. The owner of a small business retains an element of control and autonomy that is dispersed in a larger company.

EXHIBIT 1.4   One-year survival rates by firm's size

Firm Size (employees)	Survival %
0–9	77.8
10–19	85.5
20–30	93.3
100–240	95.3
250+	100.0

Small businesses tend to produce well-rounded people because they provide a greater variety of learning experiences and more potential for diversified interaction. Larger companies, on the other hand, require that their people specialize and thus limit the breadth of their working experiences. The opportunities for freedom in decision making and the variety of activities is therefore greater within a small firm. This can lead to more creative and aggressive leadership. These characteristics tend to attract good management personnel and in doing so reduce the overall chance of failure. Management people are attracted to smaller firms because: (1) advancement with smaller firms can be more accelerated; (2) in a smaller firm, personnel tend to have greater responsibilities and duties; and (3) work experience tends to be more diversified.

Disadvantages of a Small Business

As many benefits as there are to running a small business, however, the business owner must face an equal, if not greater, number of the **disadvantages of a small business,** including potential shortcomings. Some of the most obvious handicaps faced by small business are *the inability to hire qualified employees, lack of funds for expansion, tax burdens, limited or non-existent credit with suppliers, high costs for advertising, and coping with competition.* Many of these disadvantages can be directly linked to improper planning and misuse of funds. As previously mentioned, the main factors inherent in most business failures revolve around:

- Inadequate managerial ability
- Inadequate financing
- Poor competitive position

Reasons a Business Might Fail

Inadequate Management Ability

Problems exist because managers cannot specialize in any one area but rather must function with broad-based knowledge. Expert knowledge in specific functional areas does not guarantee management ability. Often management ability is a skill gained separately from functional knowledge. The best salesperson may have little interest in, or ability to, manage an organization that requires knowledge in all aspects of the business operation.

Tasks of a Small Business Owner

A small business owner is expected to efficiently manage every aspect of the business, such as the initial strategy and how the business is going to operate internally and externally. A business plan can provide assistance in resolving questions such as determining how much space is needed for operations and how much space to leave for future expansion for diversification into other lines or fields. You must also contend with employee issues such as the number needed initially, task specialization, compensation, scheduling, and the amount and extent of delegation of responsibility.

You must act as a financial adviser for the business and be able to interact well with employees, customers, and suppliers. You must possess strong management and organizational skills, which are required for the daily running of the operation. In addition to knowing your own business thoroughly, you must keep abreast of your competition, cyclical trends of your industry, and the environment in which your business is to operate. The small business operator must be aware of the external environment and the forces that impact upon his or her operations. Looked at from this perspective, it is not surprising that so many businesses fail, but that some succeed.

Good Overall Planning

As a new business owner, you must look at several factors that fall under the heading of good planning such as site analysis, good merchandising policies, thorough record keeping and expense analysis, and the determination of your breakeven point. All these factors are incorporated into a business plan, which will be discussed in Chapter 5.

Site Planning

An important reason for business failure is poor location. **Site planning is** *the determination of how a specific location is to be utilized in the most efficient manner consistent with the needs of the business.* In many industries, the site can make or break the operation. Since each industry dictates the specifics of the location, a site analysis explores the significant aspects of the potential area in relation to the product or service that the business wishes to sell. This material is discussed in Chapter 8.

Marketing

Marketing is *the selling of a product or service.* The overall presentation of the product can be incorporated into good merchandising policies. This is best explained by the four Ps of marketing strategy (price, place, product, promotion), which will be discussed in Chapter 7. Once you have both determined the product or service you wish to sell or provide and measured consumer demand, you must then calculate the price through cost accounting. At this point promotional decisions are made based on advertising expense as well as the overall need to educate the consumer to the existence of the product. This material is discussed in Chapter 7.

Record Keeping

It is extremely important that you keep complete and adequate financial records. **Record keeping** requires *maintaining detailed information about purchases, sales, orders, expenses, and cash balances* from a double-entry bookkeeping system. This information can and should be used for future planning.

Certain rules should be followed when handling finances:

1. Separate personal cash from the business.

2. The owner should receive a salary or "draw" in the case of a partnership or proprietorship.
3. Utilize a bank account for the business's funds and to deposit cash receipts daily.
4. Record incoming cash along with sources and receipt dates.
5. Pay all business expenses by check to ensure a record.
6. Obtain a cash receipt for all petty cash disbursements.

Record keeping also involves keeping track of employees, maintaining insurance records, and complying with various local, state, and federal requirements.

The firm's future stability will always be dependent upon adequate records about the past. A classic example of this was reported in *The Wall Street Journal.*[10] At one time the Long Island Railroad, one of the nation's largest commuter railroads, lost significant amounts of money because their cash position was unknown; large amounts of money owed to the railroad had not been billed; some bills were erroneously paid twice; and bond redemptions had not been recorded. The same problems arise in small businesses, but they are not as well documented. From the author's experience, most small businesses keep inadequate records. This material is discussed in Chapter 12.

Improper Financing

A new business must have adequate capital to obtain a stable position. A cash-poor firm has little or no bargaining power, and as a result it must struggle to meet creditors' demands. **Undercapitalization** means that *a new firm lacks the money to enter into the venture properly*. Undercapitalization in an ongoing firm implies that too much money is tied up in fixed assets, accounts receivable, or obsolete inventory. This material is discussed in Chapter 12.

Some common causes of financial business failure can be grouped into several categories:

- Poor sales
- High operating costs
- Poor credit and collection policies
- Too many fixed assets
- Too much of the wrong inventory
- Inflation
- Taxes
- Competition
- Government regulation
- Interest rates

Lacking proper managerial skills, it is often impossible for a manager to effectively control all of these potential failure points. Therefore, hiring an accountant (if the firm is large enough) or consulting an outside accounting firm may provide the expertise required to resolve financial problems. The Small Business Administration provides low-cost assistance for the business that cannot afford outside help. An analysis of the firm's financial records will enable an expert to advise the firm of possible strategies.

Poor Management

Poor management is the main reason businesses fail, according to Dun & Bradstreet. Dun & Bradstreet is a company that has been analyzing and reporting on the financial health of American business for well over a century and is a very credible source of information about the reasons for business failure. Businesses seem to fail for the same reasons year after year; the seven most common factors are listed in Exhibit 1.5.

In Exhibit 1.6, the last four reasons are grouped together because they are directly related to the qualifications of the owner-manager.

Dun & Bradstreet uses the elements listed in Exhibit 1.7 in each of the major categories.

Poor management encompasses incompetence. Many new small business ventures are started by people who lack extensive knowledge of many aspects of oper-

EXHIBIT 1.5   Causes of business failures

Percent of Business Failures	Cause of Failures
3.9	Neglect
4.6	Disaster
2.2	Fraud
63.5	Economic factors
1.0	Lack of experience
24.1	Poor financial practices
1.0	Lack of strategy

Source: Dun & Bradstreet, *Business Failure Record* (1993), p. 18.

EXHIBIT 1.6   External reasons why businesses fail

Cause	Percentage
Bad management	89.6
Neglect	3.9
Fraud	2.2
Disaster	4.6

Source: Dun & Bradstreet, *Business Failure Record* (1993), p. 18.

Exhibit 1.7   Causes of business failure

Neglect
Business conflicts
Family problems
Lack of commitment
Poor work habits

Disaster

Fraud

Economic Factors
High interest rates
Inadequate sales
Industry weakness
Insufficient profits
Inventory difficulties
Not competitive
Poor growth prospects
Poor location

Lack of Experience
Lack of business knowledge
Lack of line experience
Lack of managerial experience

Poor Financial Practices
Burdensome institutional debt
Heavy operating expenses
Insufficient capital

Lack of Strategy
Excessive fixed assets
Overexpansion
Receivables difficulties

Source: Dun & Bradstreet, *Business Failure Record* (1993), p. 9.

ating a business. You must become competent not only in your own field but in many related areas. Since you typically cannot afford to hire outside experts as you start out, you must rely on your own abilities.

We should also consider business owners whose experience has not provided them with a balanced background in all areas of running a business. While the average person may be an expert in one area, he or she usually lacks the experience or knowledge in other fields, which causes an imbalance in his or her management skills. It is very hard to compensate for a small business owner's deficiencies. A new business is usually strapped for money and therefore cannot afford to hire persons who have extensive knowledge in other areas. Also, many small businesses have only one manager and for efficiency or financial reasons cannot hire additional management personnel.

Many people venturing into a new business do so lacking knowledge of management principles or how to manage the day-to-day operation of a small business. Unless you have worked in the same business you are planning to start (and frequently entrepreneurs have), or you are willing to spend the time thoroughly investigating and learning a new business, your chances of success are greatly reduced. If the business has sufficient capital, one possibility would be to hire a consultant or expert in the field to help set up the business and monitor it until you have gained an adequate knowledge of its operations. This could be a costly strategy and would place the success or failure of the business in the hands of the consultant rather than the owner. The business owner who lacks sufficient capital might seek a partner who could contribute additional funds. Most small businesses need additional funds to finance operations and growth.

Requirements for Success

What then are the requirements for a successful manager? The **factors inherent in business success** are *those characteristics or operating methodologies that are defined as causing business success.* A great deal depends on the owner's own personality. Generally speaking, successful managers tend to exhibit in varying degrees the following desirable characteristics.

Energy
It takes a great deal of energy to form and operate your own business. A small business starts through the hard work and effort devoted to it. One of the greatest rewards the small business owner can achieve is developing a successful business that is a direct result of his or her own efforts.

Initiative
The small business owner must possess the entrepreneur's initiative to operate independently. In addition to having the initiative, you must also be a calculated risk taker, willing to travel an unmapped road toward potential profitability, independence, and security. Small business ventures require people who are looking for independence and creativity as opposed to the potential long-term security offered by established firms.

Organization
It is very important that from the time the venture is conceived you become meticulous about the records you maintain so that they are easily accessible in a form that is usable not only by you but also by creditors, consultants, and others who may need access to the information.

Appearance
You should possess an approachable demeanor for customers and business contacts by appearing appropriately dressed; your manner should be one that conveys a willingness to be helpful and attentive to customer needs. It is an asset if you reflect an attitude that portrays integrity and honesty.

Technical Competence
You must have, or be willing to acquire, good technical know-how of your product or service as well as a general knowledge of your industry. For example, you would naturally want to keep up on new developments that could have an effect on your business.

Administrative Ability
You must have an aptitude for running the business, including decisions concerning employee work schedules, identifying and determining employee tasks, supervising every aspect of the daily operation to ensure that it runs smoothly, and setting up and running the record-keeping portion of the business.

Good Judgment
You must develop the skill that enables you to foresee the ramifications of possible alternatives so that you have the best chance of choosing the optimal course. Learn to recognize how and when to act.

Restraint and Patience
Try to acquire the skill of not overreacting to a situation or acting prematurely. A good manager needs to be level-headed in order to calmly make effective decisions. As you start out, you must be aware of the limitations of your employees so that you do not expect them to immediately achieve expert status.

Ability to Communicate Well
This is crucial to the efficient operation of a business. You must be able to communicate with your employees. By not clearly conveying your thoughts, time, energy, customers, and inventory could be lost.

Leadership Qualities
Leadership is important in order to maintain a chain of command within your business. Your position as a small business owner involves knowing when and how to act, when to talk and when to listen, when the rules need to be strictly followed, and when you can be flexible. And above all you must develop a reliable ability to judge people and employees.

Preownership Experience
Experience you have already acquired dealing with employees, customers, and suppliers in a particular or related industry and having been exposed to the running of a similar operation in the past can be invaluable when you start your own firm.

Good Managerial Ability

As a manager you should practice good customer relations. This involves a knowledge of consumerism, which includes value, safety, adequacy, and price policies. Value entails making sure that the consumer is receiving something worthwhile for the money he or she is spending. You should also be aware of safety, both with the product and the premises; you should not only sell the consumer a product, guaranteeing its safety if properly used, but also provide the customer with a safe place in which to purchase the product. When selling the product, you should have an adequate knowledge of competitors' products as well as your own so that you can best inform the buyer about a particular product's benefits and limitations. Your business should also maintain an adequate inventory of the product, replacement parts, and if need be, easy access to repair facilities. The selling price should not be exorbitant but should be set so that your business makes a reasonable profit for producing, storing, transporting, marketing, and selling the merchandise. An astute manager, you will keep abreast of changing consumer trends, government legislation, and regulations so that you can best adapt and market the product in the face of changing situations.

Community/Ethical/Social Responsibility

The importance of adopting community, ethical, and social responsibilities as a way of doing business is becoming increasingly important to the businessperson. As an individual, the business owner may feel obligated to have high standards in the way the business is conducted. Should these be absent, however, customers may impose them from outside. In Chapter 4, which deals with the legal environment and social responsibilities, we will fully discuss these concepts.

Entrepreneurship

While many small business owners think of themselves as entrepreneurs, running a small business and being an entrepreneur are not the same thing. In fact the ability to operate an organization requires different skills and abilities than those required for being an entrepreneur. Successful long-term operation of a business requires managerial skills, while being an entrepreneur requires innovative skills. One can be a successful small business operator without being an entrepreneur. Confusion exists because nearly all entrepreneurial activities begin as a small business operation. Once the "newness" or "innovation" in the organization has settled down and production for profit begins, managerial talents take over, as shown in Exhibit 1.8.

What, then, is an entrepreneur and how is an entrepreneur different from a manager? An **entrepreneur** is *a person who has the need to build and create something new.* If the organization is to survive, the entrepreneur must be a businessperson, but not all businesspeople are entrepreneurs.

Exhibit 1.8

Changing managerial needs

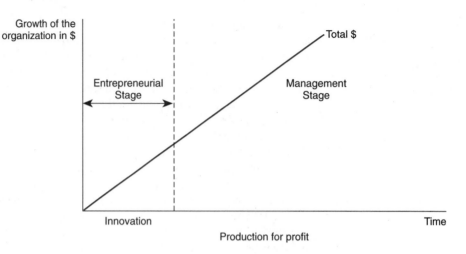

Entrepreneurs . . . . possess a strong need for control, independence, keen intuition, a need to build and create, and an ability to simplify complex problems. In addition, they are hard workers who willingly accept responsibility. They tend to be optimistic and to have an exceptionally strong desire to achieve.[11]

Entrepreneurs are a special type of individual, having specific characteristics in addition to those necessary to operate a small business. This does not mean that entrepreneurs are risk takers. In fact, many of them are very conservative in their approach to their operations. Not all small-business people are entrepreneurs nor need they be. If, however, you are an entrepreneur, you should recognize the fact and act accordingly. This is not to suggest that starting and operating a successful company should be restricted to entrepreneurs, for if the contrary is true, many more people could become successful small business operators. It is a game any-one could play.

While tests cannot predict success and should not be used to predict or define entrepreneurial ability, you should look at one of the tests, scoring yourself to iden-tify whether you could be an entrepreneur. If you score high in the test, it might indicate that you have entrepreneurial characteristics. Using Exhibits 1.9 and 1.10, you can score yourself and compare your scores to the combined responses of entrepreneurs and business managers. High scores indicate similarity to this population.

Further, even if you possess the personal characteristics necessary for entre-preneurial success, several other factors can greatly enhance your success.

First, in order to succeed you need, aside from talent, a general feeling of self-confidence and a belief in your ability to succeed. Although some may be born with self-confidence, typically it takes some years of experience to gain it. As you reach

---

EXHIBIT 1.9   **Entrepreneurial style inventory**

This self-assessment exercise is designed to assess your entrepreneurial character traits. As you complete the Inventory, give a *high rank* to those words which best characterize the level of innovativeness and creativity as well as managerial skills and abilities you bring to your working environment; and give a *low rank* to the words which are least characteristic of the way you behave.

It may be difficult to choose the words that best describe your entrepreneurial style because there are clearly no right or wrong answers. Different combinations of characteristics described in the inventory are equally good. The aim of the inventory is to characterize how you behave, not to evaluate your entrepreneurial success or ability.

Instructions

There are fifteen sets of four words listed below. Rank in order of preference each set of four words, assigning a *4* to the word which best characterizes your entrepreneurial style, a *3* to the word which next best serves to characterize your behavior, a *2* to the next most characteristic words, and a *1* to the word which is least characteristic of your workmanship qualities. You must assign a different rank number to each of the four words in each set. No ties allowed.

Character Traits of Entrepreneurs

1. ___ Innovative	___ Decisive	___ Realistic	___ Idealistic
2. ___ Creative	___ Logical	___ Systematic	___ Controlled
3. ___ Enthusiastic	___ Energetic	___ Easygoing	___ Agreeable
4. ___ Persevering	___ Persistent	___ Painstaking	___ Committed
5. ___ Imaginative	___ Bold	___ Calm	___ Tactful
6. ___ Ingenious	___ Efficient	___ Reliable	___ Modest
7. ___ Confident	___ Dominant	___ Purposeful	___ Loyal
8. ___ Understanding	___ Thoughtful	___ Dependable	___ Sensitive
9. ___ Involved	___ Responsible	___ Diplomatic	___ Cooperative
10. ___ Soft-spoken	___ Quiet	___ Conservative	___ Patient
11. ___ Stimulating	___ Objective	___ Strong	___ Prudent
12. ___ Reserved	___ Disciplined	___ Thorough	___ Consummate
13. ___ Perceptive	___ Conscientious	___ Considerate	___ Sincere
14. ___ Intelligent	___ Intellectual	___ Practical	___ Introspective
15. ___ Persuasive	___ Determined	___ Influential	___ Integrative

FIN _____   GRI _____   MIN _____   BIN _____

OD. ☐   OD. ☐   OD. ☐   OD. ☐

ID. ☐   ID. ☐   ID. ☐   ID. ☐

Scoring the Entrepreneurial Style Inventory

To obtain your score on the four dimensions measured by the Inventory (FIN) Finders, (GRI) Grinders, (MIN) Minders, and (BIN) Binders, sum each column and place the total on the line under the column. Next, for the column with your dominant style, total the values you gave the odd numbered words and then the even numbered words placing these scores in the boxes below the column. Transfer the four raw scores to the Entrepreneurial Style Profile Chart on the last page by placing a mark by the number you scored on each of the four dimensions. Connect these four marks with straight lines. For interpretation of your profile, read the following section.

Source: Joe Singer and Joan Baker, Professional Support Services, 12705 South Mur-Len, Olathe, Kansas 66062.

Exhibit 1.10

Entrepreneurial style profile

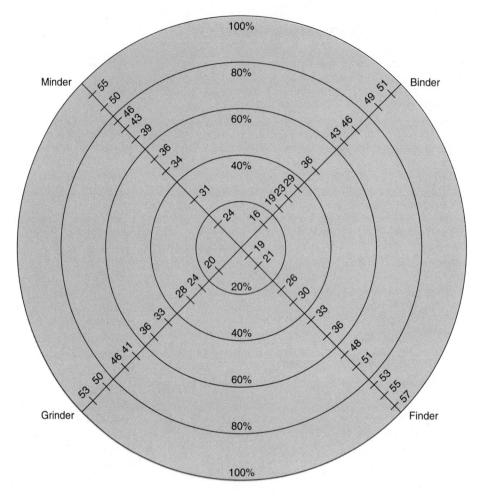

The concentric circles represent percentile scores based on the combined responses of 712 small business managers and 953 entrepreneurs. (For example, a raw score of 46 on Minder means you scored higher on this dimension than 80 percent of the managers and entrepreneurs tested. A score of 60 would indicate you scored higher than anyone in the population on which these norms are based.)

Source: Joe Singer and Joan Baker, Professional Support Services, 12705 South Mur-Len, Olathe, Kansas 66062.

the age of 30, the confidence level rises. Tied in with, and almost coincident, this is a period of free choice, as Exhibit 1.11 shows. The ability to break away from security to start a new business is highly dependent upon not having myriad personal responsibilities that make the idea of taking risks almost infeasible. If your job is going well, your family is young, or you have a high mortgage payment, you would probably not start a venture where the hours are long and the financial

Exhibit 1.11

The free choice period for the would-be entrepreneur

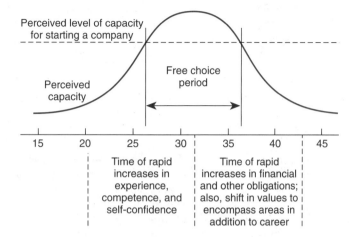

Source: Barbara Bird, *Entrepreneurial Behavior* (Glenview, Ill.: Scott, Foresman), p. 70.

Exhibit 1.12

Milestone years for beginning an entrepreneurial career

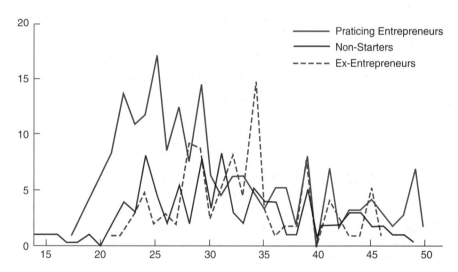

Source: "Ages of Entrepreneurs at Startup" from *Entrepreneurship: Cases & Notes,* by R. Ronstadt, p. 94. Copyright © 1984 by Lord Pu Inc. (Dover, MA).

rewards are fewer—at least for a good many years. This is true of both the entrepreneurial and the typical small business venture. In general, being an entrepreneur requires both time and financial flexibility. It is, however, ultimately rewarding and has many benefits for those choosing this path. Entrepreneurs, as a general rule, tend to be younger, with 35 percent of successful and 20 percent of unsuccessful entrepreneurs under 40 years of age. But there are many successful entrepreneurs in the 40-to-50 age bracket (see Exhibit 1.12).

ation of an environment to fulfill the needs for control and independence are the pri-
ry reasons for forming the venture rather than the profit motive. . . . The ultimate
repreneurial motivation . . . is related to the desire to build something, to express
eself to be in control, and to be independent.[12]

ll Business: A New Perspective

the economy changed in the late 1980s, people became more aware of the pitfalls in
trusting their livelihood to big business. **Small business,** an *organization that is independently owned and operated and not dominant in the field,* was viewed in a new perspective.
While it is not easy to define a small business other than in general terms, the **Small
Business Administration's guidelines,** which are *those characteristics of a firm that define
a small business,* are generally accepted. A person could avoid being laid off and be
rewarded commensurate with his or her activities by becoming a small business owner. In
fact, small business is important to the economy because it is the economy's chief job generator. Not all small businesses succeed; in fact, most fail, although there seems to be some
correlation between size and survival. If you view small business as a viable alternative to
working for a large corporation, be sure to recognize those factors inherent in business
success.

It is important to realize that while small business has many advantages, the sheer mul-
tiplicity of tasks the small business owner must confront and the relative scarcity of capital
can make small business a risky venture.

Reasons a Business Might Fail

Many factors explain the failure of small business. These include:

Lack of good overall planning
Poor site or location
Inadequate marketing
Failure to maintain useful records
Improper financing
Poor management

Most, however, can be grouped under the generic heading of inadequate management.

Requirements for Success

If you are thinking about starting a small business, you should be aware of the tasks facing
you as a small business owner. **Site planning** is *the determination of how a specific location
is to be utilized in the most efficient manner consistent with the needs of the business.*
Marketing is the *selling of a product or service.* **Record keeping** involves *maintaining
detailed information about purchases, sales, orders, expenses, and cash balances.* You
should also be cognizant of the need for energy, initiative, organization, appearance, and
technical ability.

Entrepreneurship

While these requirements appear daunting, being an **entrepreneur,** *a person who has the need to build and create something new,* requires other characteristics in addition to these. You should be certain you possess the requirements for being a small business operator or an entrepreneur.

You should not overlook the fact that in these times, all business must share social responsibility. It is incumbent upon you then to make certain that you operate in a manner consistent with all of the new social demands.

Questions

1. As a job generator, how many jobs are created by small business?
2. What percent of future employment growth will come from small business?
3. Define the term "small business."
4. How does the SBA define small business?
5. What are the survival chances of a small business?
6. Does size have anything to do with survival? Why?
7. List some advantages of being a small business owner.
8. Explain why management people are attracted to small business.
9. List the disadvantages of owning a small business.
10. What are the three most important factors inherent in small business failure? Explain why these are important.
11. What is the main reason given by Dun & Bradstreet for business failure?
12. List eight common reasons for business failure.
13. To be successful in small business, managers need to demonstrate some desirable characteristics. Name and explain six characteristics that you feel are important.
14. How important are governmental regulations in a small business operation?
15. Is the current emphasis on social responsibility important to small business? Why or why not?
16. What would be the best time in a person's life to start a small business? Why would this be true?
17. It has been said that small business is the necessary foundation of our capitalist system. Is this true? Why?

Problems

When doing these exercises, where applicable, be sure to select a specific business, preferably one where you presently or previously worked or a business you would like to own someday. If this is not possible, pick a specific organization to which you will refer. Be sure to identify the organization by name. Limit your answers to one or two pages per exercise.

1. Interview a small business owner and determine if the owner understands the difference between being an entrepreneur and a business operator. Ask the owner to choose one or the other as an accurate self-description and to explain this position.

2. Ask two business owners what they consider to be the factors inherent in their success. Compare the lists and explain the differences, if any.

3. Looking at four businesses, what in your view were the personal characteristics of the owners that contributed to success? Compare this list to the characteristics that the owners list and explain the differences.

4. Using the firms you have interviewed in questions 1, 2, and 3, classify them with respect to the SBA's definition of small business. In your opinion, is the SBA's definition realistic? Explain your answer.

5. Assume that you are running a small retail store. Prepare a report on the records you would need in order to run the firm successfully.

6. Interview six business owners and determine how much start-up or initial capital they had. Prepare a report on the adequacy of their start-up capital and the consequences of their decisions.

7. Interview three firms' owners who have recently filed for Chapter 11 bankruptcy and prepare a report on their perceived reasons for this filing.

Application Situations

1. Opportunity Strikes

As you are reading today's paper about the latest corporate downsizing (another word for "layoff"), a business broker whom you know calls, and in the ensuing conversation you learn that a tremendous opportunity exists to buy a small business. The broker tells you that if you purchase this business, you will never have to worry about being "downsized" yourself and that the business will guarantee your success in life.

Assignment

1. Answer the following questions:
   a. What advantages do you see in buying a small business? You may want to specifically address how you think you will be better off.
   b. Address the disadvantages that might manifest themselves as a result of your purchase and explain your position.
   c. Critically examine your own personal characteristics and compare them to the characteristics required of a typical small business owner. Explain any divergence and how you would cope with any problems arising from the divergence.

2. If a close friend bought a business, what advice would you offer so that failure could be avoided? Be sure to address the common causes of business failure.

3. Recognizing the difference between being an entrepreneur and a manager, analyze your own background, education, and experience and determine if you could be an entrepreneur. Make sure you recognize your strengths and weaknesses.

2. Gregory Smithson

Gregory Smithson, son of a successful business executive, grew up in a conservative family environment. He earned both a bachelor's degree and an MBA from Ivy League schools. Using the MBA as a stepping stone, he became a successful corporate executive. He often thought of leaving the "rat race," however, to start a small business. Owning and operating a small business seemed to be an ideal life.

Assignment

1. Evaluate Greg's qualifications, abilities, and potential for success.
2. If you were lending money to new entrepreneurs, would you back Greg? Indicate why you would or wouldn't. Be specific.

3. Brother's Pharmacy

The year 1993 saw one of the city's 24 family-owned drugstores become part of the CVS chain. CVS regards itself as very competitive, specifically with regard to price. Assuming that you own a small drugstore:

Assignment

1. Answer the following questions:
   a. How do you react to this event?
   b. How do you survive in this new and highly competitive arena?

Bibliography

Burck, Charles. "The Real World of the Entrepreneur." *Fortune,* April 5, 1993, p. 62.

Burr, Pat L., and Richard J. Heckman. "Why So Many Small Businesses Flop—and Some Succeed." *Across the Board,* February 1979, pp. 46–48.

Carbone, T. C. "The Challenges of Small Business Management." *Management World,* October 1980, pp. 36–37.

Clute, Ronald C. "How Important Is Accounting to Small Business Survival." *Journal of Commercial Bank Lending* 62, no. 5 (January 1980), pp. 24–28.

Comegys, Charles. "Research Needs of Prospective Entrepreneurs." *Atlanta Economic Review* 28, no. 3 (May/June 1978), pp. 19–23.

DeFilippo, Julie. "Earning and Learning: How a Student Built a Small Business." *The New York Times,* July 3, 1993, p. 26(N), p. 32(L), col. 1.

Duncan, Ian. "An Introduction to Entrepreneurship." *CMA Magazine,* November, 1991 p. 32.

Gosliano, B. Thomas, and Robert J. Warth. "Managing after Start-Up." *Management Accounting* 70, no. 8 (February 1989), pp. 27–30.

Harris, Ed. "Straight Talk about Why Businesses Fail—and How They Can Be Saved." *Canadian Business,* July 1980, pp. 156–60.

Herron, Lanny, and Harry J. Sapienza. "The Entrepreneur and the Initiation of New Venture Launch Activities." *Entrepreneurship: Theory & Practice* 17, no. 1 (Fall 1992), pp. 49–55.

Hood, Jacqueline N., and John E. Young. "Entrepreneurship's Requisite Areas of Development: A Survey of Top Executives in Successful Entrepreneurial Firms." *Journal of Business Venturing* 8, no. 2 (March 1993), pp. 115–35.

Hornaday, Robert W. "Thinking about Entrepreneurship: A Fuzzy Set Approach." *Journal of Small Business Management* 30, no. 4 (October 1992), pp. 12–23.

Hornsby, Jeffrey S; Douglas W. Naffziger; Donald F. Kuratko; Ray V. Mantangno. "An Interactive Model of the Corporate Entrepreneurship Process." *Entrepreneurship: Theory & Practice* 17, no. 2 (Winter 1993), pp. 29–37.

Kamm, Judith B., and Aaron J. Nurick. "The Stages of Team Venture Formation: A Decision-Making Model." *Entrepreneurship: Theory & Practice* 17, no. 2 (Winter 1993), pp. 17–27.

Kennedy, James; Janice Loutzenhiser; and John Chaney. "Problems of Small Business Firms: An Analysis of the SBI Consulting Program." *Journal of Small Business Management* 17, no. 1 (January 1979), pp. 7–14.

Kuratko, Donald F.; Jeffrey S. Hornsby; Douglas W. Naffziger; and Ray V. Mongtagno. "Implementing Entrepreneurial Thinking in Established Organizations." *SAM Advanced Management Journal* 58, no. 1 (Winter 1993), pp. 28–33.

McCormack, Mark H. "Starting Your Own Business." *Modern Office Technology,* September 1989, pp. 12, 14.

Mack, Toni. "Starting Your Own Business: Tortilla Wizard." *Forbes,* July 20, 1992, pp. 88–89.

Maynard, Michael. "Rebuilding Equity." *Executive Excellence,* December 1992, p. 11.

Selz, Michael. "Merger Activity of Small Firms Keeps Growing." *The Wall Street Journal,* August 23, 1993, p. B1(W), p. B1(E), col. 6.

Tjosvold, Dean, and David Weicker. "Cooperative and Competitive Networking by Entrepreneurs: A Critical Incident Study." *Journal of Small Business Management* 31, no. 1 (January 1993), pp. 11–21.

Uhland, Vicky. "The Intrepid Entrepreneur." *Colorado Business Magazine,* October 1992, p. 49.

Vanderwarf, Pieter A. "A Model of Venture Creation in New Industries." *Entrepreneurship: Theory & Practice* 17, no. 2 (Winter 1993), pp. 39–47.

Veit, Ken. "The Reluctant Entrepreneur." *Harvard Business Review* 70, no. 8 (November-December 1992), p. 40.

Warshaw, Michael. "The Mind-Style of the Entrepreneur." *Success,* April, 1993 pp. 28–33.

Endnotes

1. *The State of Small Business, 1991. Report of the President* (Washington, D.C.: U.S. Government Printing Office), p. xv.
2. Ibid., p. xvii.
3. June Case, *Boston Globe,* May 25, 1994, p. 46.
4. Ibid. p. xv.
5. *Advocate,* Spring 1992, p .4.
6. U.S. Office of Advocacy, *Small Business Job Creation in 1993,* May 1994, p. 9.
7. "Mom, Apple Pie and Small Business," *The Wall Street Journal,* August 15, 1994, p. 1
8. Jeffry A. Timmons, *New Venture Creation: Entrepreneurship in the 90's* (Burr Ridge, Ill.: Irwin, 1990), p. 11.

9. As the firm increases its level of production, unit costs tend to decrease. Simply stated, unit costs decrease as plant size increases. The larger the firm, the greater use of high-cost, specialized and/or automated machinery, which produces a high volume of product at a low unit cost.

10. "Long Island Railroad Is Said to be Losing Revenue Due to Weak Accounting System," *The Wall Street Journal,* February 10, 1971, p. 4.

11. J. Corman, B. Perles, and P. Vancini, "Motivational Factors Influencing High-Technology Entrepreneurship," *Journal of Small Business Management* 26, no. 1 (January 1988), pp. 36–42.

12. Lilles Patrick, "Who Are the Entrepreneurs?" *MSU Business Topics,* Winter 1974, pp. 5–14.

2 LEGAL FORMS OF OWNERSHIP

In this chapter you will learn about the three major legal forms of organization structures: the proprietorship, the partnership, and the corporation. The purpose of this chapter is to define each of these forms of organization and to acquaint you with the advantages and disadvantages of each. Additionally, this chapter defines and acquaints you with the generic kinds of business activity that are conducted in our country.

Chapter Learning Objectives

After completing this chapter, you should be able to:
· Choose which sector of business activity your firm will be in.
· Set up the best legal infrastructure for your business.
· Identify and define the major sectors of business activity.
· Define the following 24 key terms in order of appearance:

Proprietorship	Junior partner
Partnership	Corporation
General partners	Foreign corporation
Limited partner	Corporate charter
Partnership agreement	"S" corporation
General partnership	Limited liability corporation
Limited partnerships	Par value
Secret partner	Standard Industrial Code
Silent partner	Retailing
Dormant partner	Wholesalers
Nominal partner	Service sector
Senior partner	Manufacturing

Introduction

While the decision to own or operate a small business represents a major step in your life, it is important not to jump into the myriad operating details of such a venture before carefully considering what form of ownership your business will take. There are several organizational formats from which you can choose. Your choice will determine the amount of taxes you will pay, whether you can be sued for unpaid business debts, and whether or not the organization will survive your death or absence. Our discussion will examine the more common forms of ownership. Since there is no single correct form for an organization, you must examine the pros and cons of each form and decide which is best for you.

We will look at three organization structures for small business:

Proprietorship.

Partnership (which includes both general and limited form).

Corporation (which includes a "C" corporation and an "S" corporation).

The tools and techniques used to operate a business are universal; that is, the same rules apply to all firms. The ways in which you choose to organize your firm are not; there are pros and cons to each. The eventual form of organization you choose will depend upon your view of what is best for your unique situation. You should examine each one to determine the best choice for you and your business.

Sole Proprietorship

The **proprietorship** is an *unincorporated business owned and operated by one person.* This is the most common form of ownership, with 11.2 million single proprietorships compared to 1.6 million partnerships and 3.1 million corporations.[1] In a single proprietorship you receive all the profits of the business, but you also will bear all the costs and have unlimited liability springing from the firm's operations. When starting out, this form of business ownership is the easiest and least expensive to set up.

Advantages of Proprietorship

The reasons for the popularity of proprietorships are:

1. Ease of start-up. To secure any necessary state and local licenses and registrations, you must complete the required forms and file them with the appropriate state or local authority. You are then in business.

2. Profits. As you are the sole owner of the firm, you are free to take all the profits and use them for whatever purpose you desire. Most frequently, profits are reinvested in the business.

3. Freedom to manage as you choose. Again because you are the sole owner of the business, you have total authority to take any action you see fit. You do not

have to ask permission or, if you choose, confer with anyone. Decisions can be quick and/or entirely personal.

4. Few legal restrictions. You have the freedom to operate (subject to the appropriate licensing and regulations) anywhere in the country and to add or subtract products or services as you desire. None of these activities would violate any legal document.

5. Easy to dissolve. The ease of starting a business is only surpassed by the ease with which you can end it. You just stop doing whatever it is you were doing. You don't even need to fill out any forms. The firm exists only as long as you want it to.

6. Taxes. Since you own and operate the firm, as the owner, you, rather than the business, are taxed.

Disadvantages of Proprietorship

1. Unlimited liability. This is probably the most important disadvantage of a sole proprietorship. Since you own and operate the business, make all the decisions, and take all the profits, you and the business are viewed as one entity. There is no legal distinction between you and the business, and therefore you are liable for all its debts. If, for example, one of your vehicles is in an accident, seriously injuring someone, all of your assets are at risk. Only by having adequate and expensive insurance can you prevent this from happening.

2. Difficulty in raising capital. All businesses need money to operate and to grow. Some may also need a great deal of money to purchase inventory for seasonal variations. For example, the Christmas season may account for 90 percent of your store's yearly sales. Thus you will have to spend a great deal of money to accumulate inventory in anticipation of seasonal sales because the money to cover these purchases will only be generated at the end of the peak selling period. It may be extremely difficult for a single person to already have, or to borrow, a large sum of money. Because only you can raise money, the amount of funds available is strictly dependent upon your assets. If you are not already wealthy, your ability to borrow is restricted.

3. Maintaining the overall direction of your business. As the business expands, it becomes more complex and therefore quite difficult for one person to retain overall control in order to provide the necessary direction.

4. Demise of the firm. The death of an owner terminates the firm. As the business has no separate existence and is just an extension of the owner, when the owner ceases to function, so too does the business. Should someone else acquire the business, it will then be considered a new company.

Partnership

A **partnership** is *an association of two or more people who carry on as co-owners of a business.* There are two basic kinds of partnerships: general and limited.

General partners *participate actively in the operation of the business, sharing all the responsibility, profits, and liabilities.* A **limited partner** *has limited liability and does not take an active part in the management of the company.* A limited partner's liability extends only to the amount of money invested, not to personal assets. A limited partner must be careful, however, since if it can be determined that such a partner took an active part in the management of the business, liability becomes unlimited. A business may have a number of limited partners, but there must be at least one general partner with unlimited liability.

Forms of Partnership

Partnerships, as proprietorships, are not difficult to form. As one of the owners, you share in the profits and the right and freedom to manage. There are few legal restrictions, and the organization is easy to dissolve. You, rather than the business, will be taxed, as in a proprietorship. There are, however, some disadvantages. Each partner is liable for the debts of the organization. If your trusted partner departs without warning for warmer climates, taking all the capital of the business, the debts become your responsibility. While this may not be fair, it is legal. There may be exceptions if fraud is involved.

Further, since the partnership is nothing more than an agreement to be in business together, it can be difficult to raise capital. Why would anyone want to invest in an organization where the investor does not have ownership rights as well as the certainty of repayment? While two or more people can usually raise more money than one person can, there are limits; and as the business grows, the lack of capital can become a major problem.

Also, as the business grows, it becomes more and more difficult for the original partners to manage. Since there is limited opportunity, employees cannot be counted on to assume management obligations and tasks, as the rights of control and ownership reside with the partners. As with a sole proprietorship, death, imprisonment, or insanity automatically terminate the firm unless the partnership agreement states otherwise and a contractual clause is negotiated.

If the partnership is to continue after the death of one of the partners, the partnership can choose between two methods of ensuring the continuity of the partnership. These are:

1. The partners can arrange for the heirs to replace the deceased partner.
2. The partners can have the remaining partners buy the deceased partner's interest.

Most agreements do, and all agreements should, contain a provision with respect to a transfer of a partner's interest in the partnership.[2]

General Partnership

The **general partnership** is *one variation of the partnership vehicle wherein all partners participate actively in operating the business,* sharing all the responsibilities involved in running the firm. Perhaps the most significant responsibility from the individual's viewpoint is unlimited liability. As the business expands, liability increases correspondingly.[3] Additionally, management of the corporation becomes increasingly more complex; however, too many equal partners make decision making almost impossible.

Limited Partnership

Limited partnerships *are created in order to limit liability of the partners* as well as to facilitate the contribution of capital without incurring unlimited liability.[4] As the primary weaknesses of a partnership include unlimited liability, an inability to raise needed capital, and the difficulty of managing the partnership itself, another form of the partnership agreement was developed. The limited partnership allows people to carry on as co-owners where some of the partners have more responsibility and power in running the business. These partners (general partners), therefore, have the burden of more liability than other partners, whose roles are more limited (limited partners). In a limited partnership, at least one partner has unlimited liability and responsibility for the operation of the firm. Other partners in the organization are designated as limited partners. These limitations involve both liability as well as management obligations. Limited partners cannot take an active role in running the business. Naturally, the terms of the relationship should be specified in the partnership agreement.

The Partnership Agreement

A **partnership agreement** is a *written document that sets forth all of the terms under which the partnership is to operate.* A partnership can be created with only an oral agreement, but this is rarely a good idea. Writing down the terms of a partnership may eliminate many future disputes since the process of documenting the partnership raises and answers many questions that you might not have considered. Although there is no legal requirement for a written partnership agreement (in legal terminology called "articles of partnership"), common sense dictates that you should not go into business without one. The agreement should spell out the status, responsibilities, and authority of each partner. Even if you go into business with your best friend, do not do it without a written agreement. People often think they know what they are agreeing to only to discover later, and too late, that they never really understood the nature of their agreement. A written partnership agreement sets forth the details and terms of the partnership for the protection of each of the partners. Having a written agreement forces everyone to be specific and detailed. Also, these details do not fade with the passage of time and remain as permanent and legal reminders of what had been approved. The document will undoubtedly be referred to repeatedly in order to clarify misunderstandings.

It is useful to spell out every detail in order to avoid future misunderstandings and problems. The typical partnership agreement is described in Exhibit 2.1.

The terms covered in Exhibit 2.1 are not intended to be an exhaustive listing of possible provisions. Each partnership agreement will contain clauses that are spe-

---

EXHIBIT 2.1   Model partnership agreement

Name of the partnership.

Purpose of the business. Why did you create this business and what will the business do?

Location. Where will the business be located physically?

Duration of the partnership. How long do you think the firm will operate? It is possible to have a partnership that lasts on a continuing basis (at least as long as everyone is alive) or one that is of short duration or established for a specific purpose and/or time.

Name and legal address of all partners.

Contribution of each partner to the business. This spells out who contributed specific assets to the organization. Contributions may consist of cash, real estate, skills, contacts, or any other form of assets.

Terms specifying the distribution of profits and losses. Since the income and expenses of the partnership are treated as ordinary income and expenses as far as federal and state taxes are concerned, it is best to specify each partner's appropriate percentage of ownership and distribution. All partners need this protection. Shares of profits and/or losses may not be equal. Spell it out!

Terms specifying the compensation of the partners. Some partners may be paid a salary or commission because of their activity in the business. This compensation can be an addition to their share of the profits. Generally if one partner is more active or makes a bigger contribution to the organization, that partner is entitled to additional compensation.

Definition of profits. Since each partner is entitled to a specific percentage of the profits, it is best to know how profits are determined; which expenses are costs of doing business and which are personal. Obviously the higher the business expenses, the less profit there is to be divided.

Provisions for answering questions. How may a new partner be added or a current partner deleted? How will the partnership be dissolved or sold and how will the assets be distributed? These are all important questions that should be resolved before you begin operating your business.

Provisions governing how the absence or disability of a partner will be handled. For example, will the partnership continue? Will the salary or asset distribution remain the same? Is a disabled partner still responsible for the debts of the firm?

Provisions for altering the partnership agreement. Nothing lasts forever. With changing times and circumstances, partnership agreements should contain provisions to accommodate to change.

---

cific to the organization and its principals. In the absence of a written agreement, the terms of the Uniform Partnership Act apply.

Uniform Partnership Act

If partners lack a written partnership agreement, the Uniform Partnership Act (generally referred to as the UPA) stipulates the rights and obligations of each of the partners engaged in the operation of an organization. The act codifies the body of American law dealing with partnerships. In 1914, Pennsylvania became the first state to pass a uniform partnership act. Since then every state except Georgia, Louisiana, and Mississippi has accepted the UPA.

The Revised Uniform Partnership Act (RUPA) is a major overhaul of the UPA. It continues most of the UPA's major policies, rejecting more extreme changes in favor of a reordering of the traditional partnership relationship. Other changes involve the law of partnership breakups, which is completely reworked to give greater stability, as well as the adoption of an entity approach, a provision for the public filing of statements of partnership authority, a clarification of partners' fiduciary duties, public filings, rules on the nature and transfer of partnership property, and the authorization of partnership conversions and mergers.[5]

The UPA defines a partnership as "an association of two or more persons to carry on as co-owners of a business for profit."

A partnership has three common elements:

Common ownership.

Equal sharing of profits and losses.

The right to participate in managing the operations of the partnership.

In general, under the law, each partner has the right to:

1. Share in the management and operation of the business.
2. Share in the profits of the business.
3. Receive interest on any advance made to the business. In the initial start-up of the organization or at various times during its operation the partners may be called upon to augment the cash flow of the business (see Chapter 12). This money becomes an obligation of the business on which it must pay interest, since the owners also function as lenders to the partnership.
4. Receive compensation for expenses having to do with the business.
5. Have full access to the books and records of the partnership.
6. Receive formal accounting of all business affairs.

Obligations of the partners are:

1. Share in partnership losses.
2. Work, if necessary, without salary.
3. Abide by the majority vote of the partners' decisions regarding operation of the organization.
4. Make available to all partners all information regarding business affairs.
5. Give formal accounting of all business affairs.

Keep in mind that a partnership requires mutual trust, respect, and loyalty. Lacking these qualities, the partnership will be unlikely to succeed.

Other types of partnerships are:

Secret partner: *an owner who takes an active role in the business but who does not want to reveal his or her identity to the public.*

Silent partner: *an owner who takes an active part in the business but may be known to the public.*

Dormant partner: *an owner who plays no active role and at the same time remains unknown to the public as a partner.*

Nominal partner: *an individual who does not own the business but suggests to others by words or deed that he is a partner.*

Senior partner: *a general partner who has been with the partnership a long time and owns a large share of the business.*

Junior partner: *an individual who has been with the business a short time and is not expected to assume great responsibility for major decisions.*

Corporations

The corporate form of ownership was established to alleviate the major problems inherent in proprietorships and partnerships. Neither proprietorships nor partnerships provide for the continuation of the business when an individual owner dies or becomes incapacitated. Access to capital, beyond what may be provided by a limited circle of friends, relatives, and others, is finite. Perhaps one of the most important problems in both forms of ownership was the individual's unlimited liability for the debts of either the proprietorship or the partnership. As companies grow, problems such as these loom larger and larger on the businessperson's mind. Therefore, a form of ownership was needed that had longevity beyond that of any individual, could raise capital, and had limited liability. Thus was born the corporate form of ownership. A **corporation** is *an association of individuals united for a common purpose and permitted by law to use a common name and to change its members without dissolution of the association.*

The corporation, which carries on a business in its own name, exists as a separate entity in the eyes of the law. It can raise capital by either selling ownership (stock) or by borrowing (issuing bonds). Ownership of the corporation is established with the issuance of shares of stock; therefore, individual owners, as stockholders, have no liability for corporate debt. As an owner, you may run your business without worry that your money and possessions are in danger of being taken to satisfy a business debt. You should keep in mind that if you work for the corporation, even though you may own a portion of the stock, you are an employee. As an employee, you are paid, receive benefits, and are taxed in the same manner as every other employee.

If you choose the corporate form of organization, you must form a separate organization, which then sells portions of itself (shares) to you and to other individuals (investors). If, for example, the corporation has 100 shares of stock and sells 10 of these shares to you, you own 10 percent of the corporation. Your liability is equivalent to the value of the shares you hold in the corporation.

When a corporation is founded, it accepts all the laws, rules, and regulations of the state in which it is incorporated and does business. As required by law, the corporation must report its financial operations to the attorney general of this state. Although it is logical and sensible for you to incorporate in the state in which you do business, as states have different rules, regulations, and taxes, it might be beneficial *to incorporate in another state and be considered* a **foreign corporation** in the state in which you operate. Because of its favorable laws, Delaware is the home of many of our largest corporations. Where you incorporate will be determined by such considerations as corporate taxes, fees, and restrictions on corporate activities.

It pays to study carefully all the costs and regulations associated with incorporation and take steps to minimize them.

How to Organize a Corporation

The first step in organizing a corporation is to comply with state regulations that require a Certificate of Incorporation or a charter to be filed with the state's attorney general. A **corporate charter** is *a legal document that sets forth information about how the corporate entity intends to operate.* A corporate charter would contain the information listed in Exhibit 2.2.

Advantages of Corporations

If you choose to organize your business as a corporation, you will be able to seize certain advantages that would not be open to you under other forms of organization:

1. **Limited liability.** The corporate form of organization allows investors to limit their liability. Owners of corporate shares are liable only for the dollar value of their original or any subsequent investment. Other shareholder assets are not at risk. Protection of personal assets is a chief factor in many investment decisions, both by the owners as well as potential investors.

Many banks or other lenders, recognizing the legal protection of assets afforded to corporate borrowers, require the borrower to personally guarantee any loan to the corporate entity, making the borrower personally liable. When a company is small, it generally is not possible to avoid giving personal guarantees. As the company becomes larger and accumulates more assets, the less these guarantees will be necessary.

Limited liability however, does not apply in matters involving taxes. Nonpayment of withholding taxes pierces the corporate status and becomes the individual owner's liability. If the corporation fails to pay these taxes, as an owner, you will. "Piercing the corporate veil," where you are responsible regardless of corporate structure, is also possible in other circumstances such as waste disposal and fraud. While piercing the corporate veil, thereby bypassing the limited corporate liability is not common, it is being done much more frequently.

2. **Perpetuity.** While the sole proprietorship and the partnership dissolve with the death or disability of the individuals involved, the corporate entity does not; as a legal entity it can exist in perpetuity. The corporate entity exists beyond the lives of any individuals; business can continue as usual, despite any personal tragedies that could occur in sole proprietorships or small partnerships.

3. **Funding sources.** Based on the potential for limited liability and the fact that the corporate entity has a record of accomplishments separate from that of individuals, the corporate form of ownership makes it possible to raise money from investors. Assuming that the corporation is sound and profitable,[6] the capital that can be raised is limited only by the number of shares authorized by the corporate charter that are available. The charter can be amended as capital needs expand.

EXHIBIT 2.2   Model corporate charter

1. *Name of the corporation.* As the corporation is a separate legal entity, it must have an identity. In order to eliminate confusion or to prevent deception, the corporate name cannot be identical or even similar to that of another firm within the state's jurisdiction.

2. *Statement of purpose.* You must clearly state the purpose of the corporation. This is best done in general terms in order to have flexibility as the business develops. You might want to state the purpose of the business as "the sale and servicing of automobiles" rather than "selling Renaults."

3. *Duration of the corporation.* In general, corporations are formed for perpetuity. It is possible, however, to incorporate for a specific time period.

4. *Names and addresses of the incorporators.* The incorporators must be identified in the articles of incorporation. These incorporators are legally obligated to attest that all information given in the corporate papers is correct.

5. *Address of business.* The legal address of the principal corporate office must be supplied. All official correspondence will be sent to this address.

6. *Corporate stock authorization.* A corporation is not obligated to issue all the stock authorized in the corporate papers. The corporation must, however, identify the different classes of stock and any special rights or privileges each classification may carry with it. For example, a corporation might want to issue special preferred stock with voting rights and common stock without such rights. In this section, the incorporators also must identify whether the stock has a par or no par value. **Par value** means that *a single stock certificate would carry a monetary value.* No par means that no monetary value was assigned. In some instances, the state may require that a percentage of the stock value be deposited as escrow in a bank before incorporation. There may also be other restrictions.

7. *Preemptive rights or restrictions.* The corporate charter must provide specific details about preemptive rights or restrictions on the transfer of shares. In many cases, since corporate shares are owned by a few people, there may be limitations on how and at what value your shares may be sold and who may sell them.

8. *Name and address of the founding officers and directors of the corporation.*

9. *Rules and regulations under which the corporation will operate.* These are the by-laws of the corporation. Remember that once these are filed with the state's attorney general, you have created the corporate charter. The corporate entity is henceforth required to abide by its own rules and regulations. Once this process is complete, you then hold an organizational meeting of the stockholders to formally elect the directors who, in turn, appoint the corporate officers.

4. **Transfer of ownership.** Ownership of a corporation is determined by the shares owned. As a shareholder you do not own the corporation or its assets directly; however, you can own a share in the corporation. The organization carries on its business irrespective of share ownership. Shares can be sold or transferred to either individuals, corporations, pension funds, mutual funds, or other investment vehicles. Millions of shares are traded daily. On a particularly busy day, the New York Stock Exchange can process more than 250 million changes of ownership (shares). Despite all these stock transactions, the business of the corporation continues without any noticeable effect.

5. **Separation of ownership and management.** Too often, the growth of the corporation is limited by the skills, knowledge, expertise, or experience of the founders. The corporate form of organization allows the company to draw on an expanded pool of talent. It can utilize its officers or board of directors as sources of

funds, and with the additional capital, the company can attract and hire the best available talent. Further, the corporate form of organization allows the separation of ownership and management. As organizations grow, operating them becomes increasingly sophisticated and complex. The owners need not operate the organization. To run it in their place, they hire trained managers who may not, and probably do not, own any major share of the company. Many talented people are only too happy to work as managers. Correspondingly, many business schools are happy to train and supply managerial talent.

6. **Expansion and contraction.** Since the corporation has a life of its own and can raise needed capital, it is easy to expand as the marketplace dictates. Contraction is more difficult, however, since cutting back requires sacrifice; people lose jobs, income, and homes. The company loses size and prestige, and it is often difficult to admit that management is wrong and needs to cut back.

Disadvantages of the Corporate Form of Ownership

1. **Cost, time, and paperwork.** Creation of a corporation, an artificial entity, is not easy since it requires considerable paperwork required by the state. The state also levies a charge for participating in the process. Creation of an organization takes time and should be done carefully. Once corporate papers are filed, the organizational process is also time-consuming. In many cases, incorporation requires the services of an attorney. However, many states make it possible for the entrepreneur to incorporate by offering a "kit" containing the forms required for filing as well as detailed instructions.

Costs may range from $200 dollars for a simple incorporation to many thousands for a complex process. Most incorporations can range from $500 to $5,000 dollars. By doing the work yourself, your costs will be approximately $500 dollars.

2. **Taxation.** As a legal entity, the corporation is entitled to the same rights, privileges, and obligations as an individual. One of the obligations a corporation incurs is that of paying taxes. Like individual income, the income of the corporation is similarly taxed by federal, state, and local governments. Taxes must be paid before any owners of the corporation receive dividends, and when the owners receive dividends, since they are individuals, they pay individual income taxes as well. This double taxation is a distinct disadvantage of the corporate form of ownership.

Because governments believe corporations to be a source of considerable wealth, they are quicker to tax corporations than individuals. Corporations, however, can pass along the taxes to consumers, which become hidden in the price of the product and thus less subject to public scrutiny and outcry. In some states, corporations pay a state tax whether or not they show any profits. Corporations can be taxed at different and higher rates than individuals.

3. **Red tape, paperwork, and regulations.** Corporations seem to have an endless quota of reports and forms to file and regulations to comply with. Essentially these are hidden costs, and while a large business may be able to absorb these costs, they are a heavy burden to small business.

4. **Perils of increasing capitalization.** While it is easier to raise capital by selling additional shares of stock to other people, a problem may develop: When the corporation sells stock, each share usually has voting rights; if enough shares are sold to meet the need for capital, the owners may lose control of the organization. Venture capitalists may be willing to lend you money, but they want control of your company in return. It is not unheard of for corporate founders to lose control and even be fired or retired.

5. **Federal and state control.** As legal entities, corporations are subject to federal and state controls. In these times, government, in an effort to solve some of society's problems, creates increasingly stringent regulations covering almost every aspect of running a business. While the regulations are targeted at big business, many of these regulations may make it difficult or almost impossible to run a small business profitably.

Consider that the law requires a small painting contractor to use OSHA-approved and inspected ladders and harnesses. He or she must also use a specialized mask and have and use an air-quality tester. Meeting these requirements are added costs in addition to the mandated Worker's Comprehensive and Liability Insurance (both with high rates). These and other costs associated with other regulations add considerable overhead to many operations.

6. **Charter restrictions.** In the process of incorporation you have to state the purpose of your business. As time moves on and you find that the nature of your operation has changed, you must reflect this change by amending your corporate charter. Generally this is not a difficult process, since it is carried out at the state level. It does, however, involve more paperwork and cost.

The "S" Corporation

As discussed above, the usual form of corporation, commonly called the "C" corporation, carries some severe tax consequences. Double taxation forced by this structure can be exceedingly burdensome. In a move to equalize the tax burden for all forms of organizations, particularly for small business, in 1954 the Internal Revenue Service created a new tax entity, the Subchapter (S) Corporation now called simply the **"S" corporation,** a *corporate identity treated as an individual for income tax purposes.* In order to qualify for "S" corporate status, a company must meet certain requirements:

1. All stockholders must be individuals or certain types of estates or trusts.
2. There can be no more than 35 stockholders.
3. The business must be a domestic corporation.
4. Nonresident aliens cannot be stockholders.
5. There can be only one class of common stock.

Once these requirements are fulfilled, the corporate owners must elect to be treated as an "S" corporation. This election is formalized by filing Form 2533 with the Internal Revenue Service, generally within the first 75 days of the year. The company cannot switch between "S" and "C" corporations on an arbitrary basis.

Advantages of "S" Corporations

The primary advantage of an "S" corporation is that corporate taxes are avoided. The corporation passes on the operating profits or losses of the corporation through to the shareholder on a proportionate basis. Shareholders are taxed on the corporate income as if it were their own and pay the appropriate individual income taxes. Profits are not taxed at both the corporate and personal levels, thus avoiding double taxation. The "S" corporation achieves equity of taxation between the small business single proprietorships, partnerships, and corporations. This form of corporation became popular after the Tax Act of 1986 set corporate tax rates higher than individual tax rates. It made sense to become an "S" corporation and save money by paying fewer taxes.[7]

The following quotation from *The Wall Street Journal* was written prior to the passage of the 1993 tax act but confirms the attractiveness of the "S" corporation.

> "S" corporations are here to stay, even if personal tax rates rise. These entities aren't subject to double taxation—that is, both on corporate income and on dividends paid from that income. The income, much like a partnership's, is taxed once—to the owners personally. After 1986's tax act raised the top corporate rate (now 34 percent) above the top personal rate (now 31 percent) for the first time, hundreds of thousands of closely held businesses opted for "S" status. . . .
>
> An "S" concern has many advantages over a regular corporation besides lower income taxes. The main one . . . is that an owner's cost basis in S-company stock rises as the owner pays taxes on undistributed company income. That lowers the taxable gain if the owner sells the stock: and in most cases, the saving should offset a rise in income-tax rates.[8]

Prior to 1993, with the top personal tax rate of 31 percent and the corporate of 34 percent, it seemed that the "S" format was the sensible thing to do. The Tax Act of 1993, while it changed tax rates, did not change the fact that any decision should not be made without determining the best financial advantage. Even after the Tax Act of 1993, the "S" corporation has benefits.

> Now, it would seem the situation is reversed. The top corporate-tax rate of 35 percent compares with a top personal rate of 39.6 percent; ergo, time to incorporate. Right? Not necessarily.
>
> Because of the different paces at which corporate and personal rates rise along with income, the tax advantage can shift back and forth between the two forms of organization. The corporate rate of 34 percent, for example, begins at $75,000 of taxable income, while personal rates—on a joint return—stay at 31 percent until $140,000. So you'll have to run the numbers both ways to see which structure makes sense.[9]

In cases where the business is losing money, stockholders are allowed to deduct these losses on an individual basis.[10] These benefits are achieved while maintaining the important advantages of the Chapter "C" corporation such as limited liability and perpetuity.

Disadvantages of "S" Corporations

While not paying corporate taxes is an attractive option, there are some technicalities that might militate against an "S" corporate organization. At a lower taxable income, because of the marginal tax rates, taxes for the "C" corporation may be lower than taxes on an individual resulting from the "S" corporation pass-through. Also important is the fact that the "S" corporation cannot deduct as business expenses, for tax purposes, many fringe benefits such as insurance. These "benefits" are treated as income to the recipients and are therefore taxed accordingly. Additionally, while the typical corporation can offer a wide range of pension benefits, the "S" corporation's allowable options are fewer and perhaps less advantageous. Every state recognizes the "S" corporation for state tax purposes except Connecticut, the District of Columbia, Louisiana, New Hampshire, New Jersey, New York, Tennessee, Texas, and Vermont. Nevada, South Dakota, and Wyoming have no state income taxes.[11]

Limited Liability Corporation

Both "S" and "C" corporations provide limited liability. In doing so, however, the corporate form of organization reduces flexibility. There are rules and regulations governing corporations that result in double taxation at the "C" corporation rate as well as restrictions on the number and type of stockholders (only individuals and U.S. citizens). Partnerships would provide flexibility but not unlimited liability. A **limited liability corporation** *provides flexibility and limited liability while being treated by the IRS as a partnership.*[12] Limited liability corporations are accepted in most states and are becoming very popular.

> [Limited-liability corporations] protect you from liability just like a corporation, but you avoid the double taxation. You get the best of both worlds.[13]

Exhibit 2.3 summarizes the differences among small company structures.

EXHIBIT 2.3   Differences in small-company structures

	S Corporation	C Corporation	Partnership	Limited Liability Company
Limited liability	Yes	Yes	No	Yes
Double taxation	No	Yes	No	No
Shareholder restrictions	Yes	No	No	No
Transferability of shares	Yes	Yes	No	No

Source: "Limited Liability: A Safer Strategy for Small Business," *Business Week*, July 18, 1994, p. 90.

The Choice: "C" or "S"?

The overriding choice between a "C" or an "S" corporation should be based upon the impact on one's tax situation. The "S" corporation permits the businessperson to escape double taxation in that all income, expenses, profits, and losses pass through to the individual's personal tax base. Thus you can deduct all expenses and perhaps reduce your total tax bill. If a business shows losses, this too can work to the taxpayer's short-term advantage; but it is only fair to state that running a losing operation results in larger corporate losses and is a situation to be avoided in the long run.

Thus the "S" corporation is useful in those situations concerning start-up operations or when the business is highly profitable and would have to pay out substantial dividends. Companies are not likely to benefit from an "S" Corporation when the owners receive most of the profits as salaries or benefits.

In most cases, where provision of benefits is greater than tax saving, it may not be beneficial to either the individual or the company. Also, in extremely small companies, the "S" corporation may not be beneficial (i.e., where gross corporate income is less than $100,000). Exhibit 2.4 summarizes the advantages and disadvantages of the various business forms.

Classification of Business Firms

There are literally thousands of businesses that constitute the United States economy. To understand economic activity and make sense of the vast array of firms, it is necessary to classify them by type. Various component parts of like firms can then be compared. Trends describing the viability of each sector and its importance to the economy as a whole can be examined. Analysis of these trends and identification of business classification also aid in our choice of job or career.

The Standard Industrial Code

The Standard Industrial Classification System (SIC) has been developed to categorize, classify, and describe various business activities. SIC codes and standard industry ratios are extremely helpful in researching a business either for start-up or operating purposes. Further discussion of this topic is contained in Chapter 13. The SIC also subdivides the major categories of business activity into more detailed product, industry, or market segments. The greater the number of digits in the SIC code, the more detailed the description. Generally, there are four major business activities: retail, wholesale, service, and manufacturing. Overall retail and service operations account for the majority of all new business starts in the United States. In 1987, 1,653,811 retail and 54,788 service firms were started and accounted for 51.4 percent of all business starts.[14] Examples of SIC codes for business firms are shown in Exhibit 2.5.

EXHIBIT 2.4 Comparison of various business forms

	Sole Proprietorship	Partnership*	S Corporation**	Regular Corporation***
Restrictions on type or number of owners	One owner. The owner must be an individual.	Must have at least 2 owners.	Only individuals, estates, and certain trusts can be owners. Maximum number of shareholders limited to 35.	None, except some states require a minimum of 2 shareholders.
Incidence of tax	Sole proprietorship's income and deductions are reported on Schedule C of the individual's Form 1040. A separate Schedule C is prepared for each business.	Entity not subject to tax. Partners in their separate capacity subject to tax on their distributive share of income. Partnership files Form 1065.	Except for certain built-in gains and passive investment income when earnings and profits are present from Subchapter C tax years, entity not subject to Federal income tax. S corporation files Form 1120S. Shareholders are subject to tax on income attributable to their stock ownership.	Income subject to double taxation. Entity subject to tax, and shareholder subject to tax on any corporate dividends received. Corporation files Form 1120.
Highest tax rate	31% at individual level.	31% at partner level.	31% at shareholder level.	39% at corporate level plus 31% on any corporate dividends at shareholder level.
Choice of tax year	Same tax year as owner.	Selection generally restricted to coincide with tax year of majority partners or principal partners, or to calendar year.	Restricted to a calendar year unless IRS approves a different year for business purposes or other exceptions apply.	Unrestricted selection allowed at time of filing first tax return.
Timing of taxation	Based on owner's tax year.	Partners report their share of income in their tax year with or within which the partnership's tax year ends. Partners in their separate capacities are subject to payment of estimated taxes.	Shareholders report their shares of income in their tax year with or within which the corporation's tax year ends. Generally, the corporation uses a calendar year, but see. "Choice of tax year" above. Shareholders may be subject to payment of estimated taxes.	Corporation subject to tax at close of its tax year. May be subject to payment of estimated taxes. Dividends will be subject to tax at the shareholder level in the tax year received. Corporation may be subject to payment of estimated taxes for the taxes imposed at the corporate level.

Basis for allocating income to owners.	Not applicable (only one owner).	Profit and loss sharing agreement. Cash basis items of cash basis partnerships are allocated on a daily basis. Other partnership items are allocated after considering varying interests of partners.	Pro rata share based on stock ownership. Shareholder's pro rata share is determined on a daily basis, according to the number of shares of stock held on each day of the corporation's tax year.	Not applicable.
Contribution of property to the entity	Not a taxable transaction.	Generally not a taxable transaction.	Is a taxable transaction unless the § 351 requirements are satisfied.	Is a taxable transaction unless the § 351 requirements are satisfied.
Character of income taxed to owners	Retains source characteristics.	Conduit—retains source characteristics.	Conduit—retains source characteristics.	All source characteristics are lost when income is distributed to owners.
Basis for allocating a net operating loss to owners	Not applicable (only one owner).	Profit and loss sharing agreement. Cash basis items of cash basis partnerships are allocated on a daily basis. Other partnership items are allocated after considering varying interests of partners.	Prorated among shareholders on a daily basis.	Not applicable.
Limitation on losses deductible by owners	Investment plus liabilities.	Partner's investment plus share of liabilities.	Shareholder's investment plus loans made by shareholder to corporation.	Not applicable.
Subject to at-risk rules	Yes, at the owner level. Indefinite carryover of excess loss.	Yes, at the partner level. Indefinite carryover of excess loss.	Yes, at the shareholder level. Indefinite carryover of excess loss.	Yes, for closely held corporations. Indefinite carryover of excess loss.
Subject to passive activity loss rules	Yes, at the owner level. Indefinite carryover of excess loss.	Yes, at the partner level. Indefinite carryover of excess loss.	Yes, at the shareholder level. Indefinite carryover of excess loss.	Yes, for closely held corporations and personal service corporations. Indefinite carryover of excess loss.
Tax consequences of earnings retained by by entity	Taxed to owner when earned and increases his or her investment in the sole proprietorship.	Taxed to partners when earned and increases their respective interests in the partnership.	Taxed to shareholders when earned and increases their respective bases in stock.	Taxed to corporation as earned and may be subject to penalty tax if accumulated unreasonably.

EXHIBIT 2.4   Continued

	Sole Proprietorship	Partnership*	S Corporation**	Regular Corporation***
Nonliquidating distributions to owners	Not taxable.	Not taxable unless money received exceeds recipient partner's basis in partnership interest. Existence of § 751 assets may cause recognition of ordinary income.	Generally not taxable unless the distribution exceeds the shareholder's AAA or stock basis. Existence of accumulated earnings and profits could cause some distributions to be dividends.	Taxable in year of receipt to extent of earnings and profits or if exceeds basis in stock.
Distribution of appreciated property	Not taxable.	No recognition at the partnership level.	Recognition at the corporate level to the extent of the appreciation. Conduit—amount of recognized gain is passed through to shareholders.	Taxable at the corporate level to the extent of the appreciation.
Splitting of income among family members	Not applicable (only one owner).	Difficult—IRS will not recognize a family member as a partner unless certain requirements are met.	Rather easy—gift of stock will transfer tax on a pro rata share of income to the donee. However, IRS can make adjustments to reflect adequate compensation for services.	Same as an S corporation, except that donees will be subject to tax only on earnings actually or constructively distributed to them. Other than unreasonable compensation, IRS generally cannot make adjustments to reflect adequate compensation for services and capital.
Organizational costs	Start-up expenditures are amortizable over 60 months.	Amortizable over 60 months.	Same as partnership.	Same as partnership.
Charitable contributions	Limitations apply at owner level.	Conduit—partners are subject to deduction limitations in their own capacities.	Conduit—shareholders are subject to deduction limitations in their own capacities.	Limited to 10% of taxable income before certain deductions.
Alternative minimum tax	Applies at owner level. AMT rate is 24%.	Applies at the partner level rather than at the partnership level. AMT preferences and adjustments are passed through from the partnership to the partners.	Applies at the shareholder level rather than at the corporate level. AMT preferences and adjustments are passed through from the S corporation to the shareholders.	Applies at the corporate level. AMT rate is 20%.

ACE adjustment	Does not apply.	Does not apply.	Does not apply.	The adjustment is made in calculating AMTI. The adjustment is 75% of the excess of adjusted current earnings over unadjusted AMTI. If the unadjusted AMTI exceeds adjusted current earnings, the adjustment is negative.
Tax preference items	Apply at owner level in determining AMT.	Conduit—passed through to partners who must account for such items in their separate capacities.	Conduit—passed through to shareholders who must account for such items in their separate capacities.	Subject to AMT at corporate level.
Capital gains	Taxed at owner level using maximum 28% rate.	Conduit—partners must account for their respective shares.	Conduit, with certain exceptions (a possible penalty tax)—shareholders must account for their respective shares.	Taxed at corporate level using maximum 34% rate. No other benefits.
Capital losses	Only $3,000 of capital losses can be offset each tax year against ordinary income. Indefinite carryover.	Conduit—partners must account for their respective shares.	Conduit—shareholders must account for their respective shares.	Carried back three years and carried forward five years. Deductible only to the extent of capital gains.
§ 1231 gains and losses	Taxable or deductible at owner level. Five-year lookback rule for § 1231 losses.	Conduit—partners must account for their respective shares.	Conduit—shareholders must account for their respective shares.	Taxable or deductible at corporate level only. Five-year lookback rule for § 1231 losses.
Foreign tax credits	Available at owner level.	Conduit—passed through to partners.	Generally conduit—passed through to shareholders.	Available at corporate level only.
§ 1244 treatment of loss on sale of interest	Not applicable.	Not applicable.	Available.	Available.

EXHIBIT 2.4 Continued

	Sole Proprietorship	Partnership*	S Corporation**	Regular Corporation***
Basis treatment of entity liabilities	Includible in interest basis.	Includible in interest basis	Not includible in stock basis.	Not includible in stock basis.
Built-in gains	Not applicable.	Not applicable.	Possible corporate tax.	Not applicable.
Special allocations to owners	Not applicable (only one owner).	Available if supported by substantial economic effect.	Not available.	Not applicable.
Availability of fringe benefits to owners	None.	None.	None unless a 2% or less shareholder.	Available within antidiscrimination rules.
Effect of liquidation/redemption/ reorganization on basis of entity assets	Not applicable.	Usually carried over from entity to partner unless a § 754 election is made, excessive cash is distributed, or more than 50% of the capital interests are transferred within 12 months.	Taxable step-up to fair market value.	Taxable step-up to fair market value.
Sale of ownership interest	Treated as the sale of individual assets. Classification of recognized gain or loss depends on the nature of the individual assets.	Treated as the sale of a partnership interest. Recognized gain or loss is classified as capital under § 741, subject to ordinary income treatment under § 751.	Treated as the sale of corporate stock. Recognized gain is classified as capital gain. Recognized loss is classified as capital loss, subject to ordinary loss treatment under § 1244.	Treated as the sale of corporate stock. Recognized gain is classified as capital gain. Recognized loss is classified as capital loss, subject to ordinary loss treatment under § 1244.

*Refer to Chapters 10 and 11 for additional details on partnerships.

**Refer to Chapter 12 for additional details on S corporations.

***Refer to Chapters 2 through 9 for additional details on regular corporations.

Source: *West's Federal Taxation: 1989.* Annual ed., Comprehensive Vol., pp. 19–35.

EXHIBIT 2.5   Examples of major SIC classifications

SIC Code—Manufacturing (Major Groups)

20 Food and kindred products
21 Tobacco manufacturers
22 Textile mill products
23 Apparel and other textile products
24 Lumber and wood products
25 Furniture and fixtures
26 Paper and allied products
27 Printing and publishing
28 Chemicals and allied products
29 Petroleum and coal products

30 Rubber and miscellaneous plastic products
31 Leather and leather products
32 Stone, clay, and glass products
33 Primary metal industries
34 Fabricated metal products
35 Machinery, except electrical
36 Electric and electronic equipment
37 Transportation equipment
38 Instruments and related products
39 Miscellaneous manufacturing industries

SIC Code—Wholesale Trade (Major Groups and Subgroups)

50   Wholesale trade—durable goods
501 Motor vehicles and automotive equipment
502 Furniture and home furnishings
503 Lumber and construction materials
504 Sporting goods, toys, and hobby games
505 Metals and minerals, except petroleum
506 Electrical goods
507 Hardware, plumbing and heating equipment
508 Machinery, equipment, and supplies
509 Miscellaneous durable goods

51   Wholesale trade—nondurable goods
511 Paper and paper products
512 Drugs, proprietaries, and sundries
513 Apparel, piece goods, and notions
514 Groceries and related products
515 Farm-product raw materials
516 Chemicals and allied products
517 Petroleum and petroleum products
518 Beer, wine, and distilled beverages
519 Miscellaneous nondurable goods

SIC Code—Retail Trade (Major Groups)

52 Building materials, hardware, and farm equipment dealers
53 General merchandise group stores
54 Food stores
55 Automotive dealers and service stations

56 Apparel and accessory stores
57 Furniture and home furnishings
58 Eating and drinking places
59 Miscellaneous retail stores

SIC Code—Food Stores

54   Food stores
541   Grocery stores
5411 Grocery stores
542   Meat markets and freezer provisioners
5422 Freezer and locker meat provisioners
5423 Meat and fish (seafood) markets
543   Fruit stores and vegetable markets
5431 Fruit stores and vegetable markets
544   Candy, nut, and confectionery stores

5441 Candy, nut, and confectionery stores
545   Dairy products stores
5451 Dairy products stores
546   Retail bakeries
5462 Retail bakeries—baking and selling
5463 Retail bakeries—selling only
549   Miscellaneous food stores
5499 Miscellaneous food stores

SIC Code—Services (Major Groups)

70 Hotels and other lodging places
72 Personal services
73 Business services
75 Auto repair, services, and garages
76 Miscellaneous repair services
78 Motion pictures
79 Amusement and recreation services
80 Health services

81 Legal services
82 Educational services
83 Social services
84 Museums, botanical, zoological gardens
86 Membership organizations
88 Private households
89 Miscellaneous services

Source: Executive Office of the President, Office of Management and Budget. *Standard Industrial Classification Manual,* 1987.

Retail

Retailing generally involves *collecting a diversity of goods and/or services in one or many locations and selling these goods to the final consumer (end user).* These products are for personal or household use.[15] In general, the retailing function is to gather goods and services (any of which customers could find elsewhere) under one roof for customer convenience. Most retailers are small both in numbers of establishments and in sales per establishment. Granted there are giants in the retail trade, but only 20 percent of these had sales exceeding $1 million in 1987.[16]

Wholesale

Wholesaling, as does retailing, sells goods but not to the end user or consumer. **Wholesalers** sell to retailers and middlemen, jobbers, or other users such as institutions or industries. These institutions or industries either resell these goods or services or use them in their own operations. The function of wholesalers is to gather goods and present them for sale to their customers (retailers). In general, wholesalers are small organizations but they deal in large quantities, since their profits are based on volume. They sell many products to many retailers.

Services

Unlike the tangible goods offered by the retailing and wholesaling sectors, the **service sector** provides benefits or satisfactions that are intangible; they are not products and do not result in ownership of anything physical. For example, the services of hotels, lawyers, accountants, and doctors provide needed benefits or satisfactions, not physical products or ownership. The service sector's growth is tied to the rise in disposable income and leisure time enjoyed by the majority of U.S. citizens as the economy grows. In times of contraction, this sector will decline, since people need more of their income for the basic necessities of life.

Manufacturing

Manufacturing is *the process of making or producing goods for individual and/or business use.* Manufactured products are tangible and are desired for their own use by individuals or households or for use by wholesalers and retailers for sale to others. The service sector also needs manufactured products for use in providing their intangible benefits. Small business employment in manufacturing is important in the United States economy, and its size is almost equivalent to that of the retail trade.[17]

One of the criticisms of the current U.S. economy is that it is shifting from a high value-added to a low value-added base. The argument is often heard that the United States is losing high-wage jobs in manufacturing and gaining only in low-wage service jobs. While this argument is beyond the scope of this chapter, it may be sufficient to state that in general, these charges do not prove true. Although traditional manufacturing may be decreasing, jobs attributed to high technology are increasing and these jobs are not necessarily low paying.

Summary

Sole Proprietorship

It is important that once you choose to own and operate a small business, you utilize the proforma of legal organization. While there is no one best form of organization and frequently organization format may be dictated by tax considerations, the business operator must know which forms of organization are available and the advantages and disadvantages of each form so that an intelligent choice may be made.

The simplest form of organization is the proprietorship. The **proprietorship** is *an unincorporated business owned and operated by one person*. It is easy to start, and the business owner has the opportunity to operate the business as he or she sees fit. All the profits and losses accrue directly to the owner. This form, however, is limited by the expertise and financial resources of the owner. To expand the financial base and managerial ability, the partnership form of organization can be utilized.

Partnership

A **partnership** is *an association of two or more people who carry on as co-owners of a business*. While an oral agreement can create a partnership, it is best to spell out all the terms, obligations, and privileges of this organizational format in a written partnership agreement, leaving as little room for questions as possible. Such an agreement would also delineate *various classifications of partners;* such as **general, limited, silent, secret, dormant, nominal, senior, and junior partners** which would be defined and agreed to in the partnership agreement. Lacking a written agreement, the Uniform Partnership Act will stipulate the rights and obligations of each of the partners. This act was created so that if the partnership lacks a written agreement, there is a body of laws governing partnerships.

There are several problems with proprietorships and partnerships, namely unlimited liability, double taxation, and the cessation of these forms upon the death of a principal, which spur creation of the corporation.

Corporations

The **corporation** is *an association of individuals united for a common purpose and permitted by law to use a common name and to change its members without dissolution of the association*. Liability extends only to the amount of money an individual has invested in the corporation. Personal assets are not subject to corporate obligations.[18] This form of ownership allows for increasing the capital and managerial base of the organization and allows it to continue in perpetuity regardless of who owns, buys, or sells the stock.

The pure form of the corporation, the "C" corporation, still subjects the owners to double taxation. Operating under a **"C" corporation** means that *the owner's salary is taxed as are any corporate dividends*. To mitigate this problem, the "S" corporation was developed. An **"S" corporation** *offers all the benefits of the corporate form of organization but permits all profits or losses of the organization to be taken on the personal tax return and therefore only subject to a simple tax*; both the "S" and the "C" corporations are governed by the corporate charter, which delineates all the agreed-on governing rules by which the corporation operates. With **limited liability,** investors can *limit their liability to the dollar value of their original or any subsequent investment*. A **limited liability corporation** *provides flexibility and limited liability while being treated by the IRS as a partnership*.

Classification of Business Firms

The Standard Industrial Classification System (SIC) has been developed to categorize, classify, and describe a business. Thus a business is able to classify itself in one of the major sectors of business activity: **retail**—*selling to the ultimate consumer;* **wholesale**—*selling to the retailer;* **service**—*selling nontangible products;* and **manufacturing**—*making tangible products.*

Once the firm is classified, comparisons can be made between your business and other firms of the same type. You are thus able to monitor your performance against sector norms and to take appropriate corrective actions if needed.

To facilitate this process, the government has defined business operations using the Standard Industrial Classification, identifying the type of business you are in.

Questions

1. What is the basic difference between a corporation and the other legal forms of organization?
2. What is the difference between a limited partnership and a general partnership? Define both terms in giving your answer.
3. Define proprietorship, partnership, and corporation.
4. Which legal form of organization would you choose and why?
5. Partnerships can be created with a handshake. What problems, if any, might arise and how would you prevent these problems from occurring?
6. The death of a partner might affect the operation of the business. Why would this be true?
7. What is a subchapter "S" corporation and why would you want one?
8. "The concept of limited liability is important and this applies to all legal forms of organization." Is this a true statement? Explain your answer.
9. What was the impact of the 1986 Tax Reform Act on electing to become an "S" corporation?
10. What are the Articles of Incorporation and what purpose do they serve?
11. What is the Uniform Partnership Act and why was it necessary?
12. What are the differences between a "C" corporation and an "S" corporation?
13. Discuss the advantages and disadvantages of being a sole proprietor.
14. How does death of an owner affect the corporate form of organization?
15. Discuss the advantages of a limited liability corporation.
16. What is the Standard Industrial Classification system (SIC)?
17. How would you use the SIC to determine your business health?
18. Describe the four generic types of business activity.

Problems

When doing these exercises, where applicable, be sure to select a specific business, preferably one where you presently or previously worked or a business you would like to own someday. If this is not possible, pick a specific organization to which you will refer. Be sure to identify the organization by name. Limit your answers to one or two pages per exercise.

1. Interview a small business owner operating as a sole proprietorship. Find out why this form of organization was chosen and prepare a report for class.
2. Interview a small business operating as a partnership. Find out why this form of organization was chosen and prepare a report for class.
3. Interview a small business owner operating under the corporate form of organization. Find out why this form of organization was chosen and prepare a report for class.
4. Using the information in questions 1, 2, and 3, compare your findings and determine if there is one best form of legal organization structure for small business. Prepare a report with a summary of your findings and conclusions.
5. Ask a tax lawyer about the affect of tax considerations on the choice of organization form. Prepare a report on your findings.
6. Assume you are going into business with several of your best friends. Draw up a partnership agreement that would be appropriate.
7. You and your friends decide you would prefer the corporate form of organization. Obtain and fill out the appropriate forms.
8. Using the four basic business types—retail, service, wholesale and manufacturing—determine from census figures the best potential areas of growth.
   a. Recognizing your personal characteristics, choose the type of organization you would like to own. Prepare a report justifying your choice.
   b. Assuming that your choice in part *a* did not coincide with the area of greatest growth, would you still pursue that area? Why?
   c. Picking a company in the area of low growth, interview the owner and determine his or her outlook and future plans.

Application Situations

1. East Shore Grille

While Charles and James Eastman were identical twins and had been raised as equals, they had different personalities. Charles was an outgoing, likable person. James was more reserved and made friends less easily. After college, Charles became a salesman, James an accountant. After several years, Charles tired of selling, called James, and convinced him to go into business together running a small restaurant.

Assignment

1. Answer the following questions:
   a. What legal form of ownership would you suggest for Charles and James? Why?
   b. If you suggest the corporate form of organization, should they consider "S" corporate status? Explain.
   c. What are the chances of success in this enterprise? Justify your answer.

2. Delvin's Market

Alan Sullivan was 58 years old and had been running his retail food store for approximately 30 years. He had done a good job, and the store was extremely profitable. Alan's daughter, Moira, a recent graduate of a large East Coast university as a marketing major, asked him if they could become partners in this enterprise.

Assignment

1. Answer the following questions:
   a. Would you recommend a formal partnership agreement? Why?
   b. What would you include in the partnership agreement? Draw up a simple partnership agreement.
   c. Would another form of organization structure be preferable? Explain.

3. Sherry White

Sherry White, a successful public relations director in one of the city's largest firms, felt that she would like to earn more than the relatively conservative interest rate the bank paid on her savings. Accordingly, she called a stockbroker who recommended that she purchase a portion of a hotel construction package and become a limited partner in this venture. It was, the broker assured her, backed by one of the largest hotel chains in the country, which was the general partner.

Assignment

1. Answer the following questions:
   a. What does the difference between a general and a limited partner mean for Sherry's control of the operation? Explain your response.
   b. Should Sherry attempt to become a general partner? Discuss your answer.

Integrative Case Question—CorLu Foods

CorLu has chosen the corporate form of organization. Draw up the required corporate agreements. (Please refer to the Integrated Case "CorLu Foods.")

Bibliography

Abbott, John T. "On Starting a Practice." *Journal of Accountancy* 137, no. 6 (June 1974), pp. 61–62.

Ahlbrandt, Roger S., Jr. "Technical Assistance for Small Manufacturing Companies: Management Issues for Nonprofit Providers." *Economic Development Review* 9, no. 1 (Winter 1991), pp. 29–33.

Antonini, Joseph E., and Lawrence R. Pugh. "Strategic Partnering," *National Retail Federation,* August 1992, pp. 4–10.

Argo, Marion C. "Small Business—to Incorporate or Not to Incorporate." *Woman CPA,* January 1977, pp. 31–32.

Baum, H. James. "Small Store Retailing: Survival of the Fittest," *Retail Control,*
April/May 1992, pp. 9–12.

Blackman, Irving. "Some Important Facts about Partnerships." *National Petroleum News,*
October 1978, p. 82.

"Choosing an Organizational Form for Your Company (Part 1)." *Consulting-Specifying
Engineer* 11, no. 2 (February 1992), pp. 19–20.

Colley, Geoffrey M. "The Implications of Incorporating a Business." *Canadian Chartered
Accountant* 108, no. 4 (April 1976), pp. 71–73.

Craig, Ben, and Stuart E. Thiel. "Large Risks and the Decision to Incorporate." *Journal of
Economics & Business* 42, no. 3 (August 1990), pp. 185–94.

Daskal, Melvin H. "What Form Should Your Business Take?" *Agency Sales Magazine,*
April 1980, pp. 10–13.

Elovitz, Kenneth M. "Choosing an Organizational Form for Your Company." *Consulting-
Specifying Engineer* 11, no. 3 (March 1992), pp. 23–28.

Fevurly, Keith R., and Bryan T. Schmitt. "New Rules for S Corporations." *Best's Review,*
March 1993, pp. 51–53.

Fike, Roy F., III. "Choosing the Best Form of Business Organization." *National Public
Accountant* 19, no. 4 (April 1974), pp. 14–18.

Gault, Robert F. "Managing Customer Satisfaction for Profit." *Management Review* 82,
no. 4 (April 1993), pp. 22–24.

Gumpert, David E. "Big Company Small Company: The New American Partnership."
Forbes, July 20, 1992, p. S1.

Helms, Marilyn M.; Paula J. Haynes; and Sam D. Cappel. "Competitive Strategies and
Business Performance within the Retailing Industry." *International Journal of Retail
& Distribution Management* 20, no. 5 (September/October 1992), pp. 3–14.

Hopson, James F., and Patricia D. Hopson. "Helping Clients Choose the Legal Form for
Small Business." *Practical Accountant,* October 1990, pp. 67–84.

Keim, Gerald, and Roger Meiners. "Limited Liability: Is It Essential to the Corporate
Form?" *MSU Business Topics* 27, no. 4 (Autumn 1979), pp. 45–51.

Lefebvre, Louis A.; Jean Harvey; and Elisabeth Lefebvre. "Technological Experience and
the Technology Adoption Decisions in Small Manufacturing Firms." *R & D
Management* 21, no. 3 (July 1991), pp. 241–49.

Mitchell, Bert N. "How to Structure Your Business." *Black Enterprise,* August 1976, pp.
31–33.

Mullin, Tracy. "Small Business Power." *Stores,* June 1993, p. 10.

Salomon, Richard. "Second Thoughts on Going Public." *Harvard Business Review* 55, no.
5 (September/October, 1977), pp. 126–31.

Shockey, Houstin. "Incorporating a Going Business: Tax-Free Route Not Always the Most
Advantageous." *Taxation for Accountants* 23, no. 4 (October 1979), pp. 210–14.

"What's the Best Legal Format for Operating Your Business?" *Profit-Building Strategies
for Business Owners,* September 1991, pp. 7–8.

Endnotes

1. U.S. Department of Commerce, *Statistical Abstract of the United States* (Washington,
D.C.: U.S. Government Printing Office).

2. Ralph V. Switzer and Edward D. Jones, "Orchestrating a Continuation Provision in a
Partnership Agreement for Estate Tax Purposes," *National Public Accountant* 37, no.
12 (December 1992), pp. 30–37.

3. Consider the dissolution of a large law firm, a partnership, where each of the partners was asked to contribute $5 million in order to resolve the debt obligations of the firm.

4. For example, if an individual wants to contribute funds to the partnership, but not become a full partner, thus being liable for the obligations of the business to the total extent of his resources, he becomes a limited partner. Limited partnership does not involve operation and decision making in the company and only exposes the limited partner to loss of those resources he originally contributed.

5. Donald J. Weidner and John W. Larson, "The Revised Uniform Partnership Act: The Reporters' Overview," *Business Lawyer,* November 1993, pp. 1–44.

6. In some instances, particularly in start-up, high-tech, and bio-tech firms, corporations' future rather than current profitability may be an investor's deciding criterion.

7. The highest individual tax rate is 28 percent while the corporate is 34 percent.

8. *The Wall Street Journal,* March 17, 1993.

9. "News You Can Use," *U.S. News & World Report,* March 7, 1994, p. 88.

10. The individual can, however, deduct only the amount of his cost basis. You cannot deduct more than the corporate liability to you. For example, in any year, you cannot deduct more than the amount of money you lend to the corporation in order to keep it in business.

11. *Federal Taxes,* 2nd ed. (Warren Gorham Lamont, 1992), Section 1.08.

12. Deborah L. Jacobs, "Limited-liability Companies," *D & B Reports,* July-August 1993, p. 51.

13. Jerry Williford as quoted in "Limited Liability: A Safer Strategy for Small Business," *Business Week,* July 18, 1994, p. 90.

14. Dun & Bradstreet, *Business Record* (New York: Dun & Bradstreet Corp., 1988), p. 2.

15. The Census Bureau defines retail trade as places of business where over one-half the annual sales volume consists of the sale of merchandise for either personal or household use.

16. *Census of Retail Trade,* 1987.

17. U. S. Department of Commerce, Small Business Administration, *Small Business in the American Economy* (Washington, D.C.: U. S. Government Printing Office, 1988), p. 48.

18. Except in cases of illegal activity such as fraud or nonpayment of employment taxes.

3   BUSINESS OWNERSHIP OPTIONS

In this chapter you will learn several ways to acquire your own small business. Rather than starting your own operation from the ground floor, you might wish to buy an established business or purchase a franchise. Each of these alternatives is explored, laying out the advantages and disadvantages of each approach. While none of these approaches is perfect for everyone, your decision about the method to use will be based on your knowledge of each method and how it fits in with your desires, ambitions, personal strengths, and weaknesses.

Chapter Learning Objectives

After completing this chapter, you should be able to:

- Give reasons to consider for starting your own firm.
- Formulate ideas on starting your own firm.
- Know the questions to ask if you are considering buying an existing business.
- Recognize the advantages and disadvantages of buying a business.
- Determine what a business is worth.
- Negotiate the purchase price.
- Know where to obtain management assistance in making your initial decision and in helping you to operate your business.
- Discuss what a franchise is and the advantages and disadvantages of purchasing a franchise.
- Define the following 11 key terms in order of appearance:

Systematic innovation	Capitalized value
Book value	Weighted average
Replacement cost	Auditing

Contingent liabilities   Franchisee
Franchise   Trade regulation rule
Franchisor

Owning a Business

Previous discussions may have convinced you that it is extremely attractive to own your own business; what you own, no one can take away. You may believe that the harder you work, the greater the rewards accruing and that you can make your own hours and have more leisure. These are agreeable concepts but not entirely true.

Often owning your own business means you work harder for less money and may even have less freedom and leisure time than any job allows. It is possible that when your business grows and prospers, all the traditional things (i.e., money and leisure time) will develop. It is also possible that they will not. You should own a small business because you derive satisfaction from the enterprise and would rather be engaged in that particular activity than anything else. Regardless of the reasons, once the decision to start a small business has been made, you must decide whether to start a new venture, buy an ongoing small business, or perhaps open a franchise.

Should I start a new venture or should I buy an ongoing small business? This is a fundamental question facing many would-be small business owners that cannot be treated lightly. Whether starting or buying an existing business, one must define the specific business to enter because to do otherwise would be a costly and time-consuming mistake. This chapter will explore the different aspects of the new venture versus the buyout. The chapter will also answer the question: "How much is an established small business worth?"

The New Venture

Some people have always dreamed about founding and operating their own business. New ventures develop from a variety of sources. The specific characteristic that defines pure entrepreneurship is systematic innovation. **Systematic innovation** is *a well-defined strategy for exposing new opportunities that occur from changes in industry, social, or economic environments.*

External Causes

Changes in industry, stimulated by advancing technology and new knowledge, spur new products and services. Inventions fall into this category. Entrepreneurs who introduce new products or services to the marketplace create more business opportunities than any other source of new ventures.[1] Unfortunately, this particular kind of opportunity is neglected because many entrepreneurs do not believe that their idea is salable. Cumbersome licensing and patent procedures and the threat of imitation by large companies are reasons for not exploiting new ideas more often.

Perhaps a person stumbles across a useful idea instead of deliberately trying to invent a new product. The Post-it product by the 3M Company is an example of the accidental discovery of a new product. The decision of the 3M company to let employees use 15 percent of their time working on their own projects resulted in Spenser Silver's development of what he hoped would be a superglue. The glue didn't work as desired and was consequently neglected for some years until Art Fry, a 3M scientist, decided that he needed something with which to mark his hymnal that wouldn't slip out of the book. In sending a note about it to his boss, he used a bookmark to scribble on and Post-It was invented.[2] Soon the entire office was using the sticky memo notes, which were convenient to place anywhere without getting lost in office traffic. This was the beginning of the very successful 3M Post-it product.

Changes in perceptions are an element of the social environment. A good example is the emphasis on health activities in the 1980s. The emphasis on fitness has stimulated new ventures that have provided us with a wide variety of innovative products and services. Enormous full-service health clubs have been springing up everywhere. Equipment such as stationary bicycles and electronic rowing machines as well as magazines devoted to fitness dominate the health scene. All of these new ideas developed as a result of changing social perceptions.

Economic changes often involve opportunities that arise out of necessity. The energy crisis in the 1970s led the way for new ideas in the energy conservation arena, such as thermal windows introduced to consumers living in cold regions. Energy-efficient appliances, automobiles, and solar products are now a part of everyday life. Energy is expensive, and new ideas for reducing its cost have emerged because of an economic stimulus.

Another good example of new ideas that stem from economic change can be attributed to the labor shortage in Japan. Contrary to popular belief, it was the labor shortage, not technical superiority, that spurred the use of robots in Japan. Today's use of robotics in industry is a base from which many entrepreneurs can build new ventures.

Voluntary Self-Employment

Voluntary self-employment usually, but not always, arises out of a variety of dissatisfactions with one's present employment. Prior work experience is the most common origin of new ventures. Frequently a person, perceiving ways to modify a product or improve a service, will start a new venture from the knowledge acquired from a former workplace. In this situation, the person benefits from knowing the strengths and weaknesses of the product. The suppliers of the materials needed to produce the product may also be known. There is some risk involved, however, since this source of a new venture may have legal consequences resulting in litigation if the former employer presses charges of product infringement or breach of an employment contract. Frequently, company employment contracts specify that ideas or innovations developed while in their employ are their property. Other employment contracts contain noncompetition clauses that prohibit former employees from conducting competing business within a given number of miles. If this occurs, the entrepreneur may be forced to pay a licensing fee or be forced to cease operations entirely. These problems may be overcome legally by starting a new venture in an unrestricted area, or waiting out time restrictions by working elsewhere in the interim.

A person can also obtain the right to manufacture a product based on a patent. An example of using patent rights is shown by looking at a well-known American company, Xerox. The process of photo duplicating was developed by a professor at the University of Chicago and was further refined by the Battelle Institute, a well-known and highly respected research and development organization. Battelle subsequently offered the license to its new photo-duplicating process to a small manufacturing company, which culminated the birth of the Xerox Company.

Another example of using prior work experience is when an individual, observing the scanty competition in a particular business, goes out and duplicates that same business.

Hobbies

Hobbies, which are another way for a person to develop a start-up business, may also become a full-scale business. The person who becomes aware of a market for a particular product that originates as they enjoy their hobby may turn a spare-time activity into an opportunity for beginning a small business. Because the person has to decide whether or not to leave the security of full-time employment to pursue a hobby, a potential small business owner should research the potential of such a project.

An example of a successful entrepreneur who turned his hobby into a multi-million-dollar business is Moe Siegal. Moe Siegal loved to collect herbs and make different tea mixtures out of them. His business grew from a one-man operation into a huge manufacturing concern noted for its colorful tea boxes. Mr. Siegal's Celestial Seasonings Company has been so successful that a food-processing manufacturer bought out the business recently for more than $20 million dollars, just 15 years after it began.[3]

These are some of the different ways a new venture can come about. An initial plan for a new venture is a must. Education, experience, and research are the ingredients for a successful business idea. The true entrepreneur systematically looks for business opportunities and generates new ideas, which if they are unique, require the entrepreneur to start from scratch.[4]

The person who contemplates a new venture has to ask realistic questions about the marketplace. Is this type of business a long-term opportunity or is it a short-term fad that can be exploited? Is this a genuine business opportunity and if it is, what will I use as a wedge to enter the market? These are only a few of the many questions the newcomer has to answer before embarking on a new venture. An introduction to some of the questions and answers can be found in *The Wall Street Journal* report, "Small Business."[5]

Starting your own business rather than buying one has some advantages. The entrepreneur can select the location, employees, and avoid any undesirable precedents set by a previous owner. A start-up business can start fresh without having to follow old practices.

All aspects of a new venture have to be carefully thought out and explained in a business plan. The business plan is the most crucial factor in the organization of the new venture. We will discuss the business plan in Chapter 5.

Buying an Established Business

Many people do not want to create and nurture a new venture. For these individuals, purchasing an established business may be the best approach. The start-up process is a hectic experience, whereas the buyout has had that path cleared by the previous owner. If you have decided to buy an existing business, you can either make an active search for an acquisition or acquire a targeted business. There are two approaches to take when looking for an acquisition:

1. Find out what companies are for sale.
2. Formulate specific criteria for acquiring one of them.

Acquisitions may be found through word of mouth, by directly approaching the owner, from advertisements in local papers under the heading "Business Opportunities," in business journals such as *The Wall Street Journal,* in trade associations magazines, and business brokers.[6] Business brokers are not regulated. Therefore, before approaching a broker, investigate carefully. Check out the broker with the local chamber of commerce, the Better Business Bureau, or the state's consumer affairs office. Ask the broker for references. You may actually have the opportunity to purchase an establishment that you have targeted for some time—perhaps a local store in your neighborhood or town—or you might have a chance to buy the company where you have been working.

The specific criteria that can serve as a guide for selecting a small business to acquire should be outlined. The criteria are based on your needs and expectations. For example, you can set a price range of $75,000 to $125,000 for a business that is located within a 15-mile radius. Whatever your criteria, you must look at the factors that determine a sound business purchase.

Evaluating a business involves a background investigation by:

Personal observation.

Talking to other parties.

Talking to outside experts.

For example, the SCORE services (Senior Corps of Retired Executives), an organization that operates under the auspices of the U.S. Small Business Administration, offers free expert advice to the public about the many aspects of buying a business. SCORE has many chapters generally associated with the SBA offices in all sections of the United States. Each chapter is composed of people from nearly all industries and, upon inquiry, will refer you to a person having experience in your industry. SCORE chapters are listed in local telephone books. The SBA itself has a publication giving the potential business buyer relevant questions to ask.

Your investigation should provide answers to the important questions that form the basis of your selection criteria. A major question often neglected in a buyout situation is: Can I generate profits from this business that are in line with my income needs? The following list provides some of the questions to think about concerning a prospective buyout.

Can I manage this business? Will I enjoy it? Can I afford it?

Why is the owner selling the business? Is he or she retiring, ill, or moving on to another venture?

What is the competition in the area? Is there a similar business likely to move in around the corner?

What is the customer and neighbor attitude toward this establishment? What kind of reputation does the present owner have?

What was the profit-line trend during the past five years? This year? Are the profits consistent with the sales volume?

What is the true value of the fixed assets and in what condition are they?

Is the neighborhood surrounding the business growing or deteriorating? What are the area's nationality and politics?

As you can see, the list of important factors to consider is lengthy, but answers to these questions as well as other information you gather will help you to conclude that "Yes, this business will be successful," or "No, this is not the right business for me; I'll have to look further." These questions are not the only ones you might ask. As you study the organization and learn more about it, other more specific questions will arise. However, a buyer is often anxious and as a result may rely solely upon the financial statements of the business to arrive at a decision. The nonquantitative questions indicate that you cannot rely solely on financial statements. Also, numbers on a balance sheet can be distorted and may need to be adjusted to reflect the true value of assets, liabilities, and net profits.

The reasons the seller states for selling are not necessarily the truth or may be the truth as he or she perceives it. Additionally, there are ancillary items to consider such as the advent of foreign competition. A computer manufacturing company may be for sale, for example, because of the recent sharp decline in profits due to foreign competition or changing technology. Both foreign competition and new technology have forced many American semiconductor manufacturers into bankruptcy.

Other considerations follow that are either advantages that encourage purchase or disadvantages that would discourage acquisition.

Advantages:

The business is in an established location.

The business already has established suppliers and customers.

Profits may be earned sooner and there is less start-up time required.

The owner will often groom the buyer.

The odds of a continuing profit are high.

The business has built up goodwill.

Disadvantages:

The purchase price cannot be justified.

The buyer will inherit ill will.

The building and the layout need modernization.

The current inventory is slow-moving or obsolete.

The business is illegally located.

The seller's credit practices are poor and the result is diminished cash flow and/or uncollectible accounts.

Unwanted or unnecessary employees may come with the business.

One of the disadvantages above highlights an unjustified purchase price. In the following section, we will discuss the different methods used to determine the worth of a business.

Worth of a Small Business

What is a business worth?[7] If you were to ask, you might find that very few business owners actually know what their business is worth. However, the large number of businesses changing hands during the 1980s gave rise to the profession of business valuation. Today's small business owners realize the importance of knowing the value of their business. In the short term, the ability to obtain bank loans requires this awareness; over a longer time horizon, if you are selling a business or issuing stock, you must know exactly what your business is worth.[8]

A conscientious business valuation expert will explore information including personal, financial, and legal relations among founding or owning families; from the game plans of prospective successors to whatever local, national, and worldwide conditions exist that affect the company. A simple valuation might cost under $2,000, while one that is complicated can run as high as $50,000, depending upon the specific circumstances of the transaction.

How does one choose a business valuation expert? The best way to choose one is by talking to a network of people both within and outside your geographical area. The most important attribute for a business valuation expert is experience. At least 15 years experience in the field is a must, along with being a CPA or possessing a master of business administration degree. You can contact the American Society of Appraisers to learn more about business valuation experts.

There are other ways to find out the worth of a business. The methods discussed below are the more traditional approaches used by the small businessperson and accountants. Before considering a company for purchase, you should have at least three years of current financial statements.

Book Value

The book value method is popular among many business owners. **Book value** equals *the value of assets minus the value of liabilities.*

The problem with a selling price determined solely by book value, however, is that assets on a balance sheet differ from reality. Book value tells nothing of a business's true worth. It is calculated in purely accounting terms, leading a buyer into thinking that a business's value is more or less than it actually is. With the high inflation of the 1980s, current asset market prices generally have inflated firms far beyond book value. An adjustment to the financial reports is usually required in order to estimate the true value of a business.

Ratios based on book value have been developed to help determine the selling prices for various businesses.[9] Examples of business-specific ratios are:[10]

Business	Selling Price
Coffee shop	Book value plus 3–4 months' gross income
Cocktail lounge	Liquor license plus gross income for 3–5 months
Retail business	1–3 times book value

Using the most recent balance statement of the company you are considering, book value would be $100,000, after the following calculations

Assets		Liabilities	
Cash	$500,000	Liabilities	$200,000
Inventory	100,000		
Equipment	100,000		
Furniture and fixtures	40,000		
Goodwill	10,000	Owner's equity	$100,000
	$300,000		$300,000

Book Value = Assets − Liabilities
$300,000 − $200,000 = $100,000

Replacement Cost

Book value, as discussed above, does not reflect the true value of a business's assets. To assess the true value of a business in today's dollars, you should assume that you are starting a firm and have no assets. Everything necessary to be in business, such as inventory, equipment, office supplies, and even real estate, must be purchased at current market prices. You then list all of the firm's assets and determine from newspapers, brokers, agents, and whatever other sources necessary the purchase price of each like asset.

For example, if the company you are thinking of purchasing has a 1990 four-color printing press, what would it cost you to buy this press today? You might find its value from any of the sources listed in the preceding paragraph.

The sum of all current valuations equals the **replacement costs** of a business. In addition, intangible assets must also be examined and incorporated into the company's replacement value.[11]

Using the same balance sheet numbers, the replacement costs in today's dollars are:

	Assets	
	Book Value	*Replacement*
Cash	$50,000	$50,000
Inventory	$100,000	$130,000
Equipment	$100,000	$125,000
Furniture and fixtures	$40,000	$50,000
Goodwill	$10,000	
	$300,000	$355,000

Replacement costs reflect today's values as $355,000.

Comparable Market Analysis

This method, which compares attributes such as the number of employees, sales, demographics, locations, and profit ratios bases the value of one business on the value of other similar businesses in the area that are for sale. A neighboring business that has the greatest number of comparables forms the basis for reaching a price decision. Subsequently a price is chosen from the businesses that most closely resemble yours so that from this analysis a range of values or prices can be determined. For example, a business that is similar to the one you desire but located on the other side of town is priced at $75,000. Another similar business that is for sale one block away, is priced at $86,000. Since you know your bid has to be competitive, your purchase price should be less than the highest asking price for a similar business but higher than the lowest-priced business. The range of values for buying your desired business, then, is $75,000 to $86,000. A competitive price for the business would be $81,000. Remember, these figures can change. The business you may be interested in may be similar to the highest-priced business that is one block away, but the owner may be highly motivated to sell and therefore the offering may be toward the lower end of the price range.

When the worth of the business is set by using the comparable market analysis method, it poses problems both for the buyer and the seller. The buyer may be overpaying for a business, or the seller may be undervaluing his or her interests. In any case, both parties should be aware of the shortcomings inherent in this type of valuation. Comparable market analysis is often used in real estate transactions involving residential units. Remember, each small business is unique in its own way. The most practical application of this method is for purchasing franchise units that have a high degree of uniformity.

Capitalized Earnings

This method assumes that a buyer is not buying assets using either the book value or replacement cost methods but is actually buying the opportunity to reap yearly profits. **Capitalized value** is *the value that would bring stated earnings at a specified rate of return.* You must choose a rate of return that will compensate you for your time and effort. The value is usually cast in terms of a percentage.

As a buyer you have to remember that you have other opportunities to earn at least as much with other investment instruments such as a mutual fund or a money market fund, for example. A question that will make this method clearer to you is: "What am I willing to pay for a chance to earn this particular profit for a given number of years?"

The capitalized earnings method has its drawbacks, though. After-tax profits can be calculated in several different ways, and the bottom line on an income statement can be manipulated and the accounting process could have been changed previously because of a change in ownership, necessitating adjustments to the financial statements.

If you use this method, it is wise to average the yearly profits for the past five years using weighted averages. The **weighted average** results from *assigning the greater importance, or weight, to the previous period than the prior period.* Each of the historical periods receives less weight the further it is from the present because the factors determining profits are more important in the immediate past. To determine the weighted average for income during the past five years, multiply the most recent figure by five, the next most recent by four, the next by three, and so on ($5\times + 4\times + 3\times + 2\times + 1\times$). Next divide by 15; this average represents the most likely annual income.

Because the capitalization rate is usually higher than you could earn if you invested your money in something generally considered to be safe such as a bank account, the rate can be different for individuals as investment philosophy differs. Now that you have the average annual income and chosen a capitalization rate (investment rate), there is a formula that will give you a good idea of what the business is worth to you:

$$\text{Value} = \text{Estimated earnings/Capitalization rate}$$

For example, the last five years' earnings of the company being considered for purchase were:

1994	$12,000
1993	14,000
1992	9,000
1991	7,000
1990	10,000

Using our formula:

$$12,000 \ (5) + 14,000 \ (4) + 9,000 \ (3) + 7,000 \ (2) + 10,000 \ (1)$$

$$= 60,000 + 56,000 + 27,000 + 14,000 + 10,000$$

$$= \frac{167,000}{15} = 11,133$$

Using a reasonably conservative 6 percent earning rate, the value of the business is 11,133/0.06 = $185,000.

However, this is not the value of the small business. One has to consider the rate of return you could earn if the money to be used to acquire the business were invested elsewhere. This amount is added to your salary from your present job, and the total is deducted from the calculated value. The amount or difference between the calculated value and what you could earn elsewhere (alternative investment and salary) is the value of the business to you. Now, you may ask: "Why do I have to consider all of these factors?" This process leads up to an important question that you, the entrepreneur, must ask yourself before leaping into this venture:

> Am I willing to give up the total amount I have calculated that I would earn doing something else in order to buy this business?

Another aspect to consider is the nature of future profits. For example, sun-tanning salons enjoyed a fantastic yearly return when they were first introduced to the public. Now profits have dropped because of health warnings from the government and medical experts. To be conscious of the future is to be money wise.

Do not expect the results of different valuation methods to be identical. Each valuation methodology will appraise the business differently, since they look at it from different viewpoints. The purchaser must use these results as guidelines as to the actual business value. The business may be worth more if you really want it, less if you don't. A conservative approach might be to use the average of the different answers.

Auditing

Auditing involves the use of financial statements. **Auditing** is *the verification of a firm's financial statements by an independent party.* Since the figures on both the income and balance statements can be manipulated, the first step to be carried out when auditing records is to find out what adjustments should be made to the seller's statements. Here, the services of an accountant who will examine bank loans, leases, public records, bills owed by customers, and any other pertinent information that is the source of the numbers on the financial statements are indispensable.

An independent **audit** *will reveal the true nature of the worth of the small business.* Although a prospective buyer will often depend on an accountant's signature as a seal of approval, remember that an accountant who has handled the seller's books over the years also serves as an adviser to the seller. This is why an adjustment of audited statements is necessary. After the audit, the accountant may use any one of the methods mentioned above, or any one of the formulas that are available from a variety of financial resources.

The Final Steps in Buying a Business

Negotiate to Close

Have you ever been to a yard sale? Chances are if you have, you probably negotiated the price of a sale item. Negotiation is not limited to yard sales and small money deals. Negotiation takes place after the price has been established for the buyout.

The two main factors involved with negotiation are:

1. Your top dollar price.
2. Your target price.

The top dollar amount is the highest amount that you are willing to pay, and the target price is a realistic price that you want to pay for the business. The seller usually asks 15 to 20 percent above the actual price. This leaves room for negotiation.

A successful negotiation is one in which you view the process as a win-win situation rather than a win-lose deal. Negative features are weighted against each positive feature. When negotiating a price, keep in mind the intangible factors that are an important part of the price. Goodwill is one such intangible item. **Goodwill** is *the asset value of an established name, image, and patronage that are publicly known.* Another intangible good is the benefit of an exclusive territory.

Usually the negotiation between the buyer and seller has a lot to do with financing. As the down payment increases, the price tends to fall. Other than the financing aspect of the deal, a few good rules to follow when negotiating are:

1. Be prepared: This will let you be more in control of the negotiation process.
2. Identify your own needs: The negotiation time frame will be shortened when you know exactly what you want from the seller.
3. Let your attorney be the middleman: The attorney can keep the emotions of the buyer and seller off the bargaining table. People tend to get into arguments when opinions differ. Consequently, the deal often falls through.
4. Be ready to leave the deal: Establish your limits before the negotiation process begins. Don't accept terms that you will be very unhappy with or terms that are very unfair to you.

Many books have been written on how to negotiate in a variety of common situations. By reading these books, the buyer can benefit greatly.

The Closing

The final step involves the closing of the purchase arrangement. The entrepreneur should have an attorney make certain that there are no legal implications or contingent liabilities present. A **contingent liability** is *a claim on the business that may result from some action.* A contingent liability might be a lawsuit against the business that has not been settled. After settlement, the business may have to pay out a sum of money that would change the value of the business. An attorney will handle the transfer of title as well as any other stipulations written into the purchase agreement. Regardless of how honest both parties may be, a handshake is not sufficient to close a deal. A written contract is needed to spell out such issues as the method of payment or agreements concerning assets.

And finally, now's the time that you, the official small business owner, have been waiting for! Your business is finally ready to function under your guidance. The rest of the chapters in the text will help you with the short-term and long-term tasks of operating a successful venture.

Acquiring a Franchise

While the opportunities to own and operate a small business are satisfied by the ability of the entrepreneur to start or buy an existing business, both options entail a relatively high level of risk. Forty percent of all start-up businesses fail in the first year of operation, and 90 percent of new businesses fail in the first five years.

Buying an existing business has its limitations in that the entrepreneur is tied to a specific product or service and only with difficulty can this be changed. Also, while an ongoing business has credibility, it belongs to the former owner and the new owner must either live up to or repair the firm's reputation.

To minimize the risk and to gain, at the outset, a thoroughly tested management technique as well as an established reputation, you can purchase a franchise.[12] The franchising industry generally uses the 95/5 rate (95 percent success/5 percent failure) to indicate the relative safety and low risk of buying a franchise.[13] This figure may be misleading since, "Reliable statistics for the overall success rate of franchised restaurants simply aren't available and franchisors haven't much incentive to disprove 95/5."[14] Others, however, argue that the failure rate for franchises may be as high as 25 percent to 35 percent.[15] Regardless of the actual success rate, it seems that franchising has a lower failure rate than starting a new business.

Modern franchising began in 1898 when General Motors began franchising its dealerships. In the early 1900s, both Rexall Drugs and Howard Johnson restaurants started selling franchises. A **franchise** is *a relationship between the franchisor (seller) and the franchisee (buyer)* where the franchisor grants the franchisee the rights and licenses to sell a product or service developed by the franchisor, which may include assistance in starting or operating the business or only the right to use the corporate name or logo and for which the franchisee pays a fee (or fees). Generally, the relationship is long term and continuing. The franchisee in effect purchases a business where all the preliminary start-up work has been performed. You are handed (for a fee) a business that does not have to be built from scratch and into which you can step almost immediately with the signing of the franchise papers. Better still, the business will be well financed and established in the consumer's mind. Familiar examples of franchises are McDonald's, Burger King, and Arby's Roast Beef, and automobile dealerships such as Chevrolet or Ford. A business that is a franchise cannot be assumed to be profitable. Franchises should be evaluated in the same way as any other business opportunity.[16]

Franchises may be purchased in three major categories. You may purchase only a **trade name** such as True-Value Hardware, where you are identified with the trade name without having to distribute products exclusively under the manufacturer's name or maintain uniform operating premises or systems. You may obtain a **product franchise** whereby you purchase the right to resell specific products that are sold through an exclusive and restricted distribution network under the manufacturer's name. Examples of this type of franchise include soft drinks such as Coca-Cola and gasoline—Citgo, Sunoco, Mobil. Finally, you may purchase a **turnkey franchise** where the franchisor supplies a complete business format encompassing every aspect of the business from the product to a complete operating system including plant, equipment, marketing, accounting, and other necessary services vital to operating a specific type of business. Every aspect of the business has been preplanned. All you have to do is to follow the terms of your franchising agreement.

Franchising succeeds because it enables someone to own and operate a small business using the systems and procedures of big business.

Advantages for the Franchisor

Franchisor is the term used when referring to *the party that already owns a franchise.* Why does an organization sell a franchise? Selling franchises allows the franchisor to expand in size and scope (including geographic) using other people's money. Expansion of a corporation the size of McDonald's would have taken many more dollars and much more time than it did if McDonald's had had to finance its own growth. Every time a franchise is purchased, more cash finds its way into the franchisor's bank account. Expansion becomes money generating rather than money absorbing. Imagine people paying you for the privilege of expanding your business! Of course, you give up a large amount of the profit by doing this, but you still make more than not doing it at all. For this privilege, in addition to the original franchisee fee, you charge a perpetual percentage of the gross as royalties as well as levying additional charges to cover marketing and other expenses. Not all is easy, however. The franchisor must maintain all the service necessary to supply and to supervise franchisees in order to ensure consistent quality and profitability.

Most people have heard of McDonald's Hamburger University, where franchisees are trained in every aspect of operating a McDonald's. Additionally, McDonald's oversees and controls the method of operation of each and every location. Deviation from the McDonald's system can result in the loss of the franchise. Doing all this is costly and time-consuming. But doing it this way has been, and will continue to be, profitable for the McDonald's parent organization.

In 1988, franchise sales made up 34 percent of all retail sales. This represented an increase of 91 percent since 1980.[17] McDonald's is not the only franchisor. There are more than 5,000 franchise opportunities encompassing both large and small firms in every field,[18] which can be found in the *1994 Franchise Opportunities Guide,* a publication of the International Franchise Association.

Advantages for the Franchisee

For a relatively small fee, the **franchisee,** *the individual or party acquiring a franchise from the franchisor,* obtains expertise through the franchisor that would be too costly for his or her individual business to acquire. A franchisor may offer benefits in the following areas:

1. Financing
2. Training
3. Marketing
4. Management

Financing

While the cost of opening and running your own business seems prohibitively high, franchisors can ease the burden. In many cases, the franchisee only has to provide a down payment while the franchisor, either through a third party (bank) or its own agency, helps secure a favorable loan for the balance. Often payments are tailored specifically to the individual borrower and may be spread out or even deferred during the first few years of operation. The franchisor's name and credit rating may often persuade banks to expand credit. In some cases, the franchisor will cosign on loans.

Training

Large organizations such as McDonald's, Holiday Inn, and Burger King have their own training operations. Fledgling franchisees may spend anywhere from a few days to a few weeks at a central location, where they are taught all aspects of the business from sweeping floors to accounting, cost control, and production. Training is often carried on with manuals and updates. In most cases a franchise representative visits the operation to offer further assistance. An on-site visit has a dual purpose, since the franchisor also wants to examine and maintain the quality of its franchises.

Marketing

The franchisor charges all franchisees a percentage of the gross receipts and uses that money to advertise its name and logo nationally. Being associated with a national company has many advantages. Customers often buy goods or services because they recognize the product by its reputation and know they can depend on consistent quality and service regardless of the location. Franchisors have often refined and perfected their marketing approach and are able to maximize advertising dollars. The local franchisee can copy these techniques and be assured of predictable results, which is why franchisors insist upon standardization and quality control.

Management

When you enter into a franchise agreement, you are actually buying a ready-made business. The operating systems have been tried, tested, proven, and standardized. Theoretically, if you manage your unit just as the franchisor requires, you will be profitable. Actually, you will have a better chance to become profitable, since you will not endure a long period of trial and error while you learn the business.

Disadvantage of Franchising

There are several limitations the prospective franchisee must consider before signing up.

Costs

One of the compelling aspects of starting one's own firm can be the ability to start with limited income, in some cases zero capital. Steven Jobs started Apple Computer in a garage. Other large corporations such as the Polaroid Corporation and Head skis began the same way. Franchises, however, frequently require franchise fees and the down payment to be paid in cash. Starting a McDonald's may require the franchisee to have and invest $500,000; other franchises may require similar amounts of capital. The better known and more profitable the franchise, the more capital is required of a new franchisee; less well known or less capital-intensive operations may require less capital. Additionally, you should recognize that profits don't accumulate immediately upon opening your doors. In fact, when you start a business, you should have enough money to cover living expenses for yourself plus shortages in the business cash flow for six months to one year. If you franchise, capital requirements are higher than if you don't, but you are buying all the benefits a franchisor has to offer, which is a good investment.

Restrictions and Limitations

Entrepreneurs like the freedom of owning and operating their own business. They may run it the way they please and answer to no one but themselves. Becoming a part of a franchise means relinquishing this freedom. The other side of having all the standardization a franchise has to offer is that you must adhere to its policies and rules. You are giving up freedom for an increased certainty of success. There is nothing wrong with this approach if you recognize that your independence is limited. In fact, not operating by the franchise rules could cost you the franchise.

Once the agreement is signed, the franchisee is committed to paying, forever, all the fees and costs associated with the agreement. Frequently, you pay a percentage of gross receipts, national advertising assessments, and other required fees. You should also recognize that there are limitations on growth. A franchise gives you exclusive rights to operate within a certain well-defined area, since the franchisor will not sell another franchise in the same area. You, on the other hand, cannot expand out of this area, and consequently your growth is limited. In order to expand, you have to buy another franchise location.

Purchasing a franchise does not guarantee success and should be done with all the normal and prudent precautions to avoid being taken in by weak or nonexistent franchises from unscrupulous franchisors. While some claim that only 5 to 10 percent of franchisors are dishonest,[19] you should not purchase a franchise unless you are given the franchise contracts as well as the required disclosure statement. Do not make decisions without detailed analysis of all financial statements. Walk away if no financials are supplied. Sellers tend to predict high profits and a rosy future. Be skeptical. Even if the franchise is legitimate, profits flow only from dedication and hard work. Make certain that you interview operating franchise units and examine the physical facilities. Only then will you be able to judge whether you will be satisfied. Above all, make sure you will be happy actually working at whatever product or service your franchise provides.

Trade Regulation Rule

Recognizing that the potential for fraud and deception exists, the Federal Trade Commission enacted the Trade Regulation Rule in October 1979. This rule covers all franchisors (even those in states that do not have disclosure acts). All franchisors must disclose detailed information on their operations at the first personal meeting or at least 10 days before a franchise contract is signed or before any monies are paid.

The goal of the Federal Trade Commission is to enable the buyer to make intelligent decisions based on the franchisor's disclosure of information. Although the Federal Trade Commission requires disclosure, it does not guarantee the accuracy of the information. Therefore, when you are considering purchasing a franchise, obtaining and reviewing the information supplied should be the first step in your investigations. Familiarize yourself with the Trade Regulation Rule and make certain that you obtain all the information it stipulates.

Of necessity, the purchase involves signing a franchise contract. You as well as your attorney should review the contract and make certain that all its terms and conditions are clear and agreeable.[20] The franchisee is bound by the contract terms. The contract is written by the franchisor, who will enforce it.

If the terms are not agreeable, the best decision may be to seek out another opportunity. As there is a perceived inequity in bargaining power between franchisors and would-be franchisees, some states have passed franchise relationship laws to correct this.[21] There is no federal equivalent except for the Federal Trade Regulation Rule.

Sources of Assistance for Small Business

Now we will look at where the owner may turn for assistance in planning and organizing a business operation. For the small business manager, the major need for outside consulting is in the financial area. We will touch upon this in this chapter and explore it in depth in a later chapter. This section will focus on external sources of help that are available concerning the operation of the business.

Assistance to small businesses usually takes the form of financial consulting—advice about sales, accounting, merchandising, advertising, and other activities. The following is a list of various sources that are available for small businesses, but it is by no means a complete list.

U.S. Small Business Administration (SBA).

Minority enterprise agencies and associations.

Small business investment companies.

Venture capital firms.

Trade associations.

Federal, state, and local government agencies.

Colleges and universities.

Consulting firms.

Manufacturers interested in dealers and distributors of their product.

U.S. Small Business Administration

The U.S. Small Business Administration, formed in 1953, is now a permanent agency of the U.S. government. The SBA engages in a wide range of activities and offers several forms of assistance.

Financial Assistance

The SBA provides information to assist an individual or company in obtaining a conventional loan. If it appears that a business will not be able to get a conventional loan, the SBA might consider a participating loan with a bank or may, in a limited number of cases, make a direct loan if funds are available. Most loans, however, are made in conjunction with a bank, with the SBA guaranteeing up to 90 percent of the bank loan or $350,000, whichever is less, at an interest rate set by the bank. These limits change from time to time, and the small business owner should check with the SBA about current policy. Funds obtained with SBA assistance can be used for business expansion, construction, purchasing machinery, equipment, supplies, and materials, as well as for working capital.

Economic Opportunity Loans
The SBA provides Economic Opportunity Loans to disadvantaged businesspersons so that they may have an opportunity to own their own business. These are available to people whose incomes are too low or who cannot obtain financing because of social or economic disadvantages.

State and Local SBA Development Companies
These are organized by or under the auspices of the SBA in order to promote the expansion of small businesses within a state. Through these companies, loans are made available and underwritten by local people who put up money to finance local community development.

Disaster Loans
The SBA also provides money for businesses that have suffered damage from storms, flood, hurricanes, volcanic eruptions, and earthquakes. Money for hardships caused by urban renewal and compliance with new legislation is also available.

Lease Guarantee Program
Under this program, the SBA will insure leases obtained by a businessperson who otherwise lacks the credit rating necessary to quality for a lease on more desirable premises. This is offered to the businessperson who needs a good or improved location.

Procurement Assistance
This program allows small businesses to participate in certain federal government contracts. Some prime contractors are required to subcontract to small businesses in order to win a contract award. A number of activities associated with the procurement assistance program help the smaller business: Information meetings and seminars are held to inform the small business on how to bid; small businesses are informed of pending contracts, and efforts are made to sell surplus property to small businesses.

Management Assistance
The SBA has devised programs that provide direct management assistance to small businesses. Through training programs, the SBA conducts courses, conferences, problem clinics, and workshops. The courses help formulate policies, identify objectives, and help guide business owners in other areas. The conferences deal with specific and particular topics, whereas the clinics and workshops are concerned with, and concentrate on, problems and problem solving.

Service Corps of Retired Executives

The Service Corps of Retired Executives (SCORE) is composed of former business executives who offer their services to help the emerging small business. The process involves meeting with SCORE personnel, who will then assist the business owner and offer some suggestions generally based on the seasoned executive's background. The SCORE participants are volunteers, not paid consultants.

Minority Enterprise Agencies and Associations

The federal government has committed itself to helping develop and promote minority-owned small businesses. Assistance programs have been developed in an effort to improve the economic position of minorities, and direct funding of businesses is also available to qualified applicants. The U.S. Office of Minority Business Enterprise (OMBE) disburses most of the technical assistance provided by the federal government. The focus of this office is primarily on topics such as local business development organizations, business research centers, trade associations, and other joint programs with state and local government agencies. The agency counsels minority business owners, assists in the preparation of loan packages, and provides management and technical assistance.

Small Business Investment Companies

There are several Small Business Investment Companies (SBIC) whose primary purpose is to provide equity loans, long-term loans, and management assistance. This service is provided to those businesses that are at least 50 percent owned and managed by persons who are socially or economically disadvantaged. SBICs were formed by the Small Business Investment Act of 1958, and as of 1987 became conventional organizations. SBICs are generally interested in larger small businesses that have demonstrated definite growth potential and some type of proven track record within an established profit pattern and growth. This tends to exclude the true small business and those just starting out. The SBIC tends not to be interested in businesses that are in conventional industries or that have stabilized business growth.

Incubator Programs

An innovative service, called the Incubator Program, was created by the SBA to increase the success rate of new business by encouraging and nurturing the small business venture. The central purpose of this concept is to bring together several small firms under one roof, reducing each firm's overhead costs. The advantages to this arrangement include sharing centralized services, such as secretarial, administrative, shipping, computers, and overall facilities. It provides a new business with a buffer against administrative expenses during its early, more vulnerable stages of development. The program provides the business more latitude so that a management error that potentially might have jeopardized the firm's survival can now be regarded as a learning experience. Valuable working capital is freed up from shared overhead costs. As the name suggests, the incubator program is a nurturing period whose ultimate goal is to aid the firm as it makes the transition to more orthodox environments. Incubator programs can be developed by local communities, development organizations, corporations, or other sponsors.

Several reasons cited for establishing incubator programs include profit, use of empty buildings, job creation, redevelopment, and economic growth. The SBA provides information and a start-up booklet on the incubator program.

Venture Capital Firms

These private-sector firms make capital available to new or expanding businesses[22] under somewhat more risky situations; many provide help in organizing and operating the firm. Venture capital firms are usually interested in businesses that are stable in the short term and have substantial long-term growth. The venture capitalist bases the decision on whether or not to back a firm after performing an analysis of the risk versus the potential payoff. The use of venture capital tends to be expensive (considering the risks involved with small businesses and the high failure rate) and should be weighed only after other alternatives have been evaluated. Bankers, SBIC managers, and others in finance are all potential sources if one is looking for venture capital.

Trade Associations

Almost every type of small business is, in one form or another, identified with a trade organization, which usually offers helpful materials to members. Newsletters or magazines published by the association contain advertising targeted at that industry; they also contain useful feature articles and other information written by outside experts as well as other members. Some associations may offer training programs and other educational materials, but generally they provide self-help information. A trade association may use meetings, workshops, and other functions to introduce and circulate ideas among its members. The main purpose of trade associations is to expose members to activities and methods that are used in the industry. A trade association is focused on its members and therefore tends to be geared more to the established business than to newcomers. A new business firm can, however, make use of the accumulated experience of older firms. Typically, trade associations offer the following to their members:

The promotion of better organizational management methods (i.e., accounting and record keeping, cash flow analysis, ordering and returning policies, employee relations, etc.).

Conducting industrywide meetings to develop management leadership in the industry.

Acting as a liaison between federal and state agencies and individual members.

Providing current information to members concerning impending government legislation as well as other matters.

Offering technical advice specific to the industry.

Offering training programs and various types of workshops.

Publishing data concerning activities such as sales promotion, public education about products, and recruitment techniques.

Gathering statistics on the industry (benchmarking).

Supplying other services such as group insurance rates, credit reporting, and various economic studies.

A small business owner should seriously consider becoming a member of a trade association because the benefits derived are greater than the cost of the dues. The number of trade associations is so large that it would be impossible to list them all. Two of the best sources a manager should consult in determining which associations would best fit his or her situation are *Who's Who in Association Management* and the *National Trade and Professional Associations of the United States and Canada.* Both are published through the American Society of Association Executives.

Colleges and Universities

Another relatively unfamiliar source of help is local colleges and universities. In addition to their extensive research facilities and resources, many institutions provide specific training seminars for those interested in operating a small business. There are classes for those who need help in organizing and managing a business, as well as seminars on successful strategies employed by other businesses.

Small Business Institutes

Some 500 universities and colleges offer free consulting services to small business. These institutes are affiliated with the SBA. The educational institution uses a student team to assist the small business in any or all facets of operations.[23] Access to such services can be obtained through an SBA referral.

Consulting Firms

Management is becoming an increasingly complex and specialized activity. The small manager is more than ever expected to be an expert in all facets of business management; to survive in today's competitive environment, he or she must be knowledgeable in all areas. Since most managers are skilled in only a few areas, however, they need to seek outside expertise to compensate for their deficiencies in other areas. Many problems requiring the special abilities of consultants are intermittent and of short duration. For this reason, it would not prove cost-effective for a small business owner to permanently employ specialists on a full-time basis. A small business usually needs specialized assistance only when a serious difficulty is encountered or for periodic checkups to avoid potential problems in the future.

Management consultants are fairly expensive, but they are an excellent investment. Consultants costing $200 dollars or more per day may be needed for only a short period of time; therefore, the manager must weigh the cost of leaving the problem, or potential problem, unsolved against the cost of hiring the consultant. A management consultant's job consists primarily of two parts: (1) an analysis of the problem or weakness and (2) recommendations for solving the problem. The recommendations need not necessarily be followed exactly but should be used as a guideline, since the manager or owner is the one who ultimately decides which course of action to pursue and how it is to be implemented. Consultants are one of the best sources of assistance because while on the project the consultant can specifically focus on that particular business and the factors surrounding it. He or she can then tailor solutions for management.

A manager can locate consulting firms through their respective trade associations, word of mouth, or through yellow pages of the local telephone directory.

Suppliers and Equipment Manufacturers

A final source of help available to small business owners is their manufacturers and suppliers. These firms often have valuable information, usually available free or at a very nominal charge, that they are happy to share with their customers. They provide this service to promote the solvency of their customers; if their customers do well, the manufacturers and suppliers to that business also profit. Additionally these services also build and promote the supplier or vendor's own goodwill. Some companies have established departments or divisions to provide assistance and information to small business owners. For example, assistance in planning store layout might be available from floor covering or display manufacturers. This is both an effective and inexpensive source, which every small business owner should use.

Summary

Once you have become convinced that you want to own a small business, you need to become highly focused. What business do you want to be in? Do you wish to start a new venture, buy an existing business, or open a franchise? Purchasing a business means that you must know how to establish the value of an established small business.

The New Venture

New ventures develop from a number of sources. The specific characteristic that defines pure entrepreneurship is **systematic innovation,** a *well-defined strategy for exposing new opportunities that occur from changes in industry, social, or economic environments.* New ventures arise from perceiving change, deriving new ways to meet the change, creating new products to fulfill needs that have not been previously identified, or filling identified needs in a new way. New ventures may spring from external causes, voluntary self-employment, or hobbies. No matter how new ventures develop, it is important to note that while there are advantages to starting a new venture, doing so means it may take a long time to establish a self-sustaining business.

Buying an Established Business

A viable alternative would be to buy an established business. Purchasing an ongoing concern means that your decision has been to let someone else establish the business and build on that as a base.

Worth of a Small Business

The purchase option involves determining or setting a purchase price. The price may be set by using **book value,** which equals *the value of assets minus the value of liabilities,* **replacement cost,** which is *the sum of all current valuations,* or **capitalized value,** which is *the value that would bring stated earnings at a specified rate of return.* The results of using these methods may differ. You have to decide which method more accurately reflects the true value of the business. In doing so, always give more importance to the immediate past and ascribe less importance to the firm's historical operating results. Use **weighted averages,** which are *the results of assigning the greater importance, or weight, to the previous period than the previous period than the prior period.* When purchasing a business, its financials should be audited. **Auditing** is *the verification of a firm's financial statements by an independent party* such as an accountant or someone versed in accounting and preferably familiar with the principles of investing.

The Final Steps in Buying a Business

As there are only suggested rules or methods of evaluation, the purchase price of an established business is determined through negotiation. The final price results from balancing the positive and negative features of the business and satisfying both the buyer and the seller. **Goodwill,** which is the *publicly known asset value of an established name, image, and patronage* and **contingent liabilities,** which are *claims on the business that may result from some action,* are extremely important and may play a significant role in arriving at the final price.

Acquiring a Franchise

Purchasing a franchise will minimize the risk and enable you to gain, at the outset, an established reputation. A **franchise** is a *relationship between the franchisor (seller) and the franchisee (buyer).* Franchising enables you to start your own business with a tremendous support mechanism and infrastructure already in place. The support system, of course, has costs, and you should be aware of them, as these costs usually extend for the life of the franchise. The **Federal Trade Regulation Rule** *enables buyers to make intelligent decisions based on the franchisor's disclosure of information.*

Source of Assistance for Small Business

Assistance to small business can be provided through financial consulting—advice about sales, accounting, merchandising, advertising, and other activities. A number of sources are available to small businesses.

Questions

1. Why does an entrepreneur start a new venture rather than buy an existing firm?
2. Why would you rather buy an existing venture than start an entirely new firm?
3. How do you determine what business you should be in?
4. Having made the decision to buy an existing business, where and how would you find one?
5. What factors would you consider before buying a business?
6. List the advantages and disadvantages of buying a business.
7. How do you determine the value of the business you wish to buy?
8. What is the difference between book value and replacement value? Do you care?
9. Define "capitalized value"? Why is this concept important?
10. Do you have to audit the books of a company you plan to purchase? What would you look for in such an audit?
11. Discuss the statement that there is "one best way" to approach buying or valuing a business.
12. What is a franchise, and why is it different from other forms of business?
13. Are you an entrepreneur if you decide to purchase a franchise? Defend your position.
14. Why would you want to purchase a franchise rather than start a new venture?
15. How would you evaluate the information supplied by a franchisor?
16. What are the three major types of franchises?
17. What advantages does a franchisor derive from the sale of a franchise?
18. What are the advantages of being in an "incubator"?
19. Define the following terms: franchise, franchisor, franchisee, franchise fee, royalties.

Application Exercises

When doing these exercises, where applicable, be sure to select a specific business, preferably one where you presently or previously worked or a business you would like to own someday. If this is not possible, pick a specific organization to which you will refer. Be sure to identify the organization by name. Limit your answers to one or two pages per exercise.

1. Describe your educational and work experience and evaluate how you could apply this experience in:
   a. Buying an established business
   b. Starting a business
   c. Purchasing a franchise.

2. Interview a business owner and ask why he or she decided to buy or continue operating the firm rather than start a new venture. Report on the reasons given and whether or not you agree with these reasons.

3. Talk to the people responsible for selling franchises at a national chain such as McDonald's or Burger King and have them send you a franchise package. Evaluate the information and report to the class why you would or would not start this franchise.

4. Choose a small business whose owner you are personally familiar with and establish a value for the firm if this owner were to sell.

5. Check into the literature of small business such as periodicals and journals and find articles on new ventures. Write a report describing the source of these ideas.

6. Contact a business broker (you can find listings in the yellow pages of your telephone book or in the newspaper classified section for "Business Opportunities") and ask how the broker would value a business. Write a report about the evaluation method.

7. Under "Business Opportunities" in the newspaper, find a business for sale. Arrange an interview with the owner and write a report on the business. State why you would or would not buy the company.

8. Contact the local owner of the franchise you examined in question 4 and find out how and why the owner decided to franchise rather than buy another business or start a new venture. Prepare a report on your findings.

9. Determine the business you would like to own. Go to the SBA and find out how to:
   a. Find such a business
   b. Value such a business
   c. Obtain help in the process of locating, purchasing, and running the business.

Application Situations

1. Friendly Woods

Based upon the success of Pet Rocks, Sheila Masterson decided to start a new venture selling "Friendly Woods," small squares of oak wood with smiling faces on them. The business did well and had 75 percent increases in revenues for each of the first three years of its life. Desiring a change, Sheila put the company up for sale.

Assignment

Answer the following questions.
If you were to buy this business:

1. How would you value the company?
2. What information would you need before you could make a decision?
3. Is there some qualitative information that you might use in making a decision?

2. Mr. Zero's Barbecued Chicken Wings

Don Brown was heavily involved in defense weapons work as a specialist in a particular missile. Current events have led to a diminished demand for such missiles, and Don was laid off. Determining to never again be subject to such political events, Don looked at several franchise operations and decided that a Mr. Zero's Barbecued Chicken Wings franchise would be worth considering.

Assignment

Answer the following questions:

1. Is Don's background and experience important in making this decision?
2. What information would Don need before making a decision? Where would he get such information?
3. What information would you need before you would advise Don on the feasibility of proceeding?

Integrative Case Question—CorLu Foods

Given the information provided in the CorLu case, determine the value of the company. (Note: you may have to assume past earnings.) (Please refer to the Integrated Case "CorLu Foods.")

Bibliography

Dunn, I. John, and Robert H. Lee. "Making the Big Play: Structuring New Ventures through the Team Approach." *Pennsylvania CPA Journal* 59 (Winter 1989), pp. 10–14.

Frost, Ted S. "How to Be a Smart Business Buyer." *D&B Reports* 38 (March/April 1990), pp. 56–58.

Learned, Kevin. "What Happened before the Organization? A Model of Organization Formation." *Entrepreneurship: Theory and Practice* 17 (Fall 1992), pp. 39–48.

"Resources on Franchising." *Nation's Business* 81 (April 1993), pp. 54–55.

Schaeffer, Bruce S.; John L. Allbery; and Tim C. Myers. "Franchises Have Created New Challenges for the Estate Planner." *Taxation for Accountants* 42 (January 1989), pp. 40–42.

Strischek, Dev. "Lending to Franchises." *Commercial Lending Review* 8 (Spring 1993), pp. 10–21.

Sturgis, Ingrid. "Five Keys to Successful Franchise Ownership." *Black Enterprise,* May 1993, pp. 77–82.

Whittemore, Meg. "The Franchise Search." *Nation's Business,* April 1993, pp. 49–54.

Endnotes

1. John Case, "The Dumb Debate over Small Business and Jobs," *Boston Globe,* May 25, 1994, p. 46.
2. "Post-It: How a Maverick Got His Way," *Marketing,* October 28, 1993, p. 3.
3. Earl C. Gottschalk, Jr., "More Ex-managers Seek to Turn Hobbies into Full-Time Businesses," *The Wall Street Journal,* December 23, 1986, p. 21.

4. "100 Ideas for New Business," *Venture,* December 1987, pp. 35–70.

5. "Small Business," *The Wall Street Journal,* October 15, 1993, pp. B1–B26.

6. "Selling Your Small Company," *Business Week,* October 15, 1992, p. 101.

7. For a good discussion of the worth of a business, see James E. Schrager, "How Much Should You Pay for a Dream?" in "The Manager's Journal," *The Wall Street Journal,* August 12, 1992, p. A6.

8. Glen Cooper, "How Much Is Your Business Worth?" *In Business,* September/October 1984, pp. 50–54.

9. These ratios can be obtained from the U.S. Small Business Administration. In addition, reference materials found in public libraries such as the *Small Business Resource Directory* are helpful.

10. Also see Andrew Fineberg, "What's It Worth," *Fortune,* January, 1988, p. 30.

11. "How to Put a Dollar Value on Intangible Assets," *The Business Owner,* October 1980, p. 7.

12. Suzanne Hansmire, "A Piece of the Dream," *Boston Herald,* March 8, 1993, p. 42.

13. *Profiles in Franchising Leadership* (Laguna Hills, Calif.: Sir Speedy, Inc., 1992), p. 14.

14. "How Safe Are These Things?" *Restaurant Business,* March 20, 1992, p. 66.

15. Ibid.

16. "Evaluating Franchise Opportunities," U.S. Small Business Administration, Business Development Publication (U.S. Printing Office, 1988).

17. "Tenth Annual Franchise 500," *Entrepreneur,* January 1989, p. 114.

18. *Entrepreneurial Notes from the University of St. Thomas Center for Entrepreneurship,* April 1994, p. 3.

19. "Franchising: The Strings Attached to Being Your Own Boss," *Changing Times,* September 1984, p. 70.

20. Teri Agins, "Owning Franchises Has Pluses, but Wealth Isn't Guaranteed," *The Wall Street Journal,* October 22, 1984, p. 34.

21. Thomas M. Pitegott, "Franchise Relationship Laws," *Business Lawyer,* November 1989, pp. 289–331.

22. "Venture Capital Flow Nears Record Level," *Boston Business Journal,* July 23–29, 1993, pp. 1, 24.

23. The latest estimates provided at the 1993 annual meeting of SBIDA directors indicate that there are approximately 500 universities and colleges helping approximately 6,000 to 9,000 firms annually.

II   BUSINESS PLANNING

C H A P T E R

4 THE LEGAL ENVIRONMENT AND SOCIAL RESPONSIBILITY

In this chapter you will learn about some basics of business law, including contracts, the Uniform Commercial Code, agency relationships, and how to protect intangible assets; government regulation of free competition, consumer protection, employment practices, safety and health practices, and public welfare; how to select a lawyer; and the social and ethical responsibility of the small business to its employees, customers, suppliers, stockholders, competitors, and society in general. To be socially responsible the firm must exceed the minimum regulations set by the government. To help ensure ethical behavior, management and employees should follow the stakeholders' guide to ethical decisions.

Chapter Learning Objectives

After completing this chapter, you should be able to:
- List and explain the five elements of a contract.
- List and explain three methods of protecting intangible assets.
- Discuss five areas in which the small business must conform to government regulations.
- Describe how to select a lawyer.
- Explain what a firm must do to be socially responsible.
- Explain the difference between ethical and unethical behavior.
- Describe why the small business owner/manager needs to be the ethical leader by example, and to enforce ethical standards.
- State the stakeholders' guide to ethical decisions.
- Define the following 17 key terms in order of appearance:

Contract
Five elements of a contract
Sales contract elements
Warranty
Agent
Trademark
Patent
Copyright
Social responsibility

Stakeholders
Ethics
Ethical behavior
Unethical behavior
Whistle-blowing
Better Business Bureau
Credo
Code of ethics

Introduction

A small business owner is not expected to be a lawyer. However, *ignorance of the law is not an acceptable excuse for breaking the law.* You need sufficient knowledge of the law to avoid poor business decisions that can result in your going to court. The legal environment in which you are conducting your business has become hostile.[1] A lawsuit brought against your firm can result in punitive damages. Punitive damages serve two primary social functions: retribution and deterrence.[2] Punitive damages could result in losing your business. On the other hand, familiarity with the legal system can be used to safeguard your firm and provide opportunities for your business. Through this chapter you will learn about some fundamental legal issues in the complex legal environment. It is important, however, to understand the need to seek legal counsel from an attorney when making business decisions, and possibly to defend yourself against a lawsuit.

Basics of Business Law

In this section you will learn about contracts, the Uniform Commercial Code, agency relationships, and how to protect intangible assets.

Contracts

A **contract** is *a binding agreement creating an obligation among the parties involved.* Contract law governs the rights and obligations of the parties to the contract. Virtually every business relationship is a contract with promises to be fulfilled. The small business enters into contracts with its employees, customers, suppliers, and others. Both oral and written contracts are legally binding.[3] A valid contract must have five separate elements. The **five elements of a contract** are: *agreement, consideration, legality, capacity, and form.*

1. *Agreement:* A genuine offer of the seller must be unconditionally accepted by the buyer. An offer is a promise or commitment to do or refrain from doing some specific thing in the future. The terms must be either expressed or be capable of being implied in the offer. The offeree must voluntarily accept the terms exactly as the offeror presents them. Counteroffers can be accepted as sales contracts.

2. *Consideration:* Something of value must be received by the seller. Consideration is what the promisor requires in exchange for the promise; the exchange does not have to be fair. Consideration may be stated as a price, but it can also be a promise to do or not to do something.

3. *Legality:* The agreement and consideration must be legal to be binding. A promise to sell illegal products for a set price will not be enforceable through the legal system.

4. *Capacity:* All parties to the contract must be capable of entering into a legal contract. Under common law, minors, intoxicated people, insane people, or people otherwise unable to understand the nature of the transaction lack contractual capacity.

5. *Form:* Legally enforceable contracts may be oral or written. However, some contracts must be in written form to be enforceable. Under the statute of frauds, sales transactions of $500 or more, sales of real estate, and contracts extending for more than one year must be in writing. It is recommended that partnership agreements be written to ensure that the rights and responsibilities are clear to all parties.[4] The existence of an oral contract must be demonstrated in some way.

A breach of contract occurs when one party fails to perform as agreed. The injured party has legal remedies available. The commonly used court enforcement is to allow monetary damages in an amount that will restore the injured party to the same position he or she would have been in had the contract been performed. It is not common for the court to require specific performance, but when monetary damages are inadequate, it has been required. Courts also award consequential damages due to breach of contract when the breaching party knows the consequences of the breach. Awarding lost profits due to breach of contract is possible.

The Uniform Commercial Code

To make the laws consistent among states, the Uniform Commercial Code was developed in the 1940s. The code consists of 10 articles. See Exhibit 4.1 for a listing of the 10 UCC articles.

The small business manager should be familiar with the basics of the articles their firm performs. Because all businesses are involved in sales, only the basics of Article 2 are discussed.

When merchants are involved in the sales of goods, the UCC imposes rules that may vary from basic contract law. The code imposes special standards of conduct when merchants sell goods to one another. The **sales contract elements** include *a specified price, delivery date, place of delivery, and quantity.* However, the UCC states that a contract exists even if one or more terms of the contract required for

---

EXHIBIT 4.1   The Uniform Commercial Code Articles

1. General provisions
2. Sales
3. Commercial paper
4. Bank deposits and collections
5. Letters of credit
6. Bulk transfers
7. Documents of title
8. Investment securities
9. Secured transactions
10. Effective data and repealer

---

agreement are omitted as long as the parties intended to make a contract and there is a reasonably certain method for the court to supply the missing terms.

Common law states that businesses must stand behind their products, whether goods or services.[5] And the Magnuson-Moss Act of 1975 says that warranties offered must be clearly written. UCC Article 2 covers sales warranties and product liability. A **warranty** explains *what the business promises about its product.* When a business sells a product, it has an implied warranty (unwritten) that the product will perform for a particular purpose. The business can also have an express (written) warranty making statements about the conditions, quality, and performance of the product. Customers may like strong warranties, but they can be very expensive. Backing up warranties can present a variety of problems. Some people abuse products and demand a lot of service on warranties.

As part of the marketing function (Chapter 7) specific decisions should be made about what the warranty will cover, and then it should be clearly communicated to the target customers to avoid problems. An express warranty is often helpful to the business and its customers when the product is innovative, relatively expensive, purchased infrequently, relatively complex to repair, and sold as high quality. Five considerations when selecting a warranty policy include: (1) competitive warranties, (2) costs, (3) service capability, (4) customer perceptions, and (5) legal implications. The firm that elects to offer a written complex warranty may want to consult a lawyer for assistance in writing it. You may offer a full or limited warranty. The full warranty must state certain minimum standards such as replacement or full refund after reasonable attempts at repair.

If your products fail to meet the reasonable expectations of your customers, you can be sued. Customers, your workers, and others who may be injured by your product can also sue you for damages. Most small businesses should carry liability insurance (which you will learn about in Chapter 14) because product liability lawsuits have forced some small firms out of business.

Agency

An **agent** *represents the principal in dealing with a third party*. In a partnership each partner acts as an agent for the business. Employees are also agents when performing job-related tasks. Real estate agents and stockbrokers represent buyers and sellers as agents. Partners and employees are general agents whereas realtors and stockbrokers are special agents. The principal is liable to a third party for the performance of contracts made by agents acting within the scope of agent authority. The principal is also liable for fraudulent, negligent, and other wrongful acts of the agent that are executed within the scope of the agency relationship. The agency relationship is necessary to conduct most business transactions, but it is potentially dangerous for the small firm. Therefore, small business owners should exercise care in selecting agents and employees and clearly stipulate their authority and responsibility.

Protecting Intangible Assets

The small business can protect some of its intangible assets (which help the business succeed, but have no physical value in and of themselves) through trademarks, patents, and copyright.

Trademarks

A **trademark** is a *word, figure, or symbol used to distinguish a product*. A trademark stops other firms from using your name, but not from producing the same product under a different name. If a trademark becomes a generic name for a product, such as aspirin, thermos, yo-yo, and cellophane, it can no longer be licensed as a company's trademark. Trademarks and brand names are discussed in Chapter 7.

Patents

A **patent** is *the registered exclusive right to make, use, and sell an invention*. A U.S. patent is granted from the federal government's Patent and Trademark Office for 17 years from the date on which the patent is granted. After 17 years the patent expires and cannot be renewed. Most patents are granted for new product inventions, but design patents are also given. A U.S. patent is only granted to the true inventor, not to the person who discovers another's invention.

The process of getting a patent is complex. It normally takes 19 months to get a patent, and only 65 percent of patent applications are granted. The basic filing fee is $170 dollars for small businesses, $340 dollars for big businesses. If a patent is issued, there is an additional fee of $280 or $560 dollars plus incremental maintenance fees of $225, $445, and $670 over 17 years. If you have a registered patent attorney or patent agent file the application for you, the estimated application cost is between $1,000 and $5,000 dollars.

Copyrights

A **copyright** is *the registered right to exclusively reproduce, publish, and sell creative work.* Copyright is given for literature, drama, music, and artistic works (i.e., books, choreography, sculptures, motion pictures, music recordings). You can copyright words or other forms in which ideas are expressed, but not ideas themselves. Copyrights are granted for $10 each from the Copyright Office in the Library of Congress (Form TX). A copyright lasts for the life of the creator plus 50 years. Copyright holders can sue for damages people who reproduce their work without authorization.

Government Regulation

What are the important issues facing small business today? Two surveys of small business owners revealed that the major problem facing business is government regulation and paperwork,[6] and the four factors they consider most important but are the least satisfied with are the cost of health insurance and workers' compensation, government attitude towards business, and availability of capital.[7]

At the federal level more than 90 regulatory agencies promulgate hundreds of new rules each year. The number of state and local agencies the small business must comply with varies. Because there are so many types of regulations that vary by industry, discussion is limited to the more general ones. However, as a small business manager/owner you will have to become knowledgeable about specific regulations for your company.

Free Competition

Antitrust laws prevent a businessperson from restraining trade by monopolizing sales and setting prices or conspiring with others to do so. Unfair trade practice laws specify that businesses cannot sell products at less than their cost, and they also specify certain percentage markups. These laws were passed in part to protect the small firm from being forced out of business by large corporations.

Consumer Protection

The government has created the Federal Trade Commission to protect consumers from unfair business practices. The FTC regulates labeling, safety, packaging, advertising, truth-in-lending, fair credit reporting, equal credit opportunity, and many other activities. The Consumer Product Safety Commission sets standards for consumer products and bans hazardous products.

Employment Practices

There are laws stating that a business cannot discriminate during employment selection and promotional advancement. However, managers are responsible for checking to make sure employees have legal documentation to work in this country. Laws govern the number of hours employees can work, overtime, minimum wages, and equal pay. The National Labor Relations Board regulates labor-management relations. The Internal Revenue Service requires employers to collect federal and state income taxes from employees and to make regular payments. Employers must pay Workers' Compensation and FICA taxes.

Safety and Health Practices

The Occupational Safety and Health Administration creates required job-safety and health standards and enforces them in the workplace. OSHA requires businesses to report accidents, injuries, and illness.

Public Welfare

Public welfare is a catchall term used to refer to the general public's or society's need to be protected from business practices that result from indirect transactions with a business. They include things like zoning ordinances regulating where a firm can conduct business to help separate businesses from residential areas. Local ordinances establish standards for procedures such as sanitation for restaurants to protect the health of patrons. To protect society the Environmental Protection Agency along with state and local regulators set standards for air pollution, water pollution, solid-waste disposal, and handling of toxic substances. It is just a matter of time before the government will prohibit the sale of nonrecyclable and nonbiodegradable consumer goods.[8]

State governments establish licensing procedures for physicians, barbers, pharmacists, accountants, lawyers, and real estate salespersons, to protect society from unqualified businesspeople. Many cities also have licensing requirements such as a liquor license to start a bar or to serve drinks in an existing restaurant. Another local license/permit is required for construction to build a business or make major renovations.

Small Business Influence on Government Regulations

Several independent organizations attempt to influence lawmakers and to protect small business by lobbying to ensure that they have a role in determining which laws and regulations affecting small firms are created or defeated. Government regulations on all businesses tend to place a disproportionate burden on small companies. Due in part to the lobbying efforts of small business owners, the Regulatory Flexibility Act of 1980 requires federal agencies to fit regulatory and informational requirements to the scale of the business's ability to comply. Small businesses lobbied to have input into the Clinton administration's new health care regulations.[9] Some of the major organizations that your small business can join to help protect your interests are listed below.

National Federation of Independent Businesses (NFIB)

The NFIB is the largest of all the small business associations with a membership exceeding 500,000, the majority of which are retailers, wholesalers, and service firms.

National Small Business Association (NSB)

The NSB works hard lobbying for its 45,000 small business owners' interests.

U.S. Chamber of Commerce

The chamber is one of the central voices of the business community, lobbying at the federal, state, and local level. To specifically address the needs of small business, the chamber established the Center for Small Business (CSB) in 1977.

Trade and Professional Associations

Numerous trade and professional associations lobby for their members and provide them with many services.

Selecting a Lawyer

After reading the first two sections of this chapter, you should understand that the legal environment is very complex. A good lawyer can help the small business owner make decisions in order to keep the company from breaking laws, which may result in going to court. The small businessperson should take a proactive approach to the legal environment. Anticipate legal problems and consult an attorney before taking action. The time and expense to check the details of a contract, the terms of an invoice, or planned employment practices with a lawyer are minimal. But failure to obtain legal counsel could ultimately force the owner of the small firm out of business. One personal injury claim can wipe out the net worth of most small to medium-sized businesses.

You should hire a lawyer with small business experience, preferably in a business similar to yours, with whom you feel comfortable. When selecting a lawyer, ask other business owners who they would recommend. Commercial loan officers of banks and public accountants are also good sources of references in selecting a lawyer. Small law firms tend to be more accessible, more personal, and less expensive than large firms. Based on recommendations, interview two to five lawyers before making a selection. As you interview lawyers, make sure you feel comfortable with them so that you can create and maintain a good working relationship. Discuss the services they provide and their fees. Be sure to ask each lawyer about his or her experience representing small businesses; ask about specific experience in the areas you will seek advice. If after selecting an attorney you are not satisfied with the work, discuss the problem, and if it cannot be resolved, make a new selection.

These same basic guidelines can be applied to selecting an accountant, insurance agent, banker, and other professional advisers.

Social Responsibility

There is no universally accepted definition of social responsibility. For our purposes **social responsibility** is *the conscious effort to operate in a manner that creates a win-win situation with all stakeholders.*[10] **Stakeholders** are *those people who are affected by the firm's actions.* Some of the stakeholders include employees, customers, suppliers, and stockholders. Small businesses should create a win-win situation for employees by providing a safe working environment, compensating them reasonably, and treating them properly. The products and services offered should be safe and meet the expectations of customers at a reasonable price. In dealing with suppliers the firm should follow good business practices. The firm should earn a "reasonable return" for the stockholders/owners of the business. In other words, the small businessperson should not take unfair advantage of anyone or the environment, including competitors, to extract excessive profits. Looking out for the interest of employees tends to motivate them to do a good job, which in turn satisfies customers and suppliers. The result is repeat business, which leads to profitability. In Chapter 6 you will learn more about how a small business interacts with its stakeholders.

Should managers act in a socially responsible manner and exceed minimum legal requirements to ensure the safety of employees, customers, and the environment? Various theories concerning business's social responsibility may be separated on a single foundational question: Are businesses social institutions?[11] The debate over social responsibility continues with at least three major views.

Milton Friedman, economist and Nobel laureate, and others agree with Adam Smith's "invisible hand" doctrine and argue against social responsibility. The doctrine is based on the premise that in the long run public interests are served by individuals and businesses pursuing their own best interest in a free economy. According to Friedman, social responsibility is a fundamentally subversive doctrine; a business's only responsibility is to earn a profit without breaking the law. This view argues that time and money are wasted on social activities that do not increase the firm's profit. There has been evidence by the Congressional Budget Office and others[12] that productivity would have been slightly higher in the absence of environmental regulation in the 1970s and into the 1980s; however, the productivity loss appears to be declining. Arguments have been made that stringent government regulatory standards increase cost, which results in businesses moving production abroad or to other states with more lenient standards.

Economist Paul Samuelson and others argue in favor of social responsibility because the benefits outweigh the cost. If corporations become too detached from social priorities, society not only has the ability to further regulate these businesses but also possesses the ultimate power to cripple or destroy them. Some businesses have claimed that social responsibility is profitable. One example is 3M, which has invested millions in pollution control equipment and has saved more than $482 million worldwide.[13]

A third view is the social welfare approach, which holds that a business should act in an ethical, responsible manner even if there is no immediate, quantifiable benefit to the business to balance out the cost of taking the action. H.B. Fuller is an example of a company with this philosophy. It turned down $800,000 in annual sales by refusing to sell an industrial asbestos-filled adhesive to customers in Japan who refused to buy its alternative product.[14] In June 1993 Wal-Mart Stores unveiled a prototype ecologically sensitive environmental store. In the short run management doesn't expect the store to be cost-effective, but in the long run it hopes energy savings will make up at least part of the cost.[15]

Earlier in this chapter you learned of the need to meet minimum government standards of free competition, employee and consumer protection, safety and health, and public welfare. If the firm does not meet these standards it faces government action. However, social responsibility requires going beyond meeting these enforced minimum standards. Are businesses being socially responsible by exceeding the minimum requirements set by law? According to a recent survey study, businesses are being socially responsible. Managers report that the benefits of social responsibility outweigh the cost in the United States, and being socially responsible does not negatively effect a firm's international competitiveness.[16]

Although only 0.08 percent of all businesses in the United States employing 1,000 or more people have been the focus of most social responsibility research,[17] small businesses are taking advantage of the increased attention being given to social responsibility. Small ventures are providing environmental products. Examples include Alphatron Manufacturing, which has designed a machine used to process fish waste for use as food in aquaculture or fertilizer in organic farming. Solar Car and Electric Vehicles of America is providing six municipal utilities in Connecticut and Massachusetts with electric vehicles. The utilities found the small companies' vehicles to be more cost-effective and accessible than those from Detroit automakers. The little manufacturers are much more willing to work with the utilities to help them comply with clean air laws.[18]

Business Ethics

Business ethics are closely related to social responsibility, but they are not identical. Some experts distinguish between moral behavior and ethical behavior. Morals refer to absolute worldwide standards of right and wrong behavior, such as "Thou shalt not commit murder." Ethical behavior, on the other hand, reflects established customs and mores that may vary throughout the world and that are subject to change from time to time. For our purposes we combine the two: **ethics** is *the moral standard of right and wrong behavior.*

Ethical versus Unethical Behavior

Right behavior is considered ethical behavior, while wrong behavior is considered unethical behavior. In the business world, the difference between right and wrong behavior is not always clear. Many unethical behaviors are illegal, but not all. People have different values, which leads to behaviors that some people view as ethical while others do not. Ethics is also considered to be relative. In one situation people may feel certain behavior is ethical while the same behavior in a different situation is unethical. For example, giving someone a gift is legal, but giving a gift as a condition of attaining business (a bribe) is illegal. The line separating a gift from a bribe is not always clear. Also, ethics vary by culture, and what is legal in one country may be illegal in another country.

In your daily life, you face decisions in which you can make ethical or unethical choices. You make your choices based on the teaching of parents, teachers, friends, bosses, co-workers, and so forth. Our life experience makes up what many refer to as our conscience, which helps us to choose right from wrong. We will separate behavior into two categories: ethical and unethical. **Ethical behavior** includes *words and actions that benefit the individual or the firm and its stakeholders.* Ethical behavior creates a win-win situation for all relevant stakeholders. On the other hand, **unethical behavior** includes *words and actions that benefit the individual or firm but hurt stakeholders.* Generally, when conducting business in ways to create win-win situations, the people involved use ethical behavior. When people are trying to create an I-win-you-lose situation, they often use unethical behavior to take advantage of the other stakeholders.

A firm's ethical philosophy has an impact on its profitability. Does ethical behavior pay? In a recent survey, senior managers, business school deans, and members of Congress agreed that ethical behavior succeeds; 63 percent said that "a business enterprise actually strengthens its competitive position by maintaining high ethical standards."[19] At first one may be richly rewarded for knifing people in the back, but retaliation follows, trust is lost, and productivity declines.[20] For example, an unethical used-car dealer who intentionally lies to sell defective cars at inflated prices, taking advantage of customers, may make excessive profits in the short run. However, this dealer will not get important repeat business; in fact, the people who have been exploited discourage others from doing business with the dealer, and they may even go as far as to take the dealer to court. Unethical used-car dealers generally do not stay in business in the same location under the same name for many years. The dealer who honestly offers quality used cars at a reasonable price will get repeat business and word-of-mouth advertising and can avoid costly legal action while making a reasonable profit.

Ethics by Example

As the owner/manager of a small business you can develop standards of ethical behavior to convey to your employees. Employees take their lead from managers from the top down. If you talk about ethical behavior and back it up with action, generally, so will your employees. If you direct employees to be ethical but you are not, or if you allow or reward unethical behavior, you are sending a mixed message. If you are unethical you may end up managing a business considered unethical by its stakeholders. Actually, businesses are not ethical or unethical, only their people are.

When hiring employees, make ethics one of the qualities you are looking for. Reward ethical behavior and punish unethical behavior. Fire employees caught willfully engaging in serious unethical behavior and those who repeatedly commit less serious offenses. Encourage whistle-blowing; **whistle-blowing** occurs *when employees expose what they consider to be unethical behavior.* If you encourage whistle-blowing, employees will come to you rather than go to the government or elsewhere. To prevent unethical behavior in problem areas such as theft, make whistle-blowing part of the job. A survey found that employees would be more willing to report a colleague if such reporting were a clearly defined job responsibility for the whistle-blower and if employees helped to develop the code of conduct. Making communication part of the job is especially helpful in reducing theft at retail and food stores. In these establishments, where it's likely that co-workers know what is going on, direct supervision and other forms of external loss control are insufficient. A fast-food chain acted on this and other findings and increased antitheft prevention. As a result of their effort, food theft fell 80 percent. When it became less acceptable to steal, employees were considered to be stealing not just from the restaurant but from their crew as well.[21]

Better Business Bureaus

To promote ethical practices of all businesses in the community, companies band together to form Better Business Bureaus. The **Better Business Bureau** is *an organization that is dedicated to promoting ethical business practices within the community.* Its function is twofold: (1) It provides buying guidelines and information about a company to prospective consumers to help them make their purchasing decisions; and (2) it renders assistance by answering questions and resolving disputes concerning purchases. Many small business owners/managers set an example of ethical behavior by joining the Better Business Bureau in their community.

The Credo and Code of Ethics

The **credo** *defines and prioritizes company values and its ethical responsibilities to its stakeholders.* Probably the most publicized credo is the one developed by Johnson & Johnson. Exhibit 4.2 is a copy of Johnson & Johnson's credo. Notice that the credo prioritizes J&J's ethical responsibility to: (1) customers, (2) employees, (3) community, and (4) stockholders. Under the community section is a list of social responsibilities that go beyond meeting government regulations. The credo proves general guidance in ethical issues. Johnson & Johnson followed the ethical standards set in the credo as its executives handled the Tylenol poisoning crisis. Because J&J puts its customers first, it recalled all products in spite of the high cost. As a small business manager/owner you can adapt the J&J credo to fit the needs of your firm.

The **code of ethics** is *a written statement of the ethical standards of behavior a company expects from its employees.* Most large businesses have codes of ethics. Many large companies have hired ethics consultants to establish ethics policies and procedures for reporting and punishing violators of ethical behavior. However, such elaborate methods are often unnecessary and impractical for owners of small businesses.[22] When the firm is very small, the owner/manager's standards of ethical behavior are observed by all employees. However, as the firm grows the owner's visibility often declines, and based on its competitive situation, there comes a time when the code of ethics is advisable.

Small businesses should consider making the code of ethics part of an employee manual or as a booklet given to every new hire. Ethical policies should be broad enough to cover a wide range of behavior, but they should also be tailored

---

EXHIBIT 4.2   Our Credo: Johnson & Johnson

We believe our first responsibility is to the doctors, nurses and patients,
to mothers and fathers and all others who use our products and services.
In meeting their needs everything we do must be of high quality.
We must constantly strive to reduce our costs
in order to maintain reasonable prices.
Customers' orders must be serviced promptly and accurately.
Our suppliers and distributors must have an opportunity
to make a fair profit.

We are responsible to our employees,
the men and women who work with us throughout the world.
Everyone must be considered as an individual.
We must respect their dignity and recognize their merit.
They must have a sense of security in their jobs.
Compensation must be fair and adequate,
and working conditions clean, orderly and safe.
We must be mindful of ways to help our employees fulfill
their family responsibilities.
Employees must feel free to make suggestions and complaints.
There must be equal opportunity for employment, development
and advancement for those qualified.
We must provide competent management,
and their actions must be just and ethical.

We are responsible to the communities in which we live and work
and to the world community as well.
We must be good citizens—support good works and charities
and bear our fair share of taxes.
We must encourage civic improvements and better health and education.
We must maintain in good order
the property we are privileged to use,
protecting the environment and natural resources.

Our final responsibility is to our stockholders.
Business must make a sound profit.
We must experiment with new ideas.
Research must be carried on, innovative programs developed
and mistakes paid for.
New equipment must be purchased, new facilities provided
and new products launched.
Reserves must be created to provide for adverse times.
When we operate according to these principles,
the stockholders should realize a fair return.

---

for each department or job. A suggested format is as follows: (1) introduction, (2) code of ethics for all employees, (3) code of ethics for different categories of workers.[23] The code should give examples of ethical and unethical behavior and clearly state the consequences of unethical behavior. As a minimum all employees should read the code of ethics and sign an acknowledgement of their understanding. In addition, it is helpful to have a manager review the code with employees individually or in groups as one part of a training session.

Developing a code of ethics ignored or unenforced by managers is a waste of time. Setting an example and enforcing ethical behavior are necessary. If you want to develop a code you can obtain sample codes of ethics from Ethics Resource Center, Inc., 1025 Connecticut Avenue, N.W. Washington, DC 20036. Discuss with fellow small business owners/managers if they have codes of ethics, what they include, and ask to borrow a copy. If you haven't developed a friendship with any small business owners/managers yet, use your networking acquaintances at your next chamber of commerce breakfast, Rotary Club meeting, or Better Business Bureau contacts. You may also copy the stakeholder's guide to ethical decisions from the next section.

A Stakeholder's Guide to Ethical Decisions

When making decisions, try to create a win-win situation for all stakeholders with whom you will be dealing within the organization. (See Exhibit 4.3, the inner circle.) If you are a manager reporting to a higher-level manager, then you will have one or more superiors, subordinates, peers at your level, and people in other departments as your stakeholders. If you are the owner/manager, you will not have superiors or peers on your level. Depending upon the size of the small business, your stakeholders will be direct subordinates reporting to you and their subordinates. You may have various departments reporting to you. If you are not a manager, you do not have any subordinates.

You will often make decisions during interactions with stakeholders outside the firm (outside the inner circle in Exhibit 4.3) such as customers, suppliers, and governments. And many decisions affect stakeholders without direct interaction with them, such as stockholders, competitors, and the general public or society. When marketing to get customers, you usually want to create a win-win situation between the customer and company, which creates an I-win-and-the-competition-loses, but you should not do anything illegal or unethical to win the business. Your business may also cooperate with competitors to gain customers. For example, two small construction companies may join together to build a structure too large for either to build alone. In such situations you should create a win-win situation with your competitor by sharing the work and income fairly.

The first step when making a decision is to identify all the relevant stakeholders affected by the decision. Major stakeholders are shown in Exhibit 4.3, but a specific business may add others (major creditors) or delete some (stockholders). After identifying the relevant stakeholders, try to create a win-win situation for all of them, yourself, and your company. Answer their unanswered question: What's in it for me? Keep in mind the Golden Rule—treat others as you want them to treat you. If you have created a win-win situation and are proud to tell all the relevant stakeholders your decision, it is probably ethical. If you create an I-win-you-lose situation and are embarrassed to discuss your decision with the relevant stakeholders or you keep rationalizing it, the decision is probably unethical. A good approach to avoid I-win-you-lose unethical decisions is to get the input of stakeholders in the decision process to ensure everyone gets a fair deal.

EXHIBIT 4.3

A stakeholder's guide to ethical decisions

If you create a win-win situation and are proud to tell all the relevant stakeholders your decision, it is probably ethical. If you create an I-win-you-lose situation and are embarrassed to discuss your decision with the relevant stakeholders or you keep rationalizing it, the decision is probably unethical.

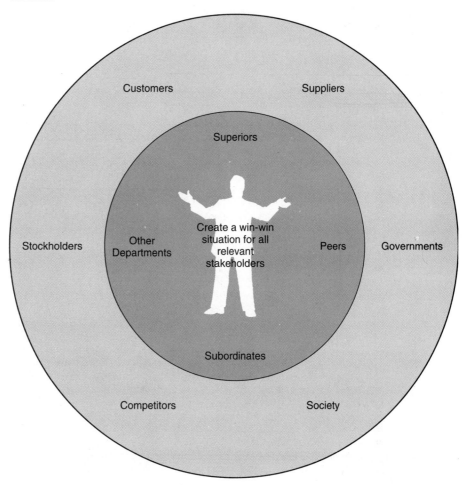

How the Law and Social and Ethical Responsibility Affect Business Planning and Implementation

If you elect to start or manage a small business, it should be clear to you that you cannot simply run your firm any way that you wish. It is clear that the small business must meet the complex regulations of federal, state, and local government (and states and cities if the firm has more than one location and/or conducts business in more than one state). You may be the boss, but if you want to stay in

EXHIBIT 4.4   How responsible and ethical is your organization?

Select an organization you work for, worked for, or are knowledgeable about. Does it try to create a win-win situation for all stakeholders? To clarify your perceptions, answer each statement below by selecting your level of agreement by writing the number 1–5 on the line before each statement. Answer as many questions as you can without guessing. Leave the others blank.

1—Strongly Agree	2—Agree	3—Neutral	4—Disagree	5—Strongly Disagree

The term *management* is used primarily to represent the top managers, but it can be any level manager, and/or all levels. Use your own discretion on what works best for you.

_____ 1. Management fully meets its contract obligations.

_____ 2. Management encourages free competition. It does not encourage taking unfair advantage of competitors such as stealing competitors' patents and/or copyrights.

_____ 3. Management does not encourage or actually restrain trade by trying to monopolize and/or fix prices.

_____ 4. The firm offers quality products and services at fair prices to its customers.

_____ 5. Management and employees listen to customers and attempt to offer products and services that meet their needs.

_____ 6. Management does not encourage or allow salespeople to use high-pressure sales tactics.

_____ 7. Management does not use or allow employees to use misleading methods to sell products. (For example, false advertising, incorrect labeling, misleading customers about product performance, unnecessarily replacing a part/product [muffler], selling more than is needed [insurance].)

_____ 8. Products are safe when used as directed.

_____ 9. Management handles customer complaints fairly.

_____ 10. Management treats employees with respect and dignity.

_____ 11. Management willingly gives employees a fair wage for their work, as compared to the same or similar jobs at competitive firms.

_____ 12. Management prohibits discrimination in hiring or promoting employees.

_____ 13. Management allows flexibility in schedules to allow employees to meet their family obligations without loss of their present job level or employment with the firm, nor does taking time off hinder career progression. (For example, some form of flextime is available to parents to provide short-term care for sick children/parents or to enable employees to handle other personal obligations. Reasonable extended time is given for childbirth.)

_____ 14. Management is committed to providing a safe and healthy work environment. It complies with, or exceeds, all OSHA standards.

_____ 15. Management is socially responsible to the communities in which it does business. (For example, managers/employees are involved in community service organizations such as the Community Way, or the firm sponsors a civic function.)

_____ 16. Management is committed to protecting the environment. It complies with, or exceeds, EPA or state regulations for air and water pollution, solid-waste disposal, and toxic substances.

_____ 17. Management encourages employees to operate in a manner that creates a win-win situation for all stakeholders.

_____ 18. Management is committed to ethical behavior and leads by example. Ethical standards are enforced.

_____ 19. Management encourages employees to treat suppliers fairly.

_____ 20. Overall, I'd say management is socially responsible and ethical and encourages employees to be too.

To determine your score add up your responses and divide this total by the number of questions answered. This is your average. The closer your average is to 1, the more social and ethical managements' behavior. The closer to 5, the less social and unethical the behavior.

Remember that this score is your perception. Others in the organization may not agree with your score. Managers tend to rate themselves higher than employees. If you are a part of management, you can use this list as a guide to social and ethical behavior. You may have all employees anonymously complete the questionnaire to compare their scores to management's. To decrease perception variations, work should be done in areas needing improvement.

business you must obey the laws, comply with the rules, and treat stakeholders in a socially responsible and ethical manner. If the small firm elects to do business internationally, the complexity increases in order to meet the regulations of foreign governments. Taking the small firm global is discussed in Chapter 15.

In the next chapter you will learn the elements that make up the business plan, and in Chapters 6 through 14 you will learn how to plan and implement the functional areas of the business plan. Social responsibility and ethics are integral parts of all business functions. As you read through this book, keep the concepts from this chapter in mind and realize that these concepts should influence behavior in each functional area of the business. But more importantly, when you actually develop and implement business plans, be sure to at least meet government regulations and create win-win situations with stakeholders to ensure social and ethical business practices.

To review the important concepts in this chapter, and to apply them to a specific organization, complete Exhibit 4.4.

Summary

Basics of Business Law

A **contract** is *a binding agreement creating an obligation among the parties involved.* A valid contract must have five separate elements. The **five elements of a contract** are: *agreement, consideration, legality, capacity, and form.* The Uniform Commercial Code was developed with 10 articles to make the laws consistent among states. The **sales contract elements** include *a specified price, delivery date, place of delivery, and quantity.* A **warranty** explains *what the business promises about its product.* An **agent** *represents the principal in dealing with a third party.* Everyone working for the firm is an agent when performing job-related tasks. There are three ways to protect intangible assets: by **trademark,** which is *a word, figure, or symbol used to distinguish a product;* by **patent,** *the registered exclusive right to make, use, and sell an invention;* and by **copyright,** *the registered right to exclusively reproduce, publish, and sell creative work.*

Government Regulation

The federal, state, and local governments have a wide range of regulations and agencies to enforce them in the areas of free competition, employment practices, safety and health practices, and public welfare.

Some of the organizations the small business can join for help with lobbying and other services are the National Federation of Independent Businesses (NFIB), National Small Business association (NSB), U.S. Chamber of Commerce, and trade and professional associations.

Selecting a Lawyer

The small business should consult a lawyer before making decisions to avoid legal problems. A major selection criterion should be experience in small business legal counseling. Select a lawyer with whom you feel comfortable developing a working relationship.

Social Responsibility

There are three major views of social responsibility. (1) A business's only responsibility is to earn a profit without breaking the law—in conducting only those activities that are profitable. (2) Business should be socially responsible because the benefits outweigh the cost. (3) Business should be socially responsible even if the cost outweighs the benefits.

To be considered socially responsible the firm must exceed the minimum standards set by the three levels of government. **Social responsibility** is *the conscious effort to operate in a manner that creates a win-win situation with all stakeholders.* **Stakeholders** are *those people who are affected by the firms' actions.* Stakeholders include employees, customers, suppliers, stockholders, society, governments, and competitors.

Business Ethics

It is generally agreed that in the long run following ethical business practices pays. **Ethics** is *the moral standard of right and wrong behavior.* Right behavior is considered ethical behavior, while wrong behavior is considered unethical behavior. The difference between right and wrong is not always clear. **Ethical behavior** includes *words and actions that benefit the individual/firm and stakeholders.* Ethical behavior creates a win-win situation for all relevant stakeholders. On the other hand, **unethical behavior** includes *words and actions that benefit the individual/firm but hurt stakeholders.*

For the firm to be considered ethical, management from the top down must lead by setting an ethical example and enforce ethical standards. Managers should encourage whistle-blowing. **Whistle-blowing** occurs *when employees expose what they consider to be unethical behavior.* The **Better Business Bureau** is *an organization that is dedicated to promoting ethical business practices within the community.*

Based on its competitive situation, at some point of growth it becomes advisable to develop a credo and/or code of ethics. The **credo** *defines and prioritizes company values and its ethical responsibilities to its stakeholders.* The **code of ethics** is *a written statement of ethical standards of behavior a company expects from its employees.*

The stakeholders' guide to ethical decisions states that if you have created a win-win situation and are proud to tell all the relevant stakeholders your decision, it is probably ethical. If you create an I-win-you-lose situation and are embarrassed to discuss your decision with the relevant stakeholders or you keep rationalizing it, the decision is probably unethical.

How the Law and Social and Ethical Responsibility Affect Business Planning and Implementation

The small business is privately owned, but it is not free to operate in a manner that exploits others. To be successful in small business, managers must operate within the legal regulations set by governments and act in a socially responsible and ethical manner with its stakeholders.

Questions

1. What is the purpose of a contract?
2. What are the five elements of a contract?
3. Are employees agents? Explain.

4. What is the difference between a trademark, patent, and copyright?

5. Do the government antitrust laws (free competition) generally help or hurt small business?

6. Should the small business person lobby? If so, how?

7. Should the small business person have a lawyer? Explain why or why not.

8. What does the term "create a win-win situation for all stakeholders" mean? Be sure to explain what a stakeholder is.

9. What is the difference between the three major views of social responsibility?

10. Should the small business person be ethical? Why or why not?

11. Why is it important for the small business owner/manager to set an ethical example and enforce ethical behavior?

12. Should employees use whistle-blowing? Why or why not?

13. What is the difference between a credo and a code of ethics?

14. Should people working in small business be more, less, or as socially and ethically responsible to its stakeholders as big business? Explain.

15. Are small business owners/managers free to operate their company any way they want to? Explain.

Application Exercises

When doing these exercises, where applicable, be sure to select a specific business, preferably one where you presently or previously worked or a business you would like to own someday. If this is not possible, pick a specific organization to which you will refer. Be sure to identify the organization by name. Limit your answer to one or two pages per exercise.

1. Give an example of how a transaction with a customer or supplier met each of the five elements of a contract.

2. Describe some of the functions you perform on the job as an agent.

3. Discuss any trademarks, patents, and/or copyrights the firm has.

4. Without identifying the firm or people by name for this question, identify any violation of government regulations of free competition, consumer protection, employment, safety and health, or public welfare you know about.

5. List the names of trade and professional associations the firm's employees belong to. Also state each association's function.

6. Is the firm you've selected socially responsible? Be sure to give specific examples of win-win or I-win-you-lose situations to support your answer.

7. Without giving names, identify ethical and unethical behavior you have observed on the job. Be sure to distinguish how ethical behavior benefited all relevant stakeholders, and the unethical behavior hurt stakeholders.

8. Does management lead by ethical example and enforce ethical behavior? Give examples to support your answer.

9. Have you ever been a whistle-blower? If yes, explain the situation. If not, and you have observed unethical behavior, why didn't you blow the whistle?

10. Does the firm have a credo and code of ethics? If yes, with the firm's permission, bring a copy to class to share. Without permission, give examples without a copy.

11. Identify the firm's major stakeholders. Who are its major customers? Who are some of its major suppliers and what do they supply? Which government agencies does the business interact with?

12. Using Exhibit 4.3, in which areas is the firm most and least socially and ethically responsible? How would you change this firm to be more socially and ethically responsible?

Application Situations

1. Munchkin Bottling

Munchkin Bottling Inc. of Van Nuys, California, has been selling about 75,000 clear tapered baby bottles per day with soda logos such as Pepsi, Dr Pepper, and 7 UP, with license permission. The baby bottles retail for $2.99. The founder, Steven Dunn, was very happy until he got letters from the Academy of Pediatric Dentistry, the California Dental Association, and the American Dental Association. Dentists are worried about tooth decay, which can result when sugary drinks, including juice, linger in the mouth. Dr. Jefferson Smith says that while the bottles do not contain soda, they imply that "it's OK to give a child a soda." These three dental associations have asked Mr. Dunn to stop putting soda logos on Munchkin baby bottles.

Steve Dunn says that the bottles carry an "explicit" warning about proper baby drinks and adds that "I think the average American parent is more intelligent than that."[24]

Assignment

Answer the following questions:

1. Does Munchkin have a contract with the soda companies? Explain.
2. Are Munchkin employees agents for the soda companies? Explain.
3. Which companies identified, if any, have trademarks?
4. Is Munchkin Bottling company in violation of consumer protection and/or safety and health regulations?
5. Should Munchkin have a lawyer?
6. According to dentists, which stakeholder(s) are winning and losing in this situation?
7. Is Munchkin being socially responsible in selling these baby bottles?
8. Is selling these baby bottles ethical or unethical behavior?
9. Will the publicity from the dentist, news media, this book, etc., be of benefit or harm to Munchkin Bottling?
10. If you were in Steven Dunn's position, would you refuse the dental associations' request and continue to sell the baby bottles with soda logos or would you accept their request and stop? If you stop selling the bottles with soda logos, would you sell the bottles without any logos or get a license to use some other logos?

2. Credo or Code of Ethics

For this application situation it is recommended that you select a business you own or would like to own someday. If you have no ideas for a business you would like to own, select a firm you presently work for or have worked for that does not have either a credo or code of ethics. Develop a credo and/or code of ethics for this business. Be sure to include some information about the firm (name, type of business, products/services, number of employees, etc.). As suggested in the text, don't reinvent the wheel; use existing credos and/or codes of ethics as your guide in the development of your own.

Integrative Case Question—CorLu Foods

Develop a legal plan for CorLu. Be sure to include any contracts you will enter into, any warranties you will offer, any agents you will have, develop a trademark(s), identify government regulations you will have to enforce, list all stakeholders, develop a code of ethics and social responsibility statement, identify trade/professional organizations owners should join. (Please refer to the Integrated Case "CorLu Foods.")

Bibliography

Clarkson, Kenneth W.; Roger LeRoy Miller; and Bonnie Blair. *West's Business Law.* St. Paul, Minn.: West Publishing Company, 1990.

"Do Good Ethics Ensure Good Profits?" *Business & Society Review,* Fall 1990, p. 4.

Ferrell, O.C. and John Fraedrich. "Understanding Pressures That Cause Unethical Behavior in Business." *Business Insights,* Spring/Summer 1990, pp. 1–4.

Fisher, Anne B. "How to Cut Your Legal Costs," *Fortune,* April 23, 1990, p. 192.

Labrecque, Thomas B. "Good Ethics Is Good Business," *USA Today Magazine,* May 1990, pp. 20–21.

Verespej, Michael A. "How to Avert a Trip to Court," *Industry Week,* March 5, 1991, p. 74.

U.S. Small Business Administration. *Introduction to Patents,* Management Aid No. 240. Washington, D.C.: U.S. Government Printing Office, 1979.

Endnotes

1. Rick Whiting, "Protecting the Power of the Idea," *Electronic Business,* February 24, 1992, pp. 24–32.
2. Fred Morgan and Jeffrey Stoltman, "The Effects of Punitive Damages Litigation on Marketing and Public Policy," *Journal of Macromarketing* 12, no. 1 (Spring 1992), pp. 30–44.
3. "Business Law for Manufacturers and Agents," *American Salesman,* February 2, 1992, pp. 19–22.

4. Eric Chase, "Owner vs. Owner: How Written Agreements Prevent Internal Legal Battles," *Small Business Reports,* September 1990, pp. 69–76.

5. J. T. Westermeir, "The Legal Environment: An Implied Promise Cannot Be Ignored," *Information Strategy: The Executive's Journal* 7, no. 2 (Winter 1991), pp. 46–47.

6. McRae Banks and Stephen Taylor, "Developing an Entrepreneur—and Small Business Owner—Defined Research Agenda," *Journal of Small Business Management* 29 (April 1991), pp. 10–18.

7. Robert N. Lussier and Joel Corman, "Factors Encouraging Start-up Business and Existing Firm Expansion: Public Policy Implications," manuscript not yet published.

8. Jacqueline Scerbinski, "Consumers and the Environment: A Focus on Five Products," *Journal of Business Strategy* 12, no. 5 (September/October 1991), pp. 44–47.

9. Jeffrey Kransney, "Bush, Clinton and Small Business," *National Public Accountant* 37, no. 10 (October 1992), pp. 14–15.

10. Robert N. Lussier, *Human Relations in Organizations: A Skill Building Approach,* (Homewood, IL: Richard D. Irwin, 1993), p. 469.

11. Richard Klonski, "Environmental Regulation and U.S. Economic Growth," *Business Horizons,* 34 (1991), pp. 9–18.

12. Antony Barbera and Virginia McConnell, "The Impact of Environmental Regulations on Industry Productivity," *Journal of Environmental Economics and Management* 18 (1990), pp. 50–65; Dale Jorgenson and Peter Wilcoxin, "Environmental Regulation and U.S. Economic Growth," *Journal of Economics* 21 (1990), pp. 314–40; Frances Cairncross, *Costing the Earth* (Boston: Harvard Business School Press, 1992).

13. Jacky Gold, "The Pioneers," *Financial World,* January 1990, pp. 56–60.

14. David Silverstein, "Managing Corporate Social Responsibility in a Changing Legal Environment," *American Business Law Journal* 25 no. 3, Summer 1987, p. 535.

15. Bob Ortega, "Wal-Mart Store Comes in Colors, But Is All Green," *The Wall Street Journal,* June 11, 1993, p. B1.

16. Robert N. Lussier and Joel Corman, "Environmental Strategy Formulation: Which Firms Should Take a Proactive Approach?" manuscript not yet published.

17. Judith Kenner Thompson and Howard Smith, "Social Responsibility and Small Business: Suggestions for Research," *Journal of Small Business Management* 29, no. 1 (January 1991), pp. 30–44.

18. "Small Business and Social Responsibility," *The Wall Street Journal,* April 14, 1993, p. B1.

19. David Vogel, "Ethics and Profits Don't Always Go Hand in Hand," *Los Angeles Times,* December 28, 1988, p. 7.

20. Roger Ricklefs, "Executives and General Public Say Ethical Behavior Is Declining in U.S.," *The Wall Street Journal,* November 2, 1983, p. 33.

21. "To Prevent Theft, Make Ratting Part of the Job," *The Wall Street Journal,* April 2, 1992, p. B1.

22. "Does Your Business Need a Code of Ethics?" *Profit-Building Strategies for Business Owners* 21, no. 4 (April 1991), pp. 15–16.

23. Ibid.

24. "Baby Bottles That Sport Soda Logos May Be Cute, But Dentists Aren't Smiling," *The Wall Street Journal,* June 10, 1993, p. A1.

5   THE BUSINESS PLAN

In this chapter, you will learn about the elements of a business plan and how to put them together systematically so that you can predict how your business will react both internally and externally to changes in the environment. The business plan is an integrated whole, but in this chapter, we will examine each part by itself. A business plan comprises many intertwined and interrelated parts. Looking at the entire document will enable you to predict how much money you will make or lose. As a final step in your business plan, you will condense the plan into an executive summary (usually the most important part of the plan); written last, it will become the first part of the plan.

Properly written, your business plan will outline all important aspects of your business and answer the following questions:

What business am I in?

What products do I sell?

Who are my customers?

Where do I secure the money to finance the company?

How do I control the company?

How do I know when and how much money I have made?

Chapter Learning Objectives

After completing this chapter, you should be able to:

· Identify and explain the intention of the main components of a business plan.
· Understand the interrelationship of the various functional elements in the business plan.

- Write an outline for a business plan, recognizing which questions are relevant to formulate and complete such a plan.
- Define the following 21 key terms in order of appearance:

Business Plan	Competition
Management	Location
Strategy formulation	Layouts
Accounting	Production/operations
Balance sheet	Human resources/personnel
Income statement	Financing
Cash flow	Controls
Capital equipment list	Breakeven analysis
Marketing	Financial ratios
Target market	Executive summary
Pricing	

Why the Business Plan Is Important

The fact that over 62 percent of all new businesses fail in the first five years of operation[1] and that almost 95 percent of the 400,000 annual small business failures can be attributed to poor management[2] underscores the need to develop a formal business plan. You should not think of starting a new business without one.[3] The **business plan** is *a written description of the firm, its objectives, and the steps necessary to achieve them.*

Planning is fundamental to all endeavors. You may be able to improvise and succeed, but you'll never know why, nor will you be able to reproduce profit-making decisions or adjust to new situations without an adequate plan. A plan tells you what you are going to do and how you are going to do it. It is your road map to success. This chapter will make it possible for you to identify all the elements that go into a business plan. It will enable you to recognize the interdependencies among the different parts of the plan and to draw some conclusions about what will happen when you put all the parts together. Mainly, you will establish a business road map that you can follow successfully to a destination. A logical, consistent, and well-thought-out business plan becomes your benchmark for judging the progress of your firm, showing you what to change if events don't turn out the way you predict.[4] Given the complexities of the world today, events probably won't turn out exactly as you predicted, and any response you make should have direction rather than being a mere reaction. You want to exercise control rather than being controlled by your environment.

A business plan is the single most important element in either starting or running your business. But planning requires a full understanding of all facets of your business; since the elements of your business plan are interconnected, making changes in one of the plan elements will require making changes in the other parts as well. A business plan will enable you to predict your firm's profits (or losses). If you consider that the primary task of a plan is to improve your business's profits, its overall importance will be clearly understood. It is essential to understand that a business plan is a primary and necessary element of your business.

A business plan is also a key element for all types of small businesses, whether yours is a start-up venture or an ongoing concern. For the start-up venture, a plan may be likened to developing a blueprint for a new building, since it is the first activity that should be undertaken before work on the structure itself begins. For an ongoing concern, a business plan can be used as a forecasting tool for future expansion and development.

A business plan should include:

- A thorough explanation of the product or service that the business will provide.
- Why this product or service will satisfy customer needs.
- Why this business will be successful.
- The potential revenue, expenses, and profits.
- The possible expansion of the business in the future.

The primary purpose behind your business plan is to thoroughly analyze the business as a whole and to make recommendations concerning potential problem areas. A plan provides you, the owner or manager, with an analysis of each aspect of the business; it reveals previously concealed problems as well as potential profit areas. A business plan also provides projections of costs, market share, production, and profits. It will assist the business owner in securing investment capital. In a thorough and logical manner, an integrated plan maps out the procedures to be followed in starting or operating a business, with each section supporting and contributing to the other sections. The sections should identify who your target market and competition are; provide a location analysis; suggest the legal form your business can take; present types of financing available as well as the associated cost requirements for capital equipment; and present accounting and inventory control systems as well as management and personnel considerations.

The ultimate success or failure of your business is based on your decisions. If you have a business plan, you will have a prototype that allows you to look at the alternatives and the consequences of your management decisions. The following sections of the chapter will discuss in detail each section of the business plan.

Developing the Business Plan

A business plan consists of the following major sections:

1. Introduction
2. Strategy formation
3. The accounting function

4. The marketing function
5. Location and layout
6. The production/operations function
7. The personnel function
8. The financing function
9. Controls
10. The executive summary (written last, placed first)

Together, these functions make up the complete business plan. While each of the functions will be explained here, each topic is so important it merits a separate chapter. A full explanation will enable you to see the relationship to your total business plan and its importance to your organization.

1. Introduction

The body of your business plan should begin with a description of the type of business that you intend to conduct. Is your business primarily service or manufacturing, retailing or wholesaling? What products or services are provided to consumers? Your plan should indicate whether the business is a start-up firm or an expansion of an ongoing concern. A business plan for a start-up company will require more extensive research in order to compile the information necessary, while an expanding firm can use its historical data to update the plan each year.

The legal form of your business must also be stated within this section. Is it a sole proprietorship, a partnership, or a corporation?[5] What are the hours of operation as well as any seasonal factors (i.e., annual period of high sales or services demanded) that may affect your business? If, for example, your business is affected by seasonal swings, you may want to incorporate another product or service to offset the negative profit swings. An example of this would be a lawn-care company that covers its profit swings in the winter by providing snow removal. If adequate profits can be earned in the spring, summer, and fall to sustain the business through the winter, then the owners may not need to consider methods of surviving through the winter. A complementary service or product, however, can enhance the resources of the firm.

Management

Some venture capitalists say that there are three important things in a business plan: management, management, and management. All other things being equal, venture capitalists would rather fund a project that has an average product but excellent management than a company with an excellent product but only average management.[6] **Management** is *the ability to accomplish objectives through the efficient use of people, capital, and equipment.* One of the main reasons new ventures fail is inadequate management. If you are writing a business plan for a venture capitalist, he or she might require personal information about management such as your formal education, your business background, and any experience you have that could be brought to bear on your firm. Any information about you that will help your

Exhibit 5.1

Sample organization chart

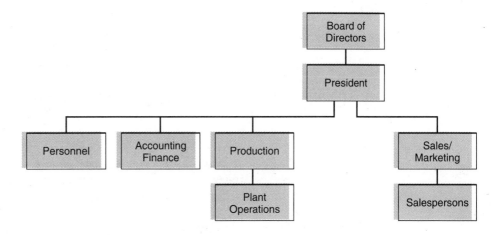

company be successful should be included within this section. Résumés of the management team also should be included in this section.

The management section should also contain an organization chart (see Exhibit 5.1) showing the primary operations such as production, accounting/finance, and sales/marketing.

Not all small businesses are corporations with boards of directors. Thus a typical noncorporate organization chart is illustrated in Exhibit 5.2.

It should also be recognized that many small businesses are not big enough to have dedicated people for each position or job function. In many small businesses, one person can, and frequently does, perform more than one function. For example, the president may also be the person in charge of sales. Production may also involve personnel, while the accounting function may be performed by an outside accountant on a weekly or monthly basis.

If you are writing a business plan for a smaller business with limited personnel, you can profit by describing the responsibilities included within each job in the firm. Each position on the organization chart should be explained in detail and show the immediate chain of command. You should also include the outside resources that will be available to you, such as accountants, lawyers, or consultants. It is important to cite all the management resources to provide yourself or potential venture capitalists with an accurate picture of the firm and its chance for survival.

2. Strategy Formation

You must determine what you are doing and where you want to be. You must ask yourself how you are going to get there. How do you get from point A to point B on your road map? Since there are many different pathways, which path should you take and how will you deal with all the internal and external pressures that divert you from your destination? Solutions to these questions are embodied in the term *strategy formation.* Strategy is your design to cope with adversities; it is a "careful

Exhibit 5.2

Sample noncorporate organization chart

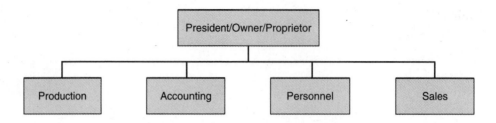

plan or method." A **strategy** is the *managerial game plan for directing and running the business.* A strategy recognizes your strengths and weaknesses; it shows how you plan to cope within the firm's environment and thus how you plan to capture the maximum profit. A new business should cite the strengths that set it apart from its competitors and will produce a profit. These strengths should include management experience and other aspects that will make the product unique. This section should present your firm's goals. This will help to determine the growth rate the company should realistically expect. It will also show how this growth rate will be achieved. Your desired rate of growth should be based upon industry standards. Statistical information can be found at trade associations, chambers of commerce, the U.S. Department of Commerce, and the Small Business Administration.[7] You will learn strategy formation details in Chapter 6.

3. Accounting

If you remember that the primary purpose of an accounting function is to enable you to keep records, to understand where your business is at any point in time, and to determine whether or not you are making money (profit), setting up an accounting system becomes much easier and more manageable. **Accounting** is *the systematic recording of the firm's income and expenditures in order to determine its financial position.* As a small business person, you must know your financial position. However, many business owners are unaware of their financial status and thus cannot make wise decisions. The fault lies with inadequate record keeping. Fundamental to any accounting system are the records that the business generates. Without good records, you cannot be up to date, much less use the tools of accounting and reporting to understand and analyze your business. A competent small business owner will be able to produce a **balance sheet,** *which shows, at a point in time, the firm's position with regard to assets, liabilities, and net worth;* **income statements (profit-and-loss statements),** *which show, over a specific time period, all the revenues and expenses that result in the profit or loss from those transactions;* and **cash flow statements,** *which show the flow of dollars from receipts into the business and expenditures made by the business.* These flows are measured only in actual dollars. Because the financial picture of an organization is the most critical part of running a business, you must be completely comfortable with the accounting system; this function is too important to be left solely to an accountant. Also needed is a **capital equipment list,** a *statement that includes the operating equip-*

ment of a firm and its corresponding dollar value. Chapter 8 will discuss the accounting function and show you how to produce these statements.

4. Marketing

The **marketing function** involves *those business activities that relate directly to determining the target market (to whom you will sell) and delivering services to those markets.* The **target market** is *the percentage of the total market to which the firm plans to sell its product.*

The Target Market

A market analysis should be conducted. Once the type of business has been established, you should determine the demographics of the marketplace. Demographics play a key role in determining the market by defining such characteristics as age, sex, profession, and income. The overall size of the market should be determined through a marketing plan. This information will allow your firm to specify its target market. After the target market has been established, you can then decide what percentage of the market you can realistically obtain. However, time, capital, and personnel will place a limit on your quest for market share.

How is the target market defined? A target market can be defined by consumer characteristics, geographic location, and size. Population, disposable income, needs, attitudes, and buying behavior are some of the factors that make up consumer characteristics. The geographic location and size of the business focus attention on the concentration of people and businesses within a specific area.

In writing your plan, you should also consider some of these questions: Is the market growing? You can answer this by looking at whether similar businesses within the market are growing. Is the market declining or stagnant? You can estimate the potential market by determining the percentage share of the market held by major competitors and then estimating the new firm's potential market share. If your firm is not new, it is important to test your target market. This can be done by personal interviewing, telemarketing surveys, and mail-in responses.

Another factor to be considered is the future growth potential of the target market. A new venture should describe the means it will use to attract and satisfy its customers. The industry as a whole should be explored to decide if your business can be supported.

Pricing

Pricing is an important aspect of the marketing plan. **Pricing** is *the determination of how much the firm will charge customers for its product(s).* The price you finally decide on should cover the cost of producing or buying the product plus a margin for profit. You can also determine pricing policies by investigating both market demand and competitors' prices. Demand and competitive pricing define the price a firm can obtain for its product. If your product or service can be substantially differentiated from competing products and a demand exists, then a higher price can be charged. Discussing marketing strategies within the business plan can reveal the means by which the firm will raise revenues to repay loans and enjoy future growth. Further discussion of pricing will be found in Chapter 7.

Competition

Once the target market has been identified, you should carefully analyze the competition in order to better meet the demands of the market segment. **Competition** is identified as *those firms selling a similar or substitute product to your target market.* If you are to be successful, you must be aware of the competition by doing an in-depth analysis so that you can identify the market niche to be exploited. Basically, a business owner studies the competition to learn what others are doing successfully and sets up business along the same lines. You should evaluate the strengths and weaknesses inherent to one industry or local area and take measures to exploit the weaknesses of the competition as well as to offer a better quality or less costly product or service. This is one way you can distinguish your business from the competition. Other ways of separating your business from the competition are by advertising, offering additional services, or using more attractive, eye-catching packaging.

Many organizations and associations can provide you with the help you need to answer questions such as who your competitors are and what the operating environment is. Most of the information they make available to the public is free. A partial list of such organizations can be found in Exhibit 5.3. These organizations can assist you by providing statistics and other information on the business environment. In Chapter 7, you will learn the details of the marketing function.

5. Location/Layout

Location

The location of your business may be the key to its success. **Location** is *the physical site and geographic area of the firm's facilities.* After deciding where you want to locate your business, you must decide between the benefits and drawbacks of buying or leasing the building. Renovations are also an important consideration. Start-up costs and information about the extent of necessary renovations should be included in the appendix of the business plan. Before the plan is completed, written estimates for the renovations should be obtained from several different contractors and should be included in the appendix, accompanied by all supporting documentation.

An area or best-use analysis should be completed by an independent specialist in order to determine why one site is preferable to another. You should include information about the types of businesses in the immediate area. The impact of the location upon your operating costs must also be analyzed. For example, locating your business in a shopping mall rather than in a storefront will result in higher overhead. The benefit of exposure to more shoppers has to be compared with the higher overhead costs. The trend toward an increase in shopping centers has in

---
EXHIBIT 5.3   Sources of information

Chambers of commerce*

Trade associations†

Small Business Association**

Banks††

State and local government agencies***

Better Business Bureaus§

Other business associations oriented to the needs of small business are:

American Small Business Association, Arlington, VA

Kessler Exchange, Northridge, CA

National Business Association, Dallas, TX

National Association of Women Business Owners, Washington, D.C.

National Association of Private Enterprise, Dallas, TX

National Association for the Self-Employed, Hurst, TX

*Virtually every town and city has its local chamber of commerce, which provides information concerning population, income, real estate, and lists of other organizations conducting business in the municipality.

†Many industries have their own trade associations. Examples of these would be the Electrical Contractors Association, Greater Boston Real Estate Board, the Massachusetts Bowling Association.

**The Small Business Association has chapters throughout the United States, and its mission is to meet the needs of the small business owner through a variety of programs. As an example, the association provides access to group health insurance coverage for employees of member firms.

††Banks, as lending institutions, can frequently supply the business owner with a large variety of data usually found in reports that the banks have produced.

***State and local government agencies produce and make available to the public a wealth of materials that are free. Although many items may be geared for general consumption, by making a few inquiries, you will uncover information that is more specialized.

§Better Business Bureaus are non-profit organizations set up in most communities that offer some information about firms doing business in their area. Most frequently they are the place where consumers register complaints about the way a business is being conducted.

many cases removed the decision of location from the entrepreneur and given it to the developers.

Layout

Layout varies according to the type of business the firm is operating. **Layout** is *the arrangement of the fixtures, equipment, and machinery in the business.* Retail stores as well as manufacturing operations equally must pay attention to where they keep certain goods, aisle size, traffic patterns, office and desk placement, plus a myriad of other factors. Once you have determined what your layout will be, you must pay equal attention to how the space is used. This requires looking at the purpose of the required procedure, process, or operation and how these purposes are to be best served. These topics are covered in detail in Chapter 8.

6. Production/Operations Function

Production/operations is *the system for transforming inputs into outputs.* This definition encompasses all types of businesses. It recognizes, for example, that many firms are engaged in producing services (i.e., educational, financial, and medical). Thus, the outputs of these firms cannot be as easily measured as the number of objects produced in a work shift. Healthy and educated people are the outputs of the production/operations process. All firms are concerned with producing output in the most efficient manner at the lowest cost. If these goals are to be reached, the firm's profits are maximized.

Production/Operations

This function is concerned with producing or making the output in the most efficient manner at lowest cost. Having achieved these goals, manufacturing cost is minimized and a firm's profit is maximized. You will have to answer some critical and crucial questions involving capital expenditures. The most important questions are the size of the physical facility and the volume it produces. Volume flows from a relevant forecast. Generally, the facility is built to accommodate the volume anticipated three to five years in the future. The length of time to which you are willing to commit depends upon how confident you are in your predictions.

After size, the facility's layout should be considered. An ideal layout should minimize the handling of materials while maximizing workers' productivity. A facility should be constructed to allow for ease of expansion or contraction. Using a good flow-process chart will facilitate this task.[8] In addition, questions such as the kind and size of equipment to buy must be answered. Additional important decisions must be made about quality control, inventory control, and finally, waste management. The production/operations function is discussed in Chapter 9.

7. The Human Resources/Personnel Function

The **human resources/personnel function** involves *recruiting, selecting, evaluating, and training the individuals who are employed by and necessary for the functioning of the firm.* The modern term for all functions pertaining to personnel is **human resource management.** A question that continually baffles and worries businesses, both large and small, is the following: "Suppose you (as a business operator/entrepreneur/manager) awoke tomorrow morning with your plant, equipment, inventory, buildings, and market intact, but without your employees. What would you do?" The answer is that nothing will be accomplished. If you had to rehire a completely new staff, the firm could fail. People are the most important component of a business.

Small businesses, in general, tend to be labor-intensive and thus personnel issues are even more critical. Depending upon the business, the nature of personnel qualifications may vary from highly skilled to unskilled. You must determine the qualification of the people needed and whether there is an adequate labor pool from which to hire. Once these needs are determined, issues such as salary, benefits, hours, and promotions must be resolved. You should also develop an organization chart along with accompanying job descriptions. The full importance of the personnel function is explained in detail in Chapter 10.

8. The Financing Function

Financing is *the process of obtaining the necessary money to operate the business.* No matter how sound or noble the dreams, no matter how common the ideas, business begins and ends with money. Money is necessary in order to begin and to continue operating. Profit, the end result, is also expressed in monetary terms. In this section of the business plan you are concerned with how and where you will obtain the money to adequately finance your business. Without this vital ingredient, your firm will fail. Because many entrepreneurs or businesspeople do not fully understand how much money they will need to run their business, they quickly become cash poor and thus fail. The act of putting together a business plan should force you to think logically and systematically, reducing all elements of the plan to your common denominator—dollars.

The most important part of any business plan is the cash flow projection, which translates your plans into the reality of dollars. Your plan should answer questions such as: How much money do you need? Where will you get this money? How will it be spent? In the case of a borrower: How soon must it be paid back? What will be left? Tools to answer these questions will be presented in Chapter 11.

9. Controls

Controls are *those methods used to ensure that the business achieves its objectives.* Operating a business means that you must have some way of knowing if you will realize your plans and aspirations for the business. As the future is uncertain, not only must you know if you have achieved your desired results but if you have not, by how much have you missed, how significant is the miss, and how will you correct your problems? These topics are more fully explained in Chapter 12. In this section we will be concerned with financial controls. These controls come from your accounting and record-keeping systems. In addition, in this chapter of the business plan you will also learn how to provide yourself or your potential investors with current financial information.

Sources and Applications of Cash
A statement of change in financial position should be included in this section. It shows the sources as well as the applications of cash within your firm. Any transaction that increases working capital is a source of cash, while any transaction which reduces cash is considered a use. This statement analyzes the effects of various transactions upon your firm's cash. A new or existing firm must have a sources and application of cash statement to demonstrate where cash originates and how it is disbursed. The transactions that can be defined as sources of cash include normal

operations, borrowing of cash, issuing of capital stock, and the sale of assets. The applications of cash include purchasing operational assets, purchasing investments, payment of debt, and payment of dividends. All transactions affecting the firm fall into one of the above-mentioned categories and can be incorporated into the statement of financial change.

Application and Expected Effect of Loan or Investment

If a new or existing business has applied for a loan or has sought outside investment, there should be a complete disclosure in the business plan of how that capital will be used. The lender, typically a bank, will require that the loan application itself also includes a complete disclosure of how the money will be spent. A complete financial analysis will not only represent the firm's past and present performance but also act as a long-range future plan.

Breakeven Analysis

A **breakeven analysis** calculates *the volume of sales sufficient to cover all fixed and variable costs. It is the point at which revenues equal costs.* A breakeven analysis is a valuable tool for making decisions regarding sales, expense control, and expansion. Both new and existing businesses must determine the point where their operations break even. A breakeven analysis, also known as a cost-volume-profit analysis, is important because it allows the firm to determine the level of operations needed to cover operating costs and to evaluate the profitability of various levels of sales. The breakeven analysis is also used in evaluating the effects of cost structure on profitability. For example, two firms with equal production and sales income volume can generate different profits because of variations in their cost structures. A firm operating at a production level *below* its breakeven is not covering operating costs, and a firm operating *above* its breakeven point is generating a profit. By taking the time to determine its breakeven point, a firm can evaluate its production and profit level. See Chapter 11 for a more detailed discussion and illustration.

Areas to Control

Certain specific areas need to be closely monitored and controlled. Inventory is one of the most important of these elements. For example, if you own a retail business, it is very costly to carry too much inventory, but carrying too little will leave you with not enough to sell. Inventory control is a balance between too much and not enough. Related to inventory control are areas where losses are incurred through crime, theft, and inventory shrinkage (by employees and customers).

Another important activity requiring control is the collection of your accounts receivable. Neglected, this can be extremely critical, since the reduction of these funds directly affects your firm's cash flow.

Finally, you must insure against various catastrophes that might affect you and your firm. Various state and federal bodies mandate that the business owner must carry insurance and will stipulate the amount of coverage required.[9] You will, as a matter of prudence, want to insure yourself against other risks such as inventory shortages, crime, and credit. These will be discussed in Chapter 13.

Financial Ratios

Throughout this chapter we have alluded to ratios that can be used to measure the operation of your business against industry standards. **Financial ratios** are *the percentage relationships of the firm that can be compared to industry averages.* You may use the following basic ratios to determine the economic condition of your business. This list represents those ratios that are used most frequently, but it is by no means all-inclusive. The ratios that will be discussed are the *current ratio,* the *quick ratio,* the *working capital ratio,* and the *proprietorship ratio.* In addition, another useful tool for control purposes is the breakeven analysis. These will be explained in more detail in Chapter 12.

10. Executive Summary

The **executive summary** is *a brief synopsis of all the key elements incorporated in the business plan.* This includes a description of the potential (or real) problems in the business and recommendations to solve these problems. Each area of concern is discussed in a brief, concise manner, followed by recommendations, costs, and return on sales. The main function of the executive summary is to identify potential problem areas and propose cost-efficient recommendations that will increase the number of products sold or services provided. It also provides the lender or investor with a complete analysis and working knowledge of the business. As the executive summary may be the only part of the plan used by the investor (lender), it needs to be powerful. A weak executive summary may turn a lender away from your plan, whereas a powerful summary may even convince the lender without going further. Although the executive summary appears at the beginning of the business plan, it must be written after the plan has been completed. This is necessary, since you can't begin to summarize until you have defined all of the necessary parameters in the business plan.

The Completed Business Plan

For a complete outline of the business plan, refer to Exhibit 5.4.

As you can see from the exhibit, the business plan is developed step-by-step. All the critical elements are examined and explained. Only after the plan is complete can you summarize. However, in presenting the business plan to a potential venture capitalist, a banker, a relative, or for your own interest, the executive summary is the first section. Its purpose is to present a clear and concise overview of the business. Anyone who wants or needs a detailed explanation can follow up by reading the pertinent section of the plan.

Exhibit 5.4   Business plan outline

Developing the Plan	*The Completed Plan*
I. The Business Plan	I. The Business Plan
1. Description of the business	1. The executive summary
2. Strategy formation	2. Description of the business
3. The accounting function	3. Strategy formation
4. The marketing function	4. The accounting function
5. Location and layout	5. The marketing function
6. The production/operation function	6. Location and layout
7. The human resources function	7. The production/operations function
8. The financing function	8. The human resources function
9. The control function	9. The financing function
10. The executive summary (written last, placed first)	10. The control function
II. Financial Data	III. Financial Data
1. Sources and applications of of funding	1. Sources and applications funding
2. Capital equipment list	2. Capital equipment list
3. Balance sheet	3. Balance Sheet
4. Breakeven analysis	4. Breakeven analysis
5. Income (profit-and-loss statement)	5. Income (profit-and-loss statement)

Summary

Why the Business Plan Is Important

The business plan is fundamental because it is a road map. It shows you the ultimate destination and how to get there. It even allows for unexpected detours and unforeseen problems. It also shows you how to change your route and still drive ahead safely. Use of a plan is necessary for new or established ventures.

Developing the Business Plan

The business plan consists of 10 parts. Each of these parts or sections deserves separate attention. Yet they are interrelated and must function as a whole if the business is to succeed.

The plan starts with the **introduction.** This section describes the type of business you intend to conduct. It goes into details such as the legal form, the hours, and the seasonality of your firm. The **management** of the firm is also specified.

The **strategy formation** section of the plan describes the game plan you will use to run the business. The business will only be successful if you are able to keep track of what you are doing and use this information to determine your financial position. **Accounting** is the term used for the necessary record keeping. From these records, you develop the **balance**

sheet, income statement, and **cash flow statements.** The balance sheet shows your financial position at a point in time and is the result of the activity shown by the income statement over a period of time. Cash flow statements show the actual income and expenses of the firm over a time period.

The purpose of any business is to sell its goods or services. **Marketing** involves all those activities relating to identifying the **target market** and delivering the goods and services to that percentage of the total market you hope to capture. How successful you are will depend upon how you **price** your product and how you deal with your competition. What you charge for your product and how you differentiate your product from your competition play an important part in your firm's profitability.

Once you know your business, decisions must be made concerning **location** and **layout.** Where you will physically site the firm and its internal arrangement of equipment and machinery also impact on the profitability of your company.

Another important factor for success will be how you recruit, train, evaluate, pay, and retain people. The **human resources/personnel** section of the plan deals with these issues. The lifeblood of the organization is money. The part of the plan that deals with **financing** answers the questions of how much money you will need and where you will obtain it.

All problems are not solved unless you make certain that you specify your firm's objectives and put in place those **controls** or methods that enable you to measure your firm's accomplishments against industry averages. This section will include a **sources and application of cash statement.** This statement will tell you where the firm's money comes from and where it is being used. An improper use of funds will become evident quickly. Using the same reasoning, you will also want to be able to track the **application** and expected effect of loans or investments to make sure you know what the loans you obtained were for and how they were used. A **breakeven analysis** will tell you the dollar volume of sales you will need to cover your total costs. Some but not all **areas to control** will be inventory, accounts receivable, and crime. **Financial ratios,** or those percentage relationships in the firm such as **current ratio, quick ratio, working capital ratio,** and **proprietorship ratio,** can be used to compare your firm's performance to industry averages.

The **executive summary** is a brief synopsis of all the elements in the business plan and can only be written last, once you know all of the plans' elements. It is, however, presented as the first part of the plan.

The Completed Business Plan

The completed business plan shows all the elements of the plan so that any interested party will be able to gain a detailed understanding of the specific business. The first part of the completed plan, the executive summary, will present the entire plan in a concise format. Reading the summary will enable you to quickly understand the broad features of the business. A detailed explanation can be found in each section.

Questions

1. What is the purpose of a business plan?
2. Why should a business plan's executive summary be written last?
3. How do financial ratios aid the owner of a small business in financial decision making?

4. Explain the purpose of the sources and applications of cash statement.

5. Explain the importance of a capital equipment list to an existing firm. To a new firm.

6. Why should a balance sheet be incorporated into a business plan?

7. What is the importance of a breakeven analysis?

8. Why should an owner project the balance sheet, income statement, and cash flow statements?

9. How is the controlling process related to the planning process?

10. To a small business what are the major advantages of a business plan? Explain.

11. Of what value is a projected cash flow to a small business? What part of the business plan does it support? Explain.

12. The specific parts of a business plan will vary, depending upon the goods and services the firm is selling. Explain.

13. What are the main parts of a business plan?

14. Why should goals be realistic and quantitative?

15. If the income statement shows that a business will be profitable, what is the need for a cash flow forecast?

Application Exercises

When doing these exercises, where applicable, be sure to select a specific business, preferably one where you now work, or worked previously. If this is not possible, pick a specific organization to which you will make reference. Be sure to identify the organization by name. Your answers should not exceed two pages per exercise.

1. Interview an established small business owner. Determine if the owner has a business plan. If a plan does exist, ask the owner if it is continually updated. If not, why not? If such a plan is not present, ask the owner why not and how he or she plans ahead. Prepare a report of your findings.

2. Interview a person who has just started or is about to start a small business and prepare a report on this person's views of the importance of a business plan.

3. Using the results of questions 1 and 2, compare and/or contrast the two viewpoints, making sure to include in your report all the good and bad points about business planning.

4. Assume you are going to start a business that will produce and sell a device that enables buyers to locate their keys. Prepare an outline of the marketing section of the business plan.

5. Assume you want to start a business tutoring high school or college students for various entrance examinations. Prepare a one-page report outlining your strategy for achieving this objective.

6. If you want to start a business selling shoelaces with fancy designs for running shoes, what would be the most important section(s) of the business plan? Prepare a report on what would be important in this section and discuss why it is important.

7. What would be your strategy for starting a business preparing résumés for students and others searching for jobs?

8. Suppose you had a universal remote control for all electronic devices. Which section of the business plan would be crucial and why? Prepare a report on your findings.

Application Situations

1. John McCulloch

John McCulloch has been running an automobile repair shop for 20 years. Each year for the past 20 years, sales have been rising. He has always been able to take enough money from the business to have a fairly comfortable lifestyle. Lately, however, he has not been able to make ends meet. John doesn't understand what is happening and why he doesn't have any money.

John asked a friend for advice and was startled when he was asked for his business plan. It seemed to John that since he had been in business for years, with things going well, there was no need for a business plan.

Assignment

1. Assuming you are John's friend, would you advise him to draw up a business plan? What should such a plan include?
2. How would a business plan have helped John and what should he do now?

2. Audrey Newton

Audrey Newton was laid off from her job in a corporate downsizing. Aware that there were relatively few job opportunities for her, Audrey decided that being self-employed was a desirable alternative to looking for a new job in another company.

Five years ago, while visiting a small Caribbean island, she discovered some excellent jams and jellies. Upon returning to this country she decided to import them for her own use. Audrey's friends also liked these jams and jellies and asked her to order some for them. Soon, she was supplying all her friends.

Audrey thought that this might be an ideal business. The demand obviously existed, and all she had to do was to order a good supply of the product, tell her friends, and wait for the orders to roll in.

Using $10,000 dollars of her savings, she ordered as much product as she could get. In the last year (her first full year of business), her sales totaled only $4,000. To pay her bills, she has borrowed money from her family.

Assignment

1. If Audrey had drawn up a business plan, what problems might she have recognized and how might she have avoided them? List these problems and explain.
2. Based upon the information given, what should she have put into her business plan that might have prevented her from getting into this situation? Be specific.
3. Will drawing up a business plan help Audrey, or is it too late? Defend your position.

3. A Healthy You

Today it seems that more and more people are concerned with their health and realize that exercise and proper diet may be determinants of longevity. Judging by the success of local health food stores, it seems that a magazine dedicated entirely to health foods and diet would be very successful.

Assignment

1. What questions does your marketing plan need to address?
2. How much money would this venture require? Would it be on the order of $1,000 or $1,000,000?
3. Estimate the amount of money required.
4. Prepare a strategy section of the business plan.

Integrated Case Question—CorLu Foods

Prepare the outline of your business plan for CorLu. You may fill in the outline as you proceed through the text. (Please refer to the Integrated Case "CorLu Foods.")

Bibliography

Adams, Eric. "Growing Your Business Plan." *Home Office Computing,* May 1991, p. 44.

Amer, Tarek S., and Craig E. Bain. "Making Small Business Planning Easier: Microcomputers Facilitate the Process." *Journal of Accountancy* 170 (July, 1990), pp. 53–60.

Boyle, Robert D., and Harsha B. Desai. "Turnaround Strategies for Small Firms." *Journal of Small Business Management* 29, no. 10 (July 1991), p. 33.

Brinckerhoff, Peter C. "Putting Together a Business Planning Team." *Non-Profit World* 9, no. 3 (May/June 1991), pp. 8–9.

Branch, Shelly. "A Good Plan Is Key to Business Success." *Black Enterprise,* November 1991, p. 68.

Brown, Caryne. "Business Busters." *Black Enterprise,* November 1992, p. 75.

Brunnen, David J. "Developing an Enterprise Culture at British Telecom." *Journal of Forecasting (UK)* 22, no. 2 (April 1989), pp. 27–36.

Bukowitz, Wendi, and Mickey Landaiche. "The Crossroads of Commitment," *Home Office Computing,* July 1991, p. 38.

"The Compleat Capacity Planner." *Capacity Management Review,* April 1992, p. 7.

Cook, Dan. "Jon Goodman on Starting Your Own Business." *New Choices for the Best Years,* March 1991, p. 80.

Crawford-Lucas, Patricia A. "Providing Business Plan Assistance to Small Manufacturing Companies." *Economic Development Review* 10, no. 1 (Winter 1992), pp. 54–58.

Daniel, Joseph E. "How to Write a Strong Business Plan." *Folio: The Magazine for Magazine Management,* March 1, 1993, p. 130.

David, Bernard J. "Doing It Your Way: Starting Your Own Business Can Be a Dream or Nightmare." *Computerworld,* April 2, 1990, pp. 87–91.

Davidson, William H. "The Role of Global Scanning in Business Planning." *Organizational Dynamics* 19, no. 3 (Winter 1991), pp. 4–16.

Dodge, H. Robert, and John E. Robbins. "An Empirical Investigation of the Organizational Life Cycle Model for Small Business Development and Survival." *Journal of Small Business Management* 30, no. 1 (January 1992), pp. 27–37.

Duncan, Ian. "Preparing Your Financing Proposal—To Get That Cash." *CMA Magazine,* February 1993, p. 32.

Foster, Gerry. "Setting Sales Goals and Marketing Strategy." *Home Office Computing,* July 1991, p. 37.

Fry, Fred L. "The Role of Incubators in Small Business Planning." *American Journal of Small Business* 12, no. 1 (Summer 1987), pp. 51–61.

Gitman, Lawrence. *Principles of Managerial Finance.* New York: Harper & Row, 1982. pp. 151–60.

"Good News, The FM Business Planning Gap Is Closing," *Facilities Design and Management,* April 1989, pp. 58–63.

"Good Plan." *Inc.,* February 1991, p. 76.

"A Helping Hand." *Small Business Reports,* January 1993, pp. 7–8.

King, Ruth A. "Developing a Business Plan." *Business and Economic Review,* July 1985, pp. 6–8.

Knight, Ray A., and Lee G. Knight. "Planning: The Key to Small Business Survival." *Management Accounting* 74, no. 8 (February 1993), pp. 33–34.

Krentz, Susanna E., and Suzanne M. Pilskaln. "Product Life Cycle: Still a Valid Framework for Business Planning." *Topics in Health Care Financing* 15, no. 6 (Fall 1988), pp. 40–48.

Kyle, Robert J., and Alfred Z. Matos. "A Winning Business Planning Process." *AACE Transactions, 1991,* pp. 15(1)–15(8).

Lee, Melissa. "Crash Courses Offer Quick Doses of Business Wisdom; Break It Gently to MBA Students, but Speedy Lessons Can Be Profitable." *The Wall Street Journal,* August 19, 1993, pp. B2(W), B2(E), col. 3.

Lyles, Marjorie A.; Inga S. Baird; J. Burdeane Orris; and Donald F. Kuratko. "Formalized Planning in Small Business: Increasing Strategic Choices." *Journal of Small Business Management* 31, no. 13 (April 1993), p. 38.

McManis, Gerald L., and Michael S. Leibman. "Integrating Human Resource and Business Planning." *Personnel Administrator,* June 1988, pp. 32–38.

Martin, Mary Dell. "Starting Your Own Business." *Accent on Living,* Winter 1991, p. 50.

Marx, Thomas G. "Removing the Obstacles to Effective Strategic Planning." *Long-Range Planning* 24, no. 24 (August 1991), pp. 21–28.

Meyer, Lurie. "What to Look For When Seeking a New Plant Site." *Modern Plastics,* July 1992, pp. 52–55.

Miller, Ernest C. "Strategic Planning Pays Off." *Personnel Journal,* April 1989, pp. 127–32.

Myers, Herbert. *Minding Your Own Business.* Homewood, Il: Dow Jones-Irwin, 1984, p. 13.

Mullins, Brenda, and Bill Mullins. "Strategic Management: A Way of Thinking," *Canadian Insurance,* December 1992, pp. 14–16.

Narchal, R. M.; K. Kittapa; and P. Bhattacharya. "An Environmental Scanning System for Business Planning." *Long-Range Planning (UK)* 20, no. 6 (December 1987), pp. 96–105.

Noland, Richard. "The Business of Planning." *Credit Union Management* 11, no. 7 (July 1988), pp. 18–22, 29.

Poelker, John S. "Developing a Comprehensive Financial Framework for Business Planning." *Bank Administration,* December 1988, pp. 44–50.

Pollan, Stephen M., and Mark Levine. "The 12 New Fundamentals of Small-Business Success." *U.S. News & World Report,* October 12, 1992, p. 65.

Rienzo, Thomas F. "Planning Deming Management for Service Organizations." *Business Horizons,* May/June 1993, pp. 19–29.

"The Road to Success: What Thriving Small Businesses Have in Common." *Profit-Building Strategies for Business Owners,* December 1989, pp. 3–5.

Rudolf, William. "Managing Raw Materials Risk." *Chemical Business,* April 1993, pp. 4–6.

Sherman, Andrew J. "Writing a Plan for Growth." *Nation's Business,* November 1991, p. 68.

Siropolis, Nicholas C. *Small Business Management.* Boston: Houghton Mifflin, 1986, pp. 153–60.

"Small Companies in Quest of Cash Face More Grilling Than Ever." *Profit-Building Strategies for Business Owners,* November 1992, pp. 3–4.

Smith, Philip L. "Tighten the Linkage between Research, Business Strategy and Marketing." *Research-Technology Management,* March/April 1988, pp. 6–8.

Steinhoff, Dan, and John F. Burgess. *Small Business Management Fundamentals.* New York: McGraw Hill, 1986, pp. 46–50.

Sullivan, Cornelius H., Jr., and Charles E. Yates. "Reasoning by Analogy; A Tool for Business Planning." *Sloan Management Review,* Spring 1988, pp. 55–60.

Sullivan, Nick. "It's 1993: Do You Know Where You're Going?" *Home Office Computing,* January 1993, p. 112.

Washer, Louise. "Marketing 101: Finding Your First Customer." *Working Woman,* October 1992, pp. 53–54, 65.

Welsch, Glenn; Robert Anthony; and Daniel Short. *Fundamentals of Financial Accounting.* Homewood, Il: Richard D. Irwin, 1984, p. 688.

Young, Peg; Alfred A. Marcus; Ronald S. Koot; and Baruch Mevorach. "Improved Business Planning through an Awareness of Political Cycles." *Journal of Forecasting (UK)* 9, no. 1 (January/February 1990), pp. 37–52.

Endnotes

1. *How to Plan and Finance Your Business* (Boston, Mass.: CBI Publishing Company, 1986), p. 4.
2. Dun & Bradstreet, *Business Failure Record* (New York: Dun and Bradstreet Company, 1993), p. 18.
3. U.S. Small Business Administration, "Business Plan for Small Manufacturer," *Management Aid, No. 2007* (Washington, D.C.: U.S. Government Printing Office, 1985), p. 2.
4. Eric Larson, "The Best-Laid Plans," *Inc.,* February, 1987, pp. 60–64.
5. Forms of ownership were discussed in Chapter 1.
6. Ruth A. King, "Developing a Business Plan," *Business and Economic Review,* July 1985.

7. There are many sources that you can use to obtain the statistics you should incorporate into your plan. If you do not have these at hand, your local public library provides a rich source of information.
8. Many computer-based flow charts are available to the small business owner to simplify this task.
9. Automobile, Workingmen's Compensation are two examples of insurance coverage mandated by law.

6   INTRODUCTION AND STRATEGY FORMULATION SECTIONS OF THE BUSINESS PLAN

In this chapter you will learn how to develop the introduction and strategy sections of the business plan. The introduction has three parts: background, management and organization, and legal form. The written strategy has three parts: environmental analysis, mission, and objectives. The strategy is based on an analysis of the internal environment (management, mission and objectives, resources, the transformation process, and structure) and the external environment (customers, competitors, suppliers, labor force, stockholders, society, technology, governments, and the economy). Through the environmental analysis you determine the strengths, weaknesses, opportunities, and threats of the firm.

Chapter Learning Objectives

After completing this chapter, you should be able to:

· Explain the interrelationship between strategy formulation and the other business plan components.
· Identify the six internal environmental components and explain them.
· Identify the nine external environmental components and explain them.
· Discuss how the external environment affects the internal environmental factors.
· Conduct an environmental analysis.
· Write a strategy for a business.
· Define the following 12 key terms in order of appearance:

Strategy	Objectives
Internal environment	Transformation process
Mission	System

Target customer   External environment
Competitive advantage Environmental analysis
Business philosophy   Interactive managers

Introduction

Back in the 1980s there was a debate about the value of strategy formulation. Two major studies were conducted. One of the studies compared higher financial performers to lower financial performers. The results revealed that the higher financial performers had clear written strategies including mission statements, while the lower performers did not.[1] A second study concluded that most organizations need to define their strategy clearly.[2] Two of the major myths about strategic planning revealed in the 1980s were: (1) Strategic plans need to be complex and based on sophisticated quantitative methods.[3] (2) Strategic planning is not important for small business.[4] Small businesses need strategic plans but they do not have to be long and complex. For most small businesses a one- to three-page strategy is all that is needed. Strategy formulation leads to better decision making, clearer communication, and greater ease in delegation.[5] Increasingly throughout the 1980s, organizations have been adopting strategic planning;[6] the trend will continue through the 1990s as small businesses continue to realize the benefits of strategy formulation.

The Interrelationship between Strategy and the Other Business Plan Components

A common starting point of business planning should be strategic-planning formulation. A **strategy** is *the managerial game plan for directing and running the business.* A strategic plan is often referred to as the outline or blueprint specifying what the business wants to do and how it is going to do it. When planning your business, work backwards. Start by stating where you want the business to be in the future, then develop the plans to get the business there.

The firm's strategic plan specifies what it wants to accomplish, while the other business-planning components (accounting, marketing, location, layout, production/operations, personnel, financing, and control) specify the details of how it will accomplish these things. However, before you can formulate a strategy, you must understand the internal and external environments and how they affect planning. You also need to conduct an environmental analysis to determine your strengths, areas for improvement, opportunities, and potential problems. So let's begin by learning about the introductory section of the business plan and the environment, then return to strategy formulation.

The Introduction Section of the Business Plan

The introduction section of the business plan includes three parts: background of the business, management and organization, and form of ownership. (1) The background of the business includes its name, address (or addresses if there is more than one location), telephone number(s), hours of operation, and a history (if any). State when the business was started or will be started. (2) List all the business's key managers and their duties and responsibilities, with their qualifications (skills, education, experience, accomplishments). If it is extensive, put résumés as exhibits in the back of the plan. If there are several departments, you should place an organization chart as an exhibit. (3) Include the form of ownership (proprietorship, partnership, or corporation), distribution of business profits (if partnership or corporation), and salaries of key managers.

The type of ownership affects your business plan. If you are a sole proprietorship, you have complete control. If you have partners, you should work together to create a mutually agreeable strategy. If you have a corporation, the board of directors should be included in the planning and accept the final business plan. You may also want to list investors', directors', and any consultants' names and qualifications in the introduction section of the business plan.

The Internal Environment

Businesses are created for the purpose of producing products and/or services for customers at a profit. The organization's **internal environment** includes *the factors that affect the firm's performance from within its boundaries.* The internal environmental factors include: management, mission and objectives, resources, the transformation process, and structure. Let's look at each separately, then put them together.

Management

Managers are responsible for the performance of the business. Managers perform the functions of planning, organizing, staffing, leading, and controlling. The leadership style and the decisions made by managers affect the performance of the business. Because managers have such an impact on the success of the business, they need to be selected carefully. We will discuss this in detail in Chapter 10, "The Human Relations/Personnel Function."

Mission

The business mission is the motivating force that moves, guides, and transports the firm to where it wants to go.[7] A clear sense of mission is the most important factor in strategic planning.[8] The mission affects managers' jobs and the structure of the organization. The mission should be developed based on the environmental analysis, to be discussed later in this chapter. The mission states the business's purpose or reason for being. The **mission** specifies *the nature of the business in the areas of product, target customer, competitive advantage, and philosophy.* Let's look at each separately.

Product

Both goods and services make up a business's product. The mission should identify the present and future products to be offered. If the firm uses some form of technology or process, it may also be identified. In the strategy section it is not necessary to list all the products; they are listed under the marketing section of the business plan and will be discussed in Chapter 7.

Target Customers

The mission should identify the specific target customers and target markets for the business's products. Trying to be all things to all people usually does not result in sales. Segment your target customers by specifying their similar needs or wants. Possible targets include young singles, ethnic groups, high-income level, retired, or college students. **Target customers** are *the segmented group of potential buyers of the firm's product.* It is also helpful to specify where these target customers are. Are you selling at retail, at wholesale, to the government, to industry, by mail? What countries, states, cities, areas, and so on do you sell in now and in the future?

Sports Illustrated magazine targets a large segment of readers. To compete head-on with them would be very difficult for the small business. However, a small business could pick a niche and offer a sports magazine to people interested in a specific sport. Notice that the product and target market should go together. If you want to start a golf magazine, you target a different reader than *Sports Illustrated.* However, the small business must be careful not to select too small a target market resulting in insufficient sales to be profitable. You need a balance.

Competitive Advantage

The **competitive advantage** *specifies how the business competes for customers.* Why should target customers buy your product rather than the competitor's? What unique advantage does the company have to offer customers? What can your business do better/different than the competition? The competitive advantage is determined based on the environmental analysis.

The firm's competitive advantage can be as simple as a convenient location or as complex as being the technology leader. However, the harder it is for the competition to copy you, the more secure is your business. For example, if you are the only Italian restaurant in town, you have a competitive advantage. But if you are very profitable, someone else may open an Italian restaurant and steal some of your business.

Price, service, and quality are common competitive advantages. However, the small business must be careful when lowering prices because it's difficult to gain the economies of scale of large business. Many customers are willing to pay for high-quality service/features. Many small businesses select a niche that the big businesses don't target by offering unique features or high quality. Domino's Pizza started as a small business with the competitive advantage of quick delivery, 30 minutes or less. With this competitive advantage, Domino's took business from the traditional sit-down Pizza Hut and the local take-out pizza parlors. Many people will agree that they can go to a local pizza parlor and get a larger, better-tasting pizza for less money. This is why the local pizza parlors are still around. They offer a competitive advantage over Domino's. But many people call Domino's because they are willing to pay for the quick delivery service.

Philosophy of Doing Business
What are the basic beliefs, values, aspirations, and priorities of the firm? What is the firm's view of itself and the way it conducts business? What is the image the firm wants its target customers and the general public to have of it? The **business philosophy** is *the specified way in which the firm conducts business.*

According to Ackoff[9] and others[10] the mission should be relevant to all stakeholders. Some of the stakeholders include employees, stockholders, customers, suppliers, governments, and the public. You'll learn more about these stakeholders throughout this chapter.

The mission statement part of the business plan should be communicated to employees and target customers. Therefore, it should be concise enough to commit its tenets to memory. Mission statements do not always include all four areas of product, target customer, competitive advantage, and philosophy. Two examples of mission statements for small businesses include:

1. The Winston is an exclusive steak house offering high-quality meals at high prices with exceptional services to high-income customers in Winston Mansion's antique ambiance.

Product: Our menu includes steaks and other meals.

Target Customer: We target the upper-income customer.

Competitive Advantage and Philosophy: The quality meal with exceptional service and antique ambiance creates a competitive advantage and philosophy of doing business. The staff is highly trained to project the Winston image.

2. This is Coalson's external mission statement given to prospective clients. Coalson Management Consultants are dedicated to training people and developing their skills in order to maximize performance and productivity on the job, while enhancing individual careers. We offer high-quality customized training and development at competitive prices.

Services: Our services are flexible in order to give clients what they want.

Target Client: We target organizations with 100–500 employees. (Smaller organizations often do not have enough managers to require in-house training, and companies with over 500 employees often have their own staff to do the training).

Competitive Advantage and Philosophy: High-quality customized training at competitive prices. Consultants stress on-the-job application of what is taught in the training sessions.

According to Deming, the major reason businesses fail is that management does not look ahead. Under management's directives, the firm produces the wrong product or service, one with no market, or one with too small a market.[11] Managers with vision develop/change the mission by offering products and services in demand by customers. You need to know your target market and give them the products they want at a profit. For example, Coalson Management Consultants' original mission was to offer training programs by renting hotel space and getting a few people from many organizations to attend. When Coalson went to businesses to sell his training services, he learned that the target market was too small in his area. He did not do a good environmental analysis. During his sales calls he learned that businesses were more interested in having consultants come on their premises and offer a custom program designed to meet their unique employee needs. Coalson completely changed his mission and became a successful small business.

Objectives

For many years writers have been saying that setting difficult objectives leads to higher levels of motivation and performance. Generally, businesses that set difficult objectives outperform those that do not set objectives. **Objectives** *state what is to be accomplished within a given period of time.* Objectives are end results; they do not state how the objective will be accomplished. How to achieve the objective is the plan. Some writers define goals and objectives differently; we do not.

Criteria for Objectives

To motivate people to high levels of performance objectives should be:

1. *Difficult but achievable.* A number of studies have shown that individuals perform better when assigned difficult objectives rather than easy ones, or are simply told "do your best." To motivate people to high levels of performance, objectives must be challenging. However, if people do not believe that the objectives are achievable, they will not be motivated to work for their accomplishment.
2. *Observable and measurable.* If people are to achieve objectives they must be able to observe and measure their progress regularly. Studies have shown that individuals perform better when their performance is measured and evaluated.
3. *Specific, with a target date.* To be motivated employees must know exactly what is expected of them and when it is expected to be completed. Employees should be given specific objectives with deadlines. However, some objectives do not require or lend themselves to target dates; for example, to keep the reject rate to under 3 percent.
4. *Participatively set when possible.* Groups that participate in setting their objectives generally out-perform groups with assigned objectives.

EXHIBIT 6.1   Writing objectives model

Infinitive + action verb + singular behavior result + target date

Example objectives for a student:
To + receive + a B as my final grade in small business management
+ in December/May 19____.
To increase my cumulative grade point average to 3.0 by May 19____.

Example objectives for managers:
To + produce + 1,000 units + per day.
To keep absences to three or less per month.
To decrease accidents by 5% during 19____.

Example objectives for a business:
To have an annual profit of $75,000 within five years, by September 1, 19____.
To develop a reputation for high-quality services within three years, by March 1, 19____.
To maintain a minimum average return on equity of 10 percent.
To sell $50,000 of our product in our first fiscal year, by August 31, 19____.
To open a second store within six months, by June 15, 19____.
To increase production from 100 to 125 units per day within three months, by May 31, 19____.

---

5. *Accepted.* For objectives to be met they must be accepted by those responsible for their attainment. Meeting the above four criteria without acceptance can lead to failure. If employees are not committed to strive for the objective, they may not meet it. Participation encourages employees to accept objectives.

Writing Objectives

Objectives should be written. To help you write objectives that meet the five criteria above, use Max E. Douglas's model shown in Exhibit 6.1.

The mission and objectives are also known as the ends the organization strives to attain. The other internal environmental factors are considered the means to achieve the ends (see Exhibit 6.2 for an illustration). Note that management develops the mission and objectives, attains resources, determines the transformation process and structure, but they are means to the end; the owners/management are not an end in and of themselves.

Resources

When running a business, it is very important to determine what resources you need, how much they will cost, where you will get them, and how you will pay for them. Morris has identified five major resources the organization can use to achieve its mission and objectives:[12]

1. *Human:* Employees are the most important resource in the business. People are responsible for achieving the organization's objectives; they are

Exhibit 6.2

Means and ends

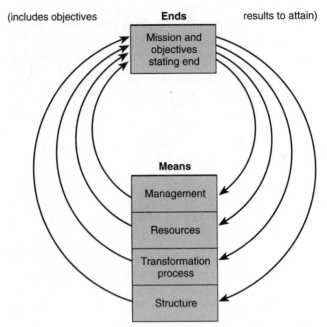

(includes objectives   **Ends**   results to attain)

Mission and objectives stating end

Means

Management

Resources

Transformation process

Structure

(includes the means by which objectives can be attained)

the ones who come up with the creative ideas that result in new businesses and products/services. Leading organizations have innovative people and use their ideas to create profits. You will learn more about human resources in Chapter 10, "The Human Relations/Personnel Function."

2. *Physical:* People use land, buildings, machines, equipment, natural resources, inventory, and so on to achieve objectives. Physical resources are often both the inputs and the transformation process to make finished goods and services. You will learn more about physical resources in Chapters 8 and 9, "Location and Layout" and "The Production/Operations Function."

3. *Intangible:* Reputation, laws, patents, trademarks, copyrights, licenses, accreditation, contracts, tariffs, quotas, and duties, can be used to enable the business to achieve its objectives. Information is also an intangible resource that is needed throughout the organization.

4. *Financial:* Organizations need cash and credit to operate. Physical and intangible resources are obtained through financing. Two major sources of finance are the acquisition of debt (credit and the sale of bonds) and equity (profits and the sale of stock). You will learn more about financing in Chapter 11, "The Financing Function."

5. *Marketing:* Marketing is used to determine potential customers, which products/services to offer them, the distribution systems to get the product

to the customer, the means of promotion to induce the customer to buy the products, and the pricing of the product. You will learn more about marketing in Chapter 7, "The Marketing Function."

The effective management team uses its combined resources in a systematic way that leads to attaining its objectives.

The Transformation Process

The **transformation process** is *the system for converting inputs into outputs.* The transformation process has four components:

1. *Inputs:* Inputs are the start-up force that provides the business with operating necessities. The inputs include the firm's resources that are converted into outputs.
2. *Outputs:* Outputs are the goods and/or services offered to customers.
3. *Process:* The transformation of the inputs into outputs.
4. *Feedback, influence, and control:* Feedback provides a means of control to ensure that the inputs and process are producing the desired results.

A small manufacturing firm like Solar Car and Electric Vehicles of America will use raw materials and components such as steel, plastic, and metal parts, rubber tires, and so on (inputs) as it makes solar and electric cars (outputs) on the assembly line (process). A service organization like Bank of Small Town will use loan application forms (inputs) to make a loan (output). The loan officer will process the application and issue the funds.

The customer for the product can be internal or external, and the output of one system can be an input to another system. For example, Solar could buy its tires from Goodyear. The tire is an output of Goodyear, an input for Solar. Solar is Goodyear's external customer. Within Solar, one department could mold fenders (its output) and send them to the assembly line as its input. Departments within the same organization are internal customers. Solar and Goodyear would be stakeholders to each other.

You will learn more about the transformation process, which is commonly called the production/operations function, in Chapter 9, "The Production/Operations Function." See Exhibit 6.3 for an illustration of the transformation process.

Note that the transformation process has a feedback loop with influence and control. If Solar cars roll off the assembly line, are test-driven, and they meet standards, the feedback is positive; keep up the good work. However, if they don't run according to standard, the feedback is negative and the inputs and/or processes must be changed to meet the standards.

Structure

An organization is a system. A **system** is *a set of two or more interacting elements in which each part affects the whole and each part is affected by at least one other*

Exhibit 6.3

The transformation process

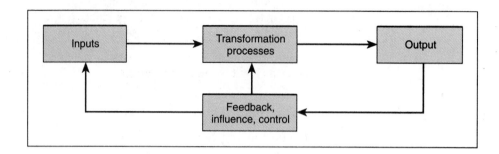

Exhibit 6.4

Internal environment components

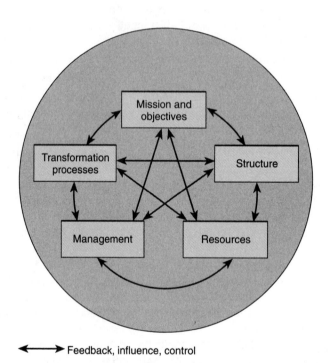

◄──────► Feedback, influence, control

part. An organization as a system is structured into departments such as finance, marketing, production, personnel, and so on. Each of these departments affects the organization as a whole, and each department is affected by the other departments. Companies structure resources to transform inputs into outputs. All of the business's resources must be structured effectively to achieve its objectives.

If the business has many managers and distinct departments, you may want to include an organization chart in the business plan introduction section as an exhibit. Place the department name and the manager of the department in the boxes. See Exhibit 6.4 for an illustration of the interrelationship between the internal environment components.

The External Environment

The organization's **external environment** includes *the factors that affect the business's performance from outside its boundaries.* Unlike the internal environment, managers have no control over what happens outside the business; yet these factors can mean the difference between the firm's success and failure. This is why the internal environmental factors should be based on the external factors. Three studies support this. The first study compared successful and failed firms. Results revealed that successful firms pay equal attention to the internal and external environments. Failures tended to ignore the external environment.[13] The second study focused on the need to balance the internal and external environment.[14] The third study revealed that small business owners/managers are more concerned with and spend more time gathering information from the external environment than large companies.[15]

Nine major external factors are: customers, competitors, suppliers, labor force/unions, stockholders, society, technology, governments, and the economy. Let's look at each separately, then put them together with the internal environment.

Customers

Customers have a major affect on the business's performance through purchasing its goods and/or services. Without customers there is no need for a business. Effective managers today realize the need to get to know their customers well and to offer them products and services that meet their needs profitably. Getting to know the target market is an important part of developing the mission statement.

Competitors

In industries that are not monopolies, the firm must compete for customers. Competitors' strategic moves affect the performance of your business. Competition is increasing as the global economy expands. To develop missions with strategies that offer a unique advantage over the competition, you must get to know your competitors.

Suppliers

Many business resources come from outside the firm. Businesses have to recruit human resources; they also buy land, buildings, machines, equipment, and natural resources from suppliers. Intangibles like patents are often awarded from outside the firm. Financing often comes from creditors like banks and through the sale of stocks and bonds to outsiders. Marketing services such as advertising and distribution are often provided by outside vendors.

Business performance is based in part on suppliers. Effective managers realize the importance of suppliers and develop close working relationships with them.

Without good reliable suppliers to provide resources, the transformation process will be adversely affected.

Labor Force/Unions

The employees of the business have a direct affect on the performance of the organization. Managers recruit human resources from the available labor force outside its boundaries. The mission of the firm, its structure, and its transformation process are major determining factors of the capability levels employees need to meet objectives. The skills needed by a high-technology firm are different from those needed by a retail store. If the firm hires employees with capability levels below standards, they will produce inferior products.

Unions are considered an external factor because they become a third party when dealing with the business. In a unionized organization it is the union rather than individual employee that negotiates an agreement with management. In nonunionized firms there may be a threat of employees organizing to form a union. Unions have the power to strike and possibly stop business operations.

Shareholders

The owners of a corporation are called shareholders. Shareholders vote for the board of directors who oversee the performance of the business. Most shareholders and directors of large corporations are generally not involved in the day-to-day operation of the firm, but they often are in small businesses. Unlike a large corporation, it is not unusual for shareholders to be the directors in small businesses. Directors hire top managers who report to them.

Society

Members of society may also pressure management of the business to change. Individuals and groups have been formed to pressure business for changes. Ralph Nader has pressured the auto industry and others to produce safer products. People who live in the area of a business do not want it to pollute the air or water or abuse the natural resources. Tougher pollution control requirements have been brought about through societal pressures.

Technology

The rate of technological change will continue to increase. Few organizations today operate as they did even a decade ago. Products and services not envisioned only a few years ago are now being mass-produced. The computer has changed the way organizations of all sizes conduct and transact business. Computers are often an essential part of operations in small business.

Changes in technology create threats and opportunities for businesses. For example, years ago there were thousands of small diaper services. But because of the large technological advance of the disposable diaper, most went out of business.

Governments

Foreign, federal, state, and local governments all set laws and regulations that businesses must obey. If the firm does not operate within the law, it can be fined and even closed. Governments create both opportunities and threats for businesses. Some years back Maine changed the legal drinking age from 21 to 18. John Thomson opened a bar targeted for the 18- to 20-year-old group and was very successful. However, a few years later the state increased the legal drinking age. John virtually lost his business overnight.

Economy

The organization has no control over inflation and interest rates, yet they have a direct impact on its performance. Generally, when the economy is growing, as measured by gross national product (GNP) and gross domestic product (GDP), businesses do better than during times of recession. In the last quarter of 1990 and the first quarters of 1991 GNP declined. The economy was in a recession for two consecutive quarters. During this period business failures increased, as reported by Dun & Bradstreet.

Environmental Analysis

Through the environmental analysis the firm assesses its internal and external environments. Through **environmental analysis** the firm *identifies its strengths and weaknesses and opportunities and threats.* This process is commonly called the SWOT analysis.[16] Before reading about SWOT see Exhibit 6.5 for an illustration of the organizational environmental factors that you are analyzing.

We are going to change from theory to practice. You are going to learn "how to" perform a SWOT analysis.

Strengths and Weaknesses

Based on the internal and external factors, how does your business compare to the competition? The way to approach this analysis is to identify the key success factors in your industry. What does it take to be successful? Key success factors vary with the type of business. Some possible factors include: quality, service, cost, price, reputation, technology, management, manufacturing, marketing, financing, location, or appearance of facilities. As you identify the key success factors, write them down, using a form like Exhibit 6.6. For each factor rate your firm and each major competitor on a scale from 1—weak, to 10—strong. If you are not sure what the key success factors are, talk to people in both the internal and external environments. The important thing in the analysis is to develop a strategy based on your strengths while you work to minimize your weaknesses.

Exhibit 6.5

*The organizational
environment*

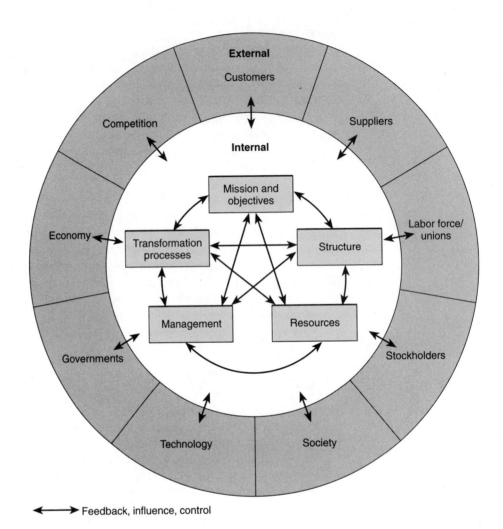

← → Feedback, influence, control

Opportunities and Threats

Based on the internal and external environments, what opportunities and threats do
you foresee? Possible areas include: market growth/decline, increasing/decreasing
competition, price and cost changes, economic expansion/contraction, government
changes in regulations, availability of supplies, increasing/decreasing substitute
products, or changing tastes/needs of customers. On a form like Exhibit 6.6 write
down the major opportunities you can take advantage of to increase size/profits,
and areas you need to watch to make sure you remain successful.

Interactive Management

Today owner/managers need to gain control over the environment.[17] According to
Ackoff,[18] **interactive managers** *design a desirable strategy and invent ways of
bringing it about.* They believe they are capable of creating a significant part of the

EXHIBIT 6.6   Environmental analysis

Strength and Weakness Analysis
Rating scale: 1 = weak, 10 = strong.

Key Success Factors	*Us*	*Competitors (list names of all major competitors)*					
1		___	___	___	___	___	___
2		___	___	___	___	___	___
.		___	___	___	___	___	___
.		___	___	___	___	___	___

Overall rating

Opportunity and Threat Analysis

Opportunities	*Threats*
1	
2	
.	
.	

List of Strengths and Weaknesses, Opportunities and Threats (priority order of a few major areas)

Strengths	*Weaknesses*	*Opportunities*	*Threats*

future and controlling the effects of their efforts on the environment. Experience is no longer the best teacher; it's too slow, ambiguous, and imprecise. Experimentation replaces experience. They try to prevent, not merely prepare for, threats and to create, not merely exploit, opportunities. Rather than react or respond, interactive managers make things happen for their benefit and that of their stakeholders. They plan to do better in the future than the best that is presently deemed possible.

Interactive managers have four principles of planning. (1) *Participative planning:* Everyone who can be affected by it has the opportunity to participate in the planning. (2) *Coordinated planning:* All aspects of a system should be anticipated simultaneously and interdependently. Departments should not each have their own separate plans. (3) *Integrated planning:* Strategic planning (selecting ends) tends to flow from the top down, and tactical planning (selecting means) tends to flow from the bottom up. Plans at all levels and time frames should be integrated with the other levels and time frames. (4) *Continuous planning:* Plans should be updated, extended, and corrected frequently. A plan's actual performance should be compared frequently with previously stated objectives. Significant deviations should be identified, and appropriate corrective action taken through the feedback, influence, and control process.

Strategy Formulation

After completing the environmental analysis, you are ready to develop the business strategy. According to Mintzberg, the strategy must achieve an essential fit between external threats and opportunities and internal competitive advantage.[19] The written strategy is the second section of the business plan. A one- to three-page strategy is long enough. The strategy section should include three parts: mission, objectives, and environmental analysis. Notice that the environmental analysis section is presented last, even though it is developed first. This is because the actual analysis is used to develop the mission and objectives and is generally of less importance to the reader.

Mission

You may use the mission statements of Winston Mansion Steak House and Coalson Management Consultants as an example to develop your own mission statement. But remember, the mission statement should be communicated to employees, consumers, and suppliers.[20] Therefore, it should be concise enough to commit its tenets to memory.

Objectives

Based on its mission, what does the business want to accomplish? It is recommended that you develop both long- and short-term objectives. Long-term objectives will take longer than one year to accomplish, while short-term objectives will be achieved in one year or less. Common areas of business objectives include sales, profitability, productivity, growth, market share, resources, and reputation. Developing too many objectives leads to unfocused attention. One to three long-term objectives and three to five short-term objectives should be enough for most small businesses. However, this is a general guide: you may want more or fewer. It is also recommended that you write the objectives in priority order to keep the focus on what is most important to the business. List the top-priority objective first and the lowest priority last for both long- and short-term objectives.

Environmental Analysis

List your firm's strengths and weaknesses, opportunities and threats as part of your strategy section. If you are seeking financing, it is often helpful to give the investor/lender a complete comparison between your business and its competitors. Exhibit 6.7 reviews the information contained in the introduction and strategy sections of the business plan.

Exhibit 6.7   The introduction and strategy section of the business plan

I. Introduction Section

a. *Background:* Company name, address(es), telephone number(s), hours of operation, and history, including date of start-up.

b. *Management and organization:* List key managers and their duties and responsibilities along with their qualifications. Include an organization chart if appropriate.

c. *Form of ownership:* Identify the form of ownership and distribution of profits and/or salaries of key managers.

II. Strategy Section

a. *Mission:* Product, target customers, competitive advantage, philosophy of doing business.

b. *Objectives (prioritized):* One to three long-term objectives and three to five short-term objectives.

c. *Environmental Analysis:* List some of the major strengths and weaknesses, opportunities and threats (SWOT).

With your strategy in hand you are now ready to move on to develop the implementation plans (accounting, marketing, location and layout, production/operations, personnel, financing, and control) to live up to the mission and achieve the objectives. However, remember that planning is an ongoing process; when making implementation plans you may realize that you have to come back to your strategy and make changes.

Summary

The Interrelationship between Strategy and the Other Business Plan Components

A **strategy** is *the managerial game plan for directing and running the business.* Your strategy states what the business will accomplish, whereas the other business-planning components specify the details of how it will accomplish these things.

The Introduction Section of the Business Plan

The introduction section of the business plan includes the background of the firm, management and organization, and form of ownership.

The Internal Environment

The organization's **internal environment** includes *the factors that affect the firm's performance from within its boundaries.* The internal environmental factors include: management, mission and objectives, resources, the transformation process, and structure. The **mission** specifies *the nature of the business in the areas of product, target customer, competitive advantage, and philosophy.* **Target customers** are *the segmented group of potential buyers of the firm's product.* The **competitive advantage** specifies *how the business competes for* *customers.* The **business philosophy** is *the specified way in which the firm conducts business.*

Objectives state *what is to be accomplished within a given period of time.* Objectives are end results; they do not state how the objective will be accomplished. The firm's mission and objectives are its ends; its management, resources, transformation process, and structure are the means to achieve these ends. The five resources the business has to achieve its mission and objectives are: human, physical, intangible, financial, and marketing.

The **transformation process** is *the system for transforming inputs into outputs.* It has four components: inputs, outputs, process, and feed back influence and control. A **system** is *a set of two or more interacting elements in which each part affects the whole and each part is affected by at least one other part.* An organization, as a system, is structured into departments such as finance, marketing, production, personnel, and so on.

The External Environment

The organization's **external environment** includes *the factors that affect the business's performance from outside its boundaries.* Nine major external factors are: customers, competition, suppliers, labor force/unions, stockholders, society, technology, governments, and the economy.

Environmental Analysis

Through the **environmental analysis** the firm *identifies its strengths and weaknesses and opportunity and threats* (SWOT). **Interactive managers** *design a desirable strategy and invent ways of bringing it about.*

Strategy Formulation

The written strategy section of the business plan includes subsections on mission, objectives, and environmental analysis. With the strategy completed you are now ready to develop the implementation plans to achieve the objectives.

Questions

1. What is a strategy? Why is it the starting point of the business plan?
2. Why is strategy formulation important to an existing and new venture?
3. List the factors in the internal environment. Explain how they interrelate.
4. Define mission. Why is it important for the existing and new venture to develop a mission statement?
5. Describe Little Caesar's Pizza's competitive advantage.
6. What purpose do objectives provide to the existing and new venture?
7. Describe the transformation process. Do all businesses have a transformation process? Is it important?
8. Identify any three of the nine external factors and state how each affects the performance of a business.

9. Is it necessary to conduct an environmental analysis? Why or why not?
10. Give an example of a strength, weakness, opportunity, and threat.

Application Exercises

When doing these exercises be sure to select a specific business, preferably one you work for or have worked for. Be sure to identify the organization by name. Keep your answers to one to two pages per exercise.

1. Write a mission statement for a specific organization. Be sure to include product/service, target customer/market, competitive advantage, and business philosophy.
2. Using Douglas's model, write one to three long-term objectives and three to five short-term objectives you personally want to accomplish.
3. For a specific organization list two to five of its most important human, physical, intangible, financial, and marketing resources. Then from your list prioritize its top three resources (1 most important, then 2 and 3).
4. Describe the production/operations process for a specific organization. State how important the efficiency of this process is to the firm.
5. For a specific organization identify its major customers, competitors, suppliers, and technology. State the effects these and the governments and economy have on this business.
6. Using Exhibit 6.6 as a guide, conduct an environmental analysis for a specific organization.

Application Situations

1. Toothpaste Mission

The American market for toothpaste is very competitive, with major national brands like Crest, Colgate, Aquafresh, Close-up, and others dominating sales. Most national brands of toothpaste are sweetened with artificial ingredients, usually saccharin; assume that the local brands in your area are too. Is it possible for a small company to start and become profitable? Assume that you are interested in starting a small toothpaste company to sell on a local level—about a 100-mile radius from your home. If your company is successful, you will expand your sales territory. You have decided that you cannot compete head-on with the national brands. You have asked yourself, "Why would anyone buy my toothpaste if it's just the same as the market leader, Crest?" Your product could possibly be cheaper, but there are already supermarket/drugstore brands available with this differentiation.

Assignment

Develop a one-page mission statement for a local toothpaste. Be sure to clearly specify the toothpaste name, target market, competitive advantage, and philosophy of doing business.

The key starting place to developing your mission statement should be your competitive advantage. "Why should people buy your toothpaste rather than the national brands?"

2. Computer Internal Environment

In 1982, Ben Rosen and L. J. Stevin invested in a company they called Gateway Technology Inc. The company name was later changed to Compaq Computer Corporation. They decided to go head-on against IBM by making a portable computer compatible with IBM's personal computer. The sales objective for their first year in business was 20,000 machines, or $35 million. Sales objectives for year two were $198 million. Year one's actual sales were 50,000 machines and $111 million. In year two sales were $329 million.

Assignment

1. When hiring managers, what qualifications do you think Rosen and Stevin would be looking for? List them.
2. Identify some of the major resources Compaq needed to be successful. Be sure to list and discuss human, physical, intangible, financial, and marketing skills as separate sections.
3. Describe Compaq's production process. Be sure to clearly identify major inputs, the transformation process, and its outputs.

Integrative Case Question—CorLu Foods

Develop the introduction section (background, management and organization, form of ownership) and strategy section (mission, objectives, environmental analysis) of CorLu's business plan. (Please refer to the Integrated Case "CorLu Foods.")

Bibliography

Flores, Michael. "The Strategic Planning Solution." *Bottomline,* June 6, 1990, pp. 32–34.

Morrisey, George. "Executive Guide to Strategic Thinking." *Executive Excellence,* June 6, 1990, pp. 5–6.

Scharf, Alan. "Secrets of Strategic Planning: Responding to the Opportunities of Tomorrow." *Industrial Management* 33, no. 1 (January/February 1991), pp. 9–10.

Specht, Pamela Hammers. "Information Sources Used for Strategic Planning Decisions in Small Firms." *American Journal of Small Business* 11, no. 4 (Spring 1987), pp. 21–34.

Thompson, Arthur, and A. J. Strickland. *Strategy Formulation and Implementation* (Homewood, Ill.: Richard D. Irwin, 1992).

Ward, John; Laurel Sorenson; and Sharon Nelton. "The Family Business: A Family Needs a Mission Statement/Ten Reasons for an Outside Board." *Nation's Business,* October 1987, pp. 45–50.

Washer, Louise. "The Business Plan That Gets the Loan." *Working Women,* January 1, 1990, pp. 37–47.

Endnotes

1. John Pearce and Fred David, "Corporate Mission Statements: The Bottom Line," *Academy of Management Executive* 1, no. 2 (May 1987), pp. 109–15.
2. Lloyd Byars and Thomas Neil, "Organizational Philosophy and Mission Statements," *Planning Review* 15, no. 4 (July/August 1987), pp. 32–35.
3. Douglas Morrill, "Strategic Planning: Maxims, Myths and Misdirections," *CPCU Journal* 40, no. 2 (June 1987), pp. 94–98.
4. Norman Scarborough and Thomas Zimmerer, "Strategic Planning for the Small Business," *Business,* (April/May/June 1987), pp. 11–19.
5. Andrew Campbell, "Does Your Organization Need a Mission?" *Leadership and Organization Development Journal* 10, no. 3 (1989), pp. 3–9.
6. James Shaffer, "Mission Statements: Why Have Them?" *Communication World,* (June 1987), pp. 14–15, 37.
7. James Reyes and Brian Kleiner, "How to Establish an Organizational Purpose," *Management Decision* 28, no. 7 (1990), pp. 51–54.
8. Karl Rye, "Will We Meet Our Goal—But Miss Our Objective?" *Telephone Engineer and Management,* October 15, 1991, pp. 66–71.
9. Russell Ackoff, "Mission Statements," *Planning Review* 15, no. 4 (July/August 1987), pp. 30–31; Andrew Campbell, "A Mission to Succeed," *Director,* February 1991, pp. 66–68.
10. Arnoldo Hax, "Redefining the Concept of Strategy and the Strategy Formation Process," *Planning Review* 18, no. 3 (May/June 1990), pp. 34–40.
11. "Dr. W. Edwards Deming 1988/1989 Winner of Dow Jones Award," *ESB,* Spring 1989, p. 3.
12. David Morris, *Marketing as a Means to Achieve Organizational Ends,* (West Haven, Conn.: University of New Haven Press, 1991), pp. 103–36.
13. Richard D'Aveni and Ian MacMillan, "Crisis and the Content of Managerial Communications: A Study of the Focus of Attention of Top Managers in Surviving and Failing Firms," *Administrative Science Quarterly* 35, no. 4 (December 1990), pp. 634–57.
14. Frank Harrison, "The Concept of Strategic Gap," *Journal of General Management* 15, no. 2 (Winter 1989), pp. 57–72.
15. Nigel Piercy and William Giles, "Making SWOT Analysis Work," *Marketing Intelligence and Planning* 7, no. 5, 6 (1989), pp. 5–7.
16. Lynn Johnson and Ralph Kuehn, "The Small Business Owner/Manager's Search for External Information," *Journal of Small Business Management* 25, no. 3 (July 1987), pp. 53–60.
17. Ray Reed, "CIM and World Class Performance—Are They Really Compatible?" *Production and Inventory Management Review* 11, no. 4 (April 1991), pp. 32–33.
18. Russell Ackoff, *Creating the Corporate Future* (New York: John Wiley, 1981).
19. Henry Mintzberg, "The Design School: Reconsidering the Basic Premises of Strategic Management," *Strategic Management Journal* 11, no. 3 (March/April 1990), pp. 171–95.
20. Donald Schimincke, "Strategic Thinking: A Perspective for Success," *Management Review* 79, no. 8 (August 1990), pp. 16–19.

III PLANNING AND IMPLEMENTATION

7   THE MARKETING FUNCTION

In this chapter you will learn about the marketing function. The marketing function begins with research to segment the market in order to identify the target customer. Through marketing research the new firm and/or product is tested for feasibility before opening the business or offering the new product. If the product is likely to be profitable, the marketing mix (product, price, place, and promotion) is developed and the sales forecast is predicted.

Chapter Learning Objectives

After completing this chapter, you should be able to:

· Explain the interrelationship between the marketing function and the other business plan components.
· Describe the importance of marketing research and its four-step process.
· Discuss the differences and advantages and disadvantages of primary and secondary data.
· Explain the difference between the target customer and target market.
· Discuss the difference between previous sales and executive opinion sales forecasting.
· Identify the four Ps of the marketing mix and describe each P in detail.
· Define the following 16 key terms in order of appearance in the chapter:

Marketing functions	Warranty
Marketing research	Packaging
Marketing research steps	Pricing
Hypothesis	Place

Survey questionnaire	Channel of distribution
Sales forecast	Promotion
Marketing mix	Sales product
Product	Publicity

The Interrelationship between the Marketing Function and the Other Business Plan Components

In Chapter 4, marketing is defined as those business activities that relate directly to determining the target market (to whom you will sell) and delivering services to those markets. We now expand upon this definition: the **marketing function** includes *identifying the target customers and product feasibility through marketing research, which leads to the development of the marketing mix—product, price, place, and promotion plans—and the sales forecast.* The marketing function is influenced by the form of ownership, social responsibility, and the legal environment. Through the business plan the strategy is formulated through the environmental analysis, which is based on marketing research. The strategy specifies how management plans to run the business in the functional areas. The marketing plans provide the information needed for the development of the strategy section of the business plan.[1] These components of the strategy are discussed in detail in this chapter.

All organizations perform the key functions of accounting and finance, marketing, production/operations, and human resources. It is critical for the small business manager to make decisions based on the firm as a system. The organization is a system because it comprises these interacting functions; each affects the other functions and the organization as a whole. The production and accounting functions are internally focused, marketing is externally focused, and personnel and financing focus on balancing both environments. Many firms have had strong separate functional areas that have failed because of the lack of coordination between these functions as a system.

Raising money depends on the marketing of a new business. To receive operating capital you must have a sound marketing plan.[2] The interrelationship between production/operations and marketing is complex and critical. To say that marketing sells what production produces is simplistic. The marketing function employs the capital resources acquired through the finance function. The firm's funds are spent on marketing research, product development, distribution of the products, and promoting the products and services. The marketing function interrelates with the production function because marketing information leads to changes in present products and new product development. A marketing forecast of sales potential must be integrated with a production forecast of capacity to provide a realistic production schedule.[3] Both the distribution system for getting the goods and services to the customers and the promotional methods used affect the personnel functions of selecting employees and determining their compensation. Pricing and credit policies affect the accounting function. Accounting data is needed to record the production and sales of the firm's products. The web of interrelationships between the functional areas is endless.

Identifying the Target Customer and Forecasting Sales through Marketing Research

In this section you will learn about marketing research, the target customer and market, product feasibility, the sales forecast, and the marketing mix.

Marketing Research

Have you ever been walking around a mall and had a person with a clipboard ask you some questions? Have you ever answered questions about the food and service in a restaurant? Have you ever bought a product, filled out, and mailed in the postcard to register your product for warranty? If you answered yes to any of these questions, you have been a part of marketing research. Marketing research is used to make sure you provide what the customer wants.

The business plan should be based on marketing research. The role of research is to reduce uncertainty in decision making. **Marketing research** is *the process of gathering and analyzing data for decision making.* The **steps in the marketing research process** are *(1) define the decision, (2) gather data, (3) analyze data, and (4) make the decision.*

Step 1: Define the Decision

The major decision the would-be business owner has to make is whether or not to start a business. The development of the business plan aids in making this decision. The completed business plan includes a projection of profit potential. The entire business plan should be based on research rather than opinion. Many new businesses have been started based on the opinion that people want a product just because the owner thinks they do, only to close because of lack of sales. When making the decision, it is important to develop questions that need to be answered. Research questions are often stated as hypotheses. A **hypothesis** is *a tentative answer to a research problem.* For example, Lynne O'Leary thought (hypothesized) there was a potential market for upside-down Cajun pickles.[4] So she decided to conduct research to test her product before opening a full-time business.

Step 2: Gather Data

Data can be classified into two types: secondary and primary. Secondary data is information that has been obtained by someone else. Secondary data is available within or outside of small businesses. Inside sources include records, files, and reports such as sales records, mailing lists, and complaint files. Outside sources include libraries, governments, chambers of commerce, Better Business Bureaus, the Small Business Association, trade associations, banks, and marketing research organizations. The advantage of secondary data is that someone else saves you the time, effort, and cost of gathering the data. The disadvantages are that the data often becomes outdated quickly and may not answer your specific research questions to help you make the decision.

Primary data is collected by the business. The disadvantages of primary data are the time, effort, and cost, but the major advantage is that the data collected is geared specifically to the decision. The two major primary information-gathering techniques include observation and survey. If Lynne O'Leary wants to know if people like her upside-down Cajun pickles, she can observe them, ask them, or both. Observation can be done by personal or mechanical approach. People or machines can record data such as the number of people shopping in a store. The **survey questionnaire** is *an instrument used to collect primary data in person, over the telephone, or by mail.*

The personal interview has the highest response rate; but it has a high cost, takes a long time to complete, and has a limited area for travel. Telephone interviewing gets the fastest response, and can cover a wide area; but you need a relatively short questionnaire (less than a 10-minute call), you cannot show visuals, and it has moderate cost. The mail questionnaire is the lowest cost, can be used for wide area coverage, and can be completed at the respondents' leisure; but mail tends to get a slow response (two to three weeks) and has the lowest response rate (around 10 percent is common).

When developing the questionnaire for survey research, care is needed to be sure the questions are clear. Try to keep questionnaires short; do not ask any question unless it has a specific purpose that will help make the decision. The multiple-choice format is commonly used. When developing the sequence of questions, start with interesting questions; leave personal questions like age and income level for the end. The questionnaire should be tested before it is used to be sure all questions are easily understood. How the data to make the decision will be analyzed should be determined before the survey is conducted, not after, as is commonly done.

When selecting the research data-gathering method, you must consider the time limit for the decision, the availability of the data, the cost versus the benefit of obtaining the data, and the type of decision. When making a decision like purchasing, you often use research to select the supplier, but after you select the supplier, you may not use research again for some time.

To make her decision Lynne would want to use primary data to determine if people like her pickles. She, or an interviewer, could go to a grocery store and get permission to display her pickles and give away samples, and possibly sell them. She can watch the expression on customers' faces as they try them, and ask them questions. See Exhibit 7.1 for a possible questionnaire that Lynn could use at the store.

Lynne would also want to ask the person responsible for purchasing the pickles at the grocery stores if the store would buy her pickles. Lynne could use the data from her survey as a selling point to the store purchaser. If people like them, but stores will not sell them, she has a problem. The more stores or other means of

EXHIBIT 7.1   Sample survey questionnaire and responses

Cajun Pickle Survey

1. Do you like the taste of the Cajun pickles better than the brand you presently buy?

Yes, definitely	Yes	Not sure	No	No, definitely not
1	2	3	4	5
(20)	(25)	(35)	(8)	(12)

2. Which statement best describes your pickle purchasing?
    1. I usually buy the lower-priced brand. (30)
    2. I usually buy the national brand that is on sale, or that I have a coupon for. (33)
    3. I usually buy the same brand, brand name_____.(37)

3. When Cajun pickles are sold, which statement best describes your purchasing plans?
    1. I'd buy them at a higher price than I pay now. (23)
    2. I'd buy them if the price is the same as I pay now. (22)
    3. I'm not sure if I'd buy them or not. (34)
    4. I would not buy them. (21)

4. How many jars of pickles do you buy per month?_____(2 average)

5. What do you think of the lids-down storage and upside-down label?
    1. I like it, it's a good idea. (27)
    2. I think it's OK. (22)
    3. I don't have a preference either way. (33)
    4. I don't like it. (18)

(Percentage of people who selected this answer out of 318 people)

interviewing potential customers, and the more people Lynne interviews, the more reliable the data to base her decision to open a full-time business.

Step 3: Analyze the Data

Data is typically analyzed qualitatively or quantitatively with statistics. One commonly used qualitative technique is the focus-group interview, which involves interviewing 6 to 10 people in an informal group setting for about a half to a full hour. The interviewer may show the group different products/packages/advertisements and/or have members try them and ask the group open-ended questions to stimulate thinking and get immediate interaction among the group members. Based on focus-group sessions, a subjective assessment is used to make the decision. One of the criticisms of this approach is the judgment needed to make the decision.

When conducting survey interviews with closed-ended questionnaires (yes/no, agree-disagree) and a large number of people (more than 25), qualitative statistical analysis is appropriate. Actually, focus groups can be used to prepare for quantitative research. For example, Lynne could have conducted a focus group with a variety of pickle tastes and packages to get the group's reaction. She could then select just one taste and package to bring to the stores for testing there. At the store she would fill out the questionnaire for each person trying her pickles. Based on the questionnaire responses, Lynne calculated the total number of people trying her pickles at five stores as 318. The response for each question is presented as a percentage of the total in Exhibit 7.1.

Step 4: Make the decision

There are usually no "hard-and-fast" rules for interpreting marketing research data. Judgment is needed in interpreting the results. We are assuming that Lynne conducted the above research and has the responses of 318 people from five different stores. Results reveal (Exhibit 7.1) that 45 percent say they would buy the pickles, and 23 percent say they would pay a premium price for them. Lynne also convinced four of the five stores to agree to buy her pickles based on this response. If you were in Lynne's position, would you open the business full-time or not? Actually, Lynne decided to open the business, and when orders exceeded 35 cases a week, she decided to broaden the market for her pickles. Bruce and Harold Wainer joined with Lynne and Edwin O'Leary to form Upside-Down Cajun Brands Inc. The name is based on the unusual packaging with the lids-down storage and upside-down label. In March 1988, Cajun Brands opened a plant in Metairie, Louisiana, and by June 1989 they were producing 1,500 cases per week of their pickles and chowchow, which are now sold in 45 states.[5]

There are market research specialists the small business person can hire to conduct research for them. However, there is a cost involved for professional help. Some colleges offer small business consulting services through Small Business Institutes using students at no labor cost to the small business owner. However, many will not do consulting for proposed start-up businesses. Check with your local colleges for services offered.

Would-be entrepreneurs often open a business based on their own opinion, or do the research themselves by asking their friends their opinion of the proposed business product and/or use friends as a focus group. But there is a danger in this approach because your friends tend to be like you, or they may not be truly honest with you because they don't want to hurt your feelings. Friends are a good starting point, but get data from people you don't know who will be objective and honest about your product.

See Exhibit 7.2 for a review of the four steps in the research process.

Target Customers and Target Market

Through the use of marketing research you want to identify your target customers and target market. The target customers are the segmented group of potential buyers of the firm's products. The target market is the percentage of the total market to whom the firm plans to sell its products.

The business plan must be built around two basic calculations—who the target customers are, and how to reach them. Defining the market should be one of the first tasks an entrepreneur completes. The most difficult part is to narrow the market down. The more specific the description of the potential customers and how to reach them, the more effectively the business plan will meet the criteria of

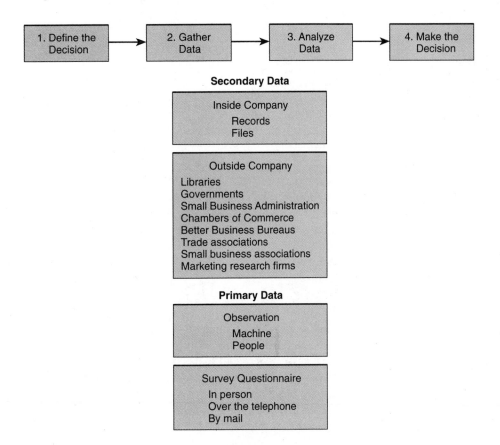

EXHIBIT 7.2

The four steps in the research process

investors.[6] For example, if you wanted to go into the insurance business, you would identify several types of insurance—health, life, auto, home, and others—and, that the insurance can be sold to businesses or consumers. The typical new small business cannot offer all types of insurance to all businesses and people; it must select a target customer from among this total market. The selection of the target should be based on marketing research to determine the strengths and weaknesses and opportunities and threats through the environmental analysis. The small business person often tries to fill the needs of customers not being met by the larger businesses, based upon its competitive advantage. In Montpelier, Vermont, National Life Insurance Company decided that the big businesses were not doing a good job of meeting the small business owners' insurance needs, so it selected this segment as its target customers. It continually gathers marketing research data.[7] National went on to be more specific by defining exactly what type of insurance and size of small business they target. In 1986, Paul Gruenberg was interested in a business in producing and selling videos. Two common segments include video-taping special events like weddings and training films for companies. Paul decided to target high schools by offering video yearbooks.[8]

There are at least three dimensions along which to segment a market into target customers: geographic, demographic, and product.

Geographic

The target market can be identified by neighborhoods, city, county, region, state, and country. Many small businesses start in a small geographic area and expand over the years. A common secondary source of geographic data are maps with zip codes.

Demographic

The target market can be identified by age, sex, family size, income, occupation, education, religion, race, nationality, social class, and other characteristics. A common secondary source of demographic data are government sources; especially helpful is the *Statistical Abstract of the United States,* which lists more than 1,000 summary tables from published sources that can help you estimate the size of markets.

Product

This is where your competitive advantage comes into play. You need to conduct research during the environmental analysis to understand your firm's strengths and weaknesses compared to its competitors, and opportunities and threats that are created by your competitive advantage. Define the benefits offered to the customer, such as fast delivery, ease of use, low cost, or high quality. Volume use of customers (heavy, medium, light, nonusers) can also be defined.

The Feasibility Study

In coordination with the target market, the small business manager must determine the potential of the product to be sold at a profit. If the target market is too small, it will not be wise to open a new venture. For example, Paul could define his yearbook target customers as high schools in Maryland with a graduating senior class of at least 200 (Paul has determined that at small schools the volume of tapes sold is not profitable). The video offers a curricular tool as well as a product at a competitive price compared to printed yearbooks. Through secondary information obtained from the Maryland State Department of Education, Paul learned that there are 204 high schools in Maryland. The total market is 204, but only those with 200 or more seniors are included in Paul's target market. He was given the estimate that 122 have 200 or more seniors. Unfortunately, identifying the total market and target are not always this easy.

After identifying the target customers and market, you have to determine if the market is large enough to profitably support your business. You also want to look at the trends of the industry. Are sales increasing, decreasing, or leveling off for your product? In Paul's video yearbook business, 122 is the target, but how many can he actually get to buy videos? Paul might also want to find out how many of these schools now have video yearbook arrangements with other sources. If the target of 122 is too small, rather than not start the business Paul might expand the geographic area to a nearby state(s). However, this would probably require more traveling or moving. Does he want to move or travel, or can he hire someone else to travel? Another option would be to offer an additional product such as wedding videos. However, Paul must calculate a different target customer and market for each different product, along with a separate marketing mix. This approach is called *multisegmentation.*

After the target customers have been selected, every part of the firm must focus its attention on attracting and retaining satisfied customers by meeting their needs. The small business should go on the offensive in an effort to increase market share by doing a better job of meeting customer needs than its competitors.[9] Market share is the percentage of the total market sales held by each competitor. Marketing research is used to understand the target customers' needs and wants. Consumer behavior research tries to better understand why people buy products. The small business owner should understand customer needs through direct contact with them, listen to complaints, and work hard to eliminate them in order to keep present customers and attract new ones.[10] Marketing will not be successful without total quality efforts throughout the entire firm.[11]

When seeking financing from outside sources, list any orders, contracts, or letters of commitment you have in the business plan. Also list the potential customers who have expressed an interest in the product. Lynne has marketing research from 318 people; the survey results can be presented along with a list of the four stores that have agreed to purchase her pickles.

Sales Forecast

After selecting the target customer and market, research is used to develop the marketing mix (blend of product, price, place, and promotion); then the sales forecast is predicted based on the marketing mix, which is explained later. Because the feasibility study is a preliminary sales forecast based on research, you will learn about it now, but remember that the sales forecast is predicted after the marketing mix is determined. The **sales forecast** is *the predicted dollars and/or units of the product that will be sold to the target customers during a given period of time.* The sales forecast is probably the most critical part of the business plan because of the system effect. To be more specific, the expenditure budget, quotas for salespeople, advertising expenditures, asset purchases of plant and equipment, hiring employees, purchasing of raw material and parts, production scheduling, making cash flow statements, developing pro forma income statements and balance sheets, and determining the breakeven point are all based on the sales forecast. In other words, the feasibility of a new venture and the future of an existing business are based on forecasted sales. The sales forecast is developed differently for the new venture vs. the existing small business.

Exhibit 7.3   **Number of pizzas sold per month in 1993**

	Jan	Feb	Mar	Apr	May	June	July	Aug	Sept	Oct	Nov	Dec
4,000												
3,800						X						
3,600					X			X				
3,400				X			X		X			
3,200			X							X	X	
3,000	X											X
2,800		X										
2,600												

Pizza Sales Revenue Per Year 1990–1997

	1990	1991	1992	1993	1994	1995	1996	1997†
$400,000								X
380,000							X	
360,000					X	X		
340,000			X					
320,000		X		X				
300,000	X							

†forecast

Sales Forecasting for the Established Small Business (Previous Sales Technique)

The existing business can use past sales to aid in predicting future sales. The common sales forecast used in an established small pizza shop would show that on a typical Saturday night it sells 100 pizzas; this figure may be adjusted for changes in the weather, seasons, and special events going on. Then the shop prepares accordingly for that night's business. This approach can be improved by looking for trends. The owner, Tony, can keep a record of how many pizzas are sold each day, week, month, or year and plot it on a simple graph. There are more complex quantitative forecasting techniques, but they are not commonly used by small businesses. See Exhibit 7.3 for an example.

Looking at Exhibit 7.3, Number of Pizzas Sold Per Month, Tony can see that sales are greater in the warmer months and can plan accordingly.

Tony's sales dropped in 1993 because a new Domino's Pizza opened in town. Domino's delivered pizza and Tony didn't. Tony didn't want to deliver pizza. After watching sales drop for several months, he added free delivery—but not within 30 minutes, and, of course, the prices of his pizzas went up to pay for the cost of free delivery. So by offering a better-tasting, larger pizza for less money than

Domino's (even though delivery is slower), customers came back and sales went up again in 1994.

Assume it is time for Tony to forecast pizza sales for 1997. Pizza sales revenue per year shows an upward trend from 1990 through 1996. Past sales can help predict future sales, but more information is needed to set the figures. Tony knows that construction of a new housing development is under way, which could increase his business. About four new houses have been built so far. Tony conducted some research and discovered that there will be about 50 new houses built. The economic forecast by the local business association Tony belongs to predicts that the economy will stay about the same in 1997; this has been discussed at meetings. The trade association Tony belongs to predicts more people will be buying take-out food during the year, and pizza sales should rise about 5 percent; Tony read this in the trade magazine he subscribes to. Based on past sales and these trends, Tony sets the sales forecast for 1997 at $400,000. The $400,000 in sales is also a challenging objective for the business to achieve. Tony is also making special plans to increase advertising as a means of increasing sales revenue.

Sales Forecasting for the New Venture or Product (Executive Opinion)
The new venture that will be opening a business, and the existing business that will be offering a different new product, cannot use past sales to predict future sales. Paul's video business is a case in point. More subjective judgment is needed to predict sales. Paul has determined the target market to be 122. Now the question becomes how many he can realistically get to agree to produce a video yearbook. Let's assume that Paul's research shows that 10 now have video yearbook arrangements at $35 per video; he called them and asked. Paul has decided to focus on the 112 without video arrangements. After making sales presentations at 10 schools, Paul has five contracts for videos. Based on the time to close a sale and time to make the videos, he plans to make presentations at 50 high schools during his first year in business. At a 50 percent closing rate, Paul forecast that he would produce videos for 25 schools in his first year, but this rate of contracts should increase as he gains experience and recommendations. So his sales forecast for the first year is 25 (schools) $\times$ 150 (average tapes sold per school) $\times$ $33 (price per tape) = $118,800 in sales revenue. In the second year he expects to keep 23 of the 25 schools (some may decide not to offer the video again, or select a competitor), and add another 20. So his year two sales forecast is 45 $\times$ 125 $\times$ $34 (price increase) = $191,250. Year three's sales forecast is 80 $\times$ 100 $\times$ $36 = $288,000. In year two Paul plans to turn a profit and use the money to expand the number of employees to increase business. Notice that Paul's projected average sale of videos per school goes down from 150, to 125, then 100. Can you think of why Paul's average drops? If you said he plans to make sales calls based on the size of the schools, starting with the larger ones and ending with the smaller ones, you are correct. Over the three-year period Paul's objective is to obtain a 66 percent (80/122) market share in Maryland. To determine the feasibility of the study, Paul must calculate the cost to run the business over the first three years and compare it to his forecasted revenue to determine profitability, or lack thereof.

Many new ventures are started with an overly optimistic sales forecast. The owner of the business plans to pay the bills based on this money coming in, only to find that the bills cannot be paid and creditors end up taking the owner to court for liquidation of the business. To avoid this scenario, it is often helpful to develop two sets of sales forecast. Start with the best reasonable sales forecast you expect. Then take this number and cut it in half. Strive for the reasonable sales forecast, but only count on half to pay your bills. This type of cushion has saved many businesses from going under. If the original forecast is accurate or underestimated, it may cause some problems, but it is easier to spend money you actually have than to pay bills with money you don't have.

It is common for the sales forecast to be wrong, especially for the new venture. However, this does not mean that the sales forecast is not useful. In fact, few creditors will lend you money without seeing a business plan that includes a sales forecast. As the firm conducts business over time, the forecast can be changed. If you develop your forecast on a computer software spreadsheet, changing it is very simple and quick.

The Marketing Mix

After conducting research to select the target customer, you need to develop the marketing mix. The **marketing mix** is *the blend of product, price, place, and promotion that best meets the needs of the target customer.* The marketing mix is often referred to as the four Ps. The selection of the marketing mix is a combination of marketing decisions in which each of the four Ps must be carefully considered and addressed fully.[12] The next four sections describe the details of each P in the marketing mix separately; however, because of the systems effect, they must all be carefully coordinated.

Product

The company product is usually the starting place for a new venture. Successful entrepreneurs tend to have an idea for a product that will satisfy unmet needs. They are really selling satisfaction rather than a product. Satisfying customer needs often requires a blend of physical goods and services. A good is a tangible item you can see and touch, whereas a service is a deed performed for the customer that cannot be kept; it is experienced, used, or consumed. Tony's Pizza offers pizza as a good, but it also offers delivery service. National Life Insurance is selling a service, but it also gives the small business owner a written copy of the policy. Paul sells the high school students the video, but the service of working with the students in the development of the yearbook is an important selling point.

So far in this book we have used the term product, but now you should realize that most products do in fact include both goods and service. A **product** is *a good and/or service offered to customers to satisfy their needs and wants.* Within the business plan each product should be clearly described with the competitive advantage explained. A product also has three important features: brand names and trademarks, warranties, and packaging.

Brand Names and Trademarks

Brand names and **trademarks** *are used to identify companies and/or products.* A good name brand can help develop sales of the product. There are nine characteristics of a good brand name you should consider when developing a company and/or product name. A brand name should be:

1. Suggestive of product benefits.
2. Short and simple.
3. Easy to spell and read.
4. Easy to recognize and remember.
5. Easy to pronounce in only one way.
6. Pleasing when read or heard.
7. Not offensive, obscene, or negative.
8. Adaptable to packaging or labeling needs.
9. Adaptable to any advertising medium.

Though not a characteristic, the name cannot be used by another business.

Lynne is developing a brand name "Upside-Down" for her products. Samuel Adams, a small brewer of beer, started by developing its brand name in the Boston area but has since been expanding its geographic presence. Important brands or trademarks you develop should be registered for protection against competitors' stealing your ideas.

Warranties

A **warranty** *explains what the business promises about its product.* Some firms use warranties to create a competitive advantage. Review Chapter 4 for the five considerations when selecting a warranty policy.

Lynne could use a standard written full warranty on her pickles similar to the one that appears on the labels of Campbell's (soups) and other companies' products: "Satisfaction guaranteed or money back." More on labeling is next.

Packaging and Labeling

Packaging involves *protecting and promoting products.* When packaging a product there is a trade-off between the cost of underprotection, which leads to damaged goods, and the cost to package the product. Generally, the higher the price of the product, the higher the quality and cost of packaging. Low-cost jewelry often comes without a box or with a thin cardboard or plastic box, whereas expensive jewelry usually comes in a nice, expensive fabric-covered box.

The package can also give the product a competitive advantage. Lynne's lids-down storage, with upside-down label, helps the pickles maintain freshness and flavor in an unusual way, while also helping to sell them.

The size of the package is also important. Will your product come in one size only? If not, how many sizes will you have? Check competitors' brands and copy them, or differentiate your product size as a competitive advantage to meet your target customers' needs. But remember the systems effect: the more package sizes, the greater the cost of production, inventory, and packaging.

Labeling is used to both identify and promote the product. The label can include information on product care, contents, directions, disposal, and other concerns. If you sell food, the Federal Trade Commission has developed guidelines for contents and nutritional information. If you plan to sell your product in supermarkets and other high-volume retailers, you may have to get a universal product code (UPC), which identifies each product with marks that can be read by electronic scanners. The fee to get the code can be expensive for the small business, so be sure to plan ahead.

Many companies put the brand name or trademark label on the outside of the product to enhance sales. Many people, especially teens, are willing to pay a lot more for a product because of its brand name or trademark on the product.

Single Product versus Product Line

Will you offer a single product or a line of products? The common approach for the small business is to start with a single product and add related products to develop a line of products. Lynne started with Cajun pickles and added Cajun chowchow. Five new products, including ketchup, were introduced in the fall 1990. In the business plan be sure to specify both present and future products.

Price

Pricing is *the determination of how much the firm will charge for its products.* Pricing the product is important because it is a key factor in the decision to buy. The price must be coordinated with the target customer, product, place, and promotion. If you are offering a high-quality, exclusive product to high-income people, a premium price is needed to project this image.

Pricing Considerations

When setting prices there are four major considerations: competition, customers, other external factors, and internal factors.

Competition

What price do the other businesses sell products for that are identical or substitutes for your product? Generally, the more your product has a unique, competitive advantage, the higher the price you can charge. Also, the more competition for identical products, the more important it is to meet competitive prices. In many industries the small business cannot compete on price with large businesses because large businesses have higher volume and greater economies of scale. A study sponsored by the National Federation of Independent Businesses that compared successful small businesses to failures reports that successful firms tend to use competitive advantages and charge higher prices, whereas the failures tend to compete on price.[13] Based on her marketing research, Lynne decided to set the price of her unique Upside-Down Cajun pickles higher than the competition. This lower-volume, higher-price strategy is called *skimming*. However, Tony offers a larger, better-tasting pizza for less than Domino's Pizza. Tony can compete on price because he does not have to pay the franchise fee. This higher-volume, lower-price strategy is called *penetrating*.

Customers

If your target customers do not view your product as having "value" (believe the product meets their needs and is worth the price), they will buy the product from your competitors rather than from you. Unfortunately, there is no magical way to determine the exact price customers are willing to pay, but research helps. Lynne asked people if they were willing to pay more for her pickles than their present brand. If there are many people who want to buy the product, especially if it is unique or new, she can charge a higher price. It is important to select products in industries whose sales are growing.

Other External Factors

In addition to competition and customers discussed above, other external environmental factors—suppliers, the labor force, stockholders, society, technology, governments, and the economy—also affect the price you can charge.

Internal Factors

Regardless of what your competitors charge, you must cover all your costs plus a margin for profit. If you cannot, don't start the business, or close it. This may sound simplistic, but there are many small businesses that underestimate their costs and end up going out of business because they cannot pay their bills.

Taking these four considerations into account, different types of businesses (producers, wholesalers and retailers, and services) use different pricing methods, and some offer credit.

Producer Pricing

The common pricing method of producers of goods is the cost-plus method. It is common to determine the cost to produce the good (labor, material, and overhead for the equipment, building, etc.), the cost of selling and administrative costs (salespeople's salary/commission, advertising, delivery, record keeping, etc.), and a profit margin. These three components are added together to get the price. However, the above considerations must be studied before setting the cost-plus price. To be competitive you may have to cut your profit margin, or with a unique product like Lynne's Cajun pickles you may set a higher margin than competitors. Every time you can cut your cost and maintain the price, your profit margin increases. Accurate records are needed to determine costs.

Wholesale and Retail Pricing

Wholesalers and retailers buy goods from the producers and sell them to their customers. While the producer must calculate the cost of the good, the wholesaler and retailer know the cost they pay to the producer. To the cost of merchandise you must add operating expenses (rent, utilities, depreciation, salaries/commissions, delivery, etc.) and a profit margin. The difference between the cost of the good and the selling price is called a markup. The markup is commonly used by wholesalers and retailers to set prices. Markup is expressed in dollars as a percentage of either cost or selling price. For example, if you buy a book for $15 and price it at $25, the markup is $10. As a percentage of retail price the markup is 40 percent (10/25), but as a percentage of cost it is 66.67 percent (10/15).

Most retailers compute markup as a percentage of the retail price because operating records are expressed as a percentage of sales; operating expenses, cost of goods sold, and profits are expressed as a percentage of total sales, not the cost of the merchandise being sold. You simply take the cost of the good and divide it by the reciprocal of the markup (100% − markup %). For example, if you pay $6 for a toy and use a markup of 35 percent, you price the toy at $9.23 ($6 / 100 − 35 = 65% or 6/0.65 = 9.23).

The math of marking up prices is easy, but setting the markup percentage is not always easy. The price has to be high enough to allow a profit, while being competitive. Through research, you can find out, or estimate, what your competitors use as markups. Many producers suggest a specific markup, or the actual selling price. Small retailers typically cannot compete on price with the large chain stores. They typically price their products higher but offer a competitive advantage (service, location, ambiance, etc.) of value to the customer for the extra cost. With a very limited product line one markup may be all that is needed, but with a variety of goods the markup should change. Generally, highly speculative and slow-moving goods (jewelry) have a higher markup than fast-moving goods with low carrying cost (grocery items).

Service Pricing

The service firm must also base prices on its cost (labor, materials, travel, etc.), operating cost (rent, utilities, etc.), and a profit margin. Services are commonly set by the job or by the hour. A laundry has a set rate to clean each item, whereas your accountant typically charges by the hour. Repair service businesses generally charge for parts and labor, but the parts are based on a retail markup and the labor is more than the pay of the mechanic to cover operating expenses and a profit. Find out what your competitors charge, but don't simply match them. Trying to compete by offering a lower price may work, but if you have a competitive advantage, you may be able to sell your services to your customers for a higher price. Be careful not to price your services too low because people may get the impression that your quality is also low and give their business to your competitors.

Credit

Will you sell your product for cash only, or will you let your customers charge? There are four major factors in the credit decision:

1. The type of business (durable goods retailers tend to offer credit; small grocers don't).
2. Credit policy of competitors (can you meet or beat them).
3. Income level of customers (higher incomes tend to get credit).
4. Working capital (can you wait to get your money?).

If you do elect to offer credit, it can be a competitive advantage. You must decide to offer your own charge account or accept national credit cards like Visa and MasterCard. They keep the records for you, but for a fee.

Place

Having a good product at a price customers are willing to pay is important, but the right place is also needed. Based on your target customers' needs, you want your product available in the right quantities and locations. **Place** includes *the distribution, transportation, and storage of the product.* The location of the business is closely related to place, and is covered in the next chapter.

Distribution

The **channel of distribution** is *the system of moving products from producers to consumers.* Consumers are the actual users of the product, and they are not necessarily the customers to which the firm sells. The producers of goods are the primary determinants of distribution. In the distribution channel wholesalers and retailers are middlepeople who get the products to their users. The producer of the product has the option of selling directly to the consumer or through a middleperson. Many industrial products are sold directly from the producer to the business as the consumer, but most consumer goods are sold through middlepeople.

Producer to Consumer

Avon products and some mail-order businesses are examples of producer-to-consumer distribution of goods. Most services (dental care, haircuts, etc.) also follow this channel of distribution. Products combining goods and services can also be sold directly to consumers. Paul sells video high school yearbooks directly to the students. Tony's can be considered a retailer producing pizza and selling it to the consumer.

Producer to Middlepeople to Consumer

When producers sell their goods to middlepeople, they perform part of the marketing mix for them. Middlepeople provide the place of sale and all or part of the promotion. The producer who wants to minimize the amount of marketing performed can use an agent. The small business that wants to minimize the number of its customers can sell to wholesalers, who in turn sell the product in smaller quantities to retailers. In our example, Lynne conducted research in grocery stores, but she decided not to sell the product there. For the proper marketing mix that fits the unique product with a premium price to the place, Lynne chose gourmet shops and delicatessens, such as Macy's and Food Emporium, as the places to sell her pickles. Lynne chose to skip the wholesalers and go directly to the retailers as her primary channel of distribution. However, she could also sell to wholesalers and start a direct mail catalog to consumers, bypassing the retailers as well. Tony could freeze his pizza and sell it to grocery stores, and Paul could sell the video yearbooks to the school store, both adding middlepeople to their channel of distribution.

Transportation

The producers of goods must get them to their customers, and someone has to pay the transportation cost. There is no such thing as free delivery; the cost is either included in the price of the product or the profit margin is cut. The three major means of transportation, in order by cost, are air (plane), land (truck and railroad), and sea (ships/barges). Pipelines are also used primarily by the petroleum industry. Each means of transportation has its advantages and disadvantages. But cost is not the major consideration; customer satisfaction is. Some products and customers require quick delivery to make the sale, while others can wait.

Producers of services often base transportation costs on supplies used and/or travel. Services that go to the customer either add the average cost of delivery as a set or minimum fee, or bill the customer directly for the charges. Jeannie has a fingernail business which is based on going to customers to manicure their nails. She charges the same rates as competitive shops. Since she has no rent to pay, she need not add charges for transportation. Customers also tip better for her service.

Storage

Storage involves holding goods from the time they are produced until they are consumed. Storage is necessary because production does not always match sales; it is used to balance supply and demand. Storage is especially important for seasonal products.

Producers hold goods until they sell them to middlepeople or consumers. Lynne must store her pickles. One advantage of using middlepeople is that they store goods until they are sold to consumers. Goods stored for sale or resale are commonly called inventory. Inventory will be discussed in Chapter 9. Service firms don't have goods to store for sale as inventory, but they do store various types of supplies, materials or equipment that is used on the jobs. Goods can be stored on the business premises or in a rented warehouse space.

Promotion

The right product, with the right price, at the right place will not sell if no one knows about it. Promotion is the process of communicating the other three Ps to target customers to inform, persuade, or remind them to buy the product. "What" is communicated depends on the target customers' needs and attitudes. "How" the messages are communicated depends on the promotional method chosen. **Promotion** includes *personal selling, advertising, sales promotion, and publicity.* We will discuss each promotional method separately, then discuss blending them.

Personal Selling

Personal selling involves direct one-on-one communication between sellers and target customers. Most personal sales are conducted face-to-face, but telephone sales (telemarketing) are growing. As part of the marketing plan management must decide:

1. How many salespeople are needed.
2. What kind of salespeople are needed.
3. What kind of sales presentation should be used.
4. How salespeople should be selected and trained.
5. How they should be motivated.

Target customers and the other three Ps in the marketing mix influence these five decisions.

Salespeople are paid by salary, commission, or a combination of the two. To many target customers the salesperson is the company. When selecting and training salespeople, cost-cutting should not be the major concern. Better-quality people generally sell more products and are worth the extra pay to attract and retain them. The effective small business salesperson can give the target customer that personal attention often not available through big business; it can be a competitive advantage.

The sales approach should be based on the marketing mix.[14] Below is an eight-step approach to personal sales that can be adapted to the situation.

1. *Prospecting:* Define your target customers clearly and go after them because they are most likely to buy your product. The telephone is a good tool for prospecting.
2. *Open:* Start by establishing rapport with the target customer. The first thing you have to do is sell yourself because people seldom buy from anyone they dislike or distrust.

3. *Listen:* Get prospects to tell you about their needs, preferences, and problems so that you can understand their situation and satisfy them.
4. *Presentation:* Explain the benefits of the product by telling prospects how the product will meet their needs/wants or solve their problem.
5. *Demonstration:* Show prospects how the product works; let them try it out. Be sure to point out your product's competitive advantage.
6. *Objections:* Ask prospects how they like the product. For different reasons, people don't always tell salespeople why they object to buying the product. Listen carefully and try to understand the person's real objection to the product and overcome it. Point out how your product will meet their needs, or do a better job of meeting their needs than the competitor's product.
7. *Close:* Ask for the order. The most common reason for losing a sale is that the seller never asks for the order. Once the buyer agrees to buy the product, stop selling it. The salesperson should be ready to close at any time during the process.
8. *Follow-up:* After the sale be sure the customer is satisfied. This step is critical for repeat business and is an excellent way to acquire referrals to new prospects.

The eight-step sales presentation should be developed and tested for its ability to attract attention, interest, desire, and action (AIDA). When preparing the presentation, determine how much of the standardized script salespeople should repeat and test it with the AIDA model. Does the presentation quickly attract the buyer's attention? Does it hold the buyer's interest? Does it create a desire to buy the product? Does it result in the action of a sales transaction? Keep working at it until it's perfected.

Advertising

While personal selling is a flexible one-on-one approach, advertising is less flexible and communicates with a large number of target customers at one time through mass media. Advertising can be cheaper than personal selling. Though it is difficult to provide concrete results from advertising, there are audited research studies that show mass selling (advertising and publicity) does work.[15] Advertising works across media, for consumer as well as industrial products, and for new and established products. It works in the short term and continues to work years later. Advertising even works to help companies through a recession, and it gives those companies a boost after the recession.[16] It works for small and large business even though the amount spent and media selected vary by size.

Advertising Objectives and Plans
There are four primary objectives of advertising:

1. To inform target customers about your business and its products.
2. To persuade customers to buy your product.

3. To remind customers about your product.
4. To influence perception of your business and products.

The four objectives are interrelated, and virtually every advertisement uses all these elements. Each ad should have a specific objective. Some ads announce sales and seek immediate action, whereas others try to build company image.

Advertising begins with the target customer. The two major planning decisions are what message to send and which media are best for reaching the target customer in the most cost-effective manner to meet the objective. Most large businesses and many small businesses employ the expertise of advertising agencies to develop the message and/or select the media for them.

The Message

The message must be appealing to target customers if it is going to persuade them to buy the product. It is common for advertisements to emphasize the product's competitive advantage. When developing and testing the message, use the AIDA model.

The Media

The most commonly used advertising media are (in order of dollars spent):

1. *Newspapers:* They allow specific geographic coverage to a broad audience at a relatively low cost for immediate responses.
2. *Television:* It is expensive to go national, but local and cable ads can be purchased at a reasonable cost for visual effect. Home shopping via cable TV is increasing in popularity.
3. *Direct mail:* It allows you to selectively reach your target market. You can develop mailing lists from directories (city, telephone, membership, etc.). There are firms that will sell you mailing lists and/or conduct the mailing for you.
4. *Radio:* It can be used to reach a narrower target market with a friendly message at the time selected.
5. *Magazines:* There are local magazine and trade publications that can be very effective at getting your message to your target customers.
6. *Outdoor:* Billboards can get a quick message across at a specified place, and the company sign is also a means of advertising.

Other sources that are less expensive include: the yellow pages and other directories, transit advertising (appealing to travelers while in town), special events (sponsoring a road race, parade), and point-of-purchase ads (displaying a Bud sign in a bar). The small business can also use cooperative advertising, in which the manufacturer shares the cost of advertising. Many manufacturers also supply free advertising packages to retailers. Another way to save money is to share advertising cost with a group of similar businesses. Many creative entrepreneurs have made agreements with advertisers to exchange products for advertising.

Choosing the "Best" Media

Not all media are equally effective for all businesses and products. The "best" medium is one that fits with the rest of the marketing plan—that is, it depends on: (1) the objective of the ad; (2) the target customers and their geographic locations; (3) the funds available; (4) the nature of the medium, which includes who it reaches, with what frequency, with what impact, at what cost. Determine if your competitors have found the best medium, and if so use it.

Advertising Budget

A major decision in the planning process is how much money to spend on advertising. Advertising should be part of the overall budget, which is discussed in Chapter 12. Four common approaches to developing the amount to be spent on advertising include:

1. *Affordability:* The owner/manager does not plan ahead and simply spends any money available on advertising.
2. *Competition:* Spend as much as the competition.
3. *Percentage of past or future sales:* One rule of thumb is to spend 10 percent of projected sales the first year, 7 percent the second year, and at least 5 percent each year thereafter.[17]
4. *The objective-and-task method:* You begin by determining the objective, then what it will cost to achieve the objective. This takes the most planning.

Steps should be taken to determine if the advertising budget is meeting the objectives. Advertising cost should be paid for by the sales and profits that they generate. If so, advertising is an investment rather than an expense.

Sales Promotion

Sales promotion refers to *promotional activities other than personal and mass selling.* Sales promotion activities are used to stimulate interest, trial, or purchase. Promotions can be aimed at the target consumer, middlepeople, or the firm's own sales force.

Consumers

Some of the commonly used sales promotion activities aimed at final consumers include: banners, streamers, free samples, calendars/key chains/magnets, point-of-purchase materials, aisle displays, contests, coupons, and trading stamps. These activities usually try to increase demand or speed up the time of purchase. The store location and trade shows are commonly used places of promotions.

Middlepeople

Some of the commonly used sales promotion (sometimes called trade promotion) activities aimed at middlepeople include: price deals, promotional allowances, sales contests, calendars, gifts, trade shows, meetings, catalogs, and merchandising aids. The objectives of promotions are commonly to encourage stocking new items, buying in larger quantity, or buying early.

Sales Force

Some of the commonly used sales promotion activities aimed at the firm's sales force include: contests, bonuses, meetings, portfolios, displays, sales aids, and training material. The objective of the promotions might be to encourage getting new customers, selling a new product, or selling the firm's whole line.

Publicity

Publicity is *any unpaid form of mass selling.* Getting the media to tell the small business's story is not only free, it can be more effective than advertising. A target customer may not pay attention to an ad, but might carefully read an article with the same information. The small business owner can send regular one-page news releases to mass media with the objective of being mentioned with other news or as a full story. Publicity is usually not cost-free; it does take time to "sell" your story to the media to get it publicized. And if you sponsor a road race, for example, you must weigh costs to conduct the race in order to get your name in the media as the sponsor.

The Promotional Blend

Dividing the marketing promotion budget is a problem, particularly in the competitive world of fast-moving consumer goods.[18] Today, most promotion blends contain both personal and mass selling, as well as sales promotions. The ratio of time, effort, and money spent on each type of promotion depends on the target customer and the other three Ps in the marketing mix. You want to aim at target customers whose needs the product meets, not all possible customers whose needs the product doesn't meet. Generally, for products that have high prices and/or are technical, personal selling is usually needed, whereas advertising can be used for low-priced, nontechnical products. Sales promotion is usually more effective with impulse products than with products that customers shop around for. A wide geographic area tends to favor mass selling and promotion, while personal selling is effective in a local market with a relatively small number of customers.

The type of business also has an impact on the promotion blend. Large producers of branded consumer products spend about equally on mass selling to consumers, personal selling to middlepeople, and sales promotion to middlepeople and consumers. Small producers and firms that offer relatively undifferentiated consumer products or industrial products put more emphasis on personal selling, with the rest of the budget going mainly to sales promotions. Wholesalers rely on personal selling almost exclusively.

Paul promotes his videos primarily through personal selling. His primary target is the principal of the high school. Tony puts more emphasis on advertising than personal selling; he plans to increase advertising to reach his sales objective. Lynne

---

EXHIBIT 7.4   **The marketing functions**

---

1. Conduct research to segment the target market and select target customers.
2. Conduct research to determine product feasibility.
3. Develop the marketing mix:

Product	*Price*	*Place*	*Promotion*
Brand names and trademarks	Producer	Distribution	Personal selling
Warranties	Wholesale and retail	Transportation	Advertising
Packaging and labeling	Service	Storage	Sales promotion
	Credit		Publicity
4. Forecast sales.			

---

relies more on sales promotion; she was sending out 300 samples a week to gourmet shops and delicatessens, and her products generated a tremendous response at the National Food Brokers' meeting.

Let's use Lynne's Upside-Down Brands company to put the marketing function concepts together. Lynne conducted marketing research to determine target customers and product feasibility. Her marketing mix includes a brand product line of Upside-Down Cajun pickles and other products that are sold in upside-down packaging and labeling at premium prices. Products are sold on credit to middlepeople in gourmet shops and delicatessens with the aid of sales promotion. Her research-based sales forecast lead to building a new plant to meet the demand.

For a review of the marketing functions, see Exhibit 7.4, but remember that you may need to develop a different marketing mix for each product that is substantially different.

Summary

The Interrelationship between the Marketing Function and the Other Business Plan Components

The **marketing function** includes *identifying the target customers and product feasibility through marketing research, which leads to the development of the marketing mix—product, price, place, and promotion plans—and the sales forecast.* Because the firm is a system, the marketing function affects the production/operations function, the accounting and finance function, and the personnel function.

Identifying the Target Customer and Forecasting Sales through Marketing Research

Marketing research is *the process of gathering data for decision making.* The **steps in the marketing research process** are: *(1) define the decision, (2) gather data, (3) analyze data, and (4) make the decision.* The decision is often stated as a **hypothesis,** a *tentative answer to a research problem.* The data gathered can be primary or secondary data. Primary data can be collected through observation or survey. The **survey questionnaire** is *an instrument used to collect primary data in person, over the telephone, or by mail.* The data can be analyzed qualitatively and/or quantitatively to make the decision.

Through the use of marketing research you want to identify your target customers and target market. The target customers are the segmented group of potential buyers of the firm's products. The target market is the percentage of the total market to whom the firm plans to sell its products.

The feasibility of the firm/product must be conducted to determined profitability. If the product has profit potential, the **marketing mix**—*the blend of product, price, place, and promotion that best meets the needs of the target customer*—is determined; it is followed by the **sales forecast**—*predicted dollars and/or units of the product that will be sold to target customers during a given period of time.* The established business can use previous sales to help predict future sales, but the new venture must rely on executive opinion.

Product

A **product** is *a good and/or service offered to customers to satisfy their needs and wants.* Most products are a combination of goods and services. The product has three features: **brand names and trademarks,** *used to identify companies and/or products;* **warranties,** which *explain what the business promises about its products;* and labeling and **packaging,** which *involves protecting and promoting products.* The firm can sell a single product or a full product line.

Price

Pricing is *the determination of how much the firm will charge for its products.* Four areas to consider include: competition, customers, other external factors, and internal factors. Producers, wholesalers and retailers, and services tend to use different pricing methods. But all must determine if they will offer credit.

Place

Place includes *the distribution, transportation, and storage of the product.* The **channel of distribution** is *the system of moving products from producers to consumers.* The channel can include direct from producer to consumer, or indirect through the use of middlepeople. Transportation should be based on meeting customers' needs, not simply cost. Storage involves holding goods from the time they are produced until they are consumed.

Promotion

Promotion *includes personal selling, advertising, sales promotion, and publicity.* Personal selling involves direct one-on-one communications between sellers and target customers. Advertising communicates with a large number of target customers at one time through mass media. Both the advertising message and media must be determined. Sales promotion refers to promotional activities other than personal and mass selling. Promotions can be aimed at customers (free samples, displays, coupons, etc.), middlepeople (price deals, gifts, trade shows, etc.), or the firm's own sales force (sales contests, etc.). **Publicity** is *any unpaid form of mass selling.* Today, most businesses offer a blend of personal selling and mass selling, as well as sales promotions.

After the marketing mix has been determined the sales forecast is predicted.

Questions

1. What is the purpose of marketing research? What is it used for?
2. What are the two classifications of data? Explain each.
3. What is a survey questionnaire, why is it used, and how is it used?
4. Explain when qualitative and quantitative data analysis are commonly used.
5. What is a feasibility study and why should the new firm/product use a feasibility study?
6. What is the difference between sales forecasting for the established versus the new small business/product?
7. Why does the manager have to select the target market before the marketing mix, and why is the marketing mix so important?
8. List and explain the three important features of a product.
9. List and explain the four considerations when pricing.
10. Explain the difference in the way producers, wholesalers and retailers, and services price their products.
11. List and explain the two major channels of distribution.
12. Describe the differences between personal selling, advertising, sales promotion, and publicity.

Application Exercises

When doing these exercises, where applicable, be sure to select a specific business, preferably where you now work, worked previously, or would like to own someday. If this is not possible, pick a specific organization to which you will make reference. Be sure to identify the organization by name. Keep your answers to one to two pages per exercise.

1. Identify the secondary and primary data collection sources used by a specific small business. List each source and explain how the data is used.
2. Develop a simple one-page questionnaire, using Exhibit 7.1 as a sample, for a new or existing product. Be sure to identify the product, state why each question is included, and how the data will help the small business.

3. For Application Exercise 2, what methods would you use to gather and analyze the data? Discuss the details of how (personal interview, telephone, mail) and where the questionnaire will be filled out, and any statistics that would be used.

4. Describe the target customers and target markets for a specific product for a specific small business.

5. Describe how a specific small business forecasts sales.

6. For Application Exercise 4, explain the marketing mix used to satisfy the target customers' needs.

7. Clearly explain the warranty for a specific small business product.

8. Explain how a specific small business prices its products.

9. Describe the channel of distribution for a specific small business product.

10. Describe the promotional blend for a specific small business product.

Application Situations

1. Toothpaste Mission

Return to Toothpaste Mission in Chapter 6 for the case data.

Assignment

Based on your mission statement, develop the marketing mix. Be sure to take the systems view, read all questions, and think about how each P affects the other Ps before you start to write out 1–4.

1. Product. What is your product's competitive advantage? What will your brand name be? What warranty will you offer, if any? How will you package the toothpaste? Draw the label.

2. Price. How does the customer, competition, and other external and internal factors affect your pricing decision? What price will you charge? Because you don't know the cost to produce each tube, base the price on competitors' prices.

3. Place. Where will your toothpaste be sold? Specify the channel of distribution, transportation, and storage of your product.

4. Promotion. How will you get the customer to buy your toothpaste? If you are not selling directly to the consumer, how will you get the middleperson to buy your product? Be sure to specify the ratio of time, effort, and money spent on personal selling, mass selling, and sales promotion.

2. Mystic Chips

Ben Greenfield had an idea for a new one-man business. So at the age of 35 he started Ben Greenfield & Associates with $60,000 out of his pocket.[9] His product was chips—a crowded market dominated by national firms as Frito-Lay, Wise, and Eagle Snacks, not to mention the regional brands. However, Ben's idea was to offer a *product* with a competitive advantage. Ben convinced the Mystic Seaport Maritime Museum, located on the Mystic River in Connecticut, to allow him to use their brand name for a 2 percent royalty for each bag of chips sold by retailers. The package label includes the trademark three-masted sailing ship

Part III *Planning and Implementation*

logo. His product is a thicker-sliced chip, seasoned with sea salt, which used to be made at sea. Ben is actually in the marketing business; he contacted a Maine processing company to mass-produce the chips for him.

The *target customers* are the upscale buyers in New England (target market) willing to pay a *price* of about 20 percent more than for other brands. Ben didn't even *place* the product all by himself; he hired a Boston food broker to help him place his chips in about 300 stores. His big break came when two major regional grocery chains, Stop & Shop Supermarkets and First National Supermarkets, agreed to stock the chips. Mystic Chips are not usually placed with the other chips on the snack-food shelves; they are found in the delicatessen or gourmet sections. This placing also allowed Ben to avoid the slotting fees to gain shelf space. His *channel of distribution* is producer to middlepeople to consumer. Ben has hired others to transport the chips, and the producer and retailer store the chips. The original *promotional* efforts were in personal selling to get the use of the brand name, then to get a processing company to make the chips and the stores to sell them, with the help of the food broker. Ben's *sales forecast* for 1993 is over $1 million in revenue. Small potatoes in the U.S. potato-chip market, which had sales of $4.3 billion in 1991.

Assignment

1. What did Ben do right and why did it work?

2. Using a historical or other well-known attraction near where you live:

   a. Come up with an idea for a product as Ben did.

   b. State the target customer and target market and how you would conduct a feasibility study. Ben's feasibility test was done at Mystic Seaport where, based on his suggestion, the chips were first made and sold. Based on successful sales at Mystic, Ben got permission to use the name on chips to be sold in retail stores. As part of your marketing research to test the feasibility of this product, develop a simple one-page questionnaire, using Exhibit 7.1 as a sample, for your product. State why each question is included and how the data will be used. What methods would you use to gather and analyze the data? Discuss the details of how (personal interview, telephone, mail) and where the questionnaire will be filled out, and any statistics that would be used.

   c. Develop the marketing mix to meet the needs of your target market.

Integrative Case Question—CorLu Foods

Develop the marketing section for CorLu's business plan. Research data has been gathered for you, but you need to analyze it and present relevant information in your business plan. Be sure to develop a complete marketing mix (product, price, place, promotion) plan. (Please refer to the Integrated Case "CorLu Foods.")

Bibliography

Boone, Louis, and David Kurtz. *Contemporary Marketing,* 7th ed. Chicago: The Dryden Press, 1992.

Evans, Joel, and Barry Berman. *Marketing,* 5th ed. New York: Macmillan, 1993.

Kotler, Philip, and Gary Armstrong. *Principles of Marketing,* 5th ed. Englewood Cliffs, NJ: Prentice Hall, 1992.

McCarthy, Jerome, and William Perreault. *Basic Marketing,* 11th ed. Homewood, Ill: Richard D. Irwin, 1993.

Pride, William, and O. C. Ferrell. *Marketing: Concepts and Strategies,* 8th ed. Boston: Houghton Mifflin, 1993.

Szabo, Joan, and Nancy Croft Baker. "Hot New Markets of the 1990s." *Nation's Business,* December 1988, p. 23.

Szabo, Joan, and Nancy Croft Baker. "How to Do Your Own Marketing Research." *Nation's Business,* December 1988, p. 24.

Endnotes

1. Alex Johne and Stephen Rowntree, "High Technology Product Development in Small Firms: A Challenge for Marketing Specialists," *Technovation,* May 1991, pp. 247–58.
2. Louise Washer, "Marketing 101: Finding Your First Customer," *Working Woman,* October 1992, pp. 53–54, 65.
3. William Ruch, Harold Fearon, David Wieters, *Fundamentals of Production/ Operations Management,* 5th ed. (St. Paul, Minn.: West Publishing, 1992), p. 12.
4. Cyndee Miller, "Cajun Craze Causes Consumers to Chow Down on Chowchow," *Marketing News,* October 23, 1989, pp. 10–11.
5. Ibid.
6. Washer, "Marketing 101: Finding Your First Customer."
7. Brendan Intinodola, "Helping Small Businesses Survive," *National Underwriter,* April 1, 1991, pp. 7, 25.
8. Bruce Posner, "Anatomy of a Start-UP: Class Pictures," *Inc.,* May 1990, pp. 72–83.
9. Mark Stevens, "Recharge Your Entrepreneurial Batteries," *Small Business Reports,* February 1991, pp. 21–23.
10. Mark Stevens, "Want to Make a Good Business Great?" *Executive Female,* July–August 1992, pp. 15–16.
11. Hank Walshak, "An Internal Consensus Can Boost External Success," *Marketing News,* June 10, 1991, p. 13.
12. Ian Duncan, "Boost Your Sales: A Results-Driven Approach," *CMA Magazine,* October 1992, p. 38.
13. Arnold Cooper, Javier Gascon, and Carolyn Woo, *New Business in America: the Firms and Their Owners,* (Washington, D.C.: The National Federation of Independent Business Foundation).
14. Mark Blessington, "Designing a Sales Strategy with the Customer in Mind," *Compensation & Benefits Review,* March/April 1992, pp. 30–42.
15. Briston Voss, "Measuring the Effectiveness of Advertising and Public Relations," *Sales & Marketing Management,* October 1992, pp. 123–24.
16. Peter Kim, "Does Advertising Work: A Review of the Evidence," *Journal of Consumer Marketing* 9, no. 4 (Fall 1992), pp. 5–21.
17. Shelby Meinhardt, "Put It in Print," *Entrepreneur,* January 1989, p. 54.
18. Hashi Syedain, "In Pursuit of the Perfect Mix," *Marketing,* October 1991, pp. 20–21.
19. Eugene Carlson, "Chips off the Old Ships Discover a Niche," *The Wall Street Journal,* April 2, 1993, p. B2.

8 LOCATION AND LAYOUT

Location and layout affect the profitability of your firm. In this chapter you will learn about the importance of the geographic location of your business and how the physical facilities of the company should be designed. You will learn some of the important factors you will need to consider in making these decisions. The final decision will balance the many different considerations, allowing you to operate profitably.

Chapter Learning Objectives

After completing this chapter, you should be able to:

- Recognize and identify important factors to consider in making a location decision.
- Assess the importance of these factors in the location decisions of retail, wholesale, service, and manufacturing firms.
- Recognize and identify different approaches to the layout of your firm.
- Determine the layout parameters for retail, wholesale, service, and manufacturing firms.
- Identify the factors affecting whether you build, buy or lease your facilities.
- Define the following 11 key terms (in order of appearance in the chapter):

Process weight loss	Leaseback leases
Derived market	Layout
Lease	Product line layout
Lessee	Process (functional) layout
Lessor	Demand items
Operating lease	

The Interrelationship between Location and Layout and Other Business Plan Components

Throughout this book we have seen that the organization is a system composed of interacting and interrelated components. Let us now see how the location and layout decisions affect and are affected by these components. Developing the organization strategies—the products and services you wish to sell and the market you wish to serve—requires making decisions about where you must locate your business. It would be inappropriate to locate a supermarket other than in the midst of its intended customer area. Marketing information helps formulate business strategy, which affects location and layout decisions.

In specific organizations common internal designs may be used to maximize profitability. These internal designs dictate specific layout patterns. Both the location and layout decisions require use of the capital resources acquired through the financial function. The accounting function must receive all such information associated with these decisions in order to determine the firm's profitability. How these costs are treated—as current cash or depreciable assets—directly affects the profitability of the firm.

In certain circumstances the production function can affect location. If you are going to market high-fashion clothing, you should plan on locating in New York.

Layout is determined by the type of production process used. Assembly lines dictate one form of layout, retailing another.

Personnel considerations also play a part in the location decision. You would not locate your organization in an area where you could not hire the right kind and number of people to employ. Labor supply is an important location consideration.

Location: A Business Decision

Because of its long-term[1] and lasting effects on profitability, a firm's location deserves thoughtful analysis.[2] While it seems to be true that a location decision is made only when the business is first established or purchased, there are times when a business will want to expand or relocate. The firm's growth might force expansion, requiring the business owner to make a decision about expanding at the same location, if possible, or moving to another area. The economy or demographics may dictate a change in location. Regardless of the reason, the location decision may involve a significant expenditure, and you will have to live with your decision for a relatively long period of time. You should know the various factors that are important in making your location decision. Knowing the criteria will explain why some companies choose to locate in a particular area and why other companies are forced to do so.

General Location Factors

Because of its effect on profitability, careful investigation is needed to reveal the good and bad aspects of any location. However, there are general factors to be considered in making your location decision. They are (1) personal preferences, (2) geographic considerations, and (3) economic aspects. Each of these factors is important, but their importance varies within the context of each specific decision.

Personal Preferences

From a strictly logical point of view, if no other consideration were allowed to influence entrepreneurs' decision making, location selection should be made in sequence. After extensive research. You would:

1. Determine the geographic region of the country best suited for your type of enterprise.
2. Pick a city within the region that would yield maximum profitability.
3. Narrow down the city location to a specific area within a city.
4. Pick the specific site in the area (see 3).

Most small business people do not have the freedom to pick up and move. Nor do they have the resources to conduct an extensive study in order to relocate. Most entrepreneurs decide to situate their business in their home community. Here they have friends, relatives, and contacts they have made. They know the banks, insurance agents, and other people who would be able to extend credit or expertise. In short, the local community often has an infrastructure that is both necessary and familiar to support the small business. It would take a great deal of effort to duplicate this infrastructure, even if you desired to do so, in a new location. Staying in your home community is not a poor decision as long as location weaknesses do not overpower the choice. For example, opening a garden and lawn care store in the middle of a city might not be practical. You might not want to open an upscale food store in a declining neighborhood.

The reason an entrepreneur might have for choosing his or her home community, however, may not preclude choosing to move elsewhere. If, for example, you've always wanted to live in the Southwest, now is the time to make the move before you start the company. The choice of where to move is yours; there are many good business locations no matter where you choose to settle.

Location Selection Criteria

Aside from personal choice, which can vary from individual to individual, there are specific factors to consider when identifying where to locate your business. There is no specific formula that allows you to weigh each criterion and come up with the ideal site. Each factor must be looked at with specific reference to your business. Examine each of the criteria and pick the location that satisfied as many as possible. Some of the factors to examine are discussed in the following subsections.

Freight Costs

The importance of freight costs increases as the value of the goods decreases in proportion to their bulk. Diamonds, for example, are expensive in proportion to their weight. Thus, diamond cutters can be located anywhere in the world. Transportation costs to ship cut diamonds to various markets are insignificant factors in the retail value of the product. Cement, on the other hand, is bulky and intrinsically of low value. It is possible to ship it long distances, but the cost of transporting it beyond a radius of 25 to 30 miles from the plant would soon make the price prohibitive. Transportation costs would increase and finally represent the bulk of the final price, reducing profit considerably.

Weight Loss

Because freight costs money, firms tend to locate, if possible, at the source of a large process weight loss. A large **process weight loss** is *the loss of raw materials that occurs naturally as an outcome of the manufacturing process.* An example of this can be seen in the typical location of steel firms. In Pennsylvania there are large supplies of coal and no significant deposits of iron ore. Although both ores are necessary, the process consumes the entire weight of the coal, which is used as fuel in the refining process. Thus, the transportation of coal, beyond any distance that is absolutely necessary, is a needless expenditure. It is cheaper to ship the iron ore from the Mesabi region of the Great Lakes to Pittsburgh for refining rather than otherwise, since you need much more coal than iron ore to produce a ton of steel. Since the coal is completely consumed in the process (five tons of coal to one ton of iron ore), you ship as little coal as possible.

Another example of location being influenced by process weight loss is that of gold refineries, which have been located as close as possible to the mines. In the refining process most of the gold ore is waste; thus it pays to refine the ore as soon as possible, thereby saving on excess transportation costs.

Proximity to Market

Manufacturing high-style garments can be done anywhere in the world, since low labor cost plays a pivotal role in generating profits. However, a garment manufacturer at the very least must have a sales office and showroom in New York City in order to service major garment buyers (the customers) who travel there to see the latest styles and to place their orders. In this case proximity to the market also facilitates faster and better customer service, not unimportant location aspects in themselves. And since many garment firms are located in New York, it is advantageous to maintain visibility along with your competition, particularly in the high-fashion, rapidly changing garment industry. Any other location is apt to leave the firm out of touch with current demand conditions.

Retail establishments sell different products in different locations. The products sold cater to the economic, religious, and ethnic composition of the surrounding population. Expensive art galleries may be found in "upscale" areas, but discount stores are rare. Retail food markets also carry products catering to the surrounding population's economic, religious, and ethnic composition.

Transportation Facilities

It is important for most businesses to be near to or on good transportation facilities such as highways, railroads, and trucking and airline terminals. Parts and raw materials are shipped to the company and finished goods are shipped out. Customers may come to the premises to view or buy the product. No less important, employees have to be able to get to work either by automobile or public transportation.

Availability of Raw Materials

Some location decisions are preordained by the need to be close to the source of raw materials. It is obvious that the only location possible for a diamond or gold mine is at the source where the ore is found. One can only grow wheat where proper growing conditions are available. These facts supersede the availability of cheap transportation and market considerations. For example, any business that involves cultivation of marine life requires location near open water. Boatyards that cater to recreational boating have to be situated in a place that boaters can reach easily.

Labor Supply

An extremely important consideration for any firm is the availability of workers.[3] Availability here refers not only to the number obtainable but also the quality and type. Because each firm needs employees trained to perform its specific tasks, it is not wise for a firm to hire just any individual.

A great source of labor for the electronic industry was the availability of industrially trained and skilled workers in and around Boston, Massachusetts. Many of these workers were available because garment, textile, and leather manufacturing firms had moved out of the area, leaving an employment vacuum with an ample supply of skilled workers. In this country, nearly all of the labor force is industrially trained; that is, the workers are accustomed to, and expect to, put in an eight-hour day every day at their place of employment.

A significant problem in less developed countries is that workers are not industrially trained. Firms must think twice about locating in an area where workers must be trained.

In some instances, where there is a need for semi- or unskilled labor, it might be advantageous to locate in a surplus labor area.

Community Attitude

A precondition for successful location is a community's attitude toward a particular firm. Although a location may be perfect in all other respects, if the community does not welcome a particular business, it should not locate there.[4] Hostility toward industry can be shown in many different ways. It is never easy to fight community ill will, and therefore it is easier, and perhaps economically more advantageous, to locate elsewhere. Communities or states that truly desire industry will do all they can to make conducting business easier. Some communities offer incentives such as financial aid or tax rebates. Reading the information published by a city's chamber of commerce, or the classified advertising in *The Wall Street Journal* or institutional advertising in magazines such as *Business Week* reveals the many communities inviting businesses to relocate by offering powerful incentives. Problems can be avoided if firms do not locate where they are not welcome. Many communities will not allow a business they deem undesirable to locate in their areas. An old village located on Cape Cod, Massachusetts, would not allow a retail food warehouse to build an outlet; Freeport, Maine, fought desperately to prevent a fast-food chain from opening.

Water Power

In addition to using water for transportation, it is advantageous to locate on or near water if it is a source of power in the manufacturing process. The supply and price of water is important to many small businesses. Restaurants, hotels, and some types of small manufacturing plants need water to carry on their businesses. The cost of water as well as the importance of keeping it clean in accordance with environmental laws is increasing. A business's location could be determined by the availability of clean, inexpensive water. Costs of water resulting from its scarcity and recent cleanup efforts have made many Boston, Massachusetts, firms consider water cost as an important factor in their location decisionmaking.

Cost of Land

In deciding where to locate, the cost of land, by itself, is a relatively unimportant factor. Since location is a long-term consideration, the purchase price of the land will be spread over many years, each year representing only a small part of the initial cost and only minimally affecting the business's total cost picture per year.

Taxes

Closely tied to land and building costs, but much more important, is the local tax structure.[5] Taxes are a continual expenditure; the higher they are the less desirable the location. This is true because the entire tax cost represents, in accountants' terms, a burden cost. The tax structure of Boston, Massachusetts, at one time was as high as $198 per thousand dollars of assessed value. This meant that a firm would have to pay out-of-pocket costs of approximately 19 percent of its asset value per year, a deciding factor that made locating in Boston remarkably unattractive. This has since been changed, and taxes are now competitive with those of other cities. No firm believes that taxes can or will be eliminated wherever it locates, but neither does the firm desire to pay higher taxes than any other similar firm in another location.

Specialized Communities

A firm's location may be predetermined by the growth and development of so-called specialized communities. Since these communities develop by meeting the needs of a specific industry, they attract more of the same industry until the communities are so specialized that it became foolish for firms to locate elsewhere. Examples of such communities are Detroit, Michigan (automobiles); Akron, Ohio (rubber products); and Grand Rapids, Michigan (furniture). The specialization of these communities means that they are able to supply the firm with required services at relatively low unit costs because of the communities' economies of scale. Firms locating in these areas have an immediate and unsurpassable cost advantage. A business that services and repairs farming equipment should be located in rural areas, where large farms can be found.

Climatic Conditions

For some businesses, climate can be a deciding factor; you can't sell air conditioners where it never gets very hot. Ski shops are generally found close to ski areas. If running a sailing school is your dream, you need access to water and warm weather.

Sister Plants or Warehouse Locations

A firm might be drawn to specific areas because of the presence of sister plants and/or warehouses. Grouping integral components together may provide advantages such as close communication and coordination; the presence of congenial business neighbors who are able and willing to supply the firm with financing, supplies, power, and transportation facilities might make certain locations more desirable than others.

Urban, Suburban, or Rural

Once the choice of the general area has been made, you must decide whether to settle in an urban, suburban, or rural location. Each locale has had its proponents. Years ago the "proper" location for any firm was in a large city. The next trend was to locate plants in rural areas, which lack city congestion, unwelcome political interference, or taxes. But since there were also no city facilities and amenities (public transportation for employees, for example), firms started moving closer to but not into the cities. Today, the most desirable location is a suburb outside of a large city. This location, it is hoped, provides the benefits and facilities of large cities and some freedom from congestion and politics. The suburban location is at present considered the most advantageous because it blends the best of both extremes.

Site Selection

Critical factors to be considered in site selection are costs, including taxes, and development, parking, customer accessibility, traffic, and neighborhood conditions. Manufacturing firms, wholesalers, and service companies need not locate in high-rent districts. Small manufacturing firms need adequate parking for employees. Retailers need adequate parking for customers and must locate where their customers can reach them.[6]

In locating your business, you should assess the importance of each location factor and determine the combination of location factors that make the best sense. The following are examples of factors affecting location of several different types of businesses.

Manufacturing Location

When locating a small manufacturing plant, several important factors to consider are (1) the market, (2) the labor force, (3) transportation, (4) raw materials, (5) site selection, and (6) community interest. These factors are important whether you are going to rent an existing facility or, because of your specific need, build to suit your specific purposes. If you are going to lease an existing facility, an industrial real estate broker can help in your deliberations.

Market

To best satisfy your market and to maximize your profit, you need to locate where it is convenient for your customers. Just because you can ship merchandise to your customers doesn't mean that you don't need parking or other amenities so that they can reach you as they wish. To determine where to locate, you need to know where your customers are. A simple geographic plot of your customers or a map will easily reveal this. It also would help you to plot the location of your competitors.

Labor

While labor may be more mobile than it was, manufacturing plants generally draw their labor supply from the immediate surrounding area. There must be enough labor in this area to supply your employment needs. Generally the population needed should provide a labor pool 10 times the size of the number of employees you anticipate; that is, there should be 10 people in the pool for each employee required. Prevailing wage rates must be comparable with your competitors'. Do not locate where living conditions such as climate are unattractive or difficult. The more benign the living conditions, the less likely you will have difficulty attracting employees.

Transportation

Unless your employees all walk to work, the area's transportation facilities such as roads or transportation systems are important. Your receipt of goods and/or raw materials coming into the factory as well as finished goods being shipped out depend heavily on the availability of airports, highways, and railroads. You should have easy access to the transportation alternatives you generally use. In the past, it was not uncommon for factories to have railroad spurs on their property. Today, however, the nation's interstate highway network has greatly increased the use of trucks as a transportation alternative.

Raw Materials

Unless they are ubiquitous and universal, you should consider the advantages you might have by being close to the source of your raw materials. In some cases, raw materials can dictate where you locate. Anytime use of raw materials involves heavy weight loss, to maximize profitability you will want to be close to the raw materials to prevent paying to ship materials that will become waste. As you plan to be in business a long time, your raw material supply and your access to it must be plentiful enough to last well into the future.

Site Selection

Even though the site may be ideal in terms of size, transportation, topography, and construction, it is no longer easy to obtain the appropriate zoning variances, licenses, and required permits. There are so many conflicting interests and desires that permit and licensing delays have become longer and longer. The opening of a McDonald's franchise in Freeport, Maine, was delayed several years while the community tried to prevent it. To secure the town's approval, McDonald's had to install the store within an existing white wood-frame structure and eliminate the golden arch outside the building. It is also possible that the required zoning changes may never come through. Do not consider a site with real or potential problems.

Community Interest

A local university's desire to expand or another university's desire to increase the seating capacity of its football stadium can provoke a blizzard of protests from neighboring communities. Be aware of the community's feelings toward your business and avoid communities that don't want you by considering areas that are seeking business development and who will not put roadblocks in the way of your plans. For example, in St. Johnsbury, Vermont, the Preservation Trust of Vermont has induced Wal-Mart to place its store, not on the outskirts of town, but in the downtown area where it would draw customers, to the benefit of other retailers.[7]

EXHIBIT 8.1   **Rating sheet on sites**

Grade each factor: 1 (lowest) to 10 (highest)
Weigh each factor: 1 (least important) to 5 (most important)

Factors	Grade	Weight
1. Centrally located to reach my market.	_____	_____
2. Raw materials readily available.	_____	_____
3. Quantity of available labor.	_____	_____
4. Transportation availability and rates.	_____	_____
5. Labor rates of pay/estimated productivity.	_____	_____
6. Adequacy of utilities (sewer, water, power, gas).	_____	_____
7. Local business climate.	_____	_____
8. Provision for future expansion.	_____	_____
9. Tax burden.	_____	_____
10. Topography of the site (slope and foundation).	_____	_____
11. Quality of police and fire protection.	_____	_____
12. Housing availability for workers and managers.	_____	_____
13. Environmental factors (schools, cultural, community atmosphere).	_____	_____
14. Estimate of quality of this site in years.	_____	_____
15. Estimate of this site in relation to my major competitor.	_____	_____

Source: U.S. Small Business Administration, *Locating or Relocating Your Manufacturing Plant.* Management Aids, Number 2.002, n.d. Copies of this Aid are available free from SBA, P.O. Box 15434, Fort Worth, TX 76119. Aids may be condensed or reproduced. They may not be altered to imply approval by SBA of any private organization, product or service. If material is reused, credit to SBA will be appreciated.

To assist you in making a decision, you should use a site rating sheet such as the one recommended by the Small Business Administration. It will help you evaluate the factors and come up with the highest-rated location.[8] Exhibit 8.1 is an example.

Retail Location

Retail locations are particularly sensitive to specific characteristics of the surrounding area. As different kinds of retail stores cater to different clienteles, it is important that the local criteria match your needs. You will need information on:

> Size of the city's trading area.
>
> Population and population trends in the trading area.
>
> Total purchasing power and the distribution of purchasing power.
>
> Total retail trade potential for different lines of trade.

Number, size, and quality of competition.

Progressiveness of competition.[9]

Once you have determined which city you are going to open in, you must then evaluate a number of factors concerning the area or the type of location you want. These factors include:

Customer attraction power of the particular store and the shopping district.

Quantitative and qualitative nature of competitive stores.

Availability of access routes to the stores.

Nature of zoning regulations.

Direction of the area expansion.

General appearance of the area.[10]

One final set of criteria should be examined concerning the specific site—or property—on which you wish to open your business. If you plan to open a large discount store, for example, you will want a site that is visible to, and accessible by, a high volume of drive-by traffic. A smaller store, however, may be appropriately located in a neighborhood where it attracts local residents. In either case, the following criteria should be kept in mind:

Adequacy and potential of traffic passing the site.

Ability of the site to intercept traffic en route from one place to another.

Complementary nature of adjacent stores.

Parking facilities or space.

Vulnerability of the site to unfriendly competition.

Cost of the site.[11]

You will want to weigh all the criteria with respect to the type of retail operation you plan to operate. For example, if yours is a discount store, you will be looking for an entirely different population than a store selling exclusive, high-price merchandise. Again, depending upon your chosen clientele, you might consider such extreme site choices as a stand-alone structure (or one in a small block of stores) or a regional mall. The former location might house a small convenience store, the latter a high-end specialty goods retail establishment.

Although you have evaluated what you earnestly believe to be all-inclusive criteria, you might want to consider the following:

How much retail, office, storage, or workroom space do you need?

Is parking space available and adequate?

Do you require special lighting, heating or cooling, or other installations?

Will your advertising expenses be much higher if you choose a relatively remote location?

Is the area served by public transportation? Is it necessary for your business that it is?

Can the area serve as a source of employees?

Is there adequate fire and police protection?

Will sanitation or utility supply be a problem?

Is exterior lighting in the area adequate to attract evening shoppers and make them feel safe?

Are customer restroom facilities available?

Is the store easily accessible?

Does the store have awnings or decks to provide shelter during bad weather?

Will crime insurance be prohibitively expensive?

Do you plan to provide pickup or delivery?

Is the trade area heavily dependent on seasonal business?

Is the location convenient to where you live?

Do the people you want for customers live nearby?

Is the population density of the area sufficient?[12]

Wholesale Locations

Wholesalers are similar to retailers in that they must locate where they have easy access to an identified market. The wholesaler's market is, however, the retailer, making it a **derived market**—*a market that springs up not from people wanting goods for their personal use but for the use those goods have in completing a demanded product or process.* Wholesalers sell only to retailers if the consumer market demands it. If there is a recession and consumers lose purchasing power, retail demand from wholesalers also falls off. There are differences in that wholesalers generally sell to a number of retailers and thus must be available in a centralized location. This gives rise to "wholesale" districts within a city. Retailers know where to go and, when buying, can visit a number of their suppliers. Wholesale locations generally are in less expensive areas, as they do not depend upon end-user consumers. Generally you will find wholesalers tend to congregate in older, less expensive areas of the city in older, multistoried buildings. Rental costs are substantially lower when you don't have to project an "image."

Wholesalers tend to group themselves together because they need to be accessible to the same retailers. Inability to secure such a location may give rise to wholesale centers outside the city. These areas can be advantageous in that they allow truck access to both the city and to suburban markets. Wholesale locations are greatly influenced by (1) the availability of large, inexpensive buildings in less costly areas within the city or beyond; and (2) proximity to other wholesalers.

Service Locations

Service businesses are similar to retail stores in that they may locate near their markets if they operate similarly to a retail business; in other words, if people or businesses have to come in for service, then the business must be both accessible and visible. The factors that drive a good retail location apply.

Operating a service where you visit customers provides more flexibility in choosing a location. For example, if you are a plumber or a piano tuner, you can have your office wherever you choose, since customers or suppliers seldom visit your premises. However, if you are dependent upon customers coming to you, accessibility is important. Locate where you want as long as your costs are kept at a minimum.

Build, Buy, or Lease

Being in a small business almost guarantees that capital will be in short supply. Most small businesses have difficulty raising capital, so any method of operation that requires less capital outlay is considered attractive. In an effort to minimize capital outlay, many firms have turned to, or at least considered, leasing.[13] A **lease** is *an agreement to rent an asset that will be used as if it were owned.* For example, many firms lease vehicles, other equipment, and buildings from third parties and use these resources in their own business. In any case, the **lessee,** who is *the party leasing the equipment,* makes periodic payments to the **lessor,** *the party that owns the equipment being leased,* for the use of the asset. Since the lessor holds title to the asset being leased, the lease payment covers both the purchase price of the equipment as well as a profit for the owner.

Who are lessors? As the popularity of leasing increases, the number of companies in the leasing business has grown. Leasing is now a billion-dollar industry. In addition to independent leasing, you can lease from companies, banks, insurance companies, and finance companies. In many instances, you can lease equipment directly from the manufacturers. As a matter of fact, you can lease almost everything you need in any business.

Advantages of Leasing

In general, the primary advantage to leasing rather than buying or building is that you get to use the asset—the building, the truck, or the computer—without making a large capital payment required for ownership. Your regular lease payments are generally less than you would pay to own the asset in question, since a lease does not require a down payment because (1) it can allow a longer term than a loan for repayment; and (2) it does not have to cover the entire cost of the asset during the term of the lease. This allows you to use as operating capital the money that you would have paid to own the asset.

Also, because of the opportunity to walk away at the end of the lease, either by prior negotiation or industry standard, your equipment may be better maintained and automatically upgraded as new technology arrives.

Equipment such as copiers, which get very hard usage, can be easily replaced at the end of the lease, which roughly corresponds to the time when they begin breaking down more frequently. Computer technology increases at such a rapid rate that purchased computers quickly become obsolete while leased computers can be exchanged at minimal cost to acquire state-of-the-art technology as it becomes available. Since the lease payments are deductible as operating expenses, there may be some tax advantage as well. Operating expenses reduce the profits upon which taxes are based.

Owned assets also have advantages in that you can treat both depreciation and investment tax credits as deductions.

Disadvantages of Leasing

When the lease period is over, you return the asset to the lessor. Whatever value it has at that time is lost to you and reverts to the owner, although the lessor can, at additional cost, extend your lease or sell you the asset. If you owned the asset, you could continue using it at no added cost. To take a current example, the monthly cost to own a new car whose original price was $25,000 dollars, with a three-year note at 10 percent, would be approximately $800 a month. To lease the same automobile for the same term, you might only have to pay $399 per month, resulting in a $400-per-month cash saving. By itself, this is attractive; however, at the end of the 36-month period, you don't own the vehicle. Its value reverts to the lessor. In effect, you have paid $14,400, and since you own nothing, you must then replace it. Of course, if you owned it, you could continue using it. Over the long run, leasing costs more than owning because included in the lease payment is a profit to the lessor, which you could avoid by buying. The same argument can be made for buying an office building or factory.

A lease is a legal obligation and as such it is generally not cancelable. If there is a cancellation clause, to effect it is fairly expensive. You will continue to pay off the lease whether or not you actually use the equipment. On the other hand, owning an asset gives you the ability to sell it and recover some of your investment.

Alternative Leases

While all leases have the same general advantages and disadvantages, leases can be classified into two categories: operating leases or sale and leaseback.

Operating Leases

Operating leases *permit you to use the equipment in your business.* While title remains with the lessor, the lessor agrees to maintain the asset and may allow cancellation. Electronic equipment, furniture, buildings, and vehicles that can be leased in this manner are written for a specific time period that is usually shorter than the life of the equipment. During this generally noncancelable term, the lessee makes payment to the lessor. Maintenance is the lessee's responsibility. When the lease period is over, the lessor recovers the property. Office space is a typical example of such a lease.

Sale or Leaseback

Sale or **leaseback leases** *are used where you already own the equipment or building and wish to generate cash to be used in other parts of the business by leasing* *the asset back to a third party.* Capital that is not tied up in assets such as real estate can then be used for operating expenses. This type of lease requires simultaneous transactions: You sell the asset to another party who then leases it back to you for a fixed time period. At the expiration of the period, you may renew the lease or repurchase the asset.

Buildings and Facilities

It was not long ago that firms rented or bought an existing building or space and fit their operation into it. As the concept of efficiency assumes more importance, the building is considered to be facilitating equipment in the production process. As such you should make sure that the facilities are appropriate to the type of business you are in. Several considerations are important.

Construction and Design

Buildings today are designed with primary consideration given to the function of the building. If the business you are in does not require heavy equipment such as that which might be needed for manufacturing, the building can be light in structure and design. If there is need for heavy equipment and machinery, make sure that the floors and walls can support the required loads. If you foresee the need for a library, make sure the building can support the weight of the books, which are heavier than you think.

Function

If you are a manufacturer, the manufacturing facilities should be on one level to facilitate material handling. Office space can be accommodated on multiple levels.

Other factors to consider are the age and condition of the building. An old building will require extensive renovation in most of its systems: heat, plumbing, air conditioning, and electrical. Further, restrooms may have to be added and/or rebuilt to conform to newer building codes. There must be an adequate number of entrances and exits. For example, retail businesses might need more entrances and exits than a factory. The importance of these factors varies with respect to the different kinds of businesses. Each factor should be analyzed so that the facilities chosen are those best suited to the organization.

Layout

Layout is *the arrangement of the physical facilities in the most efficient manner for the specific business.* Layout must be given careful consideration, since the principles of layout vary depending upon the nature of the business. To illustrate the different approaches to layout, we will examine two types of businesses—manufacturing and retail.

Manufacturing

As important as the location decision is, the decision your firm makes regarding the type of production layout it needs is even more critical. Layout is a long-term matter. As it concerns itself with the design of the production process and the placement of the equipment and machinery, layout involves heavy expenditures. Once decided, the firm must depreciate the particular type of layout decision over a long period of time; it is now locked into its decision and these costs, which must be correct, for change can be effected only at great expense.

In the past, buildings were designed from the ground up to fulfill a general function at the least possible cost, and manufacturing firms configured their production layout to fit them. Unless they are developed for speculation, buildings today are custom designed, and they are built specifically for the business that will occupy them. The most popular type of building today is the sprawling single story structure, located on a large tract of land in the suburbs. The single-floor concept permits easy and economical transportation patterns within the building itself. The land area provides shipping, parking, and expansion potential. The layout used in a building may be of the process (functional) or of the product (line) type.[14] These are the two extreme methods used and, as with extremes, most firms probably use a combination of the two. Because the type of layout depends upon the characteristics of the production process, it is necessary to define the two layout types to see where each is best utilized.

Product Line Layout

The **product line layout** is *the arrangement of machinery and personnel in the sequential order of the manufacturing process* so that the resultant production process takes in raw material at the beginning of the procedure, then works on it process by process, transferring it from station to station until it emerges as the finished product. Exhibit 8.2 illustrates a product line layout.

The material enters the process at point A where production begins and emerges at point B as a finished good. An example of such a layout is the automobile assembly line, where automobiles move from one stage of production to another, emerging in finished form at the end of the line. The use of a line layout depends upon the balance between the advantages (profit) to be gained and the disadvantages (losses) to be sustained.

Use of product layout enables a business to produce large volumes of one or a few standardized products at low unit costs. Because machines are highly specialized, expensive, and designed for a single purpose, a product layout has heavy fixed costs and is thus a relatively costly method to use. However, the more units of a product that are manufactured using product type layout, the broader the base upon which to spread these fixed costs. The relationship of fixed costs to volume is shown in Exhibit 8.3.

EXHIBIT 8.2

Product type layout

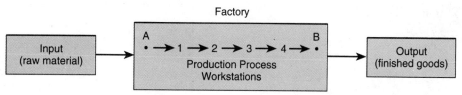

Source: Joel Corman, *Managing the Productive Process* (Morristown, N.J.: General Learning Press, 1974), p. 137.

EXHIBIT 8.3

Fixed cost to volume ratio

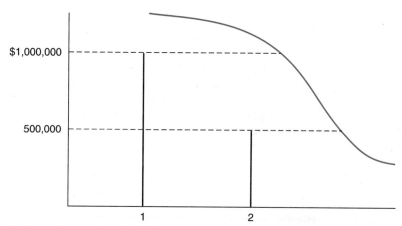

Fixed cost of product layout diminishes per unit as the number of units increases.
Source: Joel Corman, *Managing the Productive Process* (Morristown, N.J.: General Learning Press, 1974), p. 137.

At point A, the cost to manufacture one automobile is $3,000,000. At point B, because we are spreading the fixed costs over two units, the cost to manufacture two automobiles is $1,500,000. Finally, if we plan to produce 2,500,000 automobiles, the fixed cost each vehicle must bear is $1.20 per unit.

Functional Layout

In a **functional layout** *all machines are grouped according to function.* There is no predetermined route that products follow in the production process; the route is determined by the nature of the product. All products are involved in some of the same processes; however, since the products differ, they may be routed through these processes in different sequences. Exhibit 8.4 illustrates a functional layout.

If you are growing grapes and producing wine, each type of wine you are producing uses some, but not necessarily all, equipment. For example, after all grapes are picked, the white wines must have skins removed, but red wines require the grape skins to remain. Some wines are bottled immediately with screw caps; others are placed in casks for aging and are then placed in corked bottles.

EXHIBIT 8.4

*Process or
functional layout*

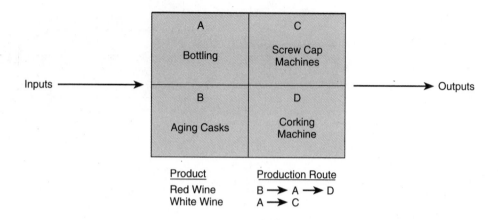

Flexibility, however, has a high cost; although there is considerable latitude in the production process, more inspection is needed to make certain that what is produced is what is desired. Close control is not possible, and economies of scale are not applicable in this process. In comparison to a product line setup, goods produced in a process layout have a high unit cost.

Both production layouts have their applicability. The use of either depends upon the product. Both have their strengths and weaknesses. It is up to you to weigh the relative costs and use either of the appropriate layouts or some combination.

Retail Layout

The function of a retail store is to maximize sales by providing customer convenience and service. Layout can facilitate this by directing the customer to those goods that provide maximum profitability. The store has to make it easy for the customer to access these goods. Studies have shown that since people entering a store are more likely to turn right rather than left, the best place to display high-profit items would be on the right side of the store as the customer enters. Generally, those goods are not **demand items,** which are *specific items that a customer needs to purchase.* They are impulse items that people want or items that people buy on the spur of the moment; they are relatively expensive, and where customers have significant differences from which to choose, they encourage weighing one item against another before purchasing. Low-margin items are generally on the left of the store. To buy the low-profit-margin items, a customer would have to walk through the store, past all of the attractive, high-profit impulse items. Thus, in a drugstore, prescription items are on the back wall, greeting cards on the left and cosmetics on the right. The middle of the store displays goods that fall between these categories such as books and candy. Exhibit 8.5 illustrates this type of layout.

In designing the layout of the retail store, you would make a scale drawing of the floor space, recognizing each area and using it for goods yielding the appropriate profit margin. This approach would produce a typical grocery store layout, as shown in Exhibit 8.6.

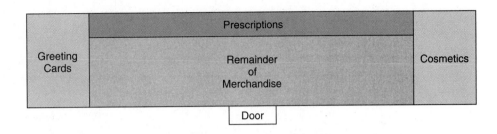

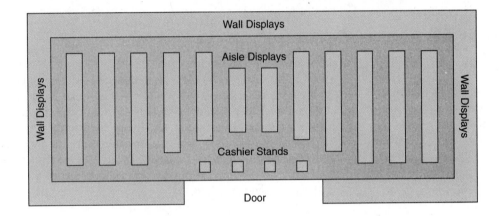

Other layout patterns can be developed, but since the objective for any retail store is to maximize profits, low-traffic areas display low-margin goods and high-traffic areas display high-profit items.

Wholesale Layout

Maximizing customer satisfaction in a wholesale operation is paramount. In most wholesale operations, because the customers usually phone, mail, or fax their orders, the wholesaler's job is to fill these orders as quickly and efficiently as possible. To do this, the wholesaler locates the faster-moving items closest to the shipping and receiving platform or dock. Slower-moving items are farther away. In filling orders, then, employees minimize the distance traveled in putting the order together. This would necessitate having wide aisles to maximize the use of material-handling equipment. Using this equipment an employee could quickly move up and down the aisles picking orders and end up at the shipping platform. Exhibit 8.7 illustrates this arrangement.

Service Layout

Because service establishments are so diverse, it is virtually impossible to describe a typical layout. A special layout will be designed to meet the needs of the business.

EXHIBIT 8.7

Typical wholesale layout

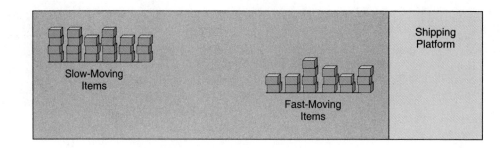

Service businesses providing direct services that customers must come to the premises to acquire, such as restaurants and hotels, have as their cornerstone customer convenience and a pleasant appearance or atmosphere. An automobile repair shop, on the other hand, may be set up much like a manufacturing company. The customer won't see and most likely is not interested in what goes on when the automobile is brought in for repairs. All the customer desires is that his or her vehicle is returned, and aside from the reception or waiting area, really doesn't care how the repair shop is arranged. Service businesses need to examine customer traffic and traffic flow before making layout decisions. Keep in mind that the needs of the business dictate the layout.

Sources of Information

Many publications aid entrepreneurs in searching for the best location. The U.S. Census Bureau puts out the following publications: *Introduction to Products and Services 1990 Census Basics,* a monthly newsletter, and *Census and You,* a monthly newsletter. The Census Bureau also publishes information about the United States, dividing it into Standard Metropolitan Statistical Areas (SMSAs). Factors about each area's population, such as age, income, home value, and education, are analyzed.

The U.S. Small Business Administration also has a number of valuable aids which include: *Practical Use of Government Statistics; Using Census Data to Select a Store Site,* and *Using Census Data in Small Plant Manufacturing.* The *American Demographics* magazine prints two booklets: *The 1990 Census: The Counting of America,* and *A Researcher's Guide to the 1990 Census.* Also quite helpful are: (1) *Sales and Marketing: Management's Survey of Buying Power;* (2) *Editor's Publishing Market Guide;* (3) Rand McNally's *Commercial Atlas and Marketing Guide;* (4) *Zip Code Atlas and Market Planner: The Survey of Buying Power,* published annually, provides a detailed breakdown of population, retail sales, spending, income, and other characteristics for census region, states, metropolitan areas, counties, and cities.

Summary

The Interrelationship between Location and Layout and Other Business Plan Components

The organization is a system of interacting and interrelated components. While location and layout are not considered to be functional areas of the firm such as accounting, finance, marketing, production/operations, and human resources/personnel, they affect and are affected by all organization components. Location is often determined by labor supply or market considerations. Layout is affected by decisions regarding production/operations. Both location and layout decisions require resources supplied by the finance function.

General Location Factors

After making the decision to operate a small business, you must consider where to locate.

If you buy an established business, you should know if its location is advantageous or you should consider changing its location, perhaps expanding to another site.

Location Selection Criteria

After your own personal preferences are examined, you want to consider such general location factors as (1) **weight loss,** *the loss of raw materials as an outcome of the manufacturing process;* (2) proximity to the market; (3) transportation facilities; (4) availability of raw materials; (5) labor supply; (6) community attitude; (7) water power; (8) land costs; (9) taxes; (10) specialized communities; (11) climatic conditions; (12) sister plants/warehouses; (13) the question of urban, suburban, or rural sites; (14) how these factors affect specific site selection.

After examining the general location factors, you will be able to apply them to specific location requirements of retail, wholesale, service, and manufacturing firms. Remember that wholesale firms are catering to a **derived market** which is *a market that springs up not from people wanting goods for their personal use but for the use those goods have in completing a demanded product or process.* Another aspect of the location decision is whether you want to buy, build, or lease your facilities. **Leasing,** which is *an agreement to rent an asset that will be used as if it were owned,* requires a contract between the **lessee,** *the party leasing the equipment* and the **lessor,** *the party that owns the equipment being leased.* In addition, you can consider an **operating lease,** which *permits you to use the equipment in your business. While title remains with the lessor, he or she agrees to maintain the asset and may allow cancellation.* **Leaseback leases** are *used where you already own the equipment or building and wish to generate cash to be used in other parts of the business by leasing the asset back to a third party.* There are arguments both for and against leasing, but your decision should be based on what is most profitable for your company.

Having committed to a building, you must develop a **layout,** the *arrangement of the physical facilities in the most efficient manner for the specific business,* for the interior in order to maximize profitability. The differences in layout for retail, wholesale, service, and manufacturing firms depends upon the demand of their customers or clients. A manufacturing firm wants to minimize production costs, while a retail store wants to ensure that customers have the opportunity to choose high-profit impulse items on entering the facility. A manufacturing firm might utilize a **product layout,** which refers to the *arrangement of the machinery and personnel in the sequential order of the manufacturing process* or a **process layout,** where *machinery is grouped according to machine function.* A retail store makes low profit on **demand items,** *specific items that a customer needs to purchase* that are accessible only after the customer passes by the high-profit impulse items. A wholesale firm's layout is dependent upon minimizing the cost of filling the derived demand order of the retailers. The location of service companies depends upon whether the customer goes to the location for service or the service people go to the customer. In the former case, service firms have to consider most of the location considerations affecting the retail store. In the latter case, it might not matter where the source company is located, except that it should be located where cost is at a minimum.

Questions

1. Location may be a significant factor for some types of firms and not for others. Why? Give several examples.

2. Is personal preference important in locating a company? Explain and justify.

3. How do most small business owners choose their location?

4. Using a specific type of business, if you were to locate a new venture, how would you select (a) the geographic area, and (b) the site within the area?

5. What factors would you consider when you evaluate a region in which to locate? Where would you find appropriate information?

6. Are there circumstances that would persuade you to locate in a declining area? What are they and how would you make your decision?

7. In locating a manufacturing plant, what factors would you consider?

8. In locating an upscale clothing store, what factors would you consider?

9. What factors should a computer sales and service operation and an asphalt manufacturing plant consider in their selection of a location? Compare the location factors you would use in each decision.

10. Would it be wise to locate your firm near others of the same kind? Why or why not?

11. What part would census information play in your location decision? Where would you get it and how would you use such information?

12. What are the advantages of buying rather than leasing your equipment or building?

13. You have been given the opportunity to plan the layout of a brand-new food store. What are the general rules you would use to enable maximum profitability?

14. Manufacturing plants need to minimize cost. How would you lay out a plant in order to minimize costs?

15. What types of businesses need to be concerned with customer accessibility? Why?

16. While keeping costs down is appropriate, a cheap location might not be the best idea. Why would this be true? Show an example where this would not be true.

17. Why is the location decision for a manufacturing plant more critical than for a retail store or service operation?

18. When does a manufacturing firm use process layout and when would it use product layout?

19. When would a manufacturing firm use general-purpose equipment and when would it use special-purpose equipment? Explain.

Application Exercises

When doing these exercises, where applicable, be sure to select a specific business, preferably one where you presently or previously worked or a business you would like to own someday. If this is not possible, pick a specific organization to which you will refer. Be sure to identify the organization by name. Limit your answers to one or two pages per exercise.

1. Pick a business you would like to own and using information such as census data, choose a region and a specific site for the business. Justify your site selection, giving advantages and disadvantages.

2. Using the information in question 1, and projecting into the future, will the site be viable for the future of the business in five years? Ten years? Why or why not, and how will you plan future relocations?

3. Interview a local small business owner and ask how the location decision was made. Cite the strengths and weaknesses of the location. Would the owner move from this site in the future?

4. Go to your local library and using demographic information about your town or city, determine what kind(s) of a business would do well in your town.

5. Indicate which of the following business would or would not do well in the town or city where you live. Justify your answer, giving the advantages and disadvantages of each site for each business: (a) barbershop; (b) beauty salon; (c) hardware and home center; (d) a restaurant specializing in Tex-Mex food; (e) low-cost clothing store; (f) gourmet food shop.

6. Visit your local supermarket and prepare a store layout. Analyze the layout for its positive and negative aspects. State your conclusions about whether the layout is a good one.

7. Visit a manufacturing plant and prepare a layout of the facility. Analyze the layout for its positive and negative aspects. State your conclusions about whether this is a good layout.

8. From your local newspaper advertising, call a local automobile dealer to compare the cost of owning and leasing a vehicle. Which method would you choose and why?

9. Locate a vacant store and ask the rental agent or the previous owner to explain why the store is vacant. By using census data, determine whether a business at this site could be successful.

Application Situations

1. Two Colleges

Two colleges, both located in the center of a large city, are at the point where a decision has to be made about future site locations. Both have outgrown their present facilities. The student bodies are similar in that both cater to and attract working commuter students. The city has excellent public transportation facilities, but like all cities, is congested and parking is virtually nonexistent. Several choices are available: (a) continue the present strategy to attract the working or commuting student; (b) change strategy and become a suburban institution attracting a residential population.

Assignment

Answer the following questions:

1. Determine the information needed to make a location decision.
2. Prepare a report for each alternative, giving the positive and negative aspects for each location.

2. Quantity Shopper

A large supermarket chain wants to choose a location for its new super-supermarket, selling in bulk at low prices.

Assignment

Prepare a report showing the factors affecting its location decision.

3. Harry Carey, Inc.

An exclusive jewelry store "High Cost, nothing but the best," is planning a new location. At present its only store is located on Rodeo Drive in Beverly Hills, California.

Assignment

Prepare a report outlining the characteristics of the Rodeo Drive location and showing where conditions exist that would support another store.

4. Sam Maxwell

Sam Maxwell, having just finished his electronics apprenticeship, has decided to open a repair service. In Center City he found a vacant store in the middle of the block in the commercial district. The city was in the midst of a decline, as people were moving out and taxes were going up. Yet the block had an apparently successful sandwich shop, a TV and appliance store, and a plumber.

Assignment

Answer the following questions:

1. What information does Sam need to make his decision?
2. Prepare a site location report for Sam, giving the reasons he should or should not locate in this area.

Integrated Case Question–CorLu Foods

1. Using the demographics supplied, is the proposed new location a good one for CorLu?
2. Draw up a layout for the proposed location. (Please refer to the Integrated Case "Corlu Foods.")

Bibliography

Bretz, E. A. "Planning, Design Approach Help Ensure Reliability." *Electrical World,* May 1992, pp. 58–60.

Brown, Stephen. "Retailing and the Importance of Micro-Locational Linkages." *Management Decision* 27, no. 5 (1989), pp. 4–11.

Cavinato, Joseph. "How to Perform a Lease v. Buy Analysis." *Distribution,* December 1988, pp. 42–45.

Chajed, Dilip; Benoit Montreuil; and Timothy J. Lowe. "Flow Network Design for Manufacturing Systems Layout." *European Journal of Operational Research* 57, no. 2, (March 11, 1992), pp. 145–61.

Duke, George W. "Warehouse/Distribution Leasing: Know When to Make a Deal." *Commercial Investment Real Estate Journal* 9, no. 4 (Fall 1990), pp. 29–33.

Finkin, Eugene F. "Strategies for More Efficient Manufacturing Operations." *Journal of Business Strategy* 11, no. 5 (September/October 1990), pp. 56–59.

Gray, Ann E.; Uday S. Karmarkar; and Abraham Seidmann. "Design and Operation of an Order-Consolidation Warehouse; Models and Application." *European Journal of Operational Research* 58, no. 1 (April 10, 1992), pp. 14–36.

Heragu, Sunderesh S. "Recent Models and Techniques for Solving the Layout Problem." *European Journal of Operational Research* 57, no. 2 (March 11, 1992), pp. 136–44.

Heragu, Sunderesh S. and Andrew Kusiak. "Efficient Models for the Facility Layout Problem." *European Journal of Operational Research* 53, no. 1 (July 5, 1991), pp. 1–13.

Houshyar, Azim, and Bob White. "Exact Optimal Solution for Facility Layout: Deciding Which Pairs of Locations Should Be Adjacent." *Computer & Industrial Engineering* 24, no. 2 (April 1993), pp. 177–87.

Johnson, John R. "Distributors Rack Up Shelving Sales." *Industrial Distribution,* March 1993, pp. 16–20.

Kaku, Bharat K., and Ram Rachamadugu. "Layout Design for Flexible Manufacturing Systems." *European Journal of Operational Research* 57, no. 2 (March 11, 1992), pp. 224–30.

McCune, Jenny C. "Tomorrow's Factory." *Management Review* 82, no. 1 (January 1993), pp. 19–23.

Masud, A.S.M., and V. Sathyana. "A CAD-based Layout Planning Procedure." *Computers & Industrial Engineering* 23, no. 1–4 (November 1992), pp. 385–88.

Montreuil, Benoit; Uday Venkatadri; and H. Donald Ratliff. "Generating a Layout from a Design Skeleton." *IIE Transactions,* January 1993, pp. 3–15.

Muroff, Cindy. "Warehouse Layouts: A Virtual Reality." *Distribution,* March 1993, pp. 84–85.

Papke, Leslie E. "Interstate Business Tax Differentials and New Firm Location." *Journal of Public Economics* 45, no. 1 (June 1991), pp. 47–68.

Rainey, Daniel V., and Kevin T. McNamara. "Determinants of Manufacturing Location: An Analysis of Locations in Indiana between 1986 and 1989." *Indiana Business Review* 67, no. 3 (Fall 1992), pp. 1–7.

Rex, Tom R. "Business Location Factors Are Clue to Economic Growth." *Arizona Business* 37, no. 2 (February 1990), pp. 8–9.

Riopel, Diana, and Andre Langevin. "Optimizing the Location of Material Transfer Stations within Layout Analysis." *International Journal of Production Economics* 22, no. 2 (November 1991), pp. 169–76.

Schwind, Gene F. "Planning for Storage: Arranging the Building Blocks." *Material Handling Engineering* 47, no. 9 (September 1992), pp. 66–86.

Sullivan, R. Lee. "Target's Customized Store Design," *Discount Merchandiser,* February 1990, p. 32.

Suskind, Peter B. "Productivity and Quality Improvement in Non-Manufacturing Activities: A Systematic Approach to Office Development." *Industrial Engineering* 21, no. 1 (January 1989), pp. 52–55.

Tamashunas, Victor M.; Jihad Labban; and David Sly. "Interactive Graphics Offer an Analysis of Plant Layout and Material Handling Systems." *Industrial Engineering* 22, no. 6 (June 1990), pp. 38–43.

"Tax Factors You Should Know When Your Company Rents Space." *Profit-Building Strategies for Business Owners,* February 1990, pp. 7–8.

Endnotes

1. Barbara Quinn, "Plant Site," *Venture,* October 1987, pp. 89–90.
2. Claire Bremer, "Engineering a Successful Renovation, Expansion or Relocation Project," *Business Age,* June 1989, p. 6.
3. Michael Selz, "Firms Battling Labor Shortages Call the Movers," *The Wall Street Journal,* January 31, 1991, pp. 115–20
4. "Food Fight," *The Wall Street Journal,* October 9, 1993, p. 1, A9.
5. "Ballot Battles over Taxes, Blue Laws, Rally Small Business Owners," *The Wall Street Journal,* October 20, 1993, pp. B1–B2.

6. U.S. Small Business Administration, "Using a Traffic Study to Select a Retail Site," *Small Marketer's Aid, No. 152* (Washington, D.C.: U.S. Government Printing Office, 1979), pp. 10–11.

7. "A Welcome Wal-Mart," *Boston Sunday Globe,* August, 21, 1994, p. 78.

8. U.S. Small Business Administration, "Locating or Relocating Your Manufacturing Plant" (Washington, D.C.: U.S. Government Printing Office, 1987), p. 6.

9. U.S. Small Business Administration, Office of Business Development. *Choosing a Retail Location* (Washington, D.C.: U.S. Government Printing Office, 1967).

10. Ibid.

11. Ibid.

12. Ibid.

13. U.S. Small Business Administration, "Should You Buy or Lease Equipment?" (Washington, D.C.: U. S. Government Printing Office, 1987), pp. 1–6.

14. James L. Riggs, *Production Systems* (New York: Wiley, 1970), pp. 219, 220.

9   THE PRODUCTION/OPERATIONS FUNCTION

In this chapter, you will learn about the importance of the production/operations function of small business. Producing quality tangible goods or services in the most efficient manner will enable firms to survive and prosper.[1] Accordingly, we will look at the definition of the product/operations function and the way firms determine how to produce products in the most efficient manner. Attention must also be given to the question of how to manage inventory and the production function so that inventory costs are at a minimum and the flow of goods or services is properly monitored. As the production of goods and services is intertwined with quality considerations, we will also examine this topic.

Chapter Learning Objectives

After completing this chapter, you should be able to:

- Define the process of the production/operations functions and identify the process of utility creation.
- Identify the components of the production process.
- Recognize some of the tools used to control the production process.
- Understand the meaning of the term inventory and how to keep its costs at a minimum.
- Be able to define the term economic order quantity (EOQ), and determine how to arrive at the lowest cost inventory.
- Identify the two approaches to production control, loading, and scheduling.
- Know how to determine the best method to use in the production process and, once you arrive at the best method, how to produce the product in the most efficient time.
- Understand the importance of quality considerations in the production process and how to integrate quality in the production process.
- Be able to define the basic approaches to quality control such as statistical quality control and sampling.

· Define the following 25 key terms in the order of appearance:

Utility	Motion study
Production/operation process	Time study
Capital	Process chart
Material resource planning (MRP)	Direct (watch) study
Just-in-time inventory system (JIT)	Predetermined time study
Economic order quantity (EOQ)	Grasp
Carrying costs	Assemble
Procurement costs	Quality
Loading	TQM
Specific production control	Statistical quality control
Master scheduling	Production/operations Variability
Perpetual loading	
Gantt chart	
PERT	

The Interrelationship between the Production/Operations Function and Other Business Plan Components

The relationship between the production/operations function and the other functional areas of accounting, finance, marketing, and human resources is critical. Defining the product or service you will provide and identifying the market and its size determines the production process you will use. To satisfy mass markets, you will need large-scale production facilities. Operating a small repair shop might require state-of-the-art test facilities or just small hand tools.

The production process must be able to meet sales forecasts provided by the marketing function. Defining the production process enables you to determine the equipment you need and how much it will cost. It also will lead you to discover what resources must be supplied by the finance function. All equipment acquired for the production/operations function must be identified by the accounting function. The accounting function also determines whether to expense or depreciate equipment expenditures—a decision that will affect the firm's profitability. Frequently, decisions about equipment acquisitions are driven by tax considerations. Once the decisions are made, however, you are then able to project your need for personnel to operate the machinery and to supervise the overall operation. This information is needed by the personnel function so that it can identify the appropriate people to hire.

Operations Management

The old definition of *production management* concerned itself only with the manufacturing process, but time and technology have forced us to enlarge the scope of production management to include any business whose function is the creation of utility, tangible or intangible. In this case, **utility** is *a good or service that is of some value to the purchaser or final consumer*. Corresponding to this change in emphasis, production management is now called "operations management."

Simply stated, if we view any organization as the creator of utility from specific resources, whatever they may be, we are able to include in the definition of production-oriented firms not only typical manufacturing firms but organizations as dissimilar as hospitals, insurance companies, or educational institutions. Instead of calling the techniques used to operate and control these firms "production management," a new term, "operations management," was devised to denote the applicability of these management techniques to industries other than manufacturing. Viewed in this manner, every business owner is also a production manager. Therefore, *a production or operations process can be described as converting inputs to outputs*. The process consists of three elements: inputs, process, and outputs, as Exhibit 9.1 illustrates.

The chief difference in managing these various production processes stems from the fact that the emphasis given to each element is determined by the nature of the individual entity in which the problem occurs. Obviously the problems of inventory maintenance in a hospital are far more critical than for an inn. But managing this process efficiently in order to produce goods or services in a timely manner is the task of any organization.

Inputs

Although all firms do not use identical inputs, every business must use four general elements: people, capital, machinery, and material. The combination of inputs differs between firms and is, of course, determined by the product or output, but all are used in some form or another as the initial step in managing operations.[2]

Exhibit 9.1

Typical operations process

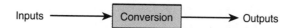

Inputs ⟶ Conversion ⟶ Outputs

People

People, often referred to as human resources, are required in every business. However, education, skill, expertise, and other desirable attributes are dependent upon the demands of the firm. Bigger and more complex firms generally require higher levels of expertise, and the demands of a professional organization may by its nature exact high levels of expertise. Legal, educational, and medical institutions are examples of organizations requiring high skill levels. Relatively low levels of education and skill may be required in other types of service occupations. In general, as the technology or educational needs of the firm increase, the skill and knowledge level demanded of the employees must keep pace. Correspondingly, the work itself tends to become less physically demanding.

Capital

Capital can be viewed in several ways. First, **capital** refers to *the physical assets of the company,* such as machinery, equipment or plant, and other assets used to produce a utility. These assets are accumulated over long periods of time and are invaluable to that specific business. If the business ceases operations, the liquidation value of these assets is often only a fraction of their value to a going concern. Secondly, a firm must have capital—in this case, cash—to pay operating expenses. There must always be enough cash to pay all expenses, even if the firm has to borrow to pay its debts. You, the entrepreneur, cannot delay paying bills indefinitely.

Materials

Any production or operation must consume material or physical goods. These goods are either used up or become part of the final product itself.[3] In manufacturing clothing, the plant needs yarn, thread, zippers, buttons, and many other associated items to produce a completed garment. In a service industry, where the good produced is often intangible, the demand for material is not quite so obvious. In an accounting firm, the primary material would be the knowledge and skills of the professional staff. In a hospital, pharmaceutical drugs, beds, and X-ray film are properly considered to be material, which contribute toward producing a healed person.

The Conversion Process

We have now identified the inputs that will be transformed into products. This procedure is known as the production/operations process, which converts one form of material to another. It can be as simple as that of a store where the actual product is not manufactured but derives its value from being available where and when the customer wants it. In this case the conversion process would involve changing the location and time of availability. Or the process can be complicated and technologically impressive, such as that involved in the production of computers or electronic components. It should be noted that production can consist of either breaking raw material down into component parts, such as in the refining of bauxite, or combining material to create final products such as garments or components.

Output

The end result of the production/operations process is the conversion of materials into the final product. It should be recognized that the production process is not pure. That is, while we are producing the goods and services we want, there are other products being created that may have unintended consequences. These products may be extremely costly to society. For example, the generation of electric power from coal has indirectly caused black-lung disease among coal miners and air pollution in areas surrounding generating plants. Although we cannot completely avoid producing unwelcome by-products, a great deal of time, energy, and money is going into determining either alternative production methods or ways to cope with these outcomes. The elements of a production process are shown in Exhibit 9.2. To ensure that the process produces goods or services in the most efficient manner, the process must be controlled. Some of the control mechanisms are also shown in Exhibit 9.2.

Material

Because foreign competition is driving American business toward increased efficiency and economy, it is not surprising that the material used in the process of creating utility has come under increasing scrutiny. The more dependent a business is on raw material in its final product, the more significant is controlling material costs. For example, a retail store may have 85 percent of its product costs dependent upon its purchase of goods for resale. If the return on sales is 5 percent, a 5 percent reduction in the material cost flows right to the bottom line. This additional savings would technically translate immediately to the profit side of the balance sheet.[4] That is, a 5 percent savings in material costs is all profit. In order to make an additional 5 percent profit, the firm would have to double its sales. Thus, small

---

EXHIBIT 9.2   Production processes and controls

Components of Production Process	Control of Production Process
1. Material	1. Quality
2. Make-buy	2. Scheduling
3. Capacity	3. Work measurement

savings in the cost of material can pay big dividends.[5] Two important topics deserve special attention. First, the firm is concerned with obtaining needed material at the right time and at the lowest price, predicated upon the ability to physically control the material it receives. Second, it must know how much to buy at any one time and when to place the order. Just as a manufacturing firm must make decisions about raw material, a hospital must make the same decisions about such items as medicine, bandages, and surgical swabs.[6]

Material Requirements Planning

Material requirements planning (MRP) is *the tool used to control the process of ordering and delivering the needed material at the right time, in the right place, and at the lowest cost*.[7] MRP's objectives encompass saving the firm money by reducing inventory levels, controlling the material needed in production, and by doing so, yielding faster delivery times, which, in turn, improves customer satisfaction.[8] A further improvement in the production process has been the introduction of the just-in-time inventory system (JIT).[9]

A **just-in-time inventory system** *delivers inventory in the production process when it is needed*. JIT techniques are the result of the demand-pull efforts of a firm to schedule production. Using this system, the actual demand triggers the production process and inventory is delivered only when needed. The advantage to this management technique is that it reduces the cost of maintaining inventory.[10] Only those materials or goods needed in the process will be delivered at the precise time they are needed. Now the company will not have capital tied up in storing and carrying inventory. A manufacturing firm would have raw material delivered when needed; a hospital, bandages and medical supplies; and a college, supplies such as copy paper and textbooks. The more dependent a firm is on materials and supplies, the more important are the savings to be realized.[11]

Make versus Buy

The small business must decide whether to make its own materials, inventory items, or component parts or to buy them from a supplier. If a firm can make everything it needs, the usual determinant of the make-or-buy decision is price. If the price of purchasing the goods is cheaper than manufacturing them, the firm will probably purchase the material in question.[12] To make an adequate analysis of the comparative advantages of making or buying, there are quantitative and nonquantitative elements that must be taken into consideration. The measurable aspects of the decision are listed in Exhibit 9.3.

Comparison of costs alone may not give a definitive answer, for other nonquantitative factors may outweigh pure price considerations. However, price becomes the significant factor if other reasons either do not exist or are unimportant. Some of the factors that may affect the firm's decision are the following:

1. At times a firm wants to keep a particular vendor in business. The firm may desire to do this because of a fear that future supplies of the product

EXHIBIT 9.3   Cost aspects: make versus buy

Make	Buy
Setup	Purchase price
Labor	Receiving cost
Material	Freight
Overhead	Inspection
Inspection	Requisition cost
Machine cost	

will be uncertain if the vendor is forced out. For example, a repair service firm may buy parts and be dependent upon one supplier; loss of that supplier could be serious.

2. Under different circumstances, the firm makes rather than buys even though the purchase price is cheaper. If the firm has idle capacity to utilize, this would be true. In this instance the contribution rate would be the determining factor.

3. The question of certainty of supply and/or production delays could cut either way, depending upon the individual situation. If the firm is busy producing its major line, it might not have the time available to produce smaller parts on schedule. Or perhaps a supplier firm cannot supply the needed quantity because of other commitments.

4. Time considerations may be a deciding factor. Regardless of price considerations, the firm might be forced to either make or buy if it or the vendor could not meet required delivery deadlines.

5. If the firm desires to keep a process secret, it would knowingly pay high manufacturing costs.

Whatever the decision, the objective of MRP is to provide the right materials at the right time and price. These materials can come from inside (self-manufacture) or outside (purchases), cost being the determining factor. Generally, if you can buy it cheaper than you can make it, do so. The converse would also be true.[13]

Inventory

Once the material arrives, there must be an adequate system to keep track of it. Arrangements must be made for adequate, secure storage facilities and effective requisition procedures. Inventory records must be kept up-to-date. The information in Exhibit 9.4 should be recorded and easily accessible. In the case of a retail clothing store, careful records must be maintained so that the styles, sizes, and colors of garments are available.

EXHIBIT 9.4

Inventory control card					
Style Name					
Style Number ———— Unit Price ———— Supplier ————			Storage Location ———— Reorder Point ———— Order Quantity (EOQ) ————		
Date	Units on Hand	P.O. Date Number	Units Rec'd.	Balance Due	Issued

Hospitals must keep track of pharmaceuticals not only for cost purposes, but in some cases to comply with state or federal regulations. However, you should not depend on paper or computer records. Mistakes can happen: parts can get mislaid. Thus, you should physically count your inventory at least once a year—more often depending upon the dollar value of the inventory involved. The more the inventory is worth, the more frequently you want to check it.

Inventory Control and EOQ

The primary questions of inventory control are (1) how much to order at any one time (economic order quantity) and (2) when to reorder (reorder point).[14] If you can answer these questions with any degree of certainty, you can keep your inventory costs at a minimum. In graphic terms, you can see the relationship between time and inventory quantity. Over time, the operations process draws down inventory. Given enough time, without any additional supply coming in or being made, you would soon run out of inventory and consequently be forced to stop production. Ideally, you'd like to have a new delivery of product parts just as you are using the last product part from your inventory. The amount delivered should be the economic order quantity (EOQ).[15] The **EOQ** is *the amount of goods whose total procurement and carrying costs are at a minimum.* Exhibit 9.5 shows the relation between time and quantity of inventory.

EXHIBIT 9.5

Relationship between time and quantity of inventory

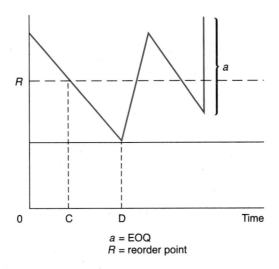

a = EOQ
R = reorder point

Time Relationship to Inventory Quantity

If you order more inventory at point *R, CD* represents the time lapse between requisition and delivery. Point *a* is the amount of goods ordered and received. You should order at point *R* if you don't want to run out of inventory. The costs of maintaining inventory fall into two categories: carrying cost and procurement cost. The ideal inventory (EOQ) quantity will minimize total costs.

Carrying Costs

Carrying costs are *those costs associated with ordering materials from the ordering cost through receiving, inspection, and storage.* They vary directly with the size of the inventory. The greater the amount of inventory, the greater the costs. The average carrying cost can be as much as 21 percent.[16] This cost component consists of:

1. Storage costs.
2. Maintenance.
3. Clerical tasks, such as preparing and filing the requisition.
4. Insurance.
5. Obsolescence.
6. Taxes.

The relation between carrying costs in annual dollars and inventory quantity (in terms of months of supply) is illustrated in Exhibit 9.6.

Procurement Costs

Procurement costs *are made up of requisition costs, follow-up tasks, and payment of invoices,* and they vary inversely with the inventory you have. The more units of inventory you procure, the cheaper the procurement costs per unit. Each time an

EXHIBIT 9.6

Relation between storage cost and quantity

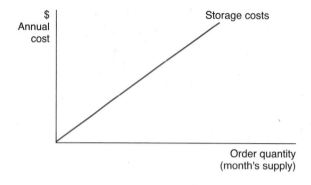

EXHIBIT 9.7

Relation between procurement costs and quantity

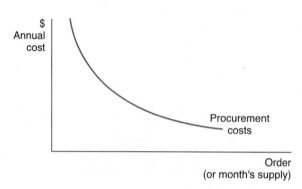

order is placed, it is subject to the same procurement costs, which are fixed and do not vary with the size of the order. Total procurement costs vary, however, with the number of times the item is purchased. The greater the supply purchased at any one time, the less the yearly procurement costs. This is shown in Exhibit 9.7.

The two cost components vary in opposite directions. Large lots minimize procurement costs while maximizing storage costs. The opposite is true for small lots. Storage costs a minimum. Procurement costs a maximum.

EOQ Determination

The object of determining the EOQ is to minimize total variable costs. Since the axes of Exhibits 9.6 and 9.7 are identical, we can superimpose one upon the other in Exhibit 9.8. Doing so enables us to add the variable costs and show a total variable cost relationship to the quantity ordered.

The minimum variable total cost occurs at the intersection of the annual storage cost and annual procurement cost. At point A, both are equal. Dropping a perpendicular to QO determines point B, the EOQ. The solution to this problem is handled in the same manner as a breakeven analysis (see Chapter 11). As there is only one point common to both relationships, the formula determining these relationships can be set equal at this point. To accomplish this, let E equal EOQ in

EXHIBIT 9.8

Relation between total variable costs and quantity

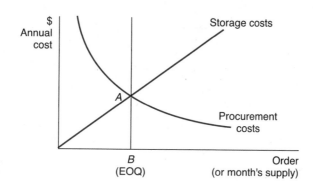

EXHIBIT 9.9

Formula used to determine EOQ

$$E = \sqrt{\frac{24P}{UI}}$$

terms of the number of months' supply to be ordered at any one time, U equal monthly dollar usage of items, P equal procurement costs in dollars, I equal inventory carrying costs per year expressed as a decimal of the total inventory costs per year. This gives us Exhibit 9.9.

Reorder Point

To properly manage inventory, you also need to know at what point to order the EOQ. That is, what quantity of inventory remaining signals the need to reorder? Two elements are important in this decision: (1) usage during lead time; and (2) safety stock desired. The combination of the two will determine the reorder point.

The definition of *lead time* is the time elapsed between the ordering of the goods and the physical delivery to the company. During this time, the company continues to use and draw down its inventory. Ideally, the moment the last unit is drawn out of storage, the new supply should be delivered. However, reality is not coincident with ideal, and operating as though it were would cause a firm to incur added costs when goods run out and production ceases.[17] It is necessary to carry a safety stock for use if the delivery of the new units of inventory is delayed or the production process and subsequent monthly usage vary.

To be certain of never running out, the company would have to carry an infinite supply. Plainly, this is impossible, but any supply less than infinite involves the risk of running out of goods and the attendant costs from lost sales and stopped production. The larger the risk a firm is willing to accept, the greater the possibility of running out.

From probability tables, a firm can choose the probability of running out and the risk it will accept. The firm decides the cost it is willing to bear and chooses the risk factor necessary. For example, you may assume that the probability of running

Exhibit 9.10

EOQ reorder point

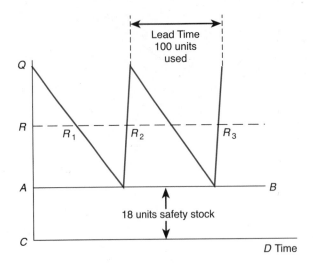

out of stock once in five years derived from probability tables is 1.8. The firm has previously calculated the cost of running out at different probability levels and has decided that it will maintain an inventory large enough to accomplish the goal of potentially running out of inventory only once in five years. Therefore, the P factor (the probability) will be used to modify the firm's safety stock. Running out less often will involve larger inventory and greater storage costs, which the firm is unwilling to bear. The firm has decided that the losses from cancellation of orders and delayed production are too great and that more frequent shortages are unacceptable. The equilibrium position is where the last dollar spent on maintaining the safety stock is equivalent to the last dollar saved. That is, on the marginal dollar, the cost of maintaining safety stock equals the cost of stockouts.

Practical experience has shown that the lead time usually varies by no more than the square root of the length of delivery time. The P factor is a modification of that variance accepted in accordance with the firm's desired goal. Thus, if for item A, usage during lead time equals 100 units, P equals 1.8 (expected frequency of stockouts once in five years), and R equals reorder point, the generalized expression for the reorder point is:

$$R = U + P \sqrt{L}$$

and the solution to utilizing the information given above is:

The firm reorders its EOQ when 118 items remain in stock. Exhibit 9.10 illustrates this.

Line *AB* shows what would occur if there were no safety stock. *CD* allows for delays and other unanticipated problems. Utilizing this safety stock allows production or sales to continue until new products or parts are delivered. The reorder point is constant, regardless of safety stock utilization.

Production Control

Necessity of Integration: Control and Planning of Facilities

In the past chapters, you have considered individual elements of the production process, such as people, materials, and machines. Unless these elements are integrated, your business cannot function as an organization.

Production/Operations

Operations are planned so that there will be a minimum number of delays and interruptions. Planning is also needed to provide management with the necessary feedback to determine whether or not the operations are progressing satisfactorily. Production/operations control coordinates the elements within the firm and produces information that management needs to determine progress, which permits management by exception.

The production control function is present in all firms, regardless of their size. In small firms the function may be performed by an individual, in large companies by a highly specialized department. Whatever the size of the organization, the duties of the function remain constant. Production/operations control must know and coordinate all the functions in the firm.

Production Control: Two Approaches

Production/operations control can be very general in approach or it can get very specific. The general approach, called **loading,** simply *assigns work to a facility.* In contrast, **scheduling** *specifies the time and sequence in which the work is to be done and develops a schedule for it.* Both methods of production control require complete knowledge of the productive process. Before you are able to load or schedule, you also must know the capacity of each production process, how long it will take to get the specific job done, material requirements, the current work load, and the operation sequence for each item. You must know how long it takes to make or buy each unit, from the beginning of the process until its completion. With this knowledge you can then balance work to be performed with the machinery, material, equipment, and people. An efficient organization will have everyone working in productive operations all the time. This plan is also important because it provides a yardstick against which progress can be measured. You are able to determine if the schedule is being met and then take corrective action if necessary.

Loading Techniques

Master Scheduling

Two general techniques are used to control the production process. **Master scheduling** *establishes a production schedule for the facility on a first-come, first-served basis.*[18] For example, if you own a small job shop printing business and you want to control production by establishing a schedule so that you can plan your time

SUPERB PRINTING CO.						
Capacity–weekly 80 hrs.					Minimum–weekly 16 hrs.	
	Week					
Job	1	2	3	4	5	6
1	18	14	9	12	24	8
2	9	16	15	6		
3	10	20	10	16		
4	30	12	18			
5	8					
6						

better, it might look like Exhibit 9.11. With this schedule, you will be able to plan personnel assignments and machinery time and determine delivery dates for customers.

In order to establish this schedule, you would need to know

1. Maximum hours available for work, which equals eighty (assume two shifts of an eight-hour day for five days);
2. Minimum number of job hours needed before you will even open for the week, which equals 16. Once you open, you must be able to cover your fixed costs.

To set up such a schedule you must take each job as it is called in and schedule it in whatever week the customer requires as long as you have available production capacity. You know how long each job takes from start to finish. You do not split jobs; that is, jobs begun in one week must be finished in the same week. Once you reach capacity for a specific week, the week is considered to be fully loaded and you then schedule work for the next week of production that has the required availability. Generally, each week is considered fully loaded at 80 to 85 percent capacity. You always leave a little slack for things like rush orders or machinery breakdowns. If everything works well and your slack time is not used, you can always do a job scheduled for the following week during the current week. You have to continually update the schedule anyway. In Exhibit 9.11, the first week, which is using 75 hours of work, is no longer available for scheduling work. Additional work can be accommodated only where there is a time slot. If a job requiring 30 hours of work had to be scheduled, delivery could not be promised before the end of week 4.

A number of PC-based computer programs can make this type of scheduling easier.[19] This approach is useful in a wide variety of firms such as copy shops or automobile repair facilities.

Exhibit 9.12

Perpetual loading

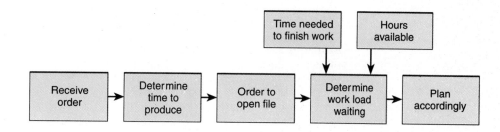

Exhibit 9.13

Gantt chart

Date	Week									
	1	2	3	4	5	6	7	8	9	10
3/4/95	//////	//////	//////	//////	////					
3/5/94	\\\\\\	\\\\\\	\\\\\\	\\\\\\	\\\\\\	\\\\\\	\\\\			

Weeks of tax returns to file, 1995 versus 1944.

Master scheduling is simple and easily understood. Its simplicity makes it easy to keep current. It can be manipulated to reschedule fairly easily. While providing an overall schedule, it doesn't give you any detailed information. The company knows that certain jobs will be accomplished in certain weeks, but not the sequence in which they will be completed nor the specific machinery and personnel used for each job.

Perpetual Loading

Perpetual loading *tabulates the time necessary to finish unfilled orders and determine how long it will take to finish this work.* If an accounting practice specializing in tax returns has 40 hours per week available and 200 hours of tax returns to file, it has 6.25 weeks of work to complete. Any tax returns desired by new clients could not be completed before the end of the sixth week. In tax season this would present a problem, and the accountant might want to hire some people so that all tax returns can be filed by the April 15 deadline. The procedure for perpetual loading is shown in Exhibit 9.12.

Gantt Chart

It might be very helpful to know how this year's work load compares to last year's for the same time period. If last year's demand showed more than 6.25 weeks of work, it might mean that demand had decreased. (One week, however, is not indicative of a trend.) This can be shown easily on a tool named after Henry Gantt, the **Gantt chart** which *shows work and how long it should take to be completed.* Exhibit 9.13 presents a typical Gantt chart.

Plotting the actual work against the forecasts would let you know whether your expectations were being met so that you could take appropriate actions. Perpetual loading is also easy to understand and maintain. It does not provide enough detail to specify the time and sequence in which the work is to be accomplished. A manufacturing plant could require more detail.

Performance Evaluation and Review Technique (PERT)

Another management production control device used is PERT, which is an acronym for Performance Evaluation and Review Technique.

PERT was developed by the Booz Allen & Hamilton Company, a management consulting firm, in connection with the Polaris program. Hence PERT—Polaris Evaluation and Rating Technique—was used to evaluate the Polaris missile program. The definition has broadened to new nomenclature, Program Evaluation and Review Technique. It is not only used in government but is required of all government contractors. Rather than being an entirely new technique, PERT actually represents a refinement of the flow chart analysis first developed by Henry Gantt.

PERT uses a sequential list of operations and the times required for each operation to establish an operations chart. This chart allows you to both plan and control. Once the plan is established, you can use it as a yardstick against which to measure actual accomplishments. This method can also be called the critical path method (CPM).

To construct a PERT network, let us use the example of a student who wants to plan his time to study for and take an examination. The first function of the PERT technique would be to develop a step-by-step plan to accomplish his purpose, as shown in Exhibit 9.14.

Exhibit 9.14 illustrates several facets of the PERT presentation: (1) necessary activities are identified; (2) relationships are shown; and (3) the required time to accomplish all tasks is identified.

The circles on the diagram signify events. An event takes no time itself. Events signify the completion of an activity. The activities are illustrated by arrows that show the direction in which the work is flowing. Attached to these activities is the time necessary to complete each one. Thus, an activity represents a specific task

EXHIBIT 9.14

PERT schematic describing studying for and taking an exam

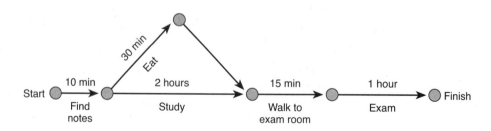

over a period of time and is bound by two events. The completion of the job or the final event in the chain is called the objective event.

The analysis of our example consists of three steps:

1. The building of the network to cover all the aspects of our problem's activities. This enables us to draw the diagram.
2. The evaluation of the plan, once it is drawn, to be sure that the steps included are reasonable and that the probability of their completion in the required time is high. In this step, any flaws in the plan should become evident. For instance, we may question the assumption that lecture notes can be found in 10 minutes.
3. The use of the plan to control the work as it proceeds. For example, eating should be finished 40 minutes after the start of the search for the lecture notes.

Thus, by checking the schematic it can be seen whether or not the student is on schedule. Adjustments then can be made accordingly.

The diagram reveals a complete picture of what must be achieved and the interrelationship of the various facets of the task. Additional information is acquired, since the time necessary for completion of each activity is also given. In this form of presentation it is easy to see problems that may develop and where the project design has been theoretical rather than practical. PERT contributes to good management by forcing the development of a clear, well-thought-out plan in advance. If the plan is not developed in advance, it cannot be diagrammed. Obviously, a diagram is much clearer and easier to understand than a written description.

Because PERT is universally applicable, you can use it to plan and diagram any job. Networks of this type may look extremely complicated; however, the theory behind any presentation is the same. Essentially, PERT is a schematic method of looking at a whole job or a task by showing the total area of concern. Its approach is to depict all the various activities necessary to complete a job from beginning to end. It also shows the relationship of these activities to one another. From these relationships and the time values attached, it is easy to calculate the total time necessary to complete the project.

Because PERT is a schematic of the project, it is possible to use the PERT system as a control device, comparing results to the plan. If the actual results do not agree with the PERT plan, the plan is changed. Thus, PERT is a planning technique, which provides its own control points. The purpose of control points is to serve the plan by identifying any disparity between actual and planned results. When planned and actual results differ, the plan must be changed.

Work Design and Work Measurement: Motion and Time Study

Several techniques management uses to establish performance standards against which to measure work fall under the heading of motion and time study. These techniques focus primarily on direct labor. The objectives of **motion study** are *to* *establish the best way to accomplish a task;* those of a **time study** are to *establish how much time it should take to accomplish the task.* In general, management's goal is to simplify work and arrive at a standard by which progress can be measured.

To differentiate further, motion study is done to eliminate ineffective and wasteful motions. Its objective is to find easier and simpler ways of performing a task. The general term motion study includes not only the motions employed by workers in performing their job but also other facets of the job such as the methods, tools, and materials used. Time study is the process of systematically recording, analyzing, and synthesizing the times required to perform a task. Time and motion study is an important management tool.

Planning and Control Techniques

Job Categories and Techniques

There are specific techniques that may be used in controlling and measuring the operations process. For ease of discussion we will break the job situation into two categories and discuss the techniques used in each. The categories are:

1. Interjob. This concerns itself with movements or operations between workstations. The following techniques can be used in this situation.
    a. Process chart
    b. Flow process chart
2. Intrajob. This concerns itself with movements or operations at a specific work station. The following techniques can be used in this situation:
    a. Simo-chart (operator or left hand/right hand chart)
    b. Man-machine chart
    c. Multiple activity chart

Process Chart

When you are focusing on a complete operation, the best approach to use is process analysis. Here the entire process is studied in an effort to determine if it is being performed in the most efficient manner. This overall analysis is done before segments of the process are analyzed. If the overall analysis were not done first, time might be spent in changing segments of the process that may be eliminated. The tool used to analyze the overall operation, called a process chart, is useful in banks, insurance companies, and financial firms in addition to manufacturing firms. It can be used efficiently to identify and control paper and information flows. Retail firms find it useful, particularly when dealing with perishable foods to prevent spoilage.

Using standardized symbols, the **process chart** *simulates on paper the operation under analysis*. The symbols used are recommended by the American Society of Mechanical Engineers:

$$O = \text{Operation}$$

This signifies that something is being done to a part or a product. An activity is being performed.

$$\Rightarrow = \text{Transportation}$$

This signifies movement of something from one location to another. It may be either the material that is being moved or it may be the worker who is moving.

$$\square = \text{Inspection}$$

This signifies a check being made on the product to determine if it meets a previously determined standard.

$$D = \text{Delay}$$

This signifies that the process has been stopped or delayed.

$$\nabla = \text{Storage}$$

This signifies that the product has been stored either to wait for another step in the process to be completed or to prevent unauthorized use.

It is a relatively simple matter using the above symbols to describe any production process. Exhibit 9.15 is a process chart that describes an existing situation in a garment factory.

Exhibit 9.15 provides an accurate and succinct record of the process. Note that there are totals given for each symbol. Thus the way to improve the production process would be to minimize all activities not adding to the product value. This means that all activities other than "operations" should be decreased. Doing so would decrease the time spent on the entire operation. Additional information such as how long it takes to perform each operation or the distance traveled to and from storage may be added if required. Any improvements in the process would make it more efficient. After studying the process, a new procedure was developed, as shown in Exhibit 9.16.

Notice that the new procedure has three operations, five transportations, four storages, one inspection, and zero delays. The present procedures had four operations, six transportations, five storages, one inspection, and one delay.

Note that a comparison between the present and the proposed procedures shows:

Exhibit 9.15

Flow chart—present method

	●	→	▲	■	◗	
(1)	●					RECEIVE ON ELEVATOR FROM WASHING
(2)		→				TO TEMPORARY STORAGE AREA
(3)			▲			STORE
(4)		→				TO SEPARATORS
(5)	●					SEPARATE
(6)		→				TRIM COMPLETED – SENT TO CUTTING ROOM
(7)			▲			STORED IN CUTTING
(8)		→				BODIES & SLEEVES SENT TO STEAMING
(9)			▲			TEMPORARY STORAGE
(10)	●					STEAM
(11)		→				TO CUTTING
(12)			▲			STORE
(13)				■		TO SEE IF ALL PIECES READY FOR PROCESSING
(14)					◗	CUTTING DISCOVERS INCORRECT TRIM
(15)	●					SEPARATE RIGHT TRIM
(16)						TO CUTTING
(17)			▲			TO CUTTING TEMPORARY STORAGE TILL WORKED AGAIN
TOTAL	4	6	5	1	1	

Exhibit 9.16

Flow chart—proposed method

	●	→	▲	■	◗	
(1)	●					RECEIVE ON ELEVATOR FROM WASHING
(2)		→				TO TEMPORARY STORAGE AREA
(3)			▲			STORE
(4)		→				TO SEPARATORS
(5)	●					SEPARATE
(6)		→				TRIM COMPLETED – SENT TO CUTTING ROOM
(7)			▲			TRIM STORED IN CUTTING ROOM
(8)		→				BODIES & SLEEVES SENT TO STEAMING
(9)			▲			TEMPORARY STORAGE
(10)	●					STEAM
(11)		→				TO CUTTING ROOM
(12)			▲			STORE IN CUTTING
(13)				■		TO SEE IF ALL PIECES READY FOR PROCESSING
TOTAL	3	5	4	1	0	

	Present	*Proposed*
Operation	4	3
Transportation	6	5
Storage	5	4
Inspection	1	1
Delay	1	0

The total savings are two operations, one transportation, one storage, and one delay. The new procedure accomplishes the same task as the old, but in fewer steps. It is more efficient and economical than the old method. Knowledge of how to change the procedure stems from the use of a general questioning approach and the knowledge of the process. You must study the process itself before you can suggest any improvements.

Earlier in this chapter we were concerned with principles and techniques that could make work easier and simpler. Attention was focused on identifying and standardizing the best method that could be used to accomplish the task with no attention paid to determining how long it should take an employee to do the job. The next step is to determine how long it should take the worker to accomplish his or her task. A time study will enable us to answer this question. The objective of time study is to arrive at an accurate, objective, and scientific standard that will permit a measure of labor. All firms, large and small, must measure labor if they are to identify and control costs. Banks, insurance companies, and automobile repair shops are a few examples.

Direct (Watch) Time Study

Direct (watch) time study is *a procedure using a stopwatch to time a task*. It is an accurate systematic and scientific method to determine the time it should take an employee to accomplish a task. The time-study engineer uses a stopwatch to time the employee on the production floor. With the information derived, a norm then can be established for the job.

Predetermined Time Standards

Predetermined time standards *are determined by using known times for all tasks in a job in order to determine how long it should take to complete it*. They are based upon the idea that there are only so many basic motion patterns. Thus, any activity or job would be the result of particular combinations of these motions. After observing many different activities an analyst can segregate such basic motions as **grasp,** *the motion that takes place when a hand or body part touches an object and* *takes control of it,* or **assemble,** *the action that takes place when parts are put together, or caused to be put together by the operator.* (Frank and Lillian Gilbreth defined 17 basic motion patterns, postulating that any job was a combination of these patterns, called "Therbligs." Essentially, this means that if basic times for these motions are known, a job can be timed by the relatively simple task of analyzing the motions necessary for completion without using a stopwatch or even going on the production floor to observe the process.

Predetermined standards are useful because the time necessary for a particular job can be discovered in advance. The firm can then make estimates and bids for new work because it is now able to predict material, manpower, machinery, and capital costs in advance.

Quality

Quality is *that combination of attributes commensurate with the price of a product or service that the customer expects.*[20] It may be defined by engineering specifications or consumer expectations.

As automobile manufacturers in the United States discovered, it is not enough to produce a product; the product must be a quality product offered at a competitive price. The watchword of today's firms must be quality, for unacceptable quality reduces sales and profits. It may also be responsible for a firm's failure, since customers will not buy inferior products. Much of today's emphasis on quality and quality control stems from the work of Dr. W. Edwards Deming, a leading figure in the development of quality control, whose theories were adopted by Japanese industry following World War II and have now been enthusiastically embraced in the United States.[21]

While much of Deming's initial work was concerned with manufacturing operations, today's markets demand a constant adherence to quality at all times by all firms. It is just as important for a hotel, dry cleaner, automobile repair shop, or accounting firm to maintain quality as it is for the traditional manufacturing firms.

> Rewards and incentives are tied to measures of customer satisfaction. And it is almost impossible to check out of a hotel, pay for a restaurant meal, or hire a car without being asked to rate the vendor's customer service.[22]

In fact, the watchword today is total quality management. **TQM** is *"a process for continuous change and improvement in everything an organization does."*[23]

TQM requires a continual commitment from everyone in the organization to improve the process involved in creating the product or service sold. Done properly, TQM involves giving people responsibility for performing their job in the best way. Small business must allow employees to contribute to the quality process. Employees must be true participants in the business. According to Deming, the people best suited to improving the job are the ones doing the job.

While it is more difficult to measure a service organization's quality than a manufacturing firm's, measures have been defined and the process in true TQM fashion is continuing to refine service measurements. For example, how many complaints does a dry cleaner get? How many checkpoints does a motel use to measure room cleanliness? These and measures like them make it possible to define quality for all firms. The quest for quality cannot and should not stop. It is a continuous job. Without this commitment, firms will fall behind in today's market.

Necessity for Inspection

Once the basic decisions have been made about the product and how to go about making or providing it, quality standards are expressed. These include engineering drawings and specifications in the case of a manufacturing enterprise or measures of quality such as number of callbacks in an automobile service firm or returns to a dry cleaner. These "specs" are the yardstick against which the product or service is measured to ensure that the production/operations process is producing the desired output.

Production/operations variability, *the variation in the attributes of products and services because of chance occurrences,* causes the firm to produce products where attributes are not identical to specifications. Inspection shows whether the performance measures up to standards. Ideally, the firm would inspect up to the point where cost of inspection equals the savings from inspection.[24]

Statistical Quality Control

Statistical quality control involves using control charts. These charts show expected and actual performance. Statistical quality control is at the heart of Deming's philosophy and the TQM concept. **Statistical quality control** *analyses samples whose attributes reveal the quality of the operation process.* As described, the primary purpose of inspection is to identify whether the quality of the product falls within certain specifications. Otherwise, the product will not be acceptable. It is necessary to specify limits, since it is impossible to produce each and every unit to exact specifications. Any operation varies because of chance occurrences. Tools wear, raw materials vary, employees become fatigued, and machines slip.

Use of Control Charts

Using statistical reasoning too complex for this text, we can derive a traditional control chart. This chart will show whether the production/operation process is producing goods or services within an acceptable range of variability. Variations within acceptable limits generally fall in an area around a specified or accepted level of performance, bounded by upper and lower control limits.

For example, if a service business were willing to accept an average of two complaints per hour, our control chart could be illustrated as shown in Exhibit 9.17.

The control chart would be used to analyze operations of the business. As long as the number of complaints falls into the area bounded by the upper and lower

Exhibit 9.17
Control chart

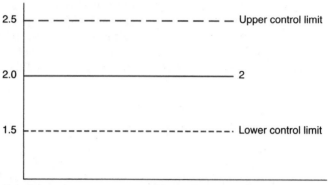

Control chart using two customer complaints per hour as sample average.

control limits, no corrective action would be required. When the operation/production process showed complaints falling outside the control limits, corrective action would be needed.

Summary

The Interrelationship between the Production/Operations Function and Other Business Plan Components

The relationship between the production/operations function and other functional areas of the firm is critical. Although marketing defines the products to be sold, decisions regarding how to produce the product may make the difference between profit and loss. The technology of producing goods or services will affect the product itself. The nature and the extent of the production function itself has a significant impact on the personnel needed and their necessary compensation; resources necessary to support the production/operations decisions can be obtained through the activities of the finance function.

Production/Operations

The main function of any business firm is to create **utility,** *a good or service that is of some value to the purchaser or final consumer,* and make a profit from its sale. To do this, you must understand that all firms need **capital,** *the physical assets of the company, such as machinery, equipment or plant,* to support the **production/operation process,** which *converts inputs into outputs.*

Inventory

Inherent in the question of utility creation is the concept of how to manage the necessary raw materials and parts needed to produce the final product. In order to be profitable, the costs of this inventory must be minimized. **Materials requirements planning (MRP),** *the* *tool used to control the process and ensure its efficiency,* is useful in this process. The **JIT** approach *delivers inventory in the production process when it is needed.*

EOQ

While looking at the question of inventory control, it is necessary to understand the concept of **EOQ,** the *amount of goods whose total costs are at a minimum,* and how you arrive at the quantity by balancing **carrying costs,** *those costs associated with ordering, receiving, inspecting, and storing materials* and **procurement costs,** which are made up of *requisition costs, follow-up tasks, and payment of invoices.*

Capacity Control

Once these decisions are made and the decision is made to produce goods or services, it is important to keep track of and control the production/operations process itself. We define the differences between **loading,** which simply *assigns work to a facility,* and **specific production control,** which *specifies the time and sequence in which the work is to be done and develops a schedule for it.* Some control techniques use **specific production controls** to *coordinate the factors of production so that the work flows through the plant in the most efficient manner.* These include **master scheduling,** which *establishes a production schedule for the facility on a first-come, first-served basis;* **perpetual loading,** which *tabulates the time necessary to finish unfilled orders and determines how long it will take to finish this work;* **Gantt charts,** which *show work and how long it will take to complete such work;* and **PERT,** which stands for *Performance Evaluation and Review Technique.*

Work Measurement

Inseparable from the questions of the production process are the questions of how to produce the product in the best way and in the least time. Overall **motion study,** which *establishes the best way to accomplish a task,* and **time study** which *establishes how much time it should take to accomplish the task,* answer these questions. The **process chart** *simulates on paper the operation under analysis,* and the **flow process chart,** a *process chart superimposed on a floor plan of your manufacturing business.* The methodology of time study requires us to understand the difference between a **direct watch study,** a *procedure using a stopwatch to time a task,* and **predetermined time standards,** which are *determined by using known times for all tasks in a job to determine how long it should take to complete the job.* This requires direct observation where predetermined standards build jobs from basic motion patterns such as **grasp,** the *motion that takes place when a hand or body part touches an object,* and **assemble,** the *action that takes place when parts are put together, or caused to be put together by the operator.*

Quality

The operations process requires close attention to **quality,** *that combination of attributes commensurate with the price of a product or service that the customer expects.* Today, **TQM,** *the process for continuous change and improvement,* is the concept most valued by management. We can use **statistical quality control** which is *the inspection procedure utilizing mathematical techniques and probability theory* to mitigate **production/operations variability,** which is *the variation in the attributes of products because of chance occurrences.*

Questions

1. Define the production process.
2. Discuss the difference, if any, between operations management and production management.
3. Describe the operations/production process for the following:
   (a) A university.
   (b) A hospital.
   (c) An insurance company.
   (d) A razor blade manufacturer.
4. What is the difference in the operations process between a manufacturing firm and a service firm?
5. It has often been said that a purchasing department is a burden cost and thus cannot contribute to the bottom line or profitability of the firm. Is this a true statement? Support your answer.
6. The timing of purchase decisions is important. Why?
7. Describe the components of total inventory costs.
8. Define *economic order quantity*. How does it minimize total inventory costs?
9. Define *reorder point*. Why is it important?
10. What is lead time?
11. How do you determine reorder points?
12. Compare inventory policies required by:
    (a) A manufacturer.
    (b) A retail store.
    (c) A service firm.
    (d) A wholesale firm.
13. Define *production/operations control*. Why is this concept important?
14. Define *scheduling* and *loading*. Comment on the similarities and differences between the two approaches.
15. Define the terms *master scheduling* and *perpetual loading*.
16. PERT is both a planning and a control technique. Defend or refute this statement.
17. Define *statistical quality control*. Is this a better control mechanism than 100 percent inspection?
18. Two techniques used to establish performance standards are time and motion study. Define these terms.

Application Exercises

When doing these exercises, where applicable, be sure to select a specific business, preferably one where you presently or previously worked or a business you would like to own someday. If this is not possible, pick a specific organization to which you will refer. Be sure to identify the organization by name. Limit your answers to one or two pages per exercise.

1. Interview a local real estate broker.
    (a) Define the broker's production/operations process.
    (b) Define "quality control" as used in broker's operations process.
    (c) What is the importance of inventory? Does the broker have any control over inventory?
    (d) Can you set time standards for the broker's operation? Develop a chart showing the various steps in the brokerage process and the time required to complete each step.
2. Visit a local manufacturing firm and define its production/operations process. Then:
    (a) Define *quality control* as used in the operations process.
    (b) What is the importance of inventory? Does the manufacturer have any control over the inventory?
3. Using the information from questions 1 and 2, identify the inputs, process, and outputs.

Application Situations

1. Paula Cromwell

Having owned a dog all her life, Paula Cromwell was attracted by an article in *The Wall Street Journal* that stated, "The care and feeding of animals is a big business." Liking animals, Paula decided to start a retail pet supply store. She found a good location in a local strip mall and for the past several years has seen her gross revenues rise 40 percent per year. However, in reviewing her financials, she found that she can't make a reasonable profit. Despite rising sales and her policy of buying inventory when she needs it, there always seems to be too much inventory remaining of products not wanted by customers.

Recently Paula requested that a student consulting team from a local university review her operation and make recommendations that would lead to profitability. The student team thought her problem was caused by her lack of attention to purchasing and inventory control.

Assignment

1. Why is purchasing important and how can it contribute to profitability?
2. What suggestions do you think the team made concerning economic order quantities and reorder points?
3. How could Paula implement the suggestions?

2. Steiner Boat Works

Whenever possible, Saul Steiner would take a break from his prestigious job as a vice president of a large advertising firm and go sailing. While sailing, he felt that he could relax and think. One day he decided to change his career to become a builder of small wooden sailboats.

Saul started building his boats only on the basis of firm orders. Each boat was handcrafted. All wood was carefully cut and fitted with care and precision. It was sanded, varnished, polished, and waxed. As demand increased, Saul hired other workers who shared his desire for and dedication to quality.

Seven years after the business began, increased demand forced him to start manufacturing the boats using assembly line techniques and production-type workers. Saul was hesitant about using productions workers, since he was afraid that his quality would suffer.

Assignment

1. Does the firm's growth make quality control easier or harder? Explain.
2. How can Saul build quality control practices into the production line?
3. Will Saul's approach to quality increase, decrease, or not have any effect on profits?

3. Owens Sweaters

Owens Sweaters, a local garment manufacturer, is having trouble making timely deliveries to customers. While all sweaters go through the same production process—knit, cut, sew, finish, pack, and ship—Betty Owens cannot seem to keep track of the production process.

Assignment

1. What production control methods would you recommend to Betty? Name and define the four types of production control techniques.
2. Prepare a production control plan for the Owens Company.

4. Corkum Realty

Corkum Realty owns and operates six large apartment houses. Vinny Green, the maintenance supervisor, is responsible for maintenance of 196 apartments. He and his staff of eight janitors do the best they can but are continually behind because, as they say, "Maintenance jobs are totally different from other jobs. Anything that can go wrong will and who knows when it will happen or how long it will take to fix it."

Assignment

1. Is the above statement true? Why or why not?
2. Can the principles of time and motion study be helpful? How would you recommend that Vinny implement these techniques?

Integrated Case Question—CorLu Foods

Prepare the inventory control system for CorLu. Make sure to indicate how to arrive at minimum inventory costs; how to control inventory and how to assure quality of products and service offered to customers. (Please refer to the Integrated Case "CorLu Foods.")

Additional Readings

Adam, Everett E., and Paul M. Swamidass. "Assessing Operations Management from a Strategic Perspective." *Journal of Management* 15, no. 2 (1989), pp. 181–203.

Bandyopadhyay, Jayanta K. "Product Design to Facilitate JIT Production." *Production and Inventory Management* 31, no. 4 (1990), pp. 71–76.

Berry, William L.; William J. Tallon; and Warren J. Boe. "Product Structure Analysis for the Master Scheduling of Assemble-to-Order Products." *International Journal of Operations & Production* 12, no. 11 (1992), pp. 24–41.

Bolwijn, P. T., and T. Kumpe. "Manufacturing in the 1990s—Productivity, Flexibility and Innovation." *Long Range Planning* 23, no. 4 (August 1990), pp. 44–57.

Bregman, Robert L. "Selecting among MRP Lot-Sizing Methods for Purchased Components When the Planning Horizon Is Limited." *Production & Inventory Management Journal* 32, no. 2 (1991), pp. 32–39.

Cavinato, Joseph. "Managing Different Types of Inventory." *Distribution,* March 1990, pp. 88–92.

———. "Textbook Approaches to Inventory Control." *Distribution,* May 1990, pp. 96, 98.

Chapman, Tim, and Doug Valenti. "Inventory and Purchasing: How to Achieve the Best Practice." *Public Utilities Fortnightly,* August 15, 1992, pp. 19–20.

Ernst & Young Quality Improvement Consulting Group. *Total Quality: An Executive's Guide for the 1990s.* Homewood, Ill.: Dow Jones–Irwin, 1990.

Evans, J. R., and W. M. Lindsay. *The Management and Control of Quality,* 2nd ed. St. Paul Minn.: West Publishing Co., 1992.

Fagan, Mark L. "Merging Purchasing with Inventory Management." *Purchasing World,* July 1990, pp. 54–55.

Fawcett, Stanley E., and Laura M. Cirou. "Just-in-Time Sourcing Techniques: Current State of Adoption and Performance Benefits" *Production & Inventory Management Journal,* First Quarter 1993, pp. 18–24.

Finkin, Eugene F. "How to Limit Inventory Expenses," *Journal of Business Strategy,* January/February 1989, pp. 50–53.

Frankel, Alan N. "When It's Not a Capital Idea, Leasing Pays Off." *Quality* 30, no. 4 (April 1989), pp. 16–19.

Gray, Clifford F. "An Integrated Methodology for Dynamic Labor Productivity Standards, Performance Control and System Audit in Warehouse Operations." *Production & Inventory Management Journal* 33, no. 3, (1992) pp. 63–67.

Gumpert, David E. "Doing More with Less." *Working Woman* 17, no. 3, (September 1992), p. 55.

"Inventory Unwelcome in '93," *Purchasing* 114, no. 2 (February), p. 22.

Hum, Sin Hoon, and Rakesh K. Sarin. "Simultaneous Product-Mix Planning, Lot Sizing and Scheduling at Bottleneck Facilities." *Operations Research* 39, no. 2, (March/April 1991), pp. 296–307.

Kanet, John J. "Real Decision Support for Production Scheduling and Control." *Production & Inventory Management* 11, no. 9, (1991), pp. 24–25.

Lankford, Ray. "Capacity Management in Complex Production Environments." *Producing & Inventory Management Review & APICS News* 10, no. 5, pp. 40–45.

Levine, Zvi A., and Boaz Ronen. "The Component Chart: A New Tool for Inventory, Purchasing, and Production Decisions." *Production and Inventory Management* 31, no. 1 (1990), pp. 8–12.

Lines, Anthony. "Inventories: The State of the Art." *Accountancy* 104, no. 1153, (September 1989), p. 130.

May, Jerrold H.; William E. Spangler; Richard E. Wendell; and Hartmut U. Zaun. "A Knowledge-Based Approach for Improving Information and Decision Making in a Small Business." *Information & Management* 21, no. 3 (October 1991), pp. 177–89.

Misterek, Susan D.A.; Kevin J. Dooley; and John C. Anderson. "Productivity as a Performance Measure," *International Journal of Operations & Production Management* 12, no. 1, (1992), pp. 29–45.

Port, Otis. "Quality: Small and Mid-Size Companies Seize the Challenge—Not a Moment Too Soon." *Business Week,* November 30, 1992, p. 66.

Pritsker, A. Alan B. "Capacity Management: The DNA of Manufacturing Systems," *APICS the Performance Advantage* 1, no. 4, (1991), pp. 4–5.

Rosander, Kurt. "Design of Production Systems for Batch Production in Short Series to Reduce Lead Time." *International Journal of Operations & Production* 12, no. 4, (1992) pp. 53–60.

Rubenowitz, Sigvard. "The Role of Management in Production Units with Autonomous Work Groups," *International Journal of Operations & Production* 12, no. 7, 8 (1992), pp. 103–16.

Seal, Gregory M. "1990's—Years of Promise, Years of Peril for U.S. Manufacturers." *Industrial Engineering,* January 1990, pp. 18–31.

Shin, Dooyoung, and Hokey Min. "Uniform Assembly Line Balancing with Stochastic Task Times in Just-in-Time Manufacturing," *International Journal of Operations & Production* 11, no. 8 (1991), pp. 23–34.

"Should You Lease Equipment or Buy It Outright?" *Profit-Building Strategies for Business Owners* 22, no. 5, (May), pp. 4–5.

Totuki, Akira. "Management Style for Tomorrow's Needs." *Journal of Business Logistics* 11, 2, (1990), pp. 1–4.

Treece, James B. "A Little Bit of Smarts, a Lot of Hard Work." *Business Week,* November 30, 1992, p. 70.

Wall, Toby D.; J. Martin Corbett; Robin Martin; Chris W. Clegg; and Paul R. Jackson. "Advance Manufacturing Technology, Work Design, and Performance: A Change Study." *Journal of Applied Psychology* 75, no. 6 (December 1990), pp. 691–97.

Willis, T. Hillman, and Jerry D. Shields. "Modifying the ABC Inventory System for a Focused Factory." *Industrial Engineering* 22, no. 5 (May 1990), pp. 38–39, 73.

Wu, Jack Andin, and Nesa L'abbe Wu. "Productivity Management of Indirect Labour through Variable Work Measurement and Control." *International Journal of Operations & Production Management* 11, no. 8 (1991), pp. 48–58.

Endnotes

1. "Building an International Business on Man-Made Rocks," *The Wall Street Journal,* September 10, 1991, p. B2.
2. John H. Sheridan, "Suppliers: Partners in Prosperity," *Industry Week,* March 19, 1990, p. 4.
3. "Close Ties with Suppliers Can Pay for Small Firms," *The Wall Street Journal,* April 3, 1991, p. B1.

4. Warren Rose, "Inventory Control," in Waltho Beacham, Richard T. Hise, and Hal N. Tungrien, *Beacham's Marketing Reference* (Washington, D.C.: Research Publishing, 1986), p. 430.
5. Nicholas Siropolis, *Small Business Management,* 4th ed. (Boston: Houghton Mifflin, 1990), p. 527.
6. E. A. Silver, and R. Paterson, *Decision Systems for Inventory Management and Production Planning,* 2nd ed. (New York: John Wiley, 1985).
7. Charlotte S. Stephens, William N. Ledbetter, and James L. Eddy, "The Best of Both Worlds: A Mainframe and Microcomputer-Based MRP-II System," *Production and Inventory Management Journal,* Third Quarter, 1990, pp. 35–41.
8. Basheier M. Khumawala, Charles Hixon, and Japhet S. Law, "MRP II in the Service Industries," *Production and Inventory Management* 27, no. 3 (1986), pp. 52–63.
9. John M. Burnham, "Some Conclusions about JIT Manufacturing," *Production and Inventory Management* 28, no. 3 (1987), pp. 7–11.
10. "Measuring Inventory Performance to Improve Profitability," *Manufacturing Insights,* November 1990 (Coopers & Lybrand Cincinnati Management Consulting Services).
11. "Wal-Mart Plans 'Just-in-Time' Delivery System," *Birmingham* (Alabama) *Post Herald,* February 14, 1989, p. B1.
12. Leon C. Megginson, Donald C. Mosley, and Paul H. Pietri, Jr., *Management: Concepts and Applications,* 4th ed. (New York: HarperCollins, 1992), p. 662.
13. Julianne Slovak, "Companies to Watch: Kimball International," *Fortune,* March 12, 1990, p. 90.
14. For an example of the use of intuition, see "Bush as the Nation's Manager," *USA Today,* February 8, 1991, pp. 1B and 2B.
15. John H. Blackstone, and James F. Cox, "Inventory Management Techniques," *Journal of Small Business Management,* April 1985, pp. 27–33.
16. National Association of Purchasing Management, *Aljuan's Purchasing Handbook* (New York: McGraw-Hill, 1982), pp. 12–17.
17. "Rarely Just in Time," *Small Business Reports,* April 1990, p. 12.
18. APICS Training Aid, *Master Production Scheduling* (Washington, D.C.: American Production and Inventory Control Society).
19. Stephens, Ledbetter, and Eddy, "The Best of Both Worlds."
20. George H. Labovitz, and Yu Sang Chang, "Learn From the Best," *Quality Progress,* May 1990, pp. 81–85.
21. W. Edwards Deming, *The New Economics for Industry, Government, Education,* (Cambridge, Mass.: MIT, Center for Advanced Studies, 1993).
22. Gary Harnell, and C. K. Prahalad, "Seeing the Future First," *Fortune,* September 5, 1994, p. 67.
23. E. I. Dupont de Nemours & Co., Inc., *Profiles in Quality: Blueprints for Action from 50 Leading Companies* (Boston: Allyn and Bacon, 1991), p. 25.
24. Steve Wernick, "TQM Keys Job Shop Profitability, Survival," *Quality,* May 1991, pp. 14–17.

10 THE HUMAN RESOURCES/ PERSONNEL FUNCTION

Staffing is one of the most important aspects of any business, particularly for small firms, which, by their nature, tend to be labor intensive and cannot exist without the appropriate people.[1] The human resources/personnel function in your organization involves all aspects of managing the people who work in your business. These tasks include:

1. Personnel planning
2. Job analysis
3. Job evaluation
4. Compensation
5. Recruiting and selecting (hiring)
6. Orienting and training
7. Legal aspects
8. Benefits

Chapter Learning Objectives

In this chapter you will consider different issues involved in staffing your business. You should be able to define the following 10 key terms in order of their appearance:

Personnel function	Internal consistency
Personnel planning	External consistency
Job description	Staffing
Job specifications	Recruiting
Job evaluations	Promotion

The Interrelationship between the Human Resources/Personnel Function and the Other Business Plan Components

Viewing business as a system, it is evident that the functional areas, which include marketing, production, personnel, finance and accounting, are interrelated. Changes in any one area impact and exert change on the others. Once you decide what you want your business to be and who your customers are, you must then determine the size of your market. Market size, in turn, dictates the machinery and equipment you need to produce the product or services you are selling. Once you know what you are producing and how it is produced, you can determine personnel needs.

Actually, you are really making this determination while you are making decisions about production and organizational structure. In an ideal situation, the personnel function will be able to recruit enough of the appropriate talent to operate your organization. Conversely, personnel can influence other functional areas. For example, if you wanted to locate a high-technology firm, you would probably choose an area such as Boston or San José because of the concentration of suitable employees. Lack of workers could also impact on your location, or, in some cases, the production technology you might use. Compensating your employees requires the finance function to supply the required resources. Accounting keeps track of all payroll and benefits and the size, and complexity of its task is directly related to the number of employees. You cannot produce anything without people, and the need for people stems from your production requirements. These requirements are determined externally. Internally, you keep track of, and pay people, through the accounting function.

There are also a number of federal laws requiring specific record keeping, such as having the Immigration and Naturalization Service's I-9 forms on file for every employee or records of required benefits such as Social Security, Workers' Compensation and unemployment.

Personnel Planning

As an entrepreneur or small business owner you expect your business to grow and prosper by selling more goods and services and at the same time see it become relatively more complex to manage. A growing firm will require not only more people to meet increasing demands but also more skilled, knowledgeable, and trained personnel to handle new tasks. If your business is to be efficient and profitable, people must be recruited, trained, compensated, and managed, but too few business owners carry out adequate or timely planning. Many hesitate adding more employees but rather demand that employees work overtime and weekends if necessary. This strategy not only causes "employee burnout" but it also makes your firm less efficient and unable to meet the demand for its products or services. Even if demand is met, the resulting products are likely to be late in delivery or of poor quality or both.[2]

Therefore, as a business owner, you should plan ahead so that you know the number of employees you will need, when you will need them, and the skills you will demand of them. Since it is highly unusual for a new employee to have exactly the skills and background you need in your business, you should establish a human resource staffing plan.[3]

If you are operating a retail store, a staffing plan could be based upon the dollar value of sales per employee. For example, last year your sales were $250,000 and you employed five people. Your average sales per person was $50,000 and the sales volume had all employees working at full capacity. Thus, when sales increase to $300,000, you should anticipate adding another employee. Thus, each employee would still equal $50,000 in sales. If your sales increase to $350,000, you will need two more people. Once you create a pro forma (see Chapter 12), you can predict how many employees you will need in the future. In recession periods, projected demand also tells you how many employees you may have to lay off in order to remain profitable. Sales dollars need not be the only criterion; you might use units sold or any other measure that enables you to determine employment levels. A personnel planning chart might look like the following:

	Sales Personnel Needed	
Sales Volume	Year	New Hires
$250,000	1994	5
300,000	1995	6
350,000	1996	7
450,000	1996	10

Before you hire new people, however, make certain that the organization is operating efficiently. It may be that you can schedule the work load more efficiently with the same number of people. You don't always have to hire new people as sales increase.

Job Analysis

Each job to be filled must be analyzed and its requirements specified so that when you hire, you know what has to be done and what requirements (training or skills) are needed for the people who will fill the job. A **job description** specifies *the duties and requirements of the job.* **Job specifications** set forth *the specific skills and training of the people hired to perform the job functions.* A job description is what the worker does; a job specification is who the worker is. Both terms fall under the overall heading of job analysis.

Once the job is so defined, it becomes easy to evaluate whether the worker is performing the exact job required and has the appropriate qualifications. People who are carrying out the annual reviews for every employee need this information as a yardstick for performance evaluation. It is also much easier to know what to pay an employee once you know what job he or she is performing. These topics will be covered later on in this chapter.

Job Descriptions

Job analysis describes both the worker and the job so that there are no questions about who is doing what within your firm. Job descriptions specify the technical requirements of the job.

A proper job description involves complete knowledge of the job being analyzed.[4] Later on when the wage is set, the duties a person is paid for performing are clear.

Job Specifications

The other facet of job analysis involves describing the personal characteristics necessary to fill the job. Exhibit 10.1 illustrates a job description and specifications for a database development manager.

When the job analysis is complete, you should interview and strive to hire only those people possessing the characteristics the job requires.[5] If your company is big enough to be specialized, the screening function is handled by the personnel department or the appropriate person making hiring decisions. As a general rule, it is not a good practice to hire people whose capabilities are greater than or less than

---

Exhibit 10.1   Sample job description and classification

Database Development Manager   Systems and Services Division

Specific Responsibilities:

Manage Development Staff; analyze and implement database systems, RECOLL, FDIC, and FMRC; work with RECOLL analysis and users to develop business/technical specifications; learn new technologies to assist in other development projects.

Qualifications Required:

3-5 years project management experience, preferably in a systems area; experience developing relational databases, preferably "DataEase" and other PC based software; excellent communications skills; highly motivated; knowledge of I/S programming standards; strong systems integration experience.

Recruiting Salary: ($42,700 - $56,000)   Grade E9   REQ #954

demanded, since the overqualified are likely to quickly become bored and frustrated and will soon leave to seek a more appropriate fit. This is a primary reason why highly qualified engineers who have been laid off in a government defense cutback have difficulty finding jobs; they are overqualified for the majority of available positions. A person whose qualifications are below what the job requires will not be able to meet production requirements. Not only will there be a loss in productivity, but what is produced frequently may be defective. A person who doesn't leave on his or her own could soon be fired.

Job Evaluation

Once the job analysis has been performed, the job evaluation performs two necessary functions. **Job evaluation** is *the process of determining the relative value of each job to the company.* It must ensure that wages are internally and externally consistent.[6] **Internal consistency** means that *high-worth jobs (to the company) get paid more than low-worth jobs, and that there are clear relationships between jobs.* **External consistency** means that *the pay structure corresponds to the community wage structure.* Although collective bargaining and additional subjective issues can enter into the setting of wages, it should not disturb the internal job structure. Exhibit 10.2 illustrates the principle of internal consistency. Line *AB* shows:

1. The relationship between pay and value of the job to the company.
2. The relationship between jobs.

Since all jobs are related to pay and to each other, the structure depicted in Exhibit 10.2 is internally consistent. The external consistency is shown by the location of *AB* on the diagram. As long as line *AB* has the same slope (i.e., showing the same relationship), it may be located higher or lower on the diagram. Although this will change the dollar amounts of compensation, it will not change the internal consistency.

EXHIBIT 10.2

Internal consistency

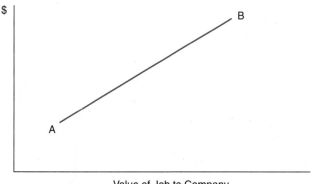

Value of Job to Company

EXHIBIT 10.3

*Differing wage
structures*

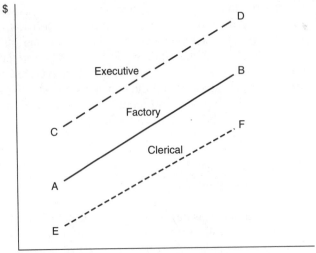

Value of Job to Company

While it is true that the same technique of job evaluation can and should be applied to all jobs, all jobs in the organization may not be covered by a single wage structure. Many classes of jobs require their own evaluation process.[7] Since executive and factory jobs vary too greatly in content to fall under one overall system, it is necessary to categorize groups of jobs and create different pay systems for different job groups. In an average organization there might be three different wage structures for the clerical, factory, and executive personnel, although in many small businesses a simple pay system might suffice. (See Exhibit 10.3.)

Job Evaluation

Wage Structure of a Typical Organization

Since the nature of job evaluation is complex and deals with a person's wages, a highly emotional subject, the people being evaluated must be convinced that the system is fair and reliable—a point that must be stressed in discussions with employees—or whatever system is set up will be doomed to fail.[8] Wage structure methods that look at the job either by considering it as a whole, such as the job-ranking method, or considering parts of jobs, such as in the point system or the factor comparison system, have proven to be fair, reliable, and workable.

The Ranking System

Whenever a company engages in a job evaluation program, the program should generally be carried out by a committee in order to avoid any prejudice or biases that a single person, consciously or unconsciously, might show. The committee

---

Exhibit 10.4   Job factors and maximum point value

Factors for Job Success and Payment	*Maximum Possible Points That Can Be Awarded*
Skill	200
Responsibility	200
Working conditions	100
Effort	200
Education	200
Total Points	1,000

should be composed of workers, union officers, and executives so that all points of view will be recognized and taken into consideration. The committee should also be composed of many people and draw on many different backgrounds and areas of expertise to avoid extremes.[9] To rank jobs, the committee, either using the job description or in some cases the job title, develops a simple ordering of jobs from highest to lowest in terms of the job's contribution to the firm. If, however, your small business is not large enough to use a committee structure, you should try to obtain as much input from other people as possible. For example, in decreasing importance the jobs might be tool-and-die maker, machinist, and sweeper. When two or more of these jobs are considered and placed in the evaluation scale, it becomes a relatively easy task to fit the rest of the jobs in by comparison with the then-known rankings for these jobs.

The Point System

Using the point system, the committee breaks down the job into those attributes that the company is paying for such as skill, responsibility, working conditions, effort, and education.[10] These attributes, called factors, may not be the only ones, but the committee should be in full agreement on whatever factors are finally selected. The committee then determines the maximum number of points that can be awarded to the highest-rated job in the company. For example, the committee might agree that the most important job in the company should be given 1,000 points. The total number of points in a company are not as important as is the agreement of the committee on the number of points to be assigned to each job.

The next step involves breaking down the total number of points so that each factor will reflect its relative importance to the success of the job. In addition to determining the maximum number of points a job can be awarded, the maximum number of points each factor will be awarded is also determined. This relative breakdown will reflect the committee's view of what is important. For example, using the above-named factors, Exhibit 10.4 may be developed.

EXHIBIT 10.5 **Point evaluation of three jobs**

Factor	Possible Points	Sweeper	Assembler	Machinist
Skill	200	10	50	150
Responsibility	200	10	50	150
Working Conditions	100	50	80	75
Effort	200	100	75	50
Education	300	0	25	175
Total Points	1,000	170	280	600

Benchmark Job Evaluation

Using the job description, the committee then evaluates each factor and awards as many points per factor as it thinks appropriate. All the job's factors are measured separately against the predetermined total possible points for each factor. A hypothetical evaluation for three jobs—sweeper, assembler, and machinist—is shown in Exhibit 10.5.

Compensation

Job evaluation is used only to determine the relative pay of each job in the organization. The outcome of job evaluation is the creation of a structure showing which jobs are more important to the company, which jobs should be paid more than others, and the degree of difference and pay between jobs. The monetary side of job evaluation—how many dollars each job is paid—is determined by a wage survey that the company conducts, including its own wage study, government surveys, and professional and trade publications.

It is important that the company also seeks the information for "benchmark" or "key" jobs that are easily recognized by everyone in the firm and the industry.[11] That is, the job descriptions describe the same job in all firms in the same industry. While it is possible for many firms to use similar job titles yet have the jobs differ in content, the content of the key jobs must be comparable for all firms. Additionally, there must be agreement that these jobs are fairly paid, that the jobs are being rewarded with a wage that adequately reflects the difficulty of the job, and that the worker accepts the wage as fair in relation to what he or she feels he or she should receive for the job. Wages for the three jobs under consideration are listed in Exhibit 10.6. The wages of these benchmark jobs can then be shown on

Exhibit 10.6 **A sample compensation plan**

Job	Wage	Point Value
Sweeper	$3.85	170
Assembler	$8.15	280
Machinist	$14.00	600

Exhibit 10.7

Use of least squares line to determine wage structure

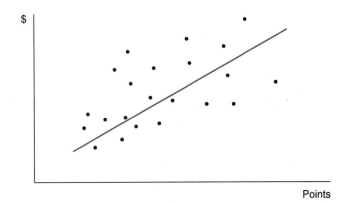

one axis of a model and the point value of the jobs on the other. A line of "best fit" can then be drawn. The usual tool used for this purpose is statistical regression analysis.[12] This information can easily be utilized and illustrated in a simple diagram: the regression line ("best fit"),[13] as shown in Exhibit 10.7.

Drawing the line in this manner immediately reveals the wage structure and its location. Once its point value is known, it then becomes a simple matter to determine the wage paid for any job. A perpendicular line is drawn up from the point value to the wage structure. Another perpendicular line is drawn from the first contact with the structure to the dollar value axis. Thus for a job value of X points, the wage rate is Y dollars, as Exhibit 10.8 shows. The same approach is also used for the ranking system.

While the preceding discussion seems to be industrially oriented and not suited for other types of business, this approach has been utilized in many small firms (using the SBA definition of *small*) and is just as easily be applied to a department store, a copy shop, or even a small bakery involving counter help, bakers, and general labor.

While the line of best fit establishes both the structure and the location, the location so established represents an average of the going rate. The location of the structure (i.e., where it is located on the chart) can be subject to union and/or

Exhibit 10.8

Determination of specific wage rate

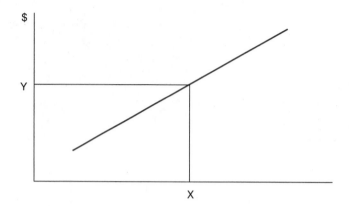

Exhibit 10.9

Determination of wage location

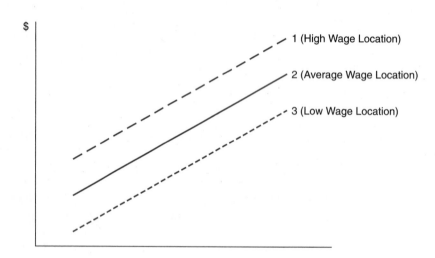

worker and employer negotiation and bargaining, as long as the shape of the structure does not change. (See Exhibit 10.9.)

The location can be either line 1, 2, or 3. If line 2 is average, the location of any company's structure can be either average, higher, or lower by agreement between parties. Location, therefore, may be subject to a power struggle, with the side winning that has the most power. Many strikes have been waged to determine which side is the most powerful and where the location of the wage structure will then be.

Influencing the location of the wage structure would be the level of wages and benefits in the community. A decision must be made by a company whether it will pay wages that are above or below the norm for the community. In most instances, the company will want to appear externally competitive with its local environment.

Many small business can use the method described above; however, some companies might find this too complex or unnecessary. Other methods of developing a wage structure can be as simple as following the prevailing wage rate—hourly or weekly—or to determine what other area workers are receiving. Employment advertising in local newspapers will provide this information as will state agencies that focus on employment and training. A firm's methods of payment may be based on hourly or productivity rates or salary. Hourly workers receive a set amount of money for every hour worked; overtime, generally over 40 hours, is paid at time and a half. Productivity pay is based upon the piecework system. Each manufactured good, insurance policy, or automobile repaired is paid a specific amount of money. Generally, workers are paid on the basis of how many goods or services they produce.

In some instances, workers may also receive incentive payments. Incentive payments are based on the production of goods or services beyond a prespecified amount.

Businesses may also pay a salary, which is a fixed amount of money per week or per month. A salary is generally paid when productivity cannot be easily measured or when the worker, for example a receptionist or a medical technician, is required to be on call at all times regardless of the demand for his or her services.

Benefits

Wages themselves are not the entire pay package. While the law mandates paying wages, employers at their option may elect to provide certain benefits either because they believe that they should or because a union or the law forces them to do so. These fringe benefits may fall under the following headings.

Economic

Pensions
In addition to the mandatory government pension plan, some employers contribute to a separate fund so that when employees retire, they will have some assurance of an independent income over and above Social Security. Contributions may be made based on a percentage of earnings or a flat payment per employee. Some employers mandate an employee-matching contribution; others do not. Employers' contributions are vested (become the employees' property) according to federal regulation. This enables the employee to keep the pension contributions even if they leave or are fired from their jobs.

Life Insurance
Employees may be offered group life insurance at reduced rates so that in the event of their death, their families have a source of income. These life insurance plans may be either wholly or partially paid by the employer.

Health and Accident Insurance

During World War II, wages were fixed and, in an effort to keep and encourage good employees, employers began paying for health care in lieu of wage increases. This practice has continued, and with the rise in the cost of health care, it has become extremely important and regarded as an entitlement. Employers may pay the entire cost or have the worker pay a portion of the premium.

Recreational

Some employers, in order to create and foster work teams and team and company loyalty, provide opportunities for worker participation in company-sponsored sports such as softball or basketball. Other events may be sponsored such as such as theater or concert performances.

Facilitative

As the number of employees increases, employers may wish to enlarge workers' benefits by supplying in-house medical services, cafeterias, or company-sponsored discount purchase plans. Employers may provide relocation assistance to upper-level executives or may provide a clearinghouse for housing opportunities in remote or high-cost areas.

Because providing benefits is expensive, the employer has to determine what portion of revenues he or she can afford to give to each employee, allocating it between direct pay and fringe benefits. These principles, techniques, and procedures are applicable in all organizations creating utility (usefulness).

The job of setting compensation is extremely important, as it defines workers' expectations and lifestyle. It is necessary to ensure equality and equity. Therefore, it demands an objective method, administered in entirely impartial manner. This does not mean that the issue of compensation is not complex. It means that under the given conditions everything that can be done is done to avoid any charges of unfairness and subjectivity.

Government Regulations and Their Impact

Government regulations impact an employer in many ways. Each employer must contribute and pay taxes based on its employees' wages. Each employer is responsible for withholding from each employee's income the employee's share of taxes and Social Security payments.

Federal Income Taxes

Any employer paying wages or salaries must withhold these taxes from employees' wages and remit the withheld monies to the government.

Workers' Compensation Insurance

To protect from the loss of income due to job related injury, employers are required, based on certain risk categories, to maintain an insurance policy that pays workers medical benefits. Further, if the worker is temporarily unable to work as a result of injuries sustained, the insurance will also provide payments in lieu of wages. Premiums for this policy are based upon a percentage of payroll.

State and Federal Unemployment Taxes

To protect workers who are laid off and willing to work, employers contribute to SUTA (State Unemployment Taxes) and FUTA (Federal Unemployment Taxes). In the event of a layoff, the worker receives income for a defined period of time. This income is meant to tide the worker over until he or she is reemployed.

FICA

Employers must withhold a certain percentage of an employee's pay to enable the employee to have a retirement income and medical benefits upon retirement. Additional coverage is at the employer's option. Additionally, the employer must match and contribute to the employee's FICA fund an amount equal to the employee's contribution.

In addition to the above categories, both federal and state governments have passed laws with rules and regulations for the social good of the working population in the country. Some of these follow:

I-9 forms. In order that employers do not hire illegal immigrants, employers must have all employees verify that they are United States citizens. This form must be available for government inspection.[14]

OSHA regulations. OSHA regulations state that the employer must provide a workplace free from hazards that are likely to cause death, physical harm, or health problems. Employers must also conform to various safety and health standards. Owners and managers who fail to comply can be charged with criminal liability under this act.[15]

Equal opportunity and employment opportunities. Under the law,[16] discrimination based on race, color, religion, sex, national origin, or age is prohibited. Sexual harassment increasingly has been recognized as an important issue in the workplace and is also illegal.

Disability regulations. It is also illegal to reject qualified applicants if the individuals can work with reasonable accommodations. Reasonable accommodations include such items as enlarged doorways and ramps.[17]

Plant closing. Under special legislation,[18] employers must give 60 days' notice for a plant closing or mass layoff. This law applies only to firms employing more than 100 people, and layoffs of 50 or more workers. While it is important, it seems to impact only minimally upon a small business.

Wage and hour laws. Starting with the Fair Labor Standards Act of 1937, legislation mandates that employers pay certain minimum hourly wage rates and generally time and a half for overtime. Also under this heading are various child labor regulations to protect children in the labor force.

Wrongful discharge legislation. Historically, the employer has had the unchallenged right to fire or to terminate employment at will. Job rights are increasingly being recognized by the courts, and employees who feel that they have been wrongfully terminated may seek legal and financial redress. An employer must be extremely careful not to be unfair in the termination process.

Recruitment and Selection of Employees

Staffing

Staffing means *placing the right people in their respective jobs.* Staffing refers to those activities affecting employees: hiring, firing, and record keeping. Staffing, which in larger businesses is primarily a personnel function, must be a function of all small business owners and operators.[19]

Recruiting

Recruiting refers to *the first step in staffing, which is finding people.* Each company tends to rely upon only a few of the many possible ways that exist for finding and recruiting employees. Common sense tells us that the greater the pool of applicants, the more likely you can find the best candidate for the position.

Techniques for recruiting employees vary from business to business and among various types of businesses. Many small retail stores tend to rely primarily on a "Help Wanted" poster in the window. Classified newspaper advertising can also be a source for locating potential candidates. In large companies or firms that are growing, accountants, lawyers, or management consultants are often used to help fill executive positions. Other sources of applicant supply could include walk-in candidates, recommendations by current employees, public and private employment agencies, schools, and advertisements in trade magazines.[20]

Selection

The process of selecting an employee for a particular position is analogous to being able to survive a series of obstacles. The potential employee can be eliminated by failing to meet a challenge; but as each hurdle or test is successfully passed, he or she becomes eligible to progress to the next level.

Many of the techniques used to recruit employees are also used as an initial step in the selection process. A system used for recruiting candidates could be a selection technique because although it serves as a vehicle to elicit candidates, the individual must in some fashion make his or her interest in employment known to the employer. Referrals by current employees are considered by many to be the best source for recruiting new employees. Current employees may have some understanding of the job; they know the company's expectations, so they are unlikely to recommend a poor candidate who might reflect poorly on them. In a tight labor market, employers frequently offer bonuses to employees for recommending other suitable candidates.

Walk-in candidates may be good potential employees since they have already evidenced interest in the company.

Advertising in newspapers, magazines, and even on television can be worded to serve as a recruiting test. An advertisement that mentions requirements such as a bachelor's degree in business administration would obviously eliminate anyone who did not possess the required degree. Listing extensive requirements reduces the number of applicants who qualify and who would respond to the advertisement. A company that advertises "no experience necessary" could receive hundreds of responses.

Private employment agencies and public agencies, such as a state's Department of Employment Services, are often used by business firms primarily because of their special interests (part-time workers, teachers, or engineers) and, more importantly, because they do much of the screening that the company itself would have to do.

School recruiting at all levels, from high school through college, is a good source of potential employees because a large group of students with similar qualifications are accessible from one source. A business that wants candidates with a business education could interview several candidates from a business school.

Two-year college graduates are good candidates for positions. These students have demonstrated their ability to learn and they recognize that success requires hard work.

The Interview

Few people are hired without being interviewed, which is a technique used to check the individual's appearance, poise, manners, and disposition as well as to elicit additional information from that which the candidate has provided on the application form.[21] Ideally the interview should take place in a quiet room, free from interruptions. Note taking by the interviewer should be avoided because it puts undue stress on the candidate, but at the close of the interview the interviewer can check appropriate items using a prepared form or makes notes about the candidate.

For many positions, not one but several interviews are required. The initial interview screens out unqualified candidates and provides a pool of candidates from which to continue the screening process or to select the person who best fits the job. In some instances, the person conducting preliminary interviews will provide candidates to the manager, who will then make the final decision.

EXHIBIT 10.10   Résumé

MAUREEN MAKEMONEY
15 TURNIP LANE
MILFORD, MA 02100
508–333–3333

OBJECTIVE	A career in public accounting focusing on audit and taxation.

AREAS OF WORK EXPERIENCE

Automated Systems	Corporate Taxation
Internal Audits	Forecasting
Budget Planning	Financial Analysis

EXPERIENCE

LIBERTY MUTUAL INSURANCE COMPANY   Boston, MA

3/xx–present

Accountant
* Participate in various activities related to book closing
* Prepare and balance journal entries to the Interactive Financial Planning System
* Assist auditors during quarterly and year-end audits
* Assist in the preparation of the annual statement

9/xx–3/xx

Assistant Investment Accountant
* Balanced over 1,200 government mortgage bonds
* Created computerized GNMA income accounting worksheet for projected vs. actual interest
* Processed short-term investments in commercial paper
* Assisted Investment Accountant in handling and filing investment acquisitions and dispositions

ROBERT D. UNDERWOOD, CPA   Boston, MA

3/XX–9/XX

Accountant
* Verified cash journals
* Reconciled bank statements
* Operated computerized spreadsheet system to assist in client audits

EDUCATION

SUFFOLK UNIVERSITY   Boston, MA

19xx

Master of Business Administration
Finance concentration
Degree awarded with honors
Member of MBA Association

19xx

Bachelor of Science in Business Administration
Accounting concentration
Financed 100% of college expenses on own
Member of Accounting Club

REFERENCES   Furnished on request

During the interview process, care should be taken to ask only those questions that are valid for the job being filled. Questions having no impact on job performance can lead to the candidate's filing a legal action against the business under the Equal Opportunity Employment Act.

EXHIBIT 10.11   Application form

D'ANGELO COMPANY

TR NAME: _____   APPLICATION FOR EMPLOYMENT

HIRED: YES ___ NO ___

NAME: _____   DATE: _____

ADDRESS: _____   SOCIAL SECURITY NUMBER: _____

_____

_____   TELEPHONE: _____

ARE YOU 18 OR OLDER? IF NOT, STATE AGE: _____

EVER APPLIED WITH D'ANGELO BEFORE? _____   WHERE: _____   WHEN: _____

IF RELATED TO ANYONE IN OUR EMPLOY, STATE NAME: _____

DO YOU HAVE ANY PHYSICAL CONDITION WHICH MAY LIMIT YOUR ABILITY TO PERFORM A PARTICULAR JOB FOR WHICH YOU ARE APPLYING? _____ IF YES, PLEASE EXPLAIN.

_____

DATE YOU CAN START: _____   DESIRED SALARY: _____

HOURS AVAILABLE:	SUN	MON	TUE	WED	THU	FRI	SAT
FROM:	_____	_____	_____	_____	_____	_____	_____
TO:	_____	_____	_____	_____	_____	_____	_____

CIRCLE LAST GRADE COMPLETED: 9   10   11   12   (HIGH SCHOOL   )

13   14   15   16   (COLLEGE   )

17+   (POST GRADUATE)

EMPLOYMENT HISTORY: LIST BELOW LAST THREE EMPLOYERS (STARTING WITH MOST RECENT)
YOU MAY INCLUDE WORK PERFORMED ON A VOLUNTARY BASIS.

DATE MONTH & YEAR	NAME & ADDRESS OF EMPLOYER	SALARY	POSITION	REASON FOR LEAVING
FROM _____ TO _____				
FROM _____ TO _____				
FROM _____ TO _____				

DURING THE PAST 7 YEARS, HAVE YOU EVER BEEN CONVICTED OF A CRIME, EXCLUDING MISDEMEANORS AND TRAFFIC VIOLATIONS?   YES _____   NO _____

IF YES, PLEASE DESCRIBE _____

IT IS UNLAWFUL IN MASSACHUSETTS TO REQUIRE OR ADMINISTER A LIE DETECTOR TEST AS A CONDITION OF EMPLOYMENT OR CONTINUED EMPLOYMENT. AN EMPLOYEE WHO VIOLATES THIS LAW SHALL BE SUBJECT TO CRIMINAL PENALTIES AND CIVIL LIABILITY

I AUTHORIZE INVESTIGATION OF ALL STATEMENTS CONTAINED IN THIS APPLICATION. I UNDERSTAND THAT MISREPRESENTATION OR OMISSION OF FACTS CALLED FOR IS CAUSE FOR DISMISSAL. FURTHER, I UNDERSTAND AND AGREE THAT NO REPRESENTATIVE OF THE COMPANY HAS AUTHORITY TO ENTER INTO ANY AGREEMENT FOR EMPLOYMENT FOR DEFINITE PERIOD AND I MAY, REGARDLESS OF THE DATE OF PAYMENT OF MY WAGES AND SALARY, BE TERMINATED AT ANY TIME WITHOUT ANY PREVIOUS NOTICE.

SIGNATURE: _____   DATE: _____

Application Forms and Résumés

The major difference between the application form and the résumé is that the application form is prepared by the company. A résumé, on the other hand, is designed and prepared by the candidate and presents his or her qualifications with special emphasis. Exhibits 10.10 and 10.11 on pages 262 and 263 are examples of a résumé and application form.

Résumés and application forms contain virtually the same information, starting off with personal data such as name, address and telephone number, education, and work experience. High school and college students lacking substantial work experience generally include their extracurricular activities and hobbies.

A résumé should be designed to meet the requirements of the potential position, emphasizing accomplishments rather than merely providing a list of dates, jobs, and titles. If an applicant responds to an advertisement for a position, the application letter generally correlates with each aspect of the job mentioned in the ad. Often the same words and active verbs, giving the feeling of strength and competency, are used.

Most application forms ask for references, but it is usually unwise to attach them to a résumé. Certain references are usually considered better than others. If an applicant is applying to a business, then references from former employers are important.

As an employer, you should always check references. The best way to check is by face-to-face contact with the reference. If this is not possible, a telephone call may be appropriate. A request that is mailed to the reference is generally the least effective way to elicit an appraisal.

You must check thoroughly the information provided on résumés and applications, since applicants, in presenting themselves in as good a light as possible, might tend to exaggerate their qualities. One firm checked on a job candidate's doctoral degree awarded by a well-known university and found that the applicant had not received it. You want to make certain that applicants really have all the education and experience they claim and that they performed well at their prior employment.

Testing

Some companies require the job applicant to take many tests. It is, however, a good idea to give a reasonable series of tests rather than to rely on only one. The ideal testing procedure should elicit the most important qualifications that have been determined from a job specification. The government will require that you be able to prove that the tests you use are predictors of job success.

A type of test that has proven useful is the performance test, where applicants are asked to perform tasks that they will be expected to perform on the job. A secretary is asked to use word-processing equipment or an auto mechanic may be asked to diagnose an engine problem.

Another type of useful test is a trade test that primarily identifies a candidate's experience by checking his or her knowledge of the language of the trade. Most trades have specific tools or equipment, and you should test to ascertain that the candidate knows the appropriate names and can identify the tools.

Aptitude tests are used to predict job success by checking the applicant's aptitude for a specific type of work; for instance, manual dexterity is measured to predict success in small-parts assembly.

Many kinds of tests are available, and you should choose the test that gives the best, most economical, and most reliable results for predicting an applicant's success on the job.

Physical Examinations

The physical examination is usually the final challenge the applicant must successfully meet. Management requires and pays for physical examinations specifically when there are job-related criteria that an employee must fulfill, such as the ability to lift certain loads or be free of disease.

Promotions

A **promotion** is *a change in position with a change in status and/or pay.* Being promoted is what most employees, especially those in management, strive for.[22]

How the selection for promotion is made is most important. Normally the person recommending a promotion is the employee's immediate superior. How one is promoted is more important because of the possibility of bias—either favorable or unfavorable. A supervisor could select an employee and promote him or her or could refrain from offering a promotion because the employee is so good that he or she is making the boss's job easier.

Most companies have a policy of promoting from within, which is good because it builds morale and loyalty to the business. Whenever this policy is seen in writing however, there always seems to be a loophole such as, "We promote from within whenever possible."

Appraisal

Many companies have instituted a periodic appraisal system not only for the purpose of promotion but also to point out any weak areas in an employee's performance. Normally, appraisals are done on a yearly basis with the exception of a six-month appraisal for new employees or employees who have been moved to a new job. Appraisals are prepared by the employee's superior and sometimes by other superiors that the employee comes in contact with. Normally the rating is never a "yes-no" answer. Usually a form is used that requires rating various traits on a one-to-five scale or on a one-to-seven scale. Some evaluations require further information for the rating. Notice that the entire system is designed to reduce bias.

Training Employees

By the time an employee is knowledgeable enough to do the job well that he or she is hired to do, the company may have spent a great deal of money, including the employee's salary while being trained, a trainer's salary, the loss of productive output, and other items of expense. Selecting and training must be done carefully, since mistakes are expensive.

Popular Methods of Training

Training employees can take many forms. (1) On-the-job training[23] is undoubtedly the oldest, most common, and most practical method of training. Not only can an employee learn by doing but he or she is also making some contribution to the firm. (2) Job rotation,[24] or transferring the operating employee from one job to another, is a useful means of education. (3) Role-playing is quite useful for training people whose job will involve dealing with other people. Salespersons, receptionists, telephone operators and all managers can be trained well using role-playing. A salesperson, for example, could sell a product or service to another person in a role-playing situation, learning the appropriate behavior and the proper way to act not only by being personally involved but also by critically observing others.

Training Assembly-Line Workers.

1. Vestibule schools: In an assembly-line process a new, inexperienced worker may not fit in; he or she might be slow and consequently slow down the entire assembly line. A stitcher in a shoe factory, for example, would be taken to a separate room with the appropriate machines and would learn the job under direct supervision. When the stitcher has learned the job and is able to perform at the required speed, he or she is returned to the assembly line with a reduced impact on the assembly line process.[25]

2. Apprenticeship:[26] Many tradespersons such as carpenters, plumbers, and electricians go through an apprenticeship. Initially, the tradesperson would be an apprentice, then a journeyman, and finally a master. Many times this apprenticeship is union controlled and requires a certain amount of classroom work along with practical experience.

Developmental Assignments

There are several forms of educational assignments for managers, varying from assigned readings in books and periodicals to courses taken for credit in colleges and universities. One of the more interesting assignments is attending a seminar normally sponsored by colleges or universities or an independent organization that specializes in training. Seminars vary in length and are offered on a daily basis or once a week for 6, 8, or 10 weeks.

Community Opportunities

The community in which potential management people live, work, and learn offers great potential for learning management skills. In school and college, one might become the president or an officer of a fraternity or business organization. The potential manager can run for public office, be active in some fraternal organization, become a scoutmaster, or in some way become actively involved with some nonbusiness-type organization in his or her community.

Some types of training are participative because fellow workers are essential to the method of training such as on-the-job training and committee assignments. Other types of training could be classified as nonparticipative because the employee learns on his or her own through study, reading assignments, and community opportunities where other company personnel are not involved.

Summary

The Interrelationship between the Human Resources/Personnel Function and the Other Business Plan Components

The personnel function is affected by the demand of the production and marketing functions since it provides the appropriate talent required to operate the business. It uses resources supplied by the finance function and coordinates with the accounting function to maintain payroll and benefit records.

The profitability of your company will be directly affected by the employees you are able to attract and retain. The personnel function in your organization involves all aspects of attracting and managing the people who work for you. Personnel planning involves defining how many and what type of employees you will need in the future. Your organization is consistently balancing its need for people with the desire to operate with as few costs as possible.

Job Analysis

Each job to be filled should be analyzed carefully so that job descriptions and job specifications can be drawn up. **Job descriptions,** which are *the duties and requirements of the job,* define the job while **job specifications,** setting forth *the specific skills and training of the people hired to perform the job functions,* define the characteristics or attributes necessary to do the job. Make certain that your company's jobs are both internally and externally consistent.

Internal Consistency and External Consistency

Internal consistency, which means that *high-worth jobs (to the company) get paid more than low-worth jobs,* involves making certain that your firm's job and pay relate their worth to the organization. **External consistency,** where *the pay structure corresponds to the community wage structure,* assures that your workers are rewarded at a rate of pay that is comparable to the market. Using either the point or the factor comparison method, **job evaluation** *ensures that wages are internally and externally consistent.*

Recruiting and Selection

Staffing, *placing the right people in their respective jobs,* includes all activities affecting employees such as **recruiting,** the *hiring of people,* and training them. Many sources can be used to recruit employees, such as newspaper advertising, referrals, and encouraging those who may walk in.

Choosing the best employee is expedited through the use of application forms in order to elicit relevant information. In addition to completing the application forms, prospective employees should submit résumés which they have prepared. Interviews, an important part of the hiring process, are helpful in gaining insight into a prospective employee's qualifications.

Once an employee is hired, it is necessary to familiarize and train them so that they can fit into your company's environment smoothly and efficiently. Training on the job is the method most frequently used. Other techniques such as attending seminars or taking courses in college can also be used. Compensation is important not just for financial reasons but for the employee's psychological health as well. In addition to financial incentives, employees should also be rewarded by being given deserved promotions and the opportunity to assume increasing levels of responsibility and authority.

It is important to remember that government regulations impact the employer in many ways from the necessary taxes to be paid to the issue of who can be employed and how the workplace must be maintained.

Questions

1. Define *job descriptions* and *job specifications.* What is the difference between them? Why are they important?

2. If you had to recruit new employees for a small business, what sources would you use?

3. How would you select a good employee? List some of the methods available.

4. How would you train a new employee? List several methods and explain each.

5. If you were to recruit a friend or classmate to work in your company, what persuasive arguments would you use?

6. Are acquaintances or relatives a good source of employees? Why or why not?

7. Many entrepreneurs hesitate to hire new employees, since this means adding overhead. How would you know when and how many new employees to hire?

8. Define *internal consistency of wages.* Why is this an important concept?

9. Define *external consistency of wages.* Why is this an important concept?

10. Define the point system and the ranking system. How would you use them to ensure both internal and external consistency?

11. Define the term *job rotation.* How might you use this technique in your firm?

12. What methods would you prefer for a training and orientation program for a small electronics company employing 95 people?

13. Prepare a job evaluation format defining several traits you might use in a small manufacturing firm. Show the traits and the relative importance of these traits for job success.

14. Why is a performance appraisal system necessary? How do you institute such a system?

15. Assume that you like a prospective employee in the initial interview. Do you think it is necessary to check references? Why or why not? How reliable are the references likely to be?

Application Exercises

When doing these exercises, where applicable, be sure to select a specific business, preferably one where you presently work or previously worked or a business you would like to own someday. If this is not possible, pick a specific organization to which you will refer. Be sure to identify the organization by name. Limit your answers to one or two pages per exercise.

1. Interview four small business owners. Have any preparations been made for management succession development? If so, outline these plans. Does the presence or lack of a management succession plan indicate any general "laws" you might apply to small business?

2. Interview an established small business owner. Determine if the owner has job descriptions and specifications. If such descriptions and specifications are not present, ask the owner how he or she knows what everyone is supposed to do. Prepare a report on your findings.

3. Using the same business as in question 2, take several of the job descriptions and job specifications and see if the jobs and people match the written specifications. If not, prepare realistic specifications. Report on your findings and include as exhibits the job descriptions and specifications. If there are no specifications, prepare the job descriptions and job specifications for two jobs in the company.

4. Interview a small business owner and find out how candidates are recruited. What sources for candidates are used? How would candidates be evaluated and on what basis would the final choice be made?

5. Using the same business as in question 4, determine how the owner trains and orients new employees so that they will acquire competency on the job and be comfortable in the company.

6. Using the same company as in question 3, discuss how employee compensation is determined, how employees are evaluated, and how raises are determined. Report on your findings.

7. Prepare a report for the business in question 4 discussing your recommendations for improving the personnel policies of the company.

8. Go to your college or university placement office and ask them to help you prepare a résumé you can use in your job search.

9. Examine your local and regional newspapers to see the job vacancies listed for small businesses. Be sure to have some criterion for judging which advertisements are for small business. Report on your findings about the kinds of jobs available.

10. Ask the owner of a business whether or not they are subject to federal, state, or local regulations concerning their workers. Include in your report items such as tax and workplace requirements.

Application Situations

1. Shelly Morris

Shelly Morris was going to graduate from a state university school of management in six months. Shelly started out as an accounting major but shifted into a management major after her summer job. Both the summer job and some lengthy discussions with her father convinced her that the future potential for longevity and salary enhancement comes from the management sector.

While in school, Shelly worked for one employer, Advanced Topographic Company, whose main products were detailed topographic maps. If a building was going to be either built or demolished, the contractor would have to know about potential problems. Shelly held several positions in the company. She began with being assigned to doing topographic surveys and summing up her findings for use by the mapmakers. She then was moved to the accounting department doing credit and debit entries. She was sure that this was a promotion. Succeeding at this job and being reviewed by her immediate superior, Shelly was given a raise and put in charge of two entry-level accounting people. The year before graduation, Shelly was asked to take charge of recruitment in the personnel department. Shelly thought she was doing well in the company and since it was a small business, felt she would be asked to stay on after graduation and grow with the organization.

Four months before she graduated, the owner was involved in a serious automobile accident and died several days later. The company ceased to exist. Shelly now had to look for a job after graduation.

Assignment

1. Prepare a résumé for Shelly to present. Keep in mind that she was active in several school organizations, was elected to class office, and ran Senior Week.
2. Based on the résumé, plan a job search strategy for Shelly pointing out where she should look for vacancies and how to report to the vacancies she found.
3. Assuming Shelly is asked to interview, how should she prepare for interviews? What questions might she be asked and what questions, if any, should she ask the interviewer?

2. Julius Sanchez

Julius Sanchez was hired as an administrative assistant in a local manufacturing company. Julius had been a business major in college. At the time he was hired last week, he was presented with a job offer and a brief outline of employee benefits. Based on the letter and his conversations with the recruiter, he decided to join the firm. Upon arrival, the recruiter assigned him to a desk and told him that he would be assisting Joe Samuels. The recruiter then left Julius sitting at his desk. After sitting there for 20 minutes, Julius asked the first person he saw where Joe Samuels was; he was told that Joe was out for the morning but would be back in several hours.

In fact, several hours later Joe returned, greeted Julius, and said, "Well, I guess I'll have to train you, although I don't know how I'll fit it into my schedule. Don't worry, though. Follow me around for several weeks and you'll be able to handle yourself."

Assignment

1. Given the above, how would you rate the company's orientation and training efforts? What are the positive and negative aspects of this approach?
2. How would you orient Julius in his new job? Develop a standard orientation program for this company.
3. From the company's approach, it seems that its total orientation relied on older, experienced workers mentoring the new workers. To what extent should a company rely on the worker to introduce and orient new employees? Is this a good approach? Will newcomers really learn how the firm works? If this approach has validity, how important should it be in the company's overall orientation program?
4. Recognizing that the company has fewer than 100 employees and no personnel manager, design a better approach, keeping in mind that you want to improve the system at no increase in expenses.

3. Tony Moore

Tony Moore worked for Donovan's Market as produce manager for 16 months before he finally asked the market manager if he could speak with him. In the manager's office, Tony explained that while he enjoyed the work and felt he was doing a good job, he hadn't had an evaluation of his performance. Keelson, the manager replied, "Don't worry, Tony. You're doing a good job. Keep it up and you'll have my job someday." Keelson then shook Tony's hand and returned to work.

Assignment

1. If you were Tony, how would you feel? Would you be justified and what are you really looking for?
2. Design a formal evaluation procedure for this market.
3. Do you think that Keelson should have been better able to handle an evaluation? Design a procedure Keelson could follow in performing employee evaluations.

Integrated Case Question—CorLu Foods

Using CorLu, draw up job descriptions and specifications for required personnel. Indicate how personnel needs might change with sales volume. Indicate compensation for each job and how you will arrive at "fair" pay rates. Justify the internal and external consistency of these rates. (Please refer to the Integrated Case, "CorLu Foods.")

Additional Readings

Bemmels, Brian, and Yonatan Reshef. "Manufacturing Employees and Technological Change." *Journal of Labor Research* 12, no. 3 (Summer 1991), pp. 231–46.
Blanchard, Ken. "Getting Work Done Right: The Five Steps of Training." *Supervisory Management,* June 1991, p. 3.

Burck, Charles. "Where Good Jobs Grow." *Fortune,* June 14, 1993, p. 22.

Burke, Thomas P., and John D. Morton. "How Firm Size and Industry Affect Employee Benefits." *Monthly Labor Review,* December 1990, p. 35.

Case, John, and Michael P. Cronin. "The Best Small Companies to Work for in America." *Inc.,* November 1992, p. 88.

Denton, D. Keith, and Barry L. Wisdom. "The Learning Organization Involves the Entire Work Force." *Quality Progress,* December 1991, pp. 69–72.

Ehrenfeld, Tom. "Cashing In." *Inc.,* July 1993, p. 69.

_____. "School's In: Teaching Job Skills Is One Thing." *Inc.,* July 1993, p. 65.

"Employee Benefits in Small Business." *Congressional Digest,* January 1993, p. 7.

"Entrepreneurial Rewards." *Forbes,* November 9, 1992, p. 240.

Fraser, Jill Andresky. "CEO's Pay Strategies." *Inc.,* June 1992, p. 121.

Grossman, Glenn M. "Life Insurance Benefits in Small Establishments and Government." *Monthly Labor Review,* October 1992, p. 33.

Hammons, Charles, and Gary A. Maddux. "The Fine-Tuned Organization." *Quality Progress,* February 1992, pp. 47–48.

Hornsby, Jeffrey S., and Donald F. Kuratko. "Human Resource Management in Small Business: Critical Issues for the 1990s." *Journal of Small Business Management* 28, no. 10 (July 1990), p. 9.

"It Doesn't Get Much Simpler Than SEP." *Nation's Business,* March 1991, p. 22.

Kanungo, Rabindra N., and Manuel Mendonca. "Evaluating Employee Compensation." *California Management Review* 31, no. 1 (Fall 1988), pp. 23–39.

Knibbs, John, and Stephen Swailes. "Implementing Performance Review and Career Planning: Part One." *Management Decision* 30, no. 1 (1992), pp. 49–53.

Kowalchuk, Reginald W. "Comments on Proposed Limitation on Deductibility of Corporate Salaries." *Tax Executive,* July/August 1992, pp. 296–97.

Mangelsdorf, Martha E. "Ground-Zero Training." *Inc.,* February 1993, pp. 82–93.

Miles, Carrie A., and Jean M. McCloskey. "People, the Key to Productivity." *HR Magazine,* February 1993, pp. 40–45.

Nordhaug, Odd. "Reward Functions of Personnel Training." *Human Relations,* May 1989, pp. 373–88.

Pouliot, Janine S. "A Hiring Bonanza: Laid-off Managers." *Nation's Business,* November 1992, p. 44.

Randall, Iris. "How to Build a Premier Sales Staff." *Black Enterprise,* February 1993, pp. 154–56.

Reddin, Bill. "Expressing Effectiveness in Terms of Outputs." *Personnel Management,* October 1989, pp. 86–91.

Rothman, Howard. "The Power of Empowerment." *Nation's Business,* June 1993, p. 49.

Sandroff, Ronni. "Are Small Companies Better?" *Working Mother,* November 1992, p. 34.

Sheehan, William J. "A CEO's Strategic Plan for Training." *Training,* November 1992, p. 86.

Sherrid, Pamela. "A Nice Reward for Sharing the Profits." *U.S. News & World Report,* November 30, 1992, p. 81.

Siemasko, Dan. "12 Steps to Jump-Starting Your Programs." *Training and Development,* May 1992, pp. 97–106.

Stevens, Mark. "Evaluating Employees from the Outside In." *Small Business Reports,* August 1990, pp. 14–16.

Szabo, Joan C. "Using ESOPs to Sell Your Firm." *Nation's Business,* January 1991, p. 59.

Thompson, Roger. "Switching to Flexible Benefits." *Nation's Business,* July 1991, p. 16.

Vaughan, Emmett J. "Recruiting Agency Employees." *Mid-America Insurance,* October 1989, pp. 18–21.

Zabriskie, Noel, and Alan Huellmantel. "Implementing Strategies for Human Resources." *Long Range Planning,* April 1989, pp. 70–77.

Endnotes

1. Barbara Marsh, "Small Firms' Disadvantage in Hiring Likely to Grow," *The Wall Street Journal,* November 27, 1989, p. B1.

2. Udayan Gupta, and Jeffrey A. Tannenbaum, "Labor Shortages Force Changes at Small Firms," *The Wall Street Journal,* May 22, 1989, p. 1B.

3. J. V. Ghorpade, *Job Analysis: A Handbook for the Human Resource Director* (Englewood Cliffs, NJ: Prentice Hall, 1988).

4. John M. Ivancevich, *Human Resource Management,* 5th ed. (Homewood, Ill.: Richard D. Irwin, 1992).

5. J. Solomon, "The New Job Interview: Show Thyself," *The Wall Street Journal,* December 4, 1989, p. B1.

6. J. N. Cleveland, K. R. Murphy, and R. E. Williams, "Multiple Uses of Performance Appraisal: Prevalence and Correlates," *Journal of Applied Psychology,* February 1989, pp. 130–35.

7. Ivancevich, *Human Resource Management.*

8. T. J. Klein, "Performance Reviews that Rate an 'A'," *Personnel,* May 1990, pp. 38–40.

9. H. H. Meyer, "A Solution to the Performance Appraisal Feedback Enigma," *Academy of Management Executives,* February 1991, pp. 68–76.

10. Roger J. Plachy, "Compensations Management: Cases and Applications," *Compensation and Benefits Review,* July 1989, p. 26.

11. R. Sneigar, "The Comparability of Job Evaluation Methods in Supplying Approximately Similar Classifications in Raising One Job Series," *Personnel Psychology,* Summer 1983, pp. 371–80.

12. Regression analysis is too complex for this text. Further information on it can be found in a statistics textbook.

13. David Belcher, *Wage and Salary Administration* (Englewood Cliffs, N.J.: Prentice Hall, 1962).

14. This regulation was mandated by the Immigration Reform Act of 1987.

15. Occupational Safety and Health Act, passed by Congress in 1970.

16. Civil Rights Act, 1964 and Age Discrimination Act, 1967.

17. Americans Disability Act, 1990.

18. Plant Closing Act, 1988.

19. "Employer Recruitment Practices," *Personnel,* May 1988, pp. 63–65; B. Schneider and N. Schmitt, *Staffing Organizations,* 2nd ed. (Glenview, Ill.: Scott Foresman, 1986); J. A. Breaugh, *Recruitment: Science and Practice* (Boston: PWS-Kent, 1992).

20. K. Groll Connolly, and P. M. Connolly, *Competing for Employees: Proven Marketing Strategies for Hiring and Keeping Exceptional People* (Lexington, Mass.: Lexington Books, 1991).

21. A. H. Eagly, R. D. Ashmore, M. G. Makhijani, and L. C. Longo, "What Is Beautiful Is Good, But . . .: A Meta-Analytic Review of Research on the Physical Attractiveness Stereotype," *Psychological Bulletin* 110, no. 1 (1991), pp. 109–28.
22. "Farewell, Fast Track," *Business Week,* December 10, 1990, pp. 192–200.
23. S. C. Gwynne, "The Right Stuff," *Time,* October 29, 1990, pp. 74–84.
24. B. G. Posner, "Role Changes," *Inc.,* February 1990, pp. 95–98.
25. G. Waddell, "Simulations: Balancing the Pros and Cons," *Training and Development Journal,* January 1982, pp. 75–80.
26. S. Overman, "Apprenticeships Smooth School to Work Transitions," *HR Magazine,* December 1990, pp. 40–43.

11   THE FINANCING FUNCTION

In this chapter you will learn the answers to two questions vital to business survival and prosperity: (1) how to estimate the amount of capital you need to fund an entrepreneurial venture or cover the operating costs of an established company and (2) what sources you can use to raise the necessary funds.[1]

It is also useful to know the level of operations at which you begin to show a profit.

Chapter Learning Objectives

After completing this chapter, you should be able to:

· Discuss the meaning and importance of the cash flow concept.
· Use pro forma statements to determine your capital needs.
· Identify sources of funds.
· Set up a cash budget using historical records generated from the business.
· Set up a cash budget using SIC codes and standard business ratios.
· Discuss the meaning of short, early, and long-term capital.
· Determine your breakeven point and what it means to your business.
· Define the following 24 key terms in order of their appearance:

Pro forma	Short-term capital
Capital requirements	Early-stage capital
Cash flow	Long-term capital
Standard industry ratios	Seed financing
SIC codes	Commercial bank
Cash deficit	Capital stock
Positive cash flow	Private placements

Operational results   Venture capital
Cash budget   SBA
Breakeven   Small Business Institute
Breakeven point   SCORE
Contribution margin   Trade credit

The Interrelationship Between the Financial Function and the Other Business Plan Components

The interrelationship between all the functional areas of the firm—accounting, financial, marketing, production/operations and personnel—are rarely more evident than when you consider the finance function. All areas of your business have demands. Production requires material, equipment, and personnel; marketing needs to advertise and promote new and old products. The demands of all functional areas are predicated upon the availability of money, and it is the finance function that must determine the organization's financial needs.

Once financial needs are known, it is the job of finance to find and tap sources for these funds. How well finance is able to do its job affects every functional area. Too little money or errors in determining financial needs can force cutbacks in any or all other functional areas. Your company cannot maximize profitability without the appropriate resources.

Determining Financial Need

Entrepreneurial/small business activities are often begun because someone has a "good" idea and thinks that pursuing this idea will provide both pleasure and profit. When you go into small business, the rewards are perceived to be multiple. Small business provides access to a lifestyle, independence, and monetary returns that cannot be achieved elsewhere. Led on by these thoughts, many people start their own business; they open a store, repair shop, or small manufacturing facility. At the outset few people consider that such an enterprise needs financial backing. In order to start and to survive in a business, the would-be businessperson must have money.

As the material in Chapter 5 explained and emphasized, you must have a business plan that forces you to think logically and systematically about what has to be done.[2] Using a systematic approach will result in creating pro forma statements (Chapter 12). These statements are key to determining the financial needs of the organization. But pro forma statements are only an estimate of what might happen given a certain defined set of circumstances and the validity of your assumptions. **Pro formas** are *guidelines against which you can measure how your assumptions relate to reality.* The future is uncertain, and while you may be asked to predict with a fair degree of confidence and certainty about the immediate future, the further you extend your predictions, the less accurate and reliable they tend to be.

As the future unfolds, events are not held constant, and you realize that conditions change in unpredictable ways. In the face of uncertainty, consider that the figures you developed are "best guesses" and treat them accordingly. Comparing your plan to what actually does happen tests the validity of your assumptions and enables you to make better—and more accurate—plans as you gain knowledge and become experienced in running the business. While the actual numbers in the future will differ from the pro formas, together both sets help formulate a good initial estimate of your financial needs.

Secondly, keep in mind that everything generally costs more than you think it will. Make sure you have a safety margin, since you will probably need it. Dollars are the common language to both creditors and debtors, enabling both sides to understand pro formas and the cash budget. Using this language, you can begin to determine your **capital requirements,** *how much money you need to go into business.*[3] While each firm has its own specific capital requirements, yours can be uniquely determined by the cash flow pro forma statement. The **cash flow pro forma statement** *translates your business plan into future or projected dollars of income and expenses.* It forces you to move systematically and logically through your plan, attaching a monetary value to every step. The act of preparing the pro forma cash flow will help determine your financial needs.

Pro forma income statements and pro forma balance sheets may be determined in the same manner as the pro forma cash flow statement. In this chapter, for ease of understanding, only the cash flow is projected. The balance sheet and income statement are examined in Chapters 12 and 13.

There are two methods you can use to determine the pro forma cash flow of your company. The first mandates using your present knowledge of the business operation and its operating history to define all the necessary expense categories and any relationships that exist between them. The second, to be discussed later, requires the use of standard industry ratios.

Each expense category has a rationale or assumption upon which it is based. For example, the assumptions to a pro forma cash flow statement in Exhibit 11.1 have been developed for a small printing company.[4] Based on these assumptions, the pro forma cash flows in Exhibit 11.2 were created.

Based upon knowledge and experience acquired over time, the projections have a solid base that has been defined by the company's operating history.

If you do not have an operating history or are dealing with a start-up operation, you may arrive at the cash flow by using **standard industry ratios,** *which are developed from data reported to trade associations or governmental units.*[5] The resulting "average" firm's financials are then used to develop ratios that can be used as a benchmark against which to measure your firm's results or to predict operating results for a new firm (see Exhibit 11.3). How to use ratios is covered in Chapter 13. Industry ratios for almost every industry are available from trade associations, federal or state government agencies, and such commercial services as Dun & Bradstreet and Robert Morris Associates (RMA). Since nearly all sources of industry ratios are based on **SIC Codes** (Chapter 2), once you know your SIC codes, it is a relatively simple process to determine your future cash flow. Since

Exhibit 11.1   Assumptions for pro forma cash flow statements

A. Beginning cash for the present period is the ending cash from the previous period.

B. Sales receipts are the total amount of sales each month.

C. Paper supplies are calculated by taking 10.4% of sales each month.

D. Outside vendors for products are calculated by taking 6.2% of sales for each month.

E. Print suppliers for products are calculated by taking 6.2% of sales for each month.

F. Freight is calculated at 1% of sales.

G. Salaries are based upon total amounts for all employees' base weekly pay multiplied by four weeks.

H. Payroll taxes are 9.82% of total salaries and paid quarterly.

I. Auto expense is calculated at 28 cents per mile and varies up to $1,000 per month.

J. Although bank charges will fluctuate, a fixed rate of $25 is used for planning purposes.

K. Commissions are based upon 10% of sales brought in by the manufacturer's rep, who is responsible for an estimated 30% of sales.

L. Dues and subscriptions are paid or renewed for magazines and printing publications and organizations.

M. Workers' compensation is based upon a yearly figure of $2,675. That number is divided by 12 to derive $222 and is prepaid in the first month.

N. Insurance on the building is $5,193; the figure fluctuates yearly. The first month consists of prepaid insurance for three months.

O. Interest expense is based upon a line of credit for an estimated annual cost of $1,517.

P. Health benefits are based upon a yearly amount of $24,175. One quarter of the total is paid in the first month.

Q. Office supplies expense is calculated by using a fixed amount.

R. The monthly lease payment on a printing press is $900 per month.

S. The monthly lease payment on a copier is $300 per month.

T. Postage is estimated at a fixed monthly cost of 1% of sales per month.

U. Professional fees for accounting and legal services fluctuate depending upon how often they are incurred. These costs are broken down as follows: accounting—$2,000; legal—$2,000. Both are shown calculated on a monthly basis.

V. Rent is a fixed amount of $2,000 each month.

W. Repairs and maintenance are based upon 1.1% of sales.

X. Machinery repairs are based upon 1.3% of sales.

Y. Sales tax is based upon 1.3% of sales.

Z. Telephone expenses are 5% of monthly sales.

AA. Utilities are 2.4% of monthly sales.

BB. Advertising and promotion is based upon $3,720 annually for Nynex yellow pages. The advertising rate for the *Patriot Ledger* is $136 and direct mail is $1,065.60. Both are paid monthly.

most sources use sales dollars as the basis for establishing the ratios (Chapter 13), accurate sales forecasting is a very important task for the business owner. (The sales forecast was examined in Chapter 7.)

Using either method, you can develop a projected cash flow. As forecast, income exceeds expenditures, and net cash balance at the conclusion of the year equals $146,540.[6]

EXHIBIT 11.2

ABC PRINTING COMPANY
Pro Forma Cash Flow Statement (monthly)
1994

	January	February	March	April	May	June	July	August	September	October	November	December
Cash receipts												
Beginning cash (A)	$ 7,000	$ 8,830	$16,770	$ 40,420	$41,810	$ 45,260	$ 76,780	$ 82,920	$ 99,890	$118,410	$131,950	$139,690
Sales receipts (B)	40,800	36,300	59,700	64,700	32,300	58,200	37,900	48,500	47,300	39,300	35,700	35,400
Total cash on hand	47,800	45,130	76,470	105,120	74,110	103,460	114,680	131,420	147,190	157,710	167,650	174,090
Cash Disbursements:												
Paper supplies (C)	$ 4,300	$ 3,600	$ 6,400	$ 6,700	$ 3,000	$ 5,400	$ 3,800	$ 5,000	$ 4,800	$ 4,000	$ 3,600	$ 3,600
Outside vendors (D)	2,600	2,200	3,900	4,000	1,900	3,300	2,300	3,100	2,900	2,400	2,200	2,200
Print suppliers (E)	1,900	1,600	3,000	3,000	1,300	2,300	1,600	2,200	2,000	1,700	1,600	1,600
Freight (F)	200	200	300	300	100	200	100	200	200	200	100	100
Salaries (G)	9,000	9,000	9,000	9,000	9,000	3,000	9,000	9,000	6,000	3,000	9,000	9,000
Payroll taxes (H)	2,300	0	0	2,700	0	0	2,700	0	2,600	0	0	0
Auto expenses (I)	300	300	200	300	200	300	200	250	300	300	300	200
Bank charges (J)	30	20	40	40	20	30	20	30	30	20	20	20
Commissions (K)	1,500	1,200	2,200	2,300	1,000	1,800	1,300	1,700	1,600	1,400	1,200	1,200
Dues and subscriptions (L)	200	0	0	0	0	200	0	0	0	0	0	0
Workers' comp. ins. (M)	2,700	0	0	0	0	0	0	0	0	0	0	0
Insurance (N)	1,000	400	400	400	400	400	400	400	400	400	400	400
Interest expense (O)	100	100	100	100	100	100	100	100	100	100	100	100
Health benefits (P)	4,800	1,800	1,800	1,800	1,800	1,800	1,800	1,800	1,800	1,800	1,800	1,800
Office expense (Q)	300	0	0	0	200	0	0	200	0	0	200	0
Printing machine lease (R)	900	900	900	900	900	900	900	900	900	900	900	900
Copier lease (S)	300	300	300	300	300	300	300	300	300	300	300	300
Postage (T)	40	40	60	70	30	50	40	50	50	40	40	40
Professional fees (U)	0	0	50	300	0	400	0	0	0	0	0	$600
Rent (V)	2,000	2,000	2,000	2,000	2,000	2,000	2,000	2,000	2,000	2,000	2,000	2,000
Repairs and maintenance (W)	800	400	700	700	300	600	400	600	500	400	400	400
Machinery repairs (X)	900	500	800	900	400	700	500	700	600	500	500	500
Sales tax (Y)	800	2,000	1,800	3,000	3,000	1,400	2,500	1,800	2,400	2,300	1,900	1,700
Taxes (other)	0	0	0	0	0	0	0	0	0	0	0	$500
Telephone (Z)	300	300	300	400	500	200	300	300	400	300	300	300
Utility (AA)	900	1,000	900	1,500	1,600	700	1,300	900	1,200	1,100	900	900
Adver. and promotion (BB)	800	500	900	600	800	600	200	0	300	0	200	0
Income taxes	0	0	0	22,000	0	0	0	0	0	0	0	0
Total cash disbursements	$38,970	$28,360	$36,050	$63,310	$28,850	$26,680	$31,760	$31,530	$28,780	$25,760	$27,960	$28,360
Ending cash balance	$8,830	$16,770	$40,420	$41,810	$45,260	$76,780	$82,920	$99,890	$118,410	$131,850	$139,690	$146,730

(continued)

EXHIBIT 11.2 *(Continued)*

ABC PRINTING COMPANY
Pro Forma Cash Flow Statement (quarterly)
1994

Cash Receipts	Quarter 1	Quarter 2	Quarter 3	Quarter 4	Annual
Beginning cash (A)	$ 7,000	$ 40,420	$ 76,780	$118,410	$ 7,000
Sales receipts (B)	136,800	155,200	133,700	110,400	536,100
Total cash on hand	143,800	195,620	210,480	228,810	543,100
Cash Disbursements					
Paper supplies (C)	$14,300	$15,100	$13,600	$11,200	$54,200
Outside vendors (D)	6,700	9,200	8,300	6,800	33,000
Print suppliers (E)	6,500	6,600	5,800	4,900	23,800
Freight (F)	700	600	500	400	2,200
Salaries (G)	27,000	21,000	24,000	21,000	93,900
Payroll taxes (H)	2,300	2,700	2,700	2,600	10,300
Auto expenses (I)	800	800	750	800	3,150
Bank charges (J)	90	90	80	60	320
Commissions (K)	4,900	5,100	4,600	3,800	18,400
Dues and Subscriptions (L)	200	200	0	0	400
Worker's comp. ins. (M)	2,700	0	0	0	2,700
Insurance (N)	1,800	1,200	1,200	1,200	5,400
Interest expense (O)	300	300	300	300	1,200
Health benefits (P)	8,400	5,400	5,400	5,400	24,600
Office expense (Q)	300	200	200	200	900
Printing machine lease (R)	2,700	2,700	2,700	2,700	10,800
Copier lease (S)	900	900	900	900	3,600
Postage (T)	140	150	140	120	560
Professional fees (U)	50	700	0	600	1,350
Rent (V)	6,000	6,000	6,000	6,000	24,000
Repairs and maintenance (W)	1,900	1,600	1,500	1,200	6,200
Machinery repairs (X)	2,200	2,000	1,800	1,500	7,500
Sales tax (Y)	4,600	7,400	6,700	5,900	24,600
Taxes (other)	0	0	0	500	500
Telephone (Z)	900	1,100	1,000	900	3,900
Utilities (AA)	2,800	3,800	3,400	2,900	12,900
Adver. and promotion (BB)	2,200	2,000	500	200	4,900
Income taxes	0	22,000	0	0	22,000
Total cash disbursement	$103,380	$118,840	$ 92,070	$ 82,080	$396,370
Ending cash balance	$ 40,420	$ 76,780	$118,410	$146,730	$146,730

As long as income exceeds expenditures, you can feel fairly comfortable. However, there are times, even in an established business, when this would not be true. Highly seasonal businesses need to accumulate a great deal of inventory at a time when sales are traditionally slow in preparation for a very short but hectic

EXHIBIT 11.3 Robert Morris Associates ratio analysis

MANUFACTURERS—ELECTRONIC COMPONENTS & ACCESSORIES. SIC# 3671 (72,74-79)

	Comparative Historical Data			Current Data Sorted by Sales					
	4/1/90–3/31/91 ALL	4/1/91–3/31/92 ALL	4/1/92–3/31/93 ALL	209(4/1–9/30/92)		338(10/1/92–3/31/93)			
# Postretirement Benefits			9					4	1
Type of Statement				0–1MM	1–3MM	3–5MM	5–10MM	10–25MM	25MM & Over
Unqualified	180	227	222	5	12	16	37	65	87
Reviewed	93	100	124	5	46	21	34	15	3
Compiled	87	80	88	15	47	11	10	4	1
Tax Returns	5	3	11	3	4	4			
Other	110	115	102	12	23	16	13	20	18
NUMBER OF STATEMENTS	475	525	547	40	132	68	94	104	109
	%	%	%	%	%	%	%	%	%
ASSETS									
Cash & Equivalents	8.6	9.3	9.5	9.5	10.4	10.0	6.5	8.5	11.8
Trade Receivables - (net)	29.4	28.0	28.9	29.7	29.6	30.7	31.6	27.6	25.6
Inventory	27.8	28.1	27.2	22.4	29.3	26.5	29.3	29.6	22.7
All Other Current	2.5	2.2	1.9	3.1	1.3	1.4	1.5	1.7	3.1
Total Current	68.2	67.6	67.6	64.8	70.6	68.7	68.9	67.4	63.2
Fixed Assets (net)	24.7	25.0	25.6	26.9	23.9	24.2	25.0	26.2	28.1
Intangibles (net)	1.9	2.1	1.7	1.3	0.9	0.6	1.0	2.7	3.1
All Other Non-Current	5.2	5.4	5.1	7.0	4.6	6.5	5.1	3.7	5.6
Total	100.0	100.0	100.0	100.0	100.0	100.0	100.0	100.0	100.0
LIABILITIES									
Notes Payable-Short Term	9.8	9.4	9.0	14.0	9.4	10.0	10.7	9.2	4.6
Cur. Mat.-L/T/D	4.3	4.3	4.3	6.5	5.2	4.0	3.5	4.0	3.6
Trade Payables	14.9	14.7	14.9	14.8	16.3	14.4	16.8	13.8	13.0
Income Taxes Payable	1.1	0.7	0.5	0.2	0.3	0.8	0.6	0.5	0.7
All Other Current	9.0	9.2	9.6	11.2	9.0	10.2	9.1	10.0	9.3
Total Current	39.0	38.3	38.3	46.7	40.3	39.3	40.7	37.3	31.2
Long Term Debt	15.4	15.0	13.5	13.7	14.9	12.4	13.1	12.7	13.7
Deferred Taxes	0.9	0.6	0.7	0.3	0.4	0.4	0.5	0.7	1.3
All Other Non-Current	2.9	3.1	3.0	2.6	2.6	4.7	2.0	3.0	3.5
Net Worth	41.8	43.0	44.5	36.7	41.9	43.1	43.6	46.2	50.3
Total Liabilities & Net Worth	100.0	100.0	100.0	100.0	100.0	100.0	100.0	100.0	100.0

(*continued*)

EXHIBIT 11.3 (Continued)

Line Item	Comparative Historical Data			Current Data Sorted by Sales					
INCOME DATA									
Net Sales	100.0	100.0	100.0	100.0	100.0	100.0	100.0	100.0	100.0
Gross Profit	33.3	32.7	32.9	41.5	37.5	33.9	30.1	28.6	30.2
Operating Expenses	28.3	27.7	28.3	37.4	34.5	29.0	26.0	23.2	24.0
Operating Profit	5.0	5.0	4.6	4.1	3.0	4.8	4.0	5.4	6.2
All Other Expenses (net)	1.7	1.5	1.3	1.2	1.1	1.6	1.0	1.7	1.5
Profit Before Taxes	3.3	3.5	3.2	2.9	1.9	3.2	3.0	3.7	4.7
RATIOS									
Current	2.9	2.8	2.9	3.1	2.9	2.9	2.6	3.4	3.3
	1.9	1.8	1.8	1.5	1.8	1.8	1.7	1.9	2.2
	1.2	1.3	1.3	0.8	1.3	1.2	1.2	1.2	1.5
Quick	1.6	1.6	1.7	2.1	1.6	1.9	1.3	1.7	2.0
	1.0	1.0	1.0	0.8	1.1	1.1	0.9	0.9	1.2
	0.6	0.6	0.7	0.4	0.6	0.6	0.6	0.7	0.8
Sales/Receivables	41 9.0	40 9.4	39 9.1	33 11.2	39 9.3	38 9.6	42 8.7	45 8.2	
	51 7.2	51 7.5	51 7.2	47 7.7	51 7.6	50 7.3	61 7.2	54 6.7	
	66 5.5	62 5.9	62 5.9	69 5.3	61 6.2	59 6.2	65 5.6	72 5.1	
Cost of Sales/Inventory	41 8.8	39 8.5	41 9.4	10 35.4	39 9.4	33 11.1	52 7.0	44 8.3	
	74 4.9	74 4.8	76 4.9	62 5.9	78 4.7	72 5.1	81 4.5	76 4.8	
	122 3.0	114 3.0	122 3.2	111 3.3	122 3.0	111 3.3	122 3.0	122 3.0	
Cost of Sales/Payables	20 18.4	22 18.0	20 16.5	11 31.9	24 15.3	23 16.0	18 20.2	26 13.9	
	33 11.2	35 10.8	34 10.4	33 11.0	38 9.6	38 9.6	32 11.3	37 10.0	
	54 6.8	52 7.2	51 7.0	79 4.6	59 6.2	50 7.3	49 7.5	52 7.0	
Sales/Working Capital	3.9	3.9	3.8	5.1	4.4	4.0	4.8	3.4	2.8
	7.2	7.4	7.0	13.5	7.4	7.3	8.9	5.9	4.9
	18.9	16.7	18.6	−16.8	16.5	19.7	23.5	20.5	10.7 / 17.5
EBIT/Interest	6.5	6.4	8.6	8.0	7.5	7.7	7.9	7.6	
	2.8	3.1	3.5	3.4	3.0	2.6	3.4	3.7	5.2
	1.1	1.1	1.3	−0.8	1.1	0.5	1.6	1.7	1.2
	(427)	(479)	(506)	(33)	(123)	(92)	(96)	(98)	
Net Profit + Depr., Dep., Amort/Cur. Mat. L/T/D	4.9	5.8	7.5	4.6	6.7	7.1	7.3	14.9	
	2.1	2.4	3.0	1.7	1.8	3.4	3.2	4.5	
	1.0	0.9	1.2	0.4	0.9	1.2	1.4	1.5	
	(252)	(270)		(49)	(34)	(54)	(67)	(58)	
Fixed/Worth	0.3	0.3	0.3	0.3	0.2	0.3	0.3	0.3	
	0.6	0.6	0.5	0.8	0.5	0.4	0.5	0.5	0.6
	1.3	1.2	1.2	8.7	1.2	1.2	1.2	1.1	1.1
Debt/Worth	0.6	0.6	0.6	0.5	0.6	0.6	0.7	0.6	0.4
	1.4	1.4	1.3	1.4	1.5	1.3	1.4	1.3	0.9
	3.4	2.9	3.1	72.7	3.2	3.0	3.0	2.9	2.9

EXHIBIT 11.3   (Concluded)

	Comparative Historical Data			Current Data Sorted by Sales					
Debt/Worth									
	0.6	0.6	0.6	0.5	0.6	0.6	0.7	0.6	0.4
	1.4	1.4	1.3	1.4	1.5	1.3	1.4	1.3	0.9
	3.4	2.9	3.1	3.2	3.2	3.0	3.0	2.9	2.9
% Profit Before Taxes/Tangible Net Worth									
	35.7	36.6	33.1	72.7	71.6	31.3	33.2	33.3	30.6
	(439) 16.5	(493) 16.2	(519) 14.7	(31) 14.8	(125) 12.1	(64) 16.4	(93) 14.7	(102) 14.8	(104) 17.8
	2.1	2.7	3.4	0.0	1.0	0.1	6.3	6.5	3.6
% Profit Before Taxes/Total Assets									
	14.9	14.4	12.9	21.2	11.6	13.1	13.0	11.7	15.6
	6.1	6.2	6.0	7.4	4.5	6.6	4.8	6.7	8.3
	0.4	0.6	1.0	−3.9	0.2	−1.3	2.1	2.1	1.3
Sales/Net Fixed Assets									
	19.4	18.3	18.3	22.1	23.1	27.6	21.9	13.5	9.3
	8.9	8.5	8.2	11.0	12.3	10.3	9.7	7.1	5.3
	4.7	4.8	4.6	5.6	5.7	5.0	5.4	4.1	3.9
Sales/Total Assets									
	2.6	2.6	2.7	3.0	2.9	2.8	3.0	2.4	1.9
	1.9	2.0	2.0	2.4	2.2	2.2	2.2	1.9	1.5
	1.4	1.4	1.4	1.5	1.6	1.6	1.6	1.3	1.1
% Depr., Depr., Amort/Sales									
	1.4	1.5	1.4	2.0	1.3	1.0	1.1	1.8	2.4
	(410) 2.7	(464) 2.6	(485) 2.6	(29) 3.5	(123) 2.3	(62) 1.9	(89) 2.0	(97) 2.7	(85) 3.4
	4.6	4.4	4.1	5.5	3.5	4.0	3.5	4.6	5.1
% Officers, Directors, Owners Comp/Sales									
	3.0	2.8	2.9	6.0	5.0	3.6	2.9	1.3	
	(135) 5.1	(143) 5.3	(164) 5.7	(15) 9.1	(55) 8.8	(37) 5.6	(35) 5.0	(14) 2.4	
	10.6	9.7	10.2	12.1	14.1	9.0	7.8	3.2	
Net Sales ($)	9480200M	13090939M	13051668M	24158M	260562M	261555M	672452M	1632642M	10200299M
Total Assets ($)	6674078M	9170171M	9063909M	12442M	146353M	135856M	367650M	1046669M	7354939M

M = $ thousand   MM = $ million

Source: Robert Morris Associates, *Annual Statement Studies* (Philadelphia, PA, 1993).

selling season later in the year. To take an extreme example, you have to spend 11 months of the year growing and accumulating Christmas trees for sales that are made primarily in the first three weeks of December. From January through December, it's all expenses, no income; you either make enough money in December to more than cover your expenses in the next 11 months or have a short-fall (deficit).

Looking at a simple example in Exhibit 11.4 of a restaurant start-up, we make the following projections: in month 0 there are no cash receipts, while there are start-up costs such as heat, light, rent and associated machinery, salary, and inventory costs of $18,420 dollars. The next month's projections show sales and reasonable expenses. Realistically, except for such fixed expenses as rent, costs vary from month to month, so it should not surprise you that as a result of start-up costs and the first several months of operation when expenses are greater than income, the yearly results show a cash deficit. A year-end deficit results from the string of monthly deficits, as shown in Exhibit 11.4. This exhibit shows the projected cash budget and its underlying assumptions.

Since you can't write checks when you are overdrawn at the bank, you must have a positive balance, with cash on hand, or you're out of business. Examining the cash projections, you discover that what will occur is a **cash deficit,** *when expenditures are greater than income.* In this case the deficit will exceed $26,000. Having this money at the beginning of the year would provide you with a **positive cash balance,** which is *the money you have in the bank enabling you to write checks and stay in business.* Although your projected deficit is only $26,675, you need a loan of $29,000 to have a contingency fund of approximately 10 percent.[7]

Borrowing money means you must pay it back. The second and succeeding months show loan payments of $940 dollars. The addition of $29,000 dollars allows for positive cash flows on both a monthly and yearly basis. You have just used your pro forma cash flow to project the amount of money you need to start up and stay in business. By the fourth month, you are showing positive cash flow derived from your operations. At the end of three years, you will have paid off the loan and will show positive cash flows. The business will then be standing on its own **operational results,** which occurs *when the operation of the business results in income being greater than expenditures on a cash basis.*

Running a deficit in the beginning stages of any business is not unusual. Although the cash projections tell you how much money you will need to cover your deficits, it is not quite that simple, since you now have to figure out where to get the cash you need (which is discussed further on).[8]

Breakeven Analysis

While the pro forma cash flow and pro forma statements may show your business to be profitable, it is helpful to know the point at which you actually began to make a profit. A useful tool to determine this point is breakeven analysis.[9] **Breakeven** occurs when *the volume of sales is sufficient to cover all fixed and variable costs; it is the point at which revenues equal costs.* The **breakeven point** is *that point at*

EXHIBIT 11.4 ABP Restaurant: Cash budget assumptions

1. Cash receipts represent current sales (85%) and collections from last month's sales on credit (15%). Thus month 2 current sales are $9,300. Collections of $1,420 represent 15% of first month sales.
2. Insurance assumes eight monthly payments.
3. Sales tax is a percentage (4%) of monthly current sales.
4. A contingency allowance is approximately 10% (rounded).
5. A loan payment is added on the bottom of the schedule.

ABP RESTAURANT
Estimated Cash Budget (Monthly)

	0	1	2	3	4	5	6	7	8	9	10	11	12	YEAR
Gross sales	0	$ 9,530	$10,940	$11,410	$12,820	$13,060	$14,000	$15,350	$14,590	$14,710	$14,470	$14,470	$14,350	$159,700
Cash receipts:														
Current sales		$8,290	9,520	9,930	11,150	11,360	12,180	13,350	12,690	12,800	12,590	12,590	12,480	138,940
A/R collections			1,240	1,420	1,480	1,670	1,700	1,820	2,000	1,900	1,910	1,880	1,880	18,900
Total receipts		$8,290	10,760	11,350	12,630	13,030	13,880	15,170	14,690	14,700	14,500	14,470	14,360	157,830
Cash disbursements:														
Direct materials		$7,000	$4,000	5,000	3,000	3,000	4,000	4,000	4,000	4,500	5,000	4,500	4,500	52,500
Rent		2,500	2,500	2,500	2,500	2,500	2,500	2,500	2,500	2,500	2,500	2,500	2,500	30,000
Labor		3,000	3,000	3,000	3,000	3,000	3,000	3,000	3,000	3,000	3,000	3,000	3,000	36,000
Utilities			1,050	1,050	1,050	1,050	1,000	1,000	1,100	1,100	1,050	1,050	1,050	11,550
Insurance		340	340	340	340	340	340	340	340					2,720
Advertising		200	200	200	200	200	200	200	200	200	200	200	200	2,400
Maintenance		140	200	200	100	80	70	80	70	80	100	140	140	1,400
Store supplies		60	30	105	50	40		30	30	30	60		30	465
Sales tax		380	440	460	510	520	560	610	580	590	580	580	570	6,380
Other taxes			220	220	480	220	220	460	220	220	330	220	220	3,030
Start-up costs	$18,420													
Total disbursements	$18,420	$13,620	11,980	13,075	11,230	10,950	11,890	12,220	12,040	12,220	12,820	12,190	12,210	146,445
Cash +/–	(18,420)	(5,330)	(1,220)	(1,725)	1,400	2,080	1,990	2,950	2,650	2,480	1,680	2,280	2,150	(7,035)
Cumulative +/–	(18,420)	(23,750)	(24,970)	(26,695)	(25,295)	(23,215)	(21,225)	(18,275)	(15,625)	(13,145)	(11,465)	(9,185)	(7,035)	(7,035)
Maximum shortage														$26,695
Contingency allowance														2,305
Cash required														$29,000
Beginning cash	$29,000	$10,580	5,250	3,090	425	885	2,025	3,075	5,085	6,795	8,335	9,075	10,415	29,000
Cash +/–	(18,420)	(5,330)	(1,220)	(1,725)	1,400	2,080	1,990	2,950	2,650	2,480	1,680	2,280	2,150	(7,035)
Less: loan payment			(940)	(940)	(940)	(940)	(940)	(940)	(940)	(940)	(940)	(940)	(940)	(10,340)
Ending cash balance	$10,580	$5,250	3,090	425	885	2,025	3,075	5,085	6,795	8,335	9,075	10,415	11,625	11,625

which the company neither makes a profit nor sustains a loss. At this point sales revenues equal the costs (expenses) necessary to generate them. This is useful information because the breakeven point also tells you the minimum level of sales you need to start or continue to operate. In addition, it illustrates the relationship between costs and revenue volume. As long as your forecasted sales are greater than the breakeven point, you may stay in business. If projected, or actual, sales drop below this point, you might decide against starting or continuing the business.

Determining the Breakeven Point (BEP)

Since the breakeven point shows the relationship between cost and volume, let's begin the analysis by identifying the components of breakeven analysis.

1. Revenue is determined by multiplying the unit sales by the unit price.
2. Fixed costs are those expenses such as rent, loan payments, or insurance premiums that do not vary with the level of production or sales.
3. Variable costs are costs such as direct labor and raw materials that vary directly with the level of production or sales.

While you recognize that some costs are semi-variable—that is, they change but not directly with the production level—for the purposes of this technique these costs must be divided into the appropriate fixed and variable components. Examples are electricity, water, and other cost components that are *fixed* for certain minimum amounts and then vary with usage.

Assume that:

$$Sales\ revenue = \$200,000\ (10,000\ units \times \$20\ each)$$
$$Variable\ cost = \$\ 40,000$$
$$Fixed\ costs = \$\ 20,000$$
$$Unit\ cost = \$\ 12.00$$

Using the formula:

$$BEP = \frac{Fixed\ cost}{1 - \dfrac{Variable\ cost}{Sales\ revenue}}$$

the breakeven point is $100,000, or 5,000 units.

$$BEP = \frac{200,000}{1 - \dfrac{40,000}{200,000}} = \$100,000$$

Graphically, this is shown in Exhibit 11.5.

Breakeven Analysis as a Management Tool

Another way of looking at and using breakeven analysis will enable you to determine your breakeven point by identifying a desired production level. **Contribution**

Exhibit 11.5

Graphic depiction of breakeven point

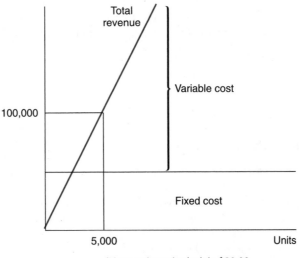

(since sales price/unit is $20.00,
then $20.00/$100,000 = 5,000)

margins are *the amount of money generated by sales volume after fixed costs are covered.* If we define our contribution as

$$\frac{Variable\ cost}{Sales\ revenue} = CM,$$

it will enable us to predict the breakeven point at various described profit levels.
Seeking a $50,000 profit, our formula would be as follows:

$$BEP = \frac{Total\ Fixed\ Cost + Desired\ Profits}{CM}$$

$$BEP = \frac{20,000 + 50,000}{0.20}$$

Breakeven point = $650,000, or 32,500 units

Thus, the breakeven point will be determined by and depend upon the profit you desire to make.[10] Although the preceding explanation of the breakeven point is presented for the business as a whole, it should be noted that in a multiproduct organization, breakeven points can be calculated by product. This can be helpful and informative if, for example, the business is losing money on one of its products; even though the consolidated breakeven may be positive, corrective action should be taken.

Types of Capital Financing

Earlier in this chapter, two questions were cited as vital to business survival. The second question of determining sources to raise necessary funds is now addressed.

Entrepreneurs can choose from three major classifications of capital to meet particular needs. The three major types of financing are:

1. Short-term capital
2. Early stage capital
3. Long-term capital

Short-Term Capital

Why would you need short-term capital? **Short-term capital** is *funds that are borrowed for less than one year.* It is used when companies have expended their initial capital. Many business owners often overlook the need for this type of capital, which develops because the owner has neglected the task of completing a projected cash flow budget statement. For example, every business has certain expenses that arise in one month and not in another, such as an insurance payment or an excessively high heating bill. If this expense is not factored into the monthly budget, the small business owner will fall short of funds.

A popular type of debt financing used by small business is trade credit, which is obtained from creditors. Trade credit is paid within 30 to 60 days, depending upon the type of business. Trade credit may also be obtained from a commercial bank, which may be a good source for a short-term loan source.

Early-Stage Capital

Early stage capital, often referred to as intermediate capital, is *funds to be paid back within a period of five years.* The need for early-stage financing usually arises as the need for working capital increases, or if accounts receivable rise and sales volume is heading upward. In any case, the business must be at the breakeven point.

For example, a business owner may decide to construct an addition on an existing structure. Projects such as these require a large amount of money, the repayment of which has to be stretched out over a longer period of time. A short-term loan to finance these needs would pinch cash flow, thereby hurting the business. Equipment loans represent a form of intermediate capital financing. These loans are paid within five years on an installment basis.

Long-Term Capital

Long-term capital *covers long-term projects lasting longer than five years and includes fixed assets and real estate purchases, expensive machinery, and franchise financing.* Expensive machinery such as numerically controlled milling machines can take as long as 10 to 15 years to be paid off. Long-term capital is capital that is borrowed for more than five years and is used mostly for major expansions or the acquisition of very expensive equipment.

Capital Requirements

A well-prepared assessment of capital needs and sources is an essential step for the small business owner. The relationships between working capital, fixed asset needs, and cash flows are sometimes confusing to the novice businessperson. Often, the entrepreneur overlooks the need to translate plans into dollars. As a result, the business owner grossly underestimates current and future capital requirements. Financial hardships and strained relationships among all parties involved are the consequences of failing to formulate a capital requirement plan, which is the cornerstone for estimating money needs. This topic is addressed in the accounting section in Chapter 12.

The entrepreneur should ask these basic questions before initiating a search for capital:

1. How much capital will I need?
2. What type of capital is required?
3. Where can I get the funds?

Traditional Sources of Venture Capital

When the entrepreneur seeks equity capital for a venture, the traditional paths of financing are usually followed. The path starts out with the entrepreneur's personal stake of money. Since initial capital is typically inadequate, the path may branch out to a number of traditional sources of equity capital such as friends, relatives, partnerships, or the sale of capital stock. Below, we will follow these traditional paths in more detail.[11]

Seed Financing

Typically, the small business owner has saved a small amount of *personal funds, which are often referred to as ownership capital, or* **seed financing.** Usually, this amount of capital is too small to start a successful venture, so it is common practice for the initial capital to include some debt. Traditionally, the owner should have at least two-thirds of the total amount.[12] Many firms fail because of the lack of ownership equity. However, if initial profits are high enough, the venture may be able to thrive on a small initial amount of seed money. A conservative approach as well as a safe one is to have enough ownership equity to ensure a margin of safety. With a larger stake in the business, the owner will be able to have greater independence and a larger share of profits. Also, investors will be more willing to finance the venture if the owner has to assume the same amount of risk.

The search for the "right" investor is frequently overlooked by many entrepreneurs. A relative or friend is the most typical source for a stake of money. However, this first choice for equity capital may not be the best source. The right investor should be one who is fully aware of the supply of funds needed to boost the business into a fairly stable operating state. The right individual will be aware of risks and have additional funds to provide if needed. Also, the right investor will have goals that are compatible with the founder. Ideally, the investor should have experience with the nature of the business and be able to offer guidance. As you see, a person who you may know casually may not be the best choice.

When times get difficult, an unsuitable investor will often call in the loan. At that point, where does the entrepreneur seek help? To avoid this trap, we will explore many other sources of venture capital that are available to the entrepreneur.

Relatives and Friends

Though this source of capital continues to be the most frequently sought by most entrepreneurs, troubles frequently arise from this type of loan.[13] Relationships may become strained during the course of the loan period, and it is not uncommon for relatives or friends to interfere with business decisions because they feel their stake in the business allows them to take an active role. Another difficulty develops when a friend or relative demands early repayment of the loan, often leading to a frantic search for capital to cover the gap left by the lender. To avoid awkward situations, the terms of the loan, which should be made on a businesslike basis, should specify the role of the lenders in the operational policies of the business. You should plan to repay loans in the shortest period of time.

Partnerships

Many business ventures are started with one or more partners in order to meet capital requirements more easily.[14] As discussed in Chapter 3, a written agreement listing the duties, responsibilities, and authority must be accepted by all partners. Some partners can be listed as being a limited partner whose main interest lies with the investment, not with the daily activities of the business. However, the limited partner should have some voice in the decisions that affect the business's viability.

Commercial Banks

Commercial banks are *banks that receive funds from depositors and then lend these funds to businesses.* Contrary to what many entrepreneurs believe about commercial bank financing, banks do offer a limited source when initial capital is needed. However, banks require a personal guarantee in the form of chattel mortgages, and most start-up ventures lack the hard assets banks seek as collateral.

Commercial banks may offer short-term loans to small businesses rather than lending on a long-term basis. In recent years, many types of financing have become available to qualified applicants. The selection of the bank should be based on the various services offered that best suit the small business owner's needs. It is to the entrepreneur's benefit to establish a good working relationship with a commercial bank in the early stages of establishment.[15]

Sale of Capital Stock

The sale of stock as a device for raising capital is not limited to large businesses. This type of financing offers an alternative source of funds after the effort to raise capital in less complicated ways has been exhausted. The sale of stock to individual investors involves the dilution of ownership, however, and should be seriously weighed as an option for raising capital.

Capital stock is *stock, or ownership shares, issued in exchange for funds needed to operate your business.* Stock, which can be sold to investors by private sale, is bought by selected individuals who may be employees and acquaintances. The advantage of a private sale of stock is that the firm does not have to comply with the laws of the Security and Exchange Commission. Equity holders, however, are able to have a voice in running the business, relative to their ownership equity position (i.e., the number of shares held relative to the total number of shares issued by the corporation). As owners, equity holders may also share in the earnings of the company.

Stock is sold to the general public at a public sale. This type of sale requires the firm to be operating as a corporation. A public sale of stock is usually carried out by a larger firm that needs additional working capital and whose owner has to keep in mind that the price of the stock is influenced by market conditions. To facilitate small business's access to the equity (stock) market, the SBA has accepted the Securities and Exchange Commission (SEC) regulations "A" and "D," which permit smaller businesses to make private placements of stock to interested groups or individuals without having to register them with the SEC. **Private placements** are *direct sales of stock (equity) positions to private investors without SEC registration and with minimal restrictions.* For example, a firm may price the stock at $13 per share on the open market, but private investors will only pay $10 per share through a direct placement.

The disadvantage of issuing public stock is that it makes the firm subject to greater regulation by the state in which the firm operates, as well as the Securities and Exchange Commission. Another disadvantage is that the small business owner may lack sufficient knowledge of the securities market and may naively enter into contracts with brokers that may not be in the best interest of the business.[16]

Venture Capital Companies

Venture capital refers to *funds that are invested in new or higher-risk enterprises, usually in return for an equity position.* Venture capital firms are a good source of capital for businesses demonstrating potential for rapid growth.[17] Venture capital firms differ from other financing sources because in seeking a higher rate of return on the initial investment, they subject themselves to high risk factors that other sources are not willing to assume. Since these investors have a large stake in the business, management counseling is available. At present, more than 800 venture capital companies operate in the United States. How does one contact a venture capital firm? Directories such as *Pratt's Guide to Venture Capital,* published by Venture Economies Inc., furnishes a list of venture capital firms.

Corporate partnering is a form of venture capital. This source of venture capital is becoming popular among large firms. By investing in small advanced-technology businesses, larger companies can keep up with fast-paced developments, a technique referred to as "windowing" in on recent entrepreneurial developments.

Venture capital firms may appear to be an excellent source of readily available capital.[18] However, the pros and cons of this type of venture capital must be considered before entering into such an arrangement:

Pros:

- Heightened credibility with customers and bankers.
- Expert managerial assistance.[19]
- Continuing source of financing.
- Smaller burden of risk.

Cons:

- Loss of substantial equity.
- Investor makes most of the decisions.
- Risk of takeover.[20]

The choice of which venture capital source to approach must be carefully thought out because the financial goals of a venture capital firm can differ from the entrepreneur's plans for his business.

Government Sponsored Agencies

The government has developed sources that sponsor the small business owner.[21] One government agency that helps to fund the entrepreneur is the Small Business Administration. Other *indirect government-sponsored agencies* include Small Business Investment Companies, commonly referred to as SBICs, and the MES-BIC program, which stands for the Minority Enterprise Small Business Investment Company. The **SBA,** *an agency of the government founded to help small businesses,* offers the most assistance with financial help and professional advice. As of 1986, the Small Business Administration made or guaranteed 361,000 business and disaster loans totaling $16 billion. The SBA oversees the functions of Small Business Investment Companies and a variety of smaller programs such as the Economic Opportunity Loan Program.

Small Business Administration Loans

The SBA guaranteed loan program is a positive commitment by the government to assist the small business owner. The program is built upon the belief that the country's small businesses help maintain a healthy economy. In addition to its guaranteed loan programs, the SBA added a program called the **Small Business Institute**

(SBI), a program that offers consulting services to the business conducted by senior-level business administration students enrolled in participating universities throughout the country. Another consulting service offered by the SBA is **SCORE** (Service Corps of Retired Executives), *an organization of people who donate their time assisting small businesses affiliated with the SBA* and who can assist the entrepreneur in writing a business plan that will facilitate obtaining a loan.

To qualify for an SBA guaranteed loan, a business applies to a commercial bank affiliated with the SBA. If the entrepreneurial venture is one the bank believes in but the entrepreneur is unable to fulfill normal bank underwriting conditions, the bank may ask the SBA for a loan guarantee. At the bank's request, the SBA will guarantee a portion of the loan. If the business later fails, the SBA is liable for the guaranteed portion of the loan.

Special Government Programs

The Economic Opportunity Loan program and the Minority Enterprise Small Business Investment Company (MESBIC) program represent special financing for minorities. The Economic Opportunity Loan program is an exclusive SBA program that lends up to $100,000 to minority business owners for up to 15 years.

The MESBIC program is owned by a private concern, usually a financial or industrial company. A MESBIC-sponsored venture may combine financing sources from the company itself, banks, and the SBA.

MESBIC companies originally began when a chief executive officer of a corporation in California proposed to offer venture capital to minority-owned small businesses. MESBICs were further developed when President Richard Nixon announced "Project Enterprise" by executive order in 1969. Nixon's order gave the Small Business Administration licensing and regulatory powers over MESBICs. Similar to SBICs, MESBICs provide managerial assistance and perform market studies on proposed projects. MESBICs invest in banks, high-tech firms, service companies, franchises, as well as other diverse ventures.

Small Business Investment Company Loans

Small Business Investment Company (SBIC) loans evolved out of the Small Business Equity Act, passed by Congress in 1958. This legislation was aimed at encouraging the private business sector to finance small businesses. SBICs are regulated and must be licensed to operate by the SBA.

Initially, SBICs almost failed. Venture capital funding during the 1960s was still an unproven concept. After many mistakes on the part of venture capitalists, SBICs were reconstructed by the late 1970s. New private venture firms were formed as limited partnerships and corporations. Principal funding now comes from insurance companies, pension funds, bank trust departments, and wealthy individuals. SBICs have been formed in most states, and most have an excellent track record of successful SBIC-sponsored ventures. Approximately 40 percent of all start-ups were financed by SBICs in 1979. However, to receive SBIC financing the entrepreneur must have a reasonable amount of equity as well as a thoroughly developed business plan.

Other federally sponsored loan programs include those sponsored by the Farmers Home Administration, the Department of Housing and Urban Development, and the Economic Development Administration. Information on these and many other programs can be obtained from the agencies. The local SBA office would be a good source of further information.

Examples of SBIC ventures are shopping center developments, fast-food franchises, cinemas, grocery stores, and drugstores. Many SBICs invest a large portion of funds in successful small businesses that are ready to expand. Financing for this type of capital requirement often originates in the form of a convertible debt structure.

State and Regional Development Companies

To develop small businesses in the community, a number of privately owned companies are sponsored by the state. The private companies desire to develop a small business community that will become, in turn, its suppliers and customers. Large manufacturing, utility, and transportation companies have traditionally been the largest contributors. To find out more about these sponsors, you can contact the local chamber of commerce or the state business development office.

There are many feasible ways the new small business can finance its operations once it is ready to serve its customers. Trade credit has been a long-time source of debt capital and remains one of the small business person's most valuable financing resource. Imagine if an owner had to pay for inventory with cash on hand! The very existence of small business would be unimaginable. Let's explore some of the debt-financing resources that are readily available when the new venture is ready to operate.

Trade Credit

Trade credit is *credit extended by a supplier.* Inventory is one of the largest investments that most small businesses have to make. An excellent source of capital comes from vendors with whom the business has dealings. This type of credit usually involves an unsecured open-book account. If the credit references of the small business owner are in good standing, the supplier ships inventory to the firm and opens up an accounts receivable record in its books. The dollar volume of trade depends on the type of buyers and suppliers.

Terms of credit are usually 30 days, although some suppliers offer a discount when the bill is paid early. A common credit term such as 2/10, net 30, means that the small business owner can take advantage of a 2 percent discount if it pays the total amount of the bill in 10 days. After the 10-day period passes, the owner has the responsibility to pay the total amount of the bill within the 30-day limit. Trade discounts can save the firm money, but failure to use credit properly will not only cost the business money but will result in the loss of a credit source as well.

A supplier is someone that the entrepreneur will have to rely on for prompt deliveries, undamaged goods, and extended credit in times of emergency. Therefore, the owner should not pick the first supplier he or she comes across. A business owner has to select suppliers carefully, taking note of their reputations. One indicator of a good supplier is that the supplier qualifies for the new European Economic Community International Standards Office (ISO) 9000 Series standards.[22]

Equipment Loans and Leases

Acquiring the equipment a business needs in order to function can be a difficult task. Because vendors routinely offer attractive installment plans, equipment can be bought on an installment basis: A 25 to 35 percent down payment is usually required with an intermediate loan period of three to five years. However, an entrepreneur should exercise caution. Just because it seems so easy to buy on installment, a new entrepreneur may easily forget that multiple small installment payments can add up. Do not buy more equipment than you can afford.

Leasing is an increasingly popular option. Companies such as IBM, Honeywell, and Xerox have been offering equipment-leasing options for many years. The advantages of leasing equipment are as follows:

- Flexibility with equipment needs and payment schedules.
- Smaller capital requirements.
- The leasing company offers maintenance service for equipment.
- Leasing offers a way to beat the obsolescence problem.

Disadvantages with leasing options are the absence of depreciation as a non-cash outlay and the higher total cost the firm will have to pay out compared to purchasing the equipment outright.

Summary

The Interrelationship between the Financial Function and the Other Business Plan Components

The financial function is critical to other functional areas, as it must supply the necessary resources to all areas if the firm is to be viable. Too little money or mistakes in determining financial needs based on input from all other functional areas can lead to cutbacks and reduce profitability.

Determining Financial Needs

In this chapter you have learned how to answer the questions of how to determine how much capital you need, where to acquire it, and how to determine when your company begins to make a profit. In order to be as precise as possible, you must be able to project **pro forma**

statements, which are *guidelines against which you can measure how your assumptions relate to reality.* Using these pro formas will enable you to predict your **cash flow,** which is a statement that *translates your business plan in future (projected) dollars.* If you don't have a financial history, you can use **standard industry ratios,** *which are developed from data reported to trade associations or governmental units,* and **SIC codes** for your firm to enable prediction. The results of your projections will indicate whether you have a **cash deficit** or a **positive cash flow.** You will identify the **operational results** of running the firm and be able to set up a **cash budget.** Using your predictions, you can determine when you make a profit by identifying your **breakeven,** which is *the volume of sales sufficient to cover all fixed and variable costs; it is the point at which revenues equal costs.* Understanding the financial needs of your business is one of the two things you need to understand.

The Search for Funds

The other facet of operating the business involves knowing when you need cash. For example you need cash at various stages of the business's growth. Your needs may be for **short-term capital** that is *borrowed for less than one year;* **long-term capital** that *covers long-term projects, fixed assets, and provides permanent working capital for real estate purchases, expensive machinery, and franchise financing;* or **early-stage capital,** *capital to be paid back within a time period of five years.* When your **capital requirements** are determined, you can use several sources for funding. You may use **seed capital,** *a small amount of personal funds that are often referred to as ownership capital* from **commercial banks.** Or the source of funds might be **venture capital,** which is *funds that are invested in new or higher-risk enterprises;* **SBICs; MESBICS;** and the SBA *indirect government-sponsored agencies.*

Questions

1. Why is a business plan so important in estimating the money needed for a new venture?
2. Why would any source of venture capital consider the business plan as an important document?
3. Why is the cash flow statement such an important part of your business plan?
4. How would you prepare a cash flow using standard industry ratios?
5. Another method of obtaining cash flow projections is to use the past history of the company. Explain this approach to cash flow and illustrate.
6. Assuming your cash flow projections are realistic, why can't you show negative balances? What do you do if negative balances occur?
7. Define *breakeven.*
8. Why is breakeven analysis a useful tool?
9. Define *fixed* and *variable* costs.
10. What basic questions should an entrepreneur ask before seeking sources of capital?
11. What is the difference between equity capital and debt capital? Which would you prefer and why?

12. What problems would you foresee in obtaining loans from friends and relatives? Under what conditions would these be a good source for funds?

13. How can your suppliers of inventory and machinery help provide initial capital for the new business?

14. Are commercial banks a good source of funds? When would you go to a commercial bank, and what business ratios would you need to present?

15. Name and discuss several governmental sources of funds. When might you go to these sources, and what documentation would you need to provide?

16. "Venture capital companies are a good source of funds." Discuss this statement, giving advantages and disadvantages of using venture capital.

17. SBA loans may be either direct or guaranteed. Define and discuss each type.

Application Exercises

When doing these exercises, where applicable, be sure to select a specific business, preferably one where you presently or previously worked or a business you would like to own someday. If this is not possible, pick a specific organization to which you will refer. Be sure to identify the organization by name. Limit your answers to one or two pages per exercise.

1. Assume you want to start a small retail store. Prepare a cash flow statement for three years, using SIC and Robert Morris Associates guidelines. Estimate the first year's sales to be between $250,000 and $1,000,000.

2. Interview a person who has just started or is about to start a business and determine if a cash flow projection was or is being developed. Prepare a report on this person's view of cash flow statements.

3. Interview three local small business owners. Find out how they obtained funds necessary to start their businesses. Keep your questions general and nonthreatening, since these people may be reluctant to provide you with actual figures.

4. Assume you have a can't-fail, profit-assured idea for a business but you need $10,000 in initial capital.

    a. Ask your friends and relatives if they would lend you money and what assurances they would want.

    b. Ask the small business loan officer at your local bank what would be required before lending you money and what the repayment requirements would be.

    c. Ask a venture capitalist if your business would be appropriate for investment and what would be demanded in return.

    d. Visit your local SBA office and ask what they would need before they would discuss a loan with you. They may have a standard loan package, including forms and instructions. Report on your findings and include the SBA package.

5. Assume you wish to start a business and you have pro formas prepared. Prepare a report on the necessity to also have a breakeven analysis. Include in your report how to arrive at the breakeven point and how the breakeven point can help you in decision making.

Application Situations

1. Al Kurrow

Al Kurrow has always loved sailing and was happiest when on the ocean in a good wind. After 15 years working in a large corporation in the shipping department, he decided to take a chance and realize his life's dream. He borrowed money to buy a sailboat so that he could set up a charter business in the Caribbean. He knew he could be successful and had already found a marina where he could operate his charter service. Until now, finances were not an important question, as Al had neither the time nor the desire to do any financial planning. His belief is that he has most of the essential ingredients for success and that success was inevitable.

Assignment

1. Based on the information provided, do you think Al needs a financial plan? Estimate his needs and draw up such a plan for the next three years.
2. Assuming you find that Al needs money, where should he get it? What would be good sources of funds for him, and what would not? Explain your choices.
3. Is his venture too small to justify financial planning? Is any venture too small? Explain your reasoning.
4. What is your opinion of Al's making this a successful venture? Explain your reasoning.

2. Sally Chin

Sally Chin had done much in the four years since leaving college. She had always had an interest in antiques and artifacts as well as a goal of managing her own business. She also had experience in buying and selling antiques as a part of her job as an assistant curator in a large city museum, but the museum was cutting back on staffing and she felt stifled. These factors led her to think about going out on her own and becoming an antiques dealer. Scouting out locations in the antique district, she found a vacant store that was perfect. Now, she thinks, might be a good time to move ahead, but this would be an entirely new business and she has no idea about where to begin. At the least, she wants to do some financial planning.

Assignment

1. Describe how Sally should start her financial planning. Where would she get basic information, and how would she use this information to plan?
2. Where would Sally get funds to support her venture? Which sources might be the best? The worst? Explain your reasoning.
3. Do you think from the information given Sally can be successful? Why or why not?

3. Mike Litt

Mike Litt went through high school in the shop course, majoring in automobile mechanics. After graduation, he worked in a service station's automobile repair business for six years. Mike thinks that it's now time he went into business for himself. He believes he has a following of people who have come to know and trust him and who would provide a good base on which to begin. After looking around for the past two years, he located an auto repair business for sale. The owner was willing to provide past financial history.

Assignment

1. How would Mike draw up his financial plan? Be specific.
2. What would be Mike's best source for funding? Explain your reasoning.

Mike made up his mind to move ahead and bought the automobile repair business he had located. His first year's experience seemed to be successful. However after examining his year-end figures, he was astounded to see that he had operated at a loss. It looked as though he didn't make enough money to cover his expenses. As he was on a very limited budget, he was worried about making it through the next year.

3. Should Mike have been surprised at these results? Why or why not? Explain your reasoning.
4. How can Mike determine when he will be making a profit? If you know of a method that will help Mike identify it, outline how Mike can use it.
5. How should Mike have planned his first three years? Explain the method Mike could have used and how he could be solvent for the first three years.

Integrated Case Question—CorLu Foods

Set up an accounting system for CorLu and develop three years of pro forma statements. Include cash flow, balance sheets, income statements and breakeven points. These statements should be monthly for the first year, quarterly for the second and bi-annually for the third. (Please refer to the Integrated Case, "CorLu Foods.")

Additional Readings

Barton, Sidney L., and Charles H. Matthews. "Small Firm Financing: Implications from a Strategic Management Perspective." *Journal of Small Business Management* 27, no. 1 (January 1989), pp. 1–7.

Brokaw, Leslie. "To Market, to Market to Buy a Fat Pig (in a Poke)." *Inc.,* May 1993, p. 160.

Carter, Richard B., and Howard E. Van Auken. "Personal Equity Investment and Small Business Financial Difficulties." *Entrepreneurship: Theory and Practice* 15, no. 2 (Winter 1990), pp. 51–60.

Cocheo, Steve. "Lenders Juggle Credit and Toxic Waste." *ABA Banking Journal,* July 1990, pp. 83–87.

Friedland, Marc. "Asset-Based Financing." *Franchising World,* January/February 1993, pp. 22–23.

Gould, Lee. "Buy, Lease, or Rent? It All Depends . . ." *Modern Materials Handling,* March 1990, pp. 52–56.

Hall, John, and Charles W. Hofer. "Venture Capitalists' Decision Criteria in New Venture Evaluation." *Journal of Business Venturing* 8, no. 1 (January 1993), pp. 25–42.

Harris, Jean E.; Stanley Keller; G. Michael Stakias; Mike Liles, Jr. "Financing the 'American Dream': ULOR SCOR(ES)." *Business Lawyer,* May 1990, pp. 1343–46.

Hirsch, Maurice L., Jr. "Break-Even Analysis: Basic Model, Variants, Extensions." *Accounting Review,* January 1993, pp. 209–10.

Hutchinson, Robert W., and Donal G. McKillop. "Banks and Small to Medium-Sized Business Financing in the United Kingdom: Some General Issues." *National Westminster Bank Quarterly Review,* February 1992, pp. 84–95.

Hyatt, Joshua. "Rewriting the Book on Entrepreneurship." *Inc.,* August 1989, pp. 86–93.

Nichols, Don. "How to Woo Your Banker." *Small Business Reports,* June 1991, pp. 41–43.

Palframan, Diane. "Why Small Banks Big (Part I)." *Management Today,* November 1989, pp. 157–64.

Posner, Bruce G. "Earning Back Your Equity." *Ideas Inc.,* March, 1993, p. 37.

Purcell, Bill. "Financing Trends in the '90s." *Manufacturing Systems,* February 1993, pp. 64–65.

Razek, Joseph R. "Gain Control of Your Organization's Finances: Break-Even Analysis." *Nonprofit World,* September/October 1989, pp. 30–33.

"Six Examples: Ways to Increase Sales and Profits." *Business Owner,* September 1990, pp. 8–11.

Szabo, Joan C. "State Funds for Start-Ups." *Nation's Business,* June 1989, pp. 42, 44.

———. "Small Firms' Credit Crunch." *Nation's Business,* July 1990, pp. 25–27.

Tarras, John. "The Search for Financing." *Restaurant Hospitality,* December 1991, p. 64.

Thompson, Kevin D. "Planning for Profit." *Black Enterprise,* April 1993, pp. 93–94.

Endnotes

1. Ronaleen R. Roha, "Raising Money for Your Small Business." *Changing Times,* May 1990, p. 45(6).
2. Bruce J. Blechman, "Make No Mistake," *Entrepreneur,* December 1991, pp. 28–31.
3. Eileen David, "Dodging the Bullet," *Venture,* December 1988, pp. 77, 79.
4. These assumptions generally appear as footnotes to the financial statements, which experienced financial specialists always read first.
5. Firms report either voluntarily to entities such as trade associations or involuntarily to the Internal Revenue Service. These reports are aggregated and a model of an "average firm" is developed.
6. Yearly sales equals $453,187.00; cash expenditures equals $409,425.54. The formula for this is income less expenditure equals net balance. See December 31 end cash flow balance in previous example.
7. Here our contingency fund is approximately 10 percent of the entire loan so that our loan is a whole dollar amount.
8. Ronald Bailey, "Them That Can, Do, Them That Can't, Forecast," *Forbes,* December 26, 1988, pp. 97–100.

9. Jack Egan, "Trump Plays His Biggest Ace," *U.S. News & World Report,* April 9, 1990, p. 41.

10. At the $50,000 profit level, you need to sell 15,250 units (20 × 15,250 = $305,000).

11. Udayan Gupta, "Venture Capital Dims for Start-Ups but Not to Worry," *The Wall Street Journal,* January 24, 1990, p. B2.

12. Elizabeth Fenner, "How to Raise the Cash You Need," *Money Guide,* Summer 1991, p. 45.

13. Gordon Williams, "Family Loans: How to Say Yes, When to Say No," *Reader's Digest,* February 1991, p. 160.

14. David R. Evanson, "Capital Gain," *Entrepreneur,* November 1991, pp. 133–36.

15. Daniel M. Clark, "Banks and Bankability," *Venture,* September 1989, p. 29.

16. Ellyn E. Spragins, "Who Needs Wall Street? *Inc.,* October 1990, pp. 159–62.

17. Ibid.

18. David J. Morrow, "An Asian Honeymoon," *International Business,* June 1991, pp. 28–32.

19. Mary-Margaret Wantuck, "The Venture Specialists," *Nation's Business,* June 1984, p. 40.

20. "Venture Capitalists Take the Reins," *Small Business Reports,* April 1990, p. 23.

21. Amy L. Weiss, "Rehabilitating a Loan Proposal," *Business Age,* October 1989, pp. 32–34.

22. The ISO 9000 Series standards are required for all firms doing business with the European Economic Community.

IV   CONTROLLING AND EVALUATING PERFORMANCE

12 THE ACCOUNTING FUNCTION

In this chapter you will learn about the importance of financial information in running your business. You will learn about the different types of financial statements you can prepare from the records you maintain of your business transactions.[1] You will learn about the fundamental accounting concepts of assets, liabilities, and owner's equity.

Financial statements commonly used in most businesses are the chart of accounts, the balance sheet, the income statement, the profit-and-loss statement, and the cash flow statement.

You will learn how to reconcile the bank statements with your checkbook balance.

Chapter Learning Objectives

After completing this chapter, you should be able to:

· Identify and construct the various financial statements to be used in your business: the balance sheet, the income statement, the cash flow statement.
· Identify the components of the financial statements.
· Understand the information presented on a bank statement.
· Perform the steps in reconciling a checking account.
· Determine the financial condition and viability of your company.
· Define the following 29 key terms in order of their appearance:

General ledger	Depreciation
Chart of accounts	Accumulated depreciation
Balance sheet	Leasehold improvements
Asset	Current liabilities
Liabilities	Accounts payable

Net worth/owner's equity   Long-term liabilities

Tangible assets   Notes payable

Intangible assets   Retained earnings

Current assets   Income statement (profit-and-loss statement)

Cash   Cost of goods sold

Accounts receivable   Gross profits

Merchandise inventory   Profits (loss)

Supplies   Canceled checks

Prepaid expenses   Fixed-asset list

Fixed assets

The Interrelationship between the Accounting Function and the Other Business Plan Components

The accounting function links all other functional areas such as production/operations, marketing, and finance. Each functional area of the company must express its needs and desires for resources in monetary terms. The accounting function records functional requirements and produces a total company demand for funds using the cash flow budget as its primary vehicle. Accounting also keeps track of sales made and bills paid by customers and bills that need to be paid from the business. Equipment and operations budgets are prepared using inputs from production/operations, marketing, finance, and personnel. The reports generated by the accounting function and the information they contain are needed in each functional area if it is to operate efficiently. Lack of a good accounting function could seriously impact on functional efficiency and company profitability.

Record Keeping

You should keep in mind that the balance sheet and income statement are compilations of the firm's activity. In order to produce these statements you need records of the business activity from which you can construct the various statements that will make use of ratios and various analytic tools that will be explained in another chapter. You must keep records:[2]

1. To construct the necessary statements.
2. To be able to compare budget figures (projected versus actual results) to see if you are on target; this will be discussed in Chapter 13.
3. To satisfy the requirements of the Internal Revenue Service (IRS), which requires record keeping.

Records should be maintained in the following areas (where applicable):

1. Sales   3 years
2. Inventory   7 years
3. Accounts Receivable   3 years
4. Accounts Payable   3 years
5. Cash   7 years
6. Payroll   10 years
7. Depreciation   Life of assets
8. Equipment   Life of assets
9. Purchases   3 years

Accounting Systems

The importance of the accounting function cannot be overemphasized.[3] You, as an entrepreneur, must be able to understand and use the accounting information to:

1. Know if your business is making a profit.
2. Compare your firm's current performance with past performance.
3. Project future performance.
4. Compare your firm's results with the results of other firms in your industry.
5. Make informed decisions about what future actions your firm should take.

The primary purpose of the accounting function is its use as a management tool that enables you to understand your company's performance and to serve as an aid in decision making.[4] Ultimately, your goal as an entrepreneur is to know if your firm is profitable; financial statements will tell you this. Thus this chapter covers the necessary information you need to know: the balance sheet, the income statement, and the cash flow statement.

While this material will enable you to understand your firm's operations, it should be clear that every firm needs an accountant or accounting advice in order to set up the books and maintain records that produce the statements you need in order to run the company.

The first task that you or your accountant will do is to review or create the chart of accounts for your business. A **chart of accounts** is *a list of all the accounts to which charges are made.* These accounts, which you name, translate your vision of how to financially measure the company into various accounts. All financial reports are generated from the chart of accounts, so a well-thought-out plan is important at the outset. All the accounts of your business are tracked in the **general ledger,** which is *a book or computer listing in which entries are made concerning all of a firm's financial transactions.* It may be computerized or a manual system.

The Balance Sheet

What do we mean when we refer to a balance sheet? A **balance sheet** is *a snapshot view of the financial value of the firm's assets, liabilities, and net worth* at a particular point in time. It is divided into two major sections: the value of the firm's resources and the claims against them. There are two types of claims against assets: (1) the claims of creditors and (2) the claims of owners, which is also known as equity. All financial statements are structured so that the assets of the firm are equal to the firm's liabilities plus the firm's net worth (sometimes referred to as owner's equity). All balance sheets are structured so that:

$$\text{Assets} = \text{Liabilities} + \text{Net worth (or owner's equity)}$$

Let us look at this equation more closely. If a firm's assets equal $5,000 and its liabilities equal $2,500, the net worth must equal $2,500. An **asset** is *a tangible item or intangible rights owned by the firm.* **Liabilities** are *the obligations or debts that the firm owes.* **Net worth,** or **owner's equity,** is *what remains and is the number that brings the equation into balance.* Further on in Exhibit 12.1 we will see exactly that this means: Total assets ($9,500,000) = Liabilities ($5,300,000) + Net worth ($4,200,000).

EXHIBIT 12.1

BROWN CORPORATION
Balance Sheet
December 31, 1994

Assets			Liabilities and Net Worth		
Current Assets			Current Liabilities		
Cash	$ 450,000		Accounts payable	$ 500,000	
Accounts receivable (net)	2,000,000		Current portion LTD	500,000	
Merchandise inventory	2,300,000		Notes payable	600,000	
Suppliers	200,000		Other	700,000	
Prepaid expenses	200,000		Total Current Liabilities		$2,300,000
Total current assets		$6,000,000	Long-Term Liabilities		
Fixed Assets			Notes payable	$1,000,000	
Fixtures	$ 800,000		Bank loan payable	1,000,000	
Vehicles	150,000		Other loans payable	1,000,000	
Equipment	100,000		Total long-term liabilities		3,000,000
Leasehold improvements	800,000		Total liabilities		$5,300,000
Building	3,000,000				
Land	450,000		Net Worth: Owner's Equity		$4,200,000
Less depreciation	(1,800,000)		Total Liabilities and Net Worth		$9,500,000
Net fixed assets		$3,500,000			
Total Assets		$9,500,000			

Assets

An asset is a tangible item or intangible rights owned by the firm. **Tangible assets** are *those things (items) that can be seen such as land, cash, equipment, and buildings.* **Intangible assets** are *items, also owned, but which cannot be seen* such as patents or copyrights.

To fully understand the balance sheet, it is necessary to define each entry (or the terms used). **Current assets** *consist of cash and any other asset that will be (or can be) converted to cash within a reasonable period of time* (generally less than one year). **Cash** refers to *bills, currency, coins, and checks on hand or in a checking or savings account.*[5] **Accounts receivable** represents *the money owed to the company for the sale of goods or services to customers.* Anytime a sale is made and the customer is given a period of time in which to pay, a receivable is created. Thirty days is a reasonable expectation for payment. Net receivables means that extending credit bears the risk of the customer's not paying for a number of reasons. Thus an allowance for nonpayment (this is determined by the industry you are in) such as 2 percent is made.[6]

Merchandise inventory is *the amount of goods the company holds for sale to customers at a particular moment.*[7]

Supplies are *those items the company holds that are used in supporting the production process.* Examples include paper, pencils, lubricating oil, light bulbs, or other similar items.

Prepaid expenses are *expenses that a company has incurred and paid for but which have not yet been consumed.* For example, most insurance policy premiums are payable in advance. The company will pay for one year's coverage, and its books will then show the amount of insurance credit still due the company. For example, if the premium is $1,200 due on January 1, this will be the credit for the company. At the end of January, the company will have used up 1/12th, or $100, so on February 1, the prepaid insurance will be $1,100; on March 1, $1,000, until December 31, when no more premium is left.

Fixed assets consist of *land, buildings, equipment, and assets that are not consumed in the production of the firm's goods and services and will usually last longer than one year.* Land is the property used by the firm in its operations. It is generally listed on the balance sheet at cost and rarely changed. In times of rapid and/or large economic change, this value may be under- or overstated. At present, the longer the land is held, the less relation to reality is its price. Generally, it shows on the balance sheet as far less than its present value.

Buildings include *the structures the firm uses;* all buildings and structures are counted. Generally these are listed at their cost at the time of purchase. However, unlike land, buildings wear out over time and are thus consumed in the production process. *Use of a fixed asset is called* **depreciation,** and **accumulated depreciation** is *the amount of a fixed asset's value that has been written off over time due to wear and tear.* How much a firm charges to depreciation every year is subject to Internal Revenue regulations. Yearly depreciation is tax deductible.[8] That is, it shows up on the income statement as a deduction or expense, and this reduces the firm's taxable income and its tax liability. Depreciation is a noncash item; that is, depreciation does not represent a "cash" expenditure. It will not affect the cash flow. However, if the firm is to recover its investment and be able to buy a new plant and new equipment when the need arises, the effects of depreciation must be covered.

Leasehold improvements are *changes made to the building or property to facilitate doing business.* These improvements generally last longer than one year and may be subject to depreciation on an annual basis.

Equipment, vehicles, and fixtures are also fixed assets and are also subject to depreciation.

Liabilities

Current liabilities are *those obligations that are due and payable in less than one year.* These include the following:

1. **Accounts payable,** which are *payments due to suppliers for inventory and/or services*[9] and which are generally due 30 days from the date of purchase.
2. **Current portion of LTD (long-term debt)** and any portion of notes or loans due within the next 12-month period.

Other current liabilities may include expenses incurred but not paid such as taxes or wages.

Long-term liabilities are *those obligations due after one year.*[10] These include all notes for loans or other obligations due in the future. **Notes payable** are *those loans due to lenders other than banks.* Bank notes payable are obligations due to a bank. Other loans may include loans on equipment or inventory.

Net Worth/Owner's Equity

Net worth may have a section called **retained earnings,** which represents *accumulated net income of the company from its inception to the present.* This amount changes every year, as it reflects a firm's net income (or net loss). The profit resulting from operations as of December 31, 1994, change net worth as of January 1, 1995, by the amount of the profits. Corporations may have a separate section in their balance sheet called retained earnings, which may or may not show owner's equity as a separate category. Retained earnings may also reflect the value of any new investment in the company by its owners. Exhibit 12.2 shows how net worth changes.

The balance sheet, by definition, always balances.

$$\text{Assets} = \text{Liabilities} + \text{Net worth}$$

Net worth is not cash, does not represent a liquidation value, and cannot be spent. In fact, it may even be a negative value if the amount a company owes is greater than its assets. It is possible for a company to continue to operate for quite some time with a negative net worth as long as its cash flow is positive. Fulfilling the equation is not just a matter of changing the net worth. Net worth reflects profits or losses.

EXHIBIT 12.2   **How net worth changes**

12/3/94	1/1/95
Income Statement	*Balance Sheet*

Sales	Assets = Liabilities
− Expenses	+
= Profits ⟶	Net Worth

Difference in Profits = Difference in Net Worth

EXHIBIT 12.3   **Double-entry bookkeeping transactions**

Purchase and Delivery of Materials

Materials in the amount of $20,000 dollars have been purchased and delivered. The invoices result in two entries:

Merchandise inventory increases $20,000
Accounts payable increases $20,000

Assets		*Liabilities*	
Merchandise inventory	+$20,000	Accounts Payable	+$20,000

Bill for Inventory Paid

The invoices for the new merchandise have been presented and now are paid. This results in two entries:

Cash decreases by $20,000
Accounts payable decreases $20,000

Assets		*Liabilities*	
Cash	−$20,000	Accounts Payable	−$20,000

Sale of Stock

The company sells $10,000 worth of stock. The two entries are:

Cash increases by $10,000
Net worth increases by $10,000

Assets		*Liabilities*	
Cash	+$10,000	Net Worth	+$10,000

The balance sheet balances because of double-entry bookkeeping. Every transaction the company undertakes is entered twice, once as a debit, once as a credit. That is, if an event is recorded on one side of the balance sheet, it must be offset by something happening on the other side in order for the balance sheet to continue balancing. Exhibit 12.3 illustrates some typical transactions.

The balance sheet always balances because its right-hand side (liabilities plus equity) tells you how the company has been financed while the left (asset) side tells you how the funds have been invested.

The Income Statement

The **income statement (profit-and-loss statement)** *shows all the revenues and expenses that result in the profit or loss from operations during a given time period.* Exhibit 12.4 provides an example.

Every time your company sells a product or a service, it receives **revenue.** Remember this amount has not been adjusted for any bad debts or discounts the company offers for paying bills early. The example shown is net of these items.

Cost of goods sold represents *the cost of the merchandise sold.* It represents the cost to you of your purchases from all sources for resale either in the same form as you bought it (a retail store which resells merchandise) or in a modified form (a manufacturer who buys raw materials and sells finished products made from the raw materials). The cost of goods sold specifically represents beginning inventory plus any purchases which increased it, minus the inventory on hand at the end of the period.

Profits (loss) is *sales minus cost of goods sold and minus operating expenses.* This is shown pretax. Taxes are what you pay to federal, state, and local govern-

Exhibit 12.4

ABC TRUCKING
Profit-and-Loss Statement
January 1, 1993 through December 31, 1993

Sales (Revenues)		$14,000,000	Operating expenses		
(Minus)			Utilities	$ 25,000	
Cost of goods sold			Telephone	15,000	
Beginning inventory	$2,500,000		Advertising	60,000	
Plus purchases	10,700,000		Rent	130,000	
(Minus) Ending inventory	2,700,000		Office supplies	50,000	
Total cost of goods sold		$10,500,000	Office labor	20,000	
Gross profit		3,500,000	Depreciation	200,000	
			Total operating expenses		500,000
			Net profit before taxes		3,000,000
			Provision for taxes		1,500,000
			Net Profit		$1,500,000

ment for the privilege of doing business; the amount is determined by a tax table and the provisions shown in Exhibit 12.4.[11]

Net profit (loss) is what is left over. This amount is added to or subtracted from owner's equity (retained earnings) as shown on the balance sheet. If this is the first balance sheet drawn up for your business, this amount becomes the first retained earnings.

On the same basis as the balance sheet, you may estimate the income statement in the future. It is then called a pro forma profit-and-loss statement.

Cash Flow Statement

The concept of cash flow was discussed in Chapter 11 and illustrated in Exhibit 11.4.[12]

The difference between the profit-and-loss and the cash flow statements is that the latter shows only actual dollars expended. Depreciation or any noncash items are not included in the cash flow statement. Thus, the net cash flow will not be equal to the profits (losses). As long as there is cash, the company can survive; that is, as long as a company can pay its bills, it can continue to operate. This would be true even for a company with a negative net worth.[13] A company without cash, even though it appears to be a good company, cannot survive, since it cannot pay its bills when they are due.[14]

A note of caution: You should not regard the balance sheet or the income statement as either precise or exact. Each is based upon estimates of various categories such as depreciation. Additionally, these statements cannot dependably convey the value (worth) of a business, since a business is worth what a buyer would pay for it should it be for sale. Its value, then, is a relative value because, in an inflationary economy, most assets (such as land) are worth more than their book value. Additionally, the value of a business as a going enterprise is considerably more than what it would be worth if you tried to sell it off (whole or piecemeal).

Bank Statements

Current business practices use the check as a medium of exchange. All receipts from sales and other income are deposited in your bank. All bills and expenses are paid by drawing on your bank account through the use of checks. Checks are simply your authorization directing your bank to use your funds to pay another party. All deposits and checks are recorded in your business's checkbook. Checkbooks come in many varieties and styles, all serving the same purpose—cash control.[15]

Because they are legal records of your business activity, all written checks should have proper documentation. When paying bills, note on each invoice the date, the amount paid, and the check number. Paid bills should then be filed alphabetically and chronologically so that if there is any question about payment, proof of payment can be furnished. The indisputable proof of payment is, of course, your canceled check. **Canceled checks** are *the checks paid to various people or*

EXHIBIT 12.5 **Bank reconciliation form**

TO HELP YOU BALANCE YOUR CHECKING ACCOUNT

1) First enter and subtract from your checkbook balance any service charge appearing on this statement. Remember to record any preauthorized or automatic transactions in your register. Then continue as follows:

2) List unpaid items

Check No.	Amount
Total	

3) List deposits made since date of last entry on this statement

Amount
Total

4) Enter requested items and add (+) or subtract (−)

Balance shown on this statement _____

Add total deposits (+) _____

Subtotal _____

Subtract total unpaid items (−) _____

Balance _____

* Your checkbook balance should agree with this final balance.

businesses that they, in turn, have presented to their banks for payment. *Upon paying these checks, the bank voids, or cancels, them so they cannot be cashed again. These canceled checks are then returned to you in your monthly statement. As in any situation where there are two sets of books, yours and the bank's, the balances in these books must agree. The process of making sure the balances agree, and taking any corrective action necessary, is called *reconciliation*. Your records and the bank's must agree. Reconciling your checking account is fundamental to maintaining accurate records. The process of reconciliation sounds more complex than it is. Most banks provide a reconciliation form and instructions for its use on the reverse side of the statement, as illustrated in Exhibit 12.5.

Exhibit 12.6   Bank reconciliation

Balance per bank statement		$2,456.23
plus deposits in transit		5,300.00
(made but not credited on bank statement)		$7,756.23
Less outstanding checks (list)		
Check #123	$100.00	
Check #127	350.00	
Check #128	351.00	
Check #129	1,200.00	
	$2,001.00	(2,001.00)
Cash balance EOM		$5,756.23
Balance per company checkbook		5,776.23
Less bank service charge		20.00
Cash balance EOM per checkbook		$5,756.23

Monthly Bank Reconciliation

To begin the process you should have:

1. Last month's bank statement with the balance reconciled.
2. This month's canceled checks.
3. Your checkbook, showing all checks written.
4. The current bank statement.

Before you begin the process of reconciliation, you should sort the checks, arranging them in numerical order. The dollar amount of each check should agree with the amount in the checkbook and on the bank statement. As you verify each canceled check, check it off in your checkbook. All checks in the statement should be recognized in the checkbook as having been paid to the recipient. Any errors should be corrected. Next, the number and dollar amount of each deposit should also be verified. The checkbook, the deposit entry, and the bank statement should agree. Any errors should be corrected at this time.

The steps for reconciliation are outlined in Exhibit 12.6. First, enter all deposits made since the date of the last entry on this statement. Because these deposits represent dollars that are in your account but do not show on the bank statement, they should be added to the bank balance. Second, since you have not reconciled items such as bank service charges and any preauthorized transactions, these should be entered in the checkbook. Bank service charges are bank fees for services provided. Preauthorized transactions might include such items as mortgage and vehicle loans that the bank is authorized to deduct automatically. Third, list and total all outstanding checks. These are the checks that have been entered in your checkbook but do not appear on the statement. They represent money that, while still in your account, is earmarked for payment and hence should not be counted in your real dollar balance. This amount is then deducted from the bank balance shown.

To the balance on the statement, you add the deposits and subtract the unpaid items. This balance should agree with the checkbook balance. The reconciliation process is neither difficult nor time-consuming and must be done monthly. Exhibit 12.6 illustrates this procedure.

Fixed Asset List

A **fixed asset list** is *a statement that itemizes the firm's operating equipment and its corresponding dollar value.* Sometimes called a capital equipment list, it should follow the statement of the sources and applications of funds. For an existing firm this is essentially an operating equipment list that itemizes all of the operating assets the firm owns. For example, a delivery service would include its trucks, mechanical equipment for truck repair, and any other equipment that is used daily in running the business. A capital equipment list is especially important to an existing firm that wishes to borrow money during low-profit periods. A list of the machinery and its value can serve as collateral when applying for a loan.

A new firm's capital equipment list will include the equipment it needs to begin operations. This list should also include estimates for each piece of equipment; it also provides a realistic picture of start-up costs and permits you to assign a priority to the equipment you will need. The capital equipment list in the business plan is important for two reasons: (1) in an existing business it serves as a complete disclosure statement, allowing investors or banks to determine the value of the firm in terms of operational assets; (2) in a new firm it estimates the start-up costs in terms of machinery needed to commence operations.

Pro Forma Statements

In building accounting statements from past information, we know what has happened. Using past knowledge to operate your firm and plan for the future means developing pro forma statements. **Pro forma statements** are *those statements based on forecasts of activities or hypothetical events.* These statements are a guide to what the company's future financial position might be. By taking the following steps as the future unfolds, you can use these statements as a control mechanism. You can:

1. Compare your actual results to your forecasted statements.
2. Determine the difference between actual and forecasted results.
3. Analyze the differences with respect to why they occurred.

The control cycle is shown in Exhibit 12.7.

Exhibit 12.7

Control cycle

1. Forecast financial.

2. Compare actual results to forecast.

3. If not equal, take corrective action.

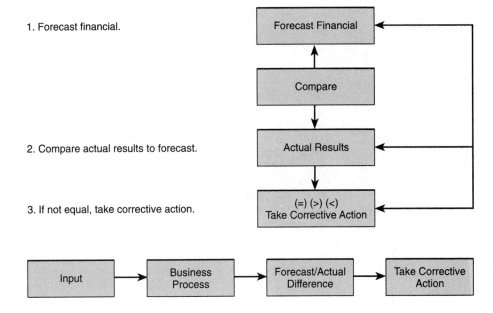

Summary

The Interrelationship between the Accounting Function and the Other Business Plan Components

The accounting function links all functional areas of the firm through its use of the common denominator of money by keeping records and producing financial statements and reports needed by the business. Lack of a good accounting function could seriously impact on functional efficiency and company profitability.

Record Keeping

To derive the information you need in order to look at your firm's activity, and to construct ratios and use analytic tools, you must keep records. The Internal Revenue Service also requires that you maintain records.

Accounting Systems

Earlier we mentioned that the first task your accountant will perform is to establish a **chart of accounts** which is *a list of all of the accounts to which charges are made* that is tailored to your business. The final service the accountant should perform is to recommend a system of internal control to prevent fraud. Operating a business means that you must know how to keep accurate and detailed business records so that you can prepare financial statements from your records. Only by using this information in the proper way, and presenting it in a commonly accepted manner, will you be able to truly understand your company's performance. All the accounts of your business are tracked in the **general ledger** which is *a book or computerized listing in which entries are made concerning all of a firm's financial transactions.* Several methods are used to present the information you require.

The Balance Sheet

You should understand the balance sheet. It essentially presents a picture of what the company owns and owes. The presentation of these facts is always in the format of **assets** which are *tangible items or intangible rights owned by the firm;* **liabilities,** which are *the obligations or debts that the firm owes;* and **net worth,** or **owner's equity,** which is *what remains and is the number that brings the equation into balance.* Assets may take several forms. They may be **tangible assets** which are *those things (items) that can be seen, such as land, equipment and buildings, and cash (bills, currency, coins or checking or savings accounts);* **intangible assets,** which are *items, also owned, but which cannot be seen, such as patents or copyrights;* **current assets,** which consist of *cash and any other asset that will be (or can be) converted to cash within a reasonable period of time* (generally less than one year); and **accounts receivable,** which represent *the money owed to the company for the sale of goods or services.* Less easily negotiable forms of assets can be **merchandise inventory,** which is the amount of goods the company holds for sale to customers at a particular moment; **supplies,** which are *those items the company holds that are of use in the production process;* **prepaid expenses,** which are *expenses that a company has incurred and paid for but which have not yet been consumed;* and **fixed assets,** consisting of *land, buildings, equipment, and assets that are not consumed in the production of the firm's goods and services* and will usually last longer than one year. To reflect present value fixed assets other than land are subject to **depreciation** and **accumulated depreciation,** which are *the amount of a building's value that has been written off over time due to wear and tear* and **leasehold improvements,** which are *changes made to the building or property to facilitate doing business.*

   Your firm also has claims against it in the form of **current liabilities,** which are *those obligations that are due and payable in less than one year;* **accounts payable,** which are *payments due to suppliers for inventory and/or services;* **long-term liabilities,** which are *those obligations due after one year;* and **notes payable,** which are *those loans due to lenders other than banks.* **Retained earnings** represent accumulated net income of the company from its inception to the present.

The Income Statement

The balance sheet presents a picture of the company at a point in time, while the **income (profit-and-loss) statement** *shows all the revenues and expenses that result in the profit or loss generated from operations during a given time period.* It depicts the **cost of goods sold,** which is *the cost of the merchandise sold.* **Gross profit** is *the difference between sales and cost of goods sold.* **Profit (loss)** from operations is *derived from sales minus cost of goods sold and minus operating expenses.* Together they show the firm's operation over a period of time. While both the income statement and the balance sheet present important information, the information contained in a cash flow statement (Chapter 11) is critical to your operations. Other information you need can be found using breakeven analysis.

Bank Statements

Because there is a time difference between when you write checks to pay your bills and when the recipients of those checks cash them, it is important to know how much money you have in the bank at all times. You use the **canceled checks,** which are *the checks written to various people or businesses that have been presented to their banks for payment and that the bank returns to you* to determine your checking account balances. Don't forget to deduct any bank service charges, which are bank fees for services provided.

Pro Forma Statements

Pro forma statements, or *statements based on forecasts of activities,* enable you to project your activities, income, and expenditures based on logical assumptions. The comparison of reality to projections and the resulting changes in your assumptions and projections are excellent control mechanisms for your company.

Fixed Asset List

As an addendum to your financial statements, you should always maintain a **fixed asset list,** which is *a statement that itemizes the firm's operating equipment and its corresponding dollar value.* Referring to this list identifies what you have and might help you to identify what you will need in the future.

Questions

1. Why is it necessary to keep good financial records? List and explain some of the reasons.
2. Do you feel that every entrepreneur or business owner needs an accountant? Justify your answer.
3. Assuming that you have an accountant, do your year-end statements tell you how to run your business? How much can your accountant help you in making business decisions? Explain your reasoning.
4. What records are required in a good accounting system?
5. Define the following: *balance sheet, income statement,* and *cash flow statement.*
6. What is the relationship between the balance sheet and the income statement?
7. How would the accounting system record a materials purchase of $40,000? Which accounts would be affected and why? Illustrate with an example.
8. How would the accounting system record a sale of stock? Which accounts would be affected and why? Illustrate with an example.
9. It is not unusual for a firm to show losses for the year but still have cash in the bank. Explain this apparent contradiction.
10. What is a canceled check?

11. Your bank statement should be reconciled on a monthly basis. What is the process of reconciliation, and why is it important? Define your terms and explain.

12. What is a capital equipment list, and why would you need one?

13. What problem might rapid growth of your firm create for your working capital and cash position? Explain.

14. Your accountant has just filed your company's tax return, which shows a profit for the past year, yet you don't have any cash to pay your bills. Is this possible? Why is this possible, and what does this mean for your future?

15. Define *pro forma statements*. Why would you want these statements? How can they be used?

16. Assume you are a bank loan officer and you realize that future projections are nothing more than best guesses. If you had to choose between a business with a well-developed set of financials and another great sure-fire opportunity that lacks financial data, which firm would you choose to fund and why?

Application Exercises

When doing these exercises, where applicable, be sure to select a specific business, preferably one where you presently work or previously worked or a business you would like to own someday. If this is not possible, pick a specific organization to which you will refer. Be sure to identify the organization by name. Limit your answers to one or two pages per exercise.

1. Interview several small businesses. Report on their accounting systems.

2. Would you say that these businesses exhibit a high or low level of sophistication with respect to their accounting systems? Explain the meaning of your findings in a report.

3. Are these, or other business like them, profitable without regard to their accounting systems? Explain your position.

4. Interview a local small business and ask if there is a cash flow pro forma for the next year. If so, present this and its assumptions to the class. If this is impossible, choose a well-defined type of business, and, using SIC codes and RMA figures, prepare a cash flow pro forma for the business.

5. Interview a local bank loan officer to ascertain his or her the degree of familiarity with small business accounting systems. What conclusions can you draw from your discussion?

6. Explain whether this information agrees with your inquiries in questions 1 and 2. Does this describe small business in general?

7. Interview a CPA who specializes in or consults to small business, and considering the information you acquired from questions 1, 2 and 6, ask how he or she compiles the year-end statements. How accurate are these statements likely to be? Report on your conclusions.

8. Prepare your own pro forma cash flow for the next two years on a monthly basis. Indicate the assumptions upon which you based your projections.

Application Situations

1. Stanley Maxwell

In addition to teaching at a local high school, Stanley Maxwell has run a very successful business selling antiques to a select group of collectors. He has never really used any formal accounting systems and is well satisfied that his income exceeds his expenditures. He his considering turning this business into a full-time activity.

Assignment

Answer the following questions:

1. What kind of accounting records should Stanley have maintained? What kind of records should he now maintain? Why?
2. Is it important for Stanley to create pro forma statements? Explain.
3. How important are pro forma cash flow statements for Stanley, and why are these statements vital to him now? Explain.

2. Susan Lew

Susan Lew, a CPA who specializes in the preparation of year-end reports for small business, has just finished visiting the Salty Sea Fish Processing plant. Susan knows that the plant, which does not pay rent, is located on farmland owned by the president's father and that the plant itself is operated by the farm workers when there is fish-processing work to be done. When there is no work at the plant, the employees work on the farm. Susan has just received a shoe box full of receipts, bank statements, and other business records.

Assignment

Answer the following questions:

1. If you were Susan, what would be your first step in making sense out of the contents of the shoe box?
2. How would you establish realistic pro formas for this business? What further information would you need and how would you use it?
3. In your opinion, is this business profitable? Explain your position.
4. If you were Susan, what recommendations would you make regarding record-keeping and accounting systems?

3. Harbor City Chemical Company

The Harbor City Chemical Company has manufactured chemical cleaning agents for 50 years. These chemicals have traditionally been manufactured using largely the same equipment. The packaging of the products, however, requires three sizes of containers. Each container size is handled by a different product line. Small containers are filled by highly automated and mechanized equipment, while the large (drum size) containers are filled by equipment that dates back to the founding of the company.

Traditionally, all the company's equipment has been carried on the books as "equipment," and depreciation has been taken on the total amount of equipment on hand. Recently, the Grand Chemical Company has considered buying Harbor City.

Assignment

Answer the following questions:

1. What information does the Grand Company need to know with respect to the equipment before it can make a purchase decision?
2. How would Grand Company go about establishing a capital equipment list?
3. What would be the significance of the capital equipment list in determining the profitability of each of the filling lines? Of the company as a whole?

4. Do-All Hardware

Scott Learner has been in the retail hardware business for several years. He generally buys supplies for the business, Do-All Hardware, from many suppliers. Scott receives approximately 40 bills per day from his suppliers. At the end of each day, Scott calls the bank for an account balance and uses this information to decide which bills to pay.

1. Is this a wise practice? Why or why not?
2. Explain what Scott should be doing to know how much money there is in his checking accounts.
3. Describe a method Scott can use to reconcile his bank accounts.

Integrated Case Question—CorLu Foods

Determine CorLu's cash flow projections. Indicate how you would obtain necessary funds. (Please refer to the Integrated Case, "CorLu Foods.")

Additional Readings

Baldwin, Carliss Y. "How Capital Budgeting Deters Innovation—and What to Do About It." *Research-Technology Management,* November/December 1991, pp. 39–45.

Bergsman, Steve. "Accounting for Small Businesses." *Black Enterprise,* November 1992, p. 37.

Bitner, Larry N., and Judith D. Powell. "Small Business Accounting Systems: Is Automation Necessary?" *National Public Accountant,* December 1989, pp. 20–24.

"Capital Investments: How to Value Every Dollar." *Business Owner,* February 1991, pp. 5–8.

Del Guidice, Victor. "Understanding the Basics of Inventory as Collateral." *Secured Lender,* July/August 1992, pp. 40, 42.

Freeman, Mark, and Kerrie Freeman. "Considering the Time Value of Money in Breakeven Analysis." *Management Accounting-London,* January 1993, pp. 50–52.

Gee, Paul. "Small Company Reporting and the Relevance Gap." *Accountancy* 111, no. 1195 (March 1993), pp. 82–83.

Hotch, Ripley. "Not Just for the Numbers." *Nation's Business,* January 1992, p. 42.

Jacobs, Vernon K. "Capital Budgeting with Lotus 1-2-3." *Journal of Accounting & EDP* 6, no. 1 (Spring 199), pp. 59–61.

Krinsky, Itzhak. "Capital Budgeting and Plant Capacity." *Engineering Costs & Production Economics* 21, no. 3, pp. 233–41.

Kuo, Horng-Ching. "How Do Small Firms Make Inventory Accounting Choices?" *Journal of Business Finance & Accounting* 20, no. 3 (April 1993), pp. 373–92.

Mamis, Robert A. "Money In, Money Out." *Inc.,* March 1993, p. 96.

McCallum, John S. "Using Net Present Value in Capital Budgeting." *Business Quarterly,* Summer 1992, pp. 66–70.

Nebel, Kenneth E. "Working Capital Financing: A Dual Approach to Generating Funds." *Journal of Commercial Bank Lending,* May 1990, pp. 30–35.

Roumi, Ebrahim, and Jacques A. Schnabel. "Evaluating Investment in Inventory Policy: A Net Present Value Framework—an Addendum." *Engineering Economist* 35, no. 3 (Spring 1990), pp. 239–46.

Salmon, Alan. "Software Update." Computers in Accounting, December 1992, pp. 69–72.

Schneider, Alan J. "Beyond Managing Cash, to Managing Cash Flow." *Financial Executive,* November/December 1988, pp. 54–57.

Smith, Michael F. "Capital Investment Budgeting." *Small Business Reports,* December 1988, pp. 80–88.

Stratton, William O. "An All-Purpose Solution for Financial Reporting." *Management Accounting,* May 1993, pp. 44–49.

Wacht, Richard F. "Capital Investment Analysis for the Small Business," *Business,* October-December 1989, pp. 27–32.

Walker, John P.; Cheryl A. Gudort; and John C. Talbott. "Contribution Margin Accounting for Small Business," *National Public Accountant,* September 1990, pp. 48–54.

Endnotes

1. Gus Gordon, *Understanding Financial Statements* (Cincinatti, Ohio: South-Western, 1992).
2. Bernard Kamoroff, "Filing Your Business Records," *In Business,* May/June 1990, p. 52.
3. Richard G. P. McMahon, and Scott Holmes, "Small Business Financial Management Practices in North America: A Literature Review," *Journal of Small Business Management,* April 1991, p. 27.
4. Daniel Kehrer, "Big Ideas for Small Business," *Changing Times,* November 1989, p. 57.

5. Roberta Maynard, "Smart Ways to Manage Cash," *Nation's Business,* August 1992, pp. 43–44.

6. Jill Andresky Fraser, "Getting Paid," *Inc.,* June 1990, pp. 58–69.

7. Jill Andresky Fraser, "Hidden Cash," *Inc.,* February 1991, pp. 81–83.

8. Eugene Willis et al., *West's Federal Taxation: Comprehensive Volume, 1993 Edition* (St. Paul, Minn.: West, 1992), p. A10.

9. "Strategies That Pay Off," *Inc.,* March 1991, p. 74.

10. M. K. Kolay, "Managing Working Capital Crises: A System Dynamics Approach," *Management Decisions* 29 (September 1991), pp. 46–52.

11. U.S. Department of the Treasury, Internal Revenue Service, *Tax Guide for Small Business,"* Publication 334 (Washington, D.C.: U.S. Government Printing Office, 1992).

12. Jill Andresky Fraser, "On Target," *Inc.,* April 1991, pp. 113–14.

13. Jeffrey M. Lademman, "Earnings, Schmernings—Look at the Cash," *Business Week,* July 24, 1989, pp. 56–57.

14. See Alan Wilson, "Effective Cash and Profit Forecasting," *The Accountant's Magazine,* August 1990, pp. 45–47.

15. Roger Ricklefs and Udayan Gupta, "Traumas of a New Entrepreneur," *The Wall Street Journal,* May 10, 1989, p. B1.

13 FINANCIAL ANALYSIS AND TAXATION

In this chapter you will learn about the tax liability that arises from the operation of your business. It is important to consider government a partner in your business and taxes a cost of being in business. All business decisions should be made with these liabilities and their consequences in mind. For example, in Chapter 3 you saw that there was a tax advantage in being a sub-chapter S corporation rather than the traditional C corporation. Some of the important taxes will be noted.

This chapter also recognizes that your firm's survival is dependent upon its profitability. Profits do not just happen; it takes careful planning and control to make certain that your company is operating in the best and most profitable manner. In order to run your business to make the greatest profit, you must use financial information that has been generated as a by-product of conducting business. Financial controls, using the financial tools discussed in Chapter 11, make it possible to identify and keep track of your firm's financial position at any moment in time and as it changes over time. With this information you can determine your firm's financial health both internally and externally in comparison to that of other similar firms.[1] Analysis of the financial statement created in Chapter 12 will enable you to control your firm's operation for maximum profitability.

Chapter Learning Objectives

After completing this chapter, you should be able to:
· Identify the most common forms of taxation.
· Identify the most common tools of financial analysis: ratios.
· Use ratios to judge your firm's internal financial health.
· Use the ratios to compare your firm to other firms in your industry.
· Use the ratios to identify problem areas.

- Identify actions you can take to correct identified problem areas.
- Examine the impact of taxes on your business decisions.
- Define the following 17 key terms in order of appearance in the chapter:

Budget	Credit trend
Budget variances	Total coverage
Standard costs	Working capital ratio
Balance sheet	Proprietorship ratio
Ratio	Breakeven analysis
Current ratio	Financial ratios
Acid test (quick ratio)	Liquidity ratios
Asset coverage ratio	Depreciation
Inventory turnover ratio	

The Interrelationship between Financial Analysis and Taxation and the Other Business Plan Components

It is the task of all functional areas of the company—accounting, finance, marketing, and personnel—to function as a smoothly operating system to ensure your company's profitability. Financial analysis examines how the company is performing, and by comparing that performance to industry standards, determines if, and how much, correction is needed. All functional areas are subject to analysis and to correction. This is a continual process. The results of this process help to maximize profitability.

Although you may operate your business as you desire, federal, state, and/or local government take a portion of the dollar you generate in the form of taxes. These taxes in turn may influence the manner in which you organize your company, what equipment you buy, how long you keep the equipment, and ultimately, your profitability. Since profits depend upon expenses, if you are allowed to deduct significantly for depreciation, your profits will be lower. Organizationally, the choice of organization form, the C or the S corporation, depends in large part upon comparative tax rates.

Additionally, any time you hire personnel, taxes such as Social Security and unemployment taxes all increase the cost of doing business and will thus have to be factored into your strategic plans.

Taxation

Everyone recognizes that living in an organized society imposes a financial cost. A government must pay for roads, defense, Social Security, and unemployment benefits. The government, which is not an inherent producer of wealth, can only pay for societal benefits by taking (taxing) money from the wealth created by producers (business organizations) and redistributing it elsewhere.[2] Although few people question the need for taxes, volumes have been published on the proper size of the "benefit" package; that is, how much should be taken from the economy in taxes and who should benefit from these taxes. Ultimately there are two sources of tax revenue: individuals and business.

As April 15 draws close, entrepreneurs, as taxpayers, see the full impact of taxes on their business and individual incomes. The imposition of taxation means reduced business and individual spending. While it is true that the government returns the money it takes out of the economy in the form of benefits, often those paying taxes do not receive an equal share of benefits. The more money paid in taxes, the less they have to spend on machinery, equipment, research, personnel, or just plain consumption. The higher the tax, the less investment, savings, or spending the business can do. Taxes are a vital consideration in business planning, and therefore it is important to know what taxes must be paid. These taxes can and will affect the survival, growth, success, and viability of the organization.[3]

Income taxes are only one form of tax. Taxes come in a variety of guises and are payable on three levels: federal, state and local. Not all forms of taxes are required at all levels, but you should be familiar with some of the various tax categories.

Income Taxes

Income taxes are *those taxes levied on the net income of the business* (defined in Chapter 12). Generally these are derived by applying a percentage determined by the taxing agency to net income.

Social Security Taxes

Social security taxes are *taxes levied on employers and employees to provide for individual retirement.* At present both the organization and the individual each pay 7.62 percent of the employees' income into the Social Security fund. Self-employed individuals pay both portions. Out of this, 1.45 percent of the Social Security tax goes to the Medicaid fund and must be accounted for separately.[4]

Unemployment Taxes

Unemployment taxes *are collected in order to insure those individuals who have lost their job.* The employer pays a percentage of the payroll into a fund, which the state then distributes to the temporarily jobless as a weekly stipend. The amount a person receives and the duration of the payments varies from state to state.

Sales Taxes

Sales taxes are *determined by a percentage of the sales price of goods and perhaps services purchased.* These are general taxes and are remitted to the state or city levying the tax.[5]

Property and Excise Taxes

Property and excise taxes are *those taxes based on ownership and are generally a percentage of the assessed value of the item.* These taxes are levied on personal or real property (such as land), automobiles, boats, inventories, and gasoline, to name a few of the taxable categories.

Budgets

Internally, one of the most powerful and common control devices is the budget.[6] While the budget appears to be identical with the historical balance sheet and income statement, it is not. Although the terms used are identical, the time frame is different. A firm's annual financial statement is a historical summary of production and other costs that have actually been incurred. The **budget** is *a preliminary written plan for future specific application whose purpose is to control future company activities.* It becomes a master plan for the overall coordination and control of the company as it moves toward achieving its objectives. Obviously there must be rational limits to the budget, since it is primarily a statement of funds to be expended. These limits are provided by the estimated sales income, since it is this income against which the expenses are drawn. Only in rare circumstances can expenses exceed income. A negative income or loss can exist for a short time and only if there are accumulated cash reserves from which to draw.

Historically, budgets were first drawn and used by state and federal governments, whose agencies had to know the amount of taxes they would gather before they could spend any funds. Although the budgeting process of American government began in 1912 in response to civic reform movements, the concept of budgeting took another 10 years to reach the business sector and finally became acceptable as a result of the influence of James Oscar McKinley's seminal book, *Budgetary Control.*[7]

It is not a coincidence that budgetary and cost accounting terminology are similar. In fact, they are designed specifically so that the budget will present accounting details that are useful in controlling budget items. While the idea of budgeting is universally applicable, each budget is uniquely and individually drawn and tailored to a specific organization's structure and objectives. It is necessary for your budget to conform to your specific business in order for it to be successfully used for planning and control.

Although it has not been explicitly mentioned previously, the budget is also a planning device. The very act of formulating expenditures requires that some thought be given to the source of cash and how it is to be expended. This activity is what is meant by planning. The outcome of the planning process, with its implications for forecasting and decision making, is a formulated budget that is then used for control purposes to ensure that the organization is proceeding according to plan. A most important caution should be kept in mind: Budgets are still only a guide to measuring progress. The normal phenomenon of "change" will cause

Exhibit 13.1

ABC COMPANY
Proposed Budget
1994
Based on sales of $1,000,000

Consolidated Budget, Fiscal 1995

Salaries	$200,000
Payroll taxes	16,000
Insurance	10,000
Motor vehicle	20,000
Telephone	5,000
Rent	40,000
Repair	10,000
Heat and light	5,000
Materials	400,000
Machinery	100,000
Advertising	70,000
Office	60,000
Total	$936,000

Budget Notes:
1. *Salaries.* Represents 5 percent increase from previous year for an across-the-board cost-of-living increase.
2. *Payroll taxes.* Computed at 8 percent of total wages.
3. *Insurance.* Includes property, vehicle, and workers' compensation.
4. *Motor Vehicle.* To cover replacement cost for sales rep's vehicle.
5. *Repairs.* Represents estimated cost for deferred building repairs.
6. *Materials.* Represents 4 percent increase from prior year required to fulfill contracts.
7. *Advertising.* Represents 2 percent decrease from prior year costs due to change in advertising strategy.
8. *Office.* Includes cost for additional computerized work station for accounting personnel.

actual dollars to deviate from the plan. Documenting and understanding the changes from plan or budget will enable you to formulate better budgets and forecasts.

Let us now look at how a budget might appear (Exhibit 13.1) if, for example, your firm envisions sales during the next fiscal year of $1 million.

The very act of determining the expense categories and the relative amount of money devoted to each category represents planning of the highest order. The budget presented in Exhibit 13.1 was a companywide budget, representing a consolidation of many smaller departmental budgets. In a large business many individuals or departments have their own budgets, each of which is a part of the whole. Frequently, the yearly budget can be, and is, broken down into smaller time segments so that during each time segment the business owner can see if spending is conforming to the desired pattern. For example, the monthly budget of a specific department might look like the one in Exhibit 13.2.

Budget Variance

The control function of the budgetary process becomes apparent when the manager examines his actual costs and compares the variance between the budgeted and the actual figures. **Budget variance** is *a deviation from the established budgetary amount,* as shown in Exhibit 13.3.

The variance column makes it clear that the budgeted numbers for that period have either been exceeded or underspent. While overspending may not be desirable, it signifies that the department has failed to meet the plan and that corrective action is needed or that significant authorized growth has occurred.

It is important that each department budget be as simple as possible so that any significant variation can be identified and corrected as soon as possible. Each budget should also be flexible, allowing for changes in the environment. A flexible budget might show the allowable expenditure pattern, dependent on estimated sales. This method of budgeting, also called variable budgeting, is illustrated in Exhibit 13.4.

Variable budgeting

The concept of the variable budget is important, since it transforms the simple budget from a passive tool into one that can respond to forecasted changes. A budget can be used to plan and control in light of many judgments about the future. It thus enables the manager to determine in advance how to respond to changing economic conditions in order to develop plans for coping with the changing future.

While the owner or entrepreneur may be willing to delegate many decisions to employees, those decisions involving fiscal matters are least likely to be shifted to a lower level in the firm. The owner is primarily responsible for raising funds and is hesitant to let others spend them. In fact, the firm may consist of a number of profit centers, but since funds are limited, the budget is a centralized umbrella under which the firm functions.

A firm can budget either for a fixed period of time, such as the next year, or it can devise a rolling budget, updating the initial budget as time passes. Using a fixed-period budget as of December 31, the business will have a budget for the next year, January 1 to December 31; it will not require additional budgeting information until it casts the budget for the following year. Using a rolling budget, a business can have a 12-month forward rolling budget. To develop a continual 12-month budget, the company prepares its budget for January 1 to December, but when January is over, an additional month—in this case January of the following year—is appended so that the business is always operating with a 12-month budget. For example, if our budget covers the period January through December 1995, when January 1995 is over, the budget will cover the period of February 1, 1995, to January 31, 1996.

EXHIBIT 13.2

ABC COMPANY Milling Department Budget Month of _____	
Wages	$2,200
Taxes	400
Materials	6,000
Repairs	500
Machinery	1,000

EXHIBIT 13.3

ABC COMPANY
Milling Department
Monthly Budget Report
Month of _____

	Budget	Actual	Budget Variance
Wages	$2,200	$2,000	$−200
Taxes	400	350	−50
Materials	6,000	7,000	+1,000
Repairs	500	200	−300
Machinery	1,000	1,000	n/c
Total	10,100	10,550	+450

EXHIBIT 13.4   Estimated sales

	$12,000/week	$15,000/week	$17,000/week
Wages	$2,200	$3,200	$4,500
Taxes	400	480	560
Material	6,000	7,000	8,500
Repair	500	500	1,000
Machinery	1,000	1,100	1,200
Total	10,100	12,280	15,760

Standard Costs

In the discussion of budgets, the term variance was introduced. This term has a second definition when we discuss standard costs. **Standard costs** are *those costs that should be incurred in the operations process if all goes according to plan and definition.* For example, by the use of time-and-motion study, we can determine how to manufacture an item, how long it should take to make it, and, knowing the wage rate, exactly what the item should cost in dollars. If a worker can make three items per hour and the wage rate is $4.85 per hour,[8] each item costs the company $1.6166 in labor. This is a standard cost. The same concept can be applied to materials, machinery, and overhead. Using this information, the organization is then able to plan on selling an item costing X dollars. This standard cost figure is used as a control device. The same costing could be applied to an insurance company. Processing the average policy could take two hours at a wage rate of $12 dollars per hour, or $24 dollars per policy.

A department manager predicts, in advance, what costs will be. This prediction is made in terms of what the standard cost *should be.* At certain set intervals, the manager then compares what the actual production costs were with what they should have been. The difference, if any, is called cost variance. **Cost variance** is *the difference between actual costs and what they should have been.* Thus, the manager might have the situation illustrated in Exhibit 13.5.

The $300 difference immediately indicates that an event, or a combination of events, has occurred so that the standard cannot be met. The differential, if it is significant, tells you that you must now look for the causes and either correct the problem or make your predictions more realistic. Setting a standard can help identify bottlenecks in your procedures. In any event, the standard has served as a control device, causing examination and change so that the organization can predict and produce with more accuracy and precision and less cost and waste.

EXHIBIT 13.5   Production Period #1

	Standard	Actual	Cost Variance
Labor	$12,000	$12,500	$500
Materials	6,000	6,000	—
Machinery	1,000	800	−200
Total	$19,000	$19,300	$+300

Ratios

Why do we use ratios?[9] Being an entrepreneur and possessing the ability to be creative will not ensure success. Your business must incorporate good management techniques and the ability to control adjustments by using the information generated by operations. All firms must have standards or guidelines against which they can measure their efforts. Controls are used to make sure the firm does what is planned. For example, if you set out to manufacture a certain number of units, did you meet your goals?

A **ratio** is *the relationship between any two numbers derived from a firm's financial statements.*[10] These relationships measure the firm's internal and external health. Analyzing the internal health of a firm requires answers to questions such as whether the firm has enough cash to cover its indebtedness or how the firm compares to other firms in the field or to average ratios of all firms in the field. The purpose of ratios is to compare the firm to a typical healthy firm in the same type of industry.

To understand the use of ratios as control tools, it is necessary to describe the two major descriptive tools that a business must use if it is to function profitably. In fact, without a balance sheet and a profit-and-loss statement, the business can only conjecture, and poorly at that, how well it is doing.[11]

As we discussed in Chapter 12, the balance sheet is a statement, at a point in time, of an organization's financial status. It shows:

1. What the organization owns.
2. What the organization owes.
3. What the stockholders own in dollar terms.
4. The value of retained earnings.

An equality results from the relationship:

Assets = Liabilities plus net worth

The Brown Corporation is a manufacturer of electrical equipment. The industry standards from RMA that are listed in Chapter 11, Exhibit 11.4, are used as a type of measurement, but unique characteristics of the Brown Corporation may give very plausible reasons for it not to measure equitably against these ratios. The balance sheet of Brown Corporation at exactly five o'clock on December 31, 1993, might look like Exhibit 13.6.

The Profit-and-Loss Statement

The profit-and-loss statement, which is also called an income statement, is just what the name implies. It shows, over the period of time considered—generally a year—how much money has been generated by sales, how much was spent to support these sales, and what is left. The remainder, of course, is profit. Since the

EXHIBIT 13.6

BROWN CORPORATION
Balance Sheet
December 31, 1994

Assets:

Current Assets

Cash	$ 450,000	
Marketable securities (at cost)	850,000	
Accounts receivable	2,000,000	
Inventory	2,700,000	
Total current assets		$6,000,000

Fixed Assets

Land	450,000	
Buildings	3,800,000	
Machinery	950,000	
Equipment	100,000	
	5,300,000	
Less: Depreciation	1,800,000	
Net fixed assets		3,500,000
Total assets		$9,500,000

Liabilities:

Current Liabilities

Accounts payable	$1,000,000	
Notes payable	600,000	
Wages payable	250,000	
Taxes payable	450,000	
Total current liabilities		2,300,000

Long-Term Liabilities

Mortgages	3,000,000	
Total liabilities		5,300,000

Owner's Equity

Common stock ($1 par value)	500,000	
Accumulated retained earnings	3,700,000	
Total equity	$4,200,000	
Total liabilities and equity		$9,500,000

primary function of any business is the creation of profit, without profit, the organization cannot survive. The profit-and-loss statement is a flow concept. It shows the result of movement over time. A typical profit and loss statement is shown in Exhibit 13.7.

Ratios are the relationships of the firm's financial figures using balance sheet and income statement information[12] that can be compared to industry averages. These ratios are used as predictive or control devices. Previously you read that cer-

EXHIBIT 13.7

BROWN CORPORATION
Profit-and-Loss Statement
For the Period Ending December 31, 1993

Net sales		$14,000,000
Cost of Sales		
Materials	$4,000,000	
Labor	3,000,000	
Overhead	3,500,000	
Total cost of goods sold		10,500,000
Gross profit		3,500,000
Less expenses:		
Selling and administration	450,000	
Supplies	50,000	
Total expenses:	500,000	
Profit from sales		$ 3,000,000
Provision for taxes		$ 1,500,000
Net profit		$ 1,500,000

tain ratios can be used to measure your business against industry standards. Ratios are excellent control devices, since they provide a very quick look at a firm's activities and enable the analyst to immediately compare a particular firm's health to the industry average. Deviation signifies the need for further research. Nothing may be wrong, but the reasons for the deviation should be examined. The object of ratio control is to make certain that the organization's performance is in line with its goals and objectives. A deviation from prediction or normality signifies that further analysis and perhaps change must take place if the organization is to reach a safe haven in the waters of the economy. The following most common ratios can be used to determine the economic condition of your business.

Liquidity Ratios

Liquidity ratios *tell if the business can meet its cash obligations as they become due.*

A prime measure of the liquidity of a firm is the **current ratio,** which *measures the ability of the business to readily convert assets into cash.* The ratio represents the firm's ability to meet its short-term debt (current liabilities) with current assets or, stated another way, the ability of the firm to pay its debts.

$$\text{Current ratio} = \frac{\text{Current assets}}{\text{Current liabilities}}$$

Assets are divided into two categories: current assets and fixed assets. Those *assets that can be converted into cash within one year* are **current assets.** Current assets may be in the form of cash or other forms of negotiable instruments such as accounts receivable. *Debts that will be due within one year* are **current liabilities.** The relationship between current assets and current liabilities is the current ratio. Typically this ratio should be at least 2 to 1 for the firm to remain viable and indicates the money that is available to cover the firm's debts. The ratio for the Brown Corporation and the RMA industry standard from Exhibit 11.4 are shown below:

$$\frac{6,000,000}{2,300,000} = 2.6 \qquad \text{RMA} = 3.4 \text{ upper quartile}$$
$$1.9 \text{ median}$$
$$1.2 \text{ lower quartile}$$

A firm is considered to be in a good position if the ratio of current assets to current liabilities is 2 to 1 or greater. Creditors would not be pleased if their coverage dips much below 2 to 1, but the stockholders would feel that coverage greater than 2 to 1 signified that too much money that could be put to other uses was being held out to pay bills. We are only talking about current assets and liabilities. The Brown Corporation above is therefore attractive to creditors and is competitive with industry standards.

The **quick ratio** or **acid test ratio** shows *the relationship between assets such as cash accounts, notes receivable, and market securities and current liabilities.* The quick ratio should be at least 1 to 1 to show the firm's ability to immediately meet and pay its current debt load.

$$\text{Quick ratio} = \frac{\text{Quick assets}}{\text{Current liabilities}}$$
$$\text{Brown:} \frac{\$3,300,000}{2,300,000} = 1.4$$
$$\text{RMA} = 1.7 \text{ upper quartile}$$
$$0.9 \text{ median}$$
$$0.7 \text{ lower quartile}$$

This ratio is important because it shows how much cash, or near cash, is instantly available to pay bills. Other items such as inventory are also short-term assets, but if a slowdown occurs, it may be difficult or impossible to dispose of them at full market value, leaving creditors with worthless paper and/or materials.[13] The firm could be bankrupt in any kind of tight credit times.

The existence of the proper ratio does not signify that a business is healthy. In Brown's case above, they are more liquid than most of the industry and appear well able to pay their debts. A high quick ratio might mean either that everything is all right or that dividends were being held back for the purposes of beefing up the ratio. If dividends were being held back, it would be exceedingly difficult to sell stock, making it a poor investment for the average stockholder.

If it is important to know the total coverage of assets and liabilities, the asset coverage ratio is used. The **asset coverage ratio** *shows how much of your debt is covered by assets.*

$$\frac{\text{Asset coverage}}{\text{ratio}} = \frac{\text{Total assets}}{\text{Total liabilities}}$$

$$\text{Brown:} \frac{\$9,500,000}{5,300,000} = 1.8 \qquad \text{RMA} = 1.8$$

There is no fixed value for this ratio, since the desired value depends upon the industry average and how secure the creditors are. Brown meets the industry average, which satisfies its creditors. The relationship is different for different industries.

Leveraging Ratios

These measure financing by a firm's owners against that supplied by creditors. A low-leverage ratio means that the business owners supply less of the funds needed by the business and that creditors provide more of the firm's financing. Consequently, with less money invested, the firm is less affected by poor economic times. During good times, however, the profit potential is lower. On the other hand, firms that are highly leveraged are more susceptible to downturns, but return greater profits in good times.[14]

$$\frac{\text{Debt to}}{\text{net worth}}_{\text{ratio}} = \frac{\text{Total liabilities}}{\text{Net worth}}$$

$$\text{Brown:} \frac{5,300,000}{4,200,000} = 1.3 \qquad \begin{array}{l}\text{RMA} = 0.6 \text{ upper quartile}\\ \phantom{\text{RMA} = } 1.3 \text{ median}\\ \phantom{\text{RMA} = } 2.9 \text{ lower quartile}\end{array}$$

In the event of a liquidation, this ratio indicates the ability of a firm to meet its obligations to owners and creditors. It shows what the business owes and what it owns. Generally, the higher the ratio, the less protection afforded creditors. Brown's ratio shows a good balance by falling on the median ratio for their industry.

$$\frac{\text{Net fixed asset}}{\text{to net worth}}_{\text{ratio}} = \frac{\text{Net fixed assets}}{\text{Net Worth}}$$

$$\text{Brown:} \frac{3,500,000}{4,200,000} = 0.8 \qquad \begin{array}{l}\text{RMA} = 0.3 \text{ upper quartile}\\ \phantom{\text{RMA} = } 0.5 \text{ median}\\ \phantom{\text{RMA} = } 1.1 \text{ lower quartile}\end{array}$$

This ratio reveals how much of net worth is represented by fixed assets. If the ratio is too high, it sends a danger signal since there then might not be enough money to pay current bills. Further, the more net worth is represented by fixed assets, the less money could be recovered in hard times, since fixed assets rarely sell at full value when they must be sold. They are usually only valuable at full dollar amounts to the organization while it is a going concern. Brown shows more of its net worth tied up in fixed assets than that of the industry. As you recall, we pointed out that plausible reasons unique to individual business can cause variations from industry standards. In Brown's case, it could be that all its fixed assets are relatively new; because they have not been depreciated, they reflect a higher fixed asset value than the industry standard. Further investigation is needed to explain this variation.

$$\text{Debt ratio} = \frac{\text{Total debts}}{\text{Total assets}}$$

$$\text{Brown:} \frac{\$5,300,000}{9,500,000} = 0.56$$

$$\text{RMA} = \frac{53.8\%}{100\%} = 0.54$$

This ratio measures the percentage of total funds in the business that are provided by creditors. A high ratio means that the business is highly leveraged; that is, as the ratio increases, the creditors provide a higher percentage of the business's funds. As a business owner, you want the highest ratio possible, since it means that you have invested fewer personal funds. Correspondingly, creditors favor a lower ratio. This would mean you have more investment in the business and are likely to work harder to make the firm a success. In case of a business failure, a creditor would have less to lose. Brown's ratio is competitive with the industry and represents a good balance of debts to assets.

Operating Ratios

Operating ratios enable you to evaluate business performance, indicating how efficiently the firm is operating. By using these ratios and comparing them to the average ratios of firms in your field, you have an indicator of changes you might have to implement for increased efficiency.

The inventory turnover ratio measures the number of times inventory is turned over during the year.

$$\frac{\text{Inventory}}{\text{turnover ratio}} = \frac{\text{Cost of sales}}{\text{Inventory}}$$

$$\text{Brown:} \frac{\$10,500,000}{2,700,000} = 3.9 \qquad \text{RMA} = 7.0 \text{ upper quartile}$$
$$4.5 \text{ median}$$
$$3.0 \text{ lower quartile}$$

$$\frac{\text{Days}}{\text{inventory}} = \frac{365}{\text{Inventory turnover ratio}}$$

$$\text{Brown:} \frac{365}{3.9} = 93.6 \text{ days} \qquad \text{RMA} = 52 \text{ upper quartile}$$
$$81 \text{ median}$$
$$122 \text{ lower quartile}$$

Both ratios indicate how long the inventory remains on the corporate shelves. A ratio of three would mean each piece of inventory stayed on the shelves four months before being sold. This means that the firm must keep its money tied up in inventory and cannot use it for other operating purposes. This has ramifications for pricing policy, since the inventory must be stored and maintained and the cost of inventory thus varies with how long the firm must store it. Also, the longer merchandise sits on the shelves, the higher the price it must return in the market. Someone, usually the consumer, must pay. This might be one reason antiques are so expensive; by the time someone who wants a special piece is found (generally three years), the article has run up large storage and investment costs that must be offset.

Again, there is no absolute best value for this ratio. The acceptability of a firm's ratio depends upon what is average and normal for the industry. Deviation from normality is a danger signal that means that unless there is a good excuse for contrary behavior, corrective action must take place. In Brown's case, further investigation and/or corrective action is necessary. Some of the procedures discussed in Chapter 11 may be relative to Brown's case.

A pair of ratios that measure the number of times receivables turn over during the year are as follows:

$$\frac{\text{Receivables}}{\text{turnover ratio}} = \frac{\text{Net sales}}{\text{Accounts receivable}}$$

Brown: $\dfrac{\$14,000,000}{2,000,000} = 7$ RMA = 8.7 upper quartile
7.2 median
5.6 lower quartile

If the ratio increases, it means that more credit is being extended, and unless the firm has a good reason, or a great deal of money, there will not be enough money to pay bills, since the firm's cash flow will be markedly reduced.[15] If this ratio is allowed to get too large, the organization could experience cash flow difficulties.

Another way to look at the receivable turnover ratio is to determine the average number of days an account receivable is outstanding. The average collection period is determined by:

$$\frac{\text{Days sales}}{\text{outstanding ratio}} = \frac{365}{\text{Receivables turnover ratio}}$$

Brown: $\dfrac{365}{7} = 52$ RMA = 42 upper quartile
51 median
65 lower quartile

The higher this ratio is, the faster your money turns over and the shorter the time between the sale of goods and the receipt of cash. The higher this number, the less cash you need to have in reserve in order to run the business. Brown's ratios are in line with industry standards.

A good measure of the ability of your company to generate sales in relation to your assets is the total assets turnover ratio.

$$\frac{\text{Total assets}}{\text{turnover ratio}} = \frac{\text{Net sales}}{\text{Total assets}}$$

Brown: $\dfrac{\$14,000,000}{9,500,000} = 1.5$ RMA = 2.4 upper quartile
                                                      1.9 median
                                                      1.3 lower quartile

Using this ratio to compare your business to other firms' ratios tells you whether or not you are generating enough sales for your assets. A ratio below the industry average indicates that you must take some action to generate more sales. Brown should investigate the causes of this low ratio and take action to generate greater sales.

$$\frac{\text{Working capital}}{\text{turnover ratio}} = \frac{\text{Net sales}}{\text{Current assets} - \text{Current liabilities}}$$

Brown: $\dfrac{\$14,000,000}{6,000,000 - 2,300,000} = 3.8$ RMA =   3.4 upper quartile
                                                            5.9 median
                                                            20.5 lower quartile

This ratio tells you how efficiently you use your working capital to generate sales.[16] Again, a low number may indicate inefficiency, but you have to be careful because a number that is too high, on the other hand, may indicate that you have insufficient working capital. In any business, particularly in a small business, it is critical to have enough working capital. Brown's ratio is relatively high and warrants investigation for underlying causes.

Also referred to as the owner's equity ratio, the **proprietorship ratio** shows *the relationship between what the owner has invested in the firm and the total assets being used by the firm.* It is calculated by dividing the owner's investment by the amount of total assets.

$$\frac{\text{Owner's equity}}{\text{ratio}} = \frac{\text{Owner's equity}}{\text{Total assets}}$$

Brown: $\dfrac{\$4,200,000}{9,500,000} = 0.44$ RMA = 0.46

There are many more ratios that a business can use in analyzing its operation. Most firms that maintain an adequate current ratio, quick ratio, working capital ratio, and a competitive proprietorship ratio will present a sound financial structure. Other specific ratios can also help you control business operations; using them will enable you to gauge the health of your business and show you how to take corrective action if necessary.

Profitability Ratios

These ratios describe how profitable the firm is. They measure the bottom line and therefore they are a measure of success.[17] In general, the higher the profit, the more efficiently and successfully you are managing your company. A ratio that measures the return on sales is:

$$\frac{\text{Profit}}{\text{to net worth}} = \frac{100 \times \text{Net profit}}{\text{Net worth}}$$

Brown: $\dfrac{100 \times \$1,500,000}{4,200,000} = 35$ RMA = 33.3 upper quartile
14.8 median
6.5 lower quartile

The resulting percentage indicates the amount of profit per dollar of sales by looking at the dollars left over after all expenses have been paid. If the industry average is above yours, it may mean that your prices are too low, your costs are too high, or perhaps both. You want this number to be as high as possible, but remember that this, as with all ratios, must be used in conjunction with all the other information you have. For example, you should also consider such things as assets, inventory turnover, and capital ratios. Brown is in good shape with this ratio, but it is possible that its profitability is resulting from lack of sufficient capital. So again, further investigation into these numbers is advisable.

$$\frac{\text{Net profit to}}{\text{total asset ratio}} = \frac{100 \times \text{Net profit}}{\text{Total assets}}$$

Brown: $100 \times \dfrac{\$1,500,000}{9,500,000} = 16$ RMA = 11.7 upper quartile
6.7 median
2.1 lower quartile

This ratio measures the rate of return of assets. If this rate is lower than you could obtain in an alternative investment, perhaps you should invest elsewhere, since this represents the percentage of your investment being returned to you annually as generated by your assets. Brown's ratio is much higher than the industry standard, warranting further investigation.

In general, Brown measures quite well to its industry as portrayed by RMA standard ratios. As has been noted, several areas need further examination. Because the ratios involving inventory, fixed assets, and profitability differ from industry medians, this may indicate Brown is a relatively new enterprise with high undepreciated asset values, inventory controls which may need tightening, and a possible shortage of capital.

Using these ratios for internal control purposes will enable you to identify potential problems before they occur. Knowing the meaning of the ratios also points to the possible actions you can take to remedy problems. Ratios are also useful in the comparison of your business to industry averages. Several organizations compare and publish industry averages against which to measure your performance. Several of the more well known publishers are:

1. Dun & Bradstreet
2. Robert Morris Associates
3. Bank of America
4. Government agencies
5. Trade associations

Most libraries either have these reference materials on hand, can access them through computer networks, or direct you to them. As a small business owner, you should strive to equal if not exceed industry averages. Keep in mind, though, that these ratios are averages and your deviation from them does not automatically mean that you have problems but rather that you should consider *why* your results differ. Recognize that your ratios may differ from standards for perfectly valid reasons. At least you will understand your company and its performance.

Tax Considerations and Record Keeping

Record Keeping

The taxes you pay are based on the records you maintain.[18] If government deems that you have paid insufficient taxes or has some question about your taxes, it can, and will, examine your company's financial records. For your own protection, and to make certain that you don't overpay, you should keep adequate and detailed records. Anytime you cannot document your numbers, the IRS can disallow deductions and increase your tax bill.[19] Accurate record keeping also provides advantages for you as a manager. As this chapter has demonstrated, you can improve management control using the information generated by your operations. Additionally, should you need credit, it is a rare bank or venture capital company that will lend you money without examining your records quite carefully.

Tax Considerations

While some taxes seem quite straightforward, taxes, by their very existence, impact upon your business decisions. A complete explanation of how taxes influence your decisions is far beyond the scope of this book and certainly subject to the fact that as tax laws change, the impact on decision making shifts. Therefore, this section will examine only a few topics that may be crucial in your decisions.

Taxes and Profitability

You have learned in Chapter 11 that the profits of your company are determined by the equation:

Sales minus the cost of goods sold minus operating expenses
equals net profit or loss.

Since taxes are based on the *profits* of your operations, you should be well acquainted with the class of expenditures allowed for deduction. The more legal expenses you can deduct, the lower will be your profit and the fewer taxes you will pay. Many entrepreneurs are unfamiliar with allowable deductions and thus may pay more taxes than necessary. The IRS accepts as deductible expenses that are ordinary and necessary to the operation of your business. Knowing what deductions you are legally entitled to plus understanding the contents of your business records should enable you to identify all the expenses allowed in order to minimize your tax bill.

Allowable Business Expenses

Cost of Goods Sold

As indicated, this includes all costs in making or buying the goods or services you sell. Typically, this represents costs associated with the production process, such as material, supplies, labor, freight, and overhead. The first four costs are direct costs; that is, they vary directly with the volume produced. Other indirect costs such as overhead and general administrative costs cannot be attributed directly to the production process except by allocation. The more accurately you recognize all production costs, the more likely your taxes will be minimized.

Salaries

Salaries are the compensation you pay your employees for the service they perform. All compensation must be ordinary, necessary, and reasonable. Further, you cannot pay for work not performed. You can deduct all compensation paid and incurred in the current taxable year.

Rent

Rent is the cost to you for the use of property. There have been, and still are, qualifications to meet if you deduct part of your home used as an office. It is best to consult a tax attorney or accountant to make certain you are in compliance.

Depreciation

Depreciation is the yearly cost of the use of an asset with a life longer than one year. Any asset with a life of one year or less may be deducted as a business expense in the year of its use. Assets with a life of longer than one year may only have a portion of their total costs deducted. Here the government has permitted you to choose between several methods of depreciation. The more you depreciate an asset in any time period by shortening its depreciable life, the higher your expenses and the lower your taxes.[20] Again, this question is complex and you should seek expert advice.

Automobile Expenses

The IRS permits you to deduct the costs of an automobile or other vehicles used in carrying on normal business activities. In the case of an automobile, only business-related expenses may be deducted.

Bad Debts

The IRS permits you to deduct as a business expense any uncollectible receivables you may incur. The amount you lost is a bad debt. This loss must have been real, and you must be able to demonstrate that you have taken steps to collect the debt. If you have bad debts and can document them as expenses, your profit will be affected.

Travel and Entertainment

Part of the cost of doing business may involve being away from the main office either buying or selling. Those costs of being away from home for more than a day qualify for deductions. Be aware that these travel costs must be reasonable and ordinary or they will not be allowed. Some costs are not fully deductible, such as business lunches or cruise ship excursions, and any item that could classify as a personal expense is not allowed. Keep good records so that you do not lose anything to which you are entitled.[21]

Interest

While you may not deduct interest, the charge for borrowed money, your company may deduct the interest it pays on loans and any borrowed funds necessary to operate the business. There are some exclusions to this general rule. Check the IRS regulations frequently.

Taxes

You are allowed to deduct taxes you pay to state, local, and foreign governments as business expenses. Taxes include sales taxes; property taxes, which are taxes based on the assessed value of property; and employment taxes such as FICA (Social Security), FUTA (Federal Unemployment Taxes), and state unemployment taxes. All of these taxes must be calculated and paid or you are violating the law.

Miscellaneous Expenses

These are expenses incurred in operating your company, some of which may be specific to your organization. You should identify all such expenses and deduct them. The questions of which miscellaneous expenses are allowable and which are not and to what extent you may deduct these expenses are complex and should be discussed with your tax adviser.

Effects of Taxes on the Form of Ownership

Chapter 2 discussed the difference between the C corporation and the S corporation. The S corporation possesses tax benefits worth examining. To restate: The S corporation permits you to pass through the corporate structure all revenues and expenses accruing to the corporation so that they can be taxed on your individual tax return. It allows you to bypass double taxation and thereby to minimize your tax bill. For example, if you choose the C corporate form of organization, its profits are taxed at corporate tax rates. If the company then declares dividends, these are taxed at personal tax rates. If your corporate profit is $10,000 and corporate tax rates are 40 percent, you pay $4,000 in taxes. Of the $6,000 remaining, if you declare dividends of $6,000, you pay personal taxes of $1,680 (28 percent of $6,000). Your total tax bill is $5,680. Using the S corporation, all income is treated as personal income, and assuming a 28 percent tax bracket, you are liable for only $2,800 in taxes, a savings of $2,880. Exhibit 13.8 highlights this difference.

Tax savings alone is a powerful reason to use the S corporation form of organization. However, the Tax Act of 1993 may make this election less favorable, as the individual tax rates have been increased. As the tax laws change, the organization form you choose can make a big difference in your tax liability.

The previous discussions should serve to acquaint you with some of the tax issues to consider in your decision making. It is best to seek expert advice, since mistakes can be costly.

Exhibit 13.8 Comparison of tax liability from $10,000

C Corporation		S Corporation	
$10,000	Profit	$10,000	Profit
.40	*Corporate tax rate*	.28	*Personal tax rate*
4,000	Tax paid	2,800	Tax paid
6,000	Dividend paid	6,000	Dividend paid
.28	Taxable at *personal rate*	.00%	n/a:included above
1,680	Tax paid on dividend	0	Tax paid on dividend
$5,680	Total taxes paid	$2,800	Total taxes paid

Summary

Interrelationship between Financial Analysis and Taxation and Other Parts of the Business Plan

Taxes may affect your overall profitability by lowering your profits by taking larger amounts for depreciation. Additionally, the difference between personal and corporate tax rates will affect your choice of corporate structure. Your business must also pay many taxes for items such as retirement and unemployment. Financial analysis is used to examine how the company is performing and to determine if and how much correction is needed. Financial analysis, by comparing the firm's ratios to industry standards, is a continual process.

Taxation

It is inevitable that the freedom you enjoy in owning and operating your own business must be supported by governmental and societal responsibility in the form of taxes. You should learn about the various types of taxes because they are a necessary business expense and will affect your profitability.

While the object of any business is to make a profit, you should realize that this profit is treated and taxed as income. Thus you pay **income tax,** or *those taxes levied on the net income of the business.* You are also responsible for paying your share of an employee's **Social Security taxes,** which are *taxes levied on employers and employees to provide for individual retirement,* and **unemployment taxes,** which are *collected in order to insure those individuals who have lost their job.* **Sales taxes,** which are *determined by a percentage of the sales price of goods and perhaps services purchased,* are also applied to your purchases, as are taxes on **property** and any **excise taxes,** which are *taxes based on the assessed value of property.*

Budgets

While you cannot control the fact that your business must pay taxes, it is incumbent on you to use the financial information your business generates to analyze and control your firm in order to maximize profitability. Pro forma statements or budgets cannot be accurate, since it is impossible to predict the future. What you can do, however, is to compare what actually happens with your predictions, discovering **variances,** *deviations from the established budgetary amounts,* which will enable you to determine how to change what you are doing in response to reality. As part of your management control, you establish **standard costs,** *those costs that should be incurred in the operations process if all goes according to plan and definition,* against which to measure your actual performance. You then take corrective action if necessary.

You will know if corrective action is necessary because **cost variances** will be immediately evident.

Ratios

You also have guidelines in the form of various average industry ratios against which to measure your firm's performance. While you don't have to meet all the ratios to still be an average firm, these ratios can assist you in understanding your firm's performance with reference to other firms. These ratios serve as an indication of the health and profitability of your firm in many ways.

Some key ratios reveal different aspects of your firm's operations. You should be aware of these ratios and their uses.

Ratios are constructed from information supplied by the **balance sheet** and the **profit-and-loss statements.** The first group of ratios used in the analysis of your business are the **liquidity ratios.** This ratio group consists of the **current ratio,** which *measures the ability of the business to readily convert assets into cash;* the **acid test (quick ratio),** which shows *the relationship between assets such as cash, notes and accounts receivable, and market securities to current liabilities;* and the **asset coverage ratio,** *which shows how much of your debt is covered by assets.* **Leveraging ratios** are important, as they show how well you are using your financial resources. This group of ratios consists of the **debt to net worth ratio,** the **fixed assets to net worth ratio,** and the **debt ratio. Operating ratios** are extremely important, since they measure your efficiency and provide significant information. This ratio group consists of the **inventory turnover ratio,** which *serves as an indication of how often merchandise is turning over;* **receivables turnover;** and **days sales outstanding.** Also in this group are the **total asset turnover,** the **turnover of working capital,** and the **proprietorship ratio,** which *shows the relationship between what the owner has invested in the firm and the total assets being used by the firm.*

The final group of ratios you should know about are the **profitability ratios.** These define the bottom line and indicate, as a total measurement, how well you are doing. These ratios are the **profit margin ratio** and the **net worth ratio.**

Record Keeping and Tax Considerations

Concomitant with achieving profitability are tax liabilities. Taxes are based on profits. Profits are always determined after deducting allowable **business expenses.** The more legal expenses you can deduct, the lower will be your profit. Lower profits mean you pay less in taxes. Some categories of IRS allowable expenses are **cost of goods sold, salaries, depreciation,** and **bad debts.** Additionally acceptable are **travel and entertainment, interest, taxes,** and **miscellaneous.**

While tax laws shift focus over time, these laws impact on the form of ownership that is most advantageous. Presently, whether you choose the C or the S corporate form of ownership depends upon the relationship between your individual tax rates and the corporate tax rate. You should chose the corporate organization form that minimizes your taxes.

Questions

1. What is the chief difference between historical balance sheets and a firm's income statements and its budget?
2. How would you go about setting up a budget for your firm? What information would you need and how would you use it?
3. How would you use the budget as a control device?
4. What is the importance of a variance from the budget, and what steps do you take when a variance occurs?
5. Define the term *operating ratio.* How would you use ratios in your business for making decisions?

6. Define and explain the meaning of *liquidity ratios.*

7. Define and explain the meaning of *leveraging.*

8. Explain the current ratio. Would a ratio of 1 to 1 be considered a "good" current ratio? Why or why not?

9. What is the difference between the current ratio and the acid test ratio? If you were a supplier to the business, which ratio would you use and why?

10. What does the inventory turnover ratio tell you? What would be a satisfactory inventory ratio?

11. Extending your credit terms would affect your credit sales ratio. What does this ratio tell you?

12. Define the *proprietorship ratio.* What is the standard usually accepted as being good for this ratio?

13. As taxes increase, what effect would this have on the health of the business?

14. How important are taxes in business planning? Explain your position.

15. Identify the different taxes that a small business would have to pay.

16. To quickly judge the overall health of a firm, which three ratios would you use, and what would be considered good ratios?

Application Exercises

When doing these exercises, where applicable, be sure to select a specific business, preferably one where you presently work or previously worked or a business you would like to own someday. If this is not possible, pick a specific organization to which you will refer. Be sure to identify the organization by name. Limit your answers to one or two pages per exercise.

1. Select a specific business you are familiar with and develop standard ratios that you would consider to be important for the business using sources such as Robert Morris Associates or Dun & Bradstreet.

2. Interview a local bank loan officer to find out what ratios are considered important and what values for these ratios are sought in judging business health.

3. Compare the information you located in questions 1 and 2. Are the ratios being considered the same or are they different? Explain the differences or similarities.

4. Interview an established small business person and obtain a copy of the firm's financial statements, current or past. Using this information:
   (a) Compare the ratios used in this chapter.
   (b) Using Robert Morris Associates or Dun & Bradstreet, find the industry ratios for this type of business.
   (c) Compare the information in parts (a) and (b) and make appropriate recommendations for the business.

5. Ask several small business owners what effect taxes have on their business decisions. What would the impact of tax increases be? Report to the class.

6. Interview a small business owner and report to the class on the impact of taxes on the firm's record keeping.

Application Situations

1. Networth Company

Networth Company, founded by Peter Jurgen in 1984 after he graduated from college, was a retail store specializing in selling expensive fabric to a wealthy clientele. In its first three years the firm saw sales increase by 50 percent, 75 percent, and 100 percent. In those years Peter was only able to show net profits of under 6 percent, while the average profits for the industry were 14 percent. He attributed this to the unusually high start-up costs and the expensive property he had leased on the most expensive street in the city. It would, he thought, take several years before everything would fall into place and he would be at least competitively profitable.

In 1987, however, there was a recession, and Peter's sales dropped in two successive years by 25 percent in the first year and 30 percent in the second. Profits became nonexistent. While not panicking, Peter decided to revise his credit policies. Previously he allowed 30 days net on his bills. Now he allowed 45 days. Also recognizing that his customers might not have as much discretionary income as before, he relaxed enforcement. His average collection period ratio was now 60 days. Given enough time, he was sure that this strategy would turn the company around.

Assignment

Answer the following questions:

1. Does the fact that Peter's 6 percent profit fail to match industry standards signal a problem for the company? How would you measure profits? As a result of your findings, what would you recommend?
2. Are you comfortable with Peter's rented facilities? Support your position and indicate the effect that a change of facilities might have on profits.
3. Is it too late for Peter's plan to save the company or is his timing wrong? Defend your opinion.

2. Jay's Antiques

Jay's Antiques, long a fixture in the antique district, managed to turn a respectable profit for 50 years. Jay, now reaching retirement age, began the process of transferring the business and responsibility for decision-making to his children, Sam and Beth. Both had been in the business for five years and while they were happy, they disagreed with several of the policies Jay followed. For example, they were certain that Jay's approach to buying inventory was too conservative. Jay studied the market and bought only those items that were selling. He gave little consideration to future trends. Sam and Beth thought that the only inventory Jay acquired was already presold, since nothing Jay bought remained unsold for longer than 30 days. This approach often resulted in a sparse inventory, leaving clients with a small selection. Slowly, they began to buy more inventory so that buyers would have a wide range of choices. Sam, studying all the journals and economic predictions, bought inventory which, while not currently popular, would be good for future sales.

Assignment

Answer the following questions:

1. Based upon the above information, what ratios would be affected by the change in policy, and how would these ratios change? Explain and be specific.
2. What does the term "respectable profit" tell you? If you were in the antique business, how would you measure success? Explain the measurements you would use and give several examples.
3. As a result of Beth and Sam's strategy, what do you think will happen to the business, and why? Explain your position, and as a result of your conclusions, make some recommendations to Beth and Sam.

3. Zenotek

"Profit doesn't mean anything to me. As a measure of my success, it is lacking. All that matters is that I have enough cash to pay my bills." This statement was often made as Priscilla paid the bills incurred by her small manufacturing firm. Her company, Zenotek, manufactured high-capacity chips for use in many of today's appliances, including computers and consumer durable goods such as washing machines, ovens, and even office machines. Because technology is continually changing, Priscilla has to continue upgrading her facility with newer, more modern manufacturing equipment.

The future appeared bright, and equipment manufacturers' terms were generous. If she wanted to, and she often did, she could extend the payout on machinery to 30 or 40 years. As a result of her firm's success, Priscilla bought a large building lot in a good suburb and erected a state-of-the-art building. Her office and those of her administrative staff were spacious and expensively furnished.

Assignment

Answer the following questions:

1. Which of the ratios discussed in the text could be affected? How would these ratios be affected with respect to industry averages?
2. What recommendations would you make to Priscilla given her beliefs as evidenced by her statements and the result of the ratios?
3. In your opinion, what is the likelihood of the firm's survival or is it too late? Explain your position.

4. Dan Espinosa

On a recent trip to Spain, Dan Espinosa happened to visit a series of small towns and villages where they manufactured silk print fabrics the likes of which could not be found in the United States. Upon returning, Dan convinced a close friend, Matt Ross, to co-found a business to import the silk fabric. Dan was certain of profits from this venture. Both men agreed that the corporate form of organization was best, and the Madon Company was founded. Neither Dan nor Matt realized that they were subject to many different taxes and hadn't given this aspect of the business much thought. Dan seemed vaguely to recall something about an S corporation and taxation, but he wasn't certain. Matt thought that the best way to mitigate the tax problem was not to keep any records and therefore they would not owe taxes.

1. Explain to Dan what he should have known about an S corporation and how tax structures should affect his decision about using the S corporate form.
2. Is Matt's thinking correct? Could this approach lead to trouble? How would you advise Matt to set up, keep, and maintain corporate records? Which records would be important in determining Madon's corporate tax liability?

Integrated Case Question—CorLu Foods

Using ratio analysis, compare CorLu to industry standards and indicate any corrective action needed. Determine CorLu's breakeven point. (Please refer to the Integrated Case, "CorLu Foods.")

Additional Reading

Aaron, Hugh. "Cap Gains? Small Change to Small Start-Ups." *The Wall Street Journal,* August 12, 1993, pp. A13(W), A13(E), col. 4.

Brophy, David, and Joel Shulman. "Financial Factors Which Stimulate Innovation." *Entrepreneurship: Theory and Practice* 17, no. 2 (Winter 1993), pp. 61–75.

Brown, Richard N. "Accounting for Sole Proprietor Income Taxes." *National Public Accountant,* September 1989, pp. 32–34.

Carlson, Eugene, "Small Businesses Gaze Hungrily at Sweeter Tax Provision; Higher Expensing Ceiling, Retroactive Too, Promises an Array of Breaks." *The Wall Street Journal,* July 29, 1993, pp. B2(W), B2(E), col. 3.

Carlson, Eugene, and Jeanne Saddler. "Clinton Seeks Small-Business Support for Budget Plan; Administration's All-out Effort Seeks to Portray Proposal as Boon to Firms." *The Wall Street Journal,* July 22, 1993, pp. B2(W), B2(E), col. 3.

Coker, John W., and Robert D. Hayes. "Lenders' Perceptions of Income-Tax-Basis Financial Reporting by Small Business." *Journal of Small Business Management* 30, no. 3 (July 1992), pp. 66–76.

Davidson, Wallace N., III, and Dipa Dutia. "Debt, Liquidity and Profitability Problems in Small Firms." *Entrepreneurship: Theory and Practice* 16, no. 1 (Fall 1991), pp. 53–64.

Ellentuck, Albert B. "An Accelerated Schedule for Certain Taxpayers." *Nation's Business,* February 1992, p. 65.

"Financial Ratios That Tell You How Well Your Business Is Doing." *Profit-Building Strategies for Business Owners,* February 1991, pp. 6–8.

Frazer, Jill Andresky. "Tax Strategies: Like-kind Exchanges." *Inc.,* August 1991, p. 91.

Green, Gary L., Jr. "Built-in Gains for 'S' Corporations." *National Public Accountant,* May 1993, p. 34.

Hale, David. "Small Business, Tax Plan's Victim," *The Wall Street Journal,* July 30, 1993, pp. A10(W), A8(E), col. 4.

Lunzer Kritz, Francesca; Leonard Wiener; and James Popkin. "A Bonus for Small Businesses." *U.S. News & World Report,* May 13, 1991, p. 95.

Marder, Melvin, and Calvin Engler. "Change from Sole Proprietorship to a Corporation May Result in Unexpected Tax." *Taxation for Accountants,* May 1989, pp. 292–96.

"New Rules Conform 'S' Corp. and Partnership Income." *Taxation for Accountants,* April 1993, p. 233.

Padwe, Gerald W. "Smaller Can Be Better." *Nation's Business,* January 1990, p. 69.

Ryans, Cynthia. "Resources." *Journal of Small Business Management* 30, no. 5 (July 1992), p. 77.

Rutman, Gail. "Should You Go Corporate." *Nation's Business,* May 1990, p. 46.

Stern, Linda. "10 Smart Tax-Saving Tips for Small Businesses." *Home Office Computing,* December 1990, p. 26.

Szabo, Joan C. "Tax-Saving Tips for Small Firms." *Nation's Business,* March 1992, p. 29.

Teitell, Conrad. "What Looks Like a Corporation, Smells Like a Corporation, but Is Taxed Like a Partnership or Sole Proprietorship?" *Trusts and Estates,* November 1989, pp. 63–64.

Tibergien, Mark C. "Business Planning for the Planner." *Best's Review,* February 1992, pp. 67–70.

"Treasury Signs Up." *The Wall Street Journal,* July 6, 1993, pp. A12(W), A12(E), col. 1.

Watson, Harry. "The Effects of Taxation on Partnership Investment." *Journal of Public Economics* 36, no. 1(June 1988), pp. 111–26.

Weicholz, Jacob. "Many Happy Returns." *The New York Times Magazine,* March 22, 1992, p. 10A, col. 1.

Zagorin, Adam. "How the Small-Business Owner Gets Clobbered." *Time,* July 12, 1993, p. 32.

Endnotes

1. Consult "The Five Cardinal Rules of Financial Control," *Inc.,* May 1992, for other characteristics.
2. Dean Croushore, "How Big Is Your Share of Government Debt?" *Business Review,* November–December 1990, p. 3.
3. Jill Andresky Fraser, "Planning Ahead: Estate Planning Isn't Just for Your Heirs; It Can Save Your Company," *Inc.,* August 1989, pp. 125–27.
4. John D. McClain, "Social Security Recipients to Receive Bigger Checks," *Mobile* (Alabama) *Register,* October 16, 1992, p. 5–A.
5. Eugene Carlson, "Catalog Firms Resist Pressure to Collect States' Use Taxes," *The Wall Street Journal,* July 2, 1985, p. 35.
6. Tom Richman, "The Language of Business," *Inc.,* February 1990, pp. 41–50.
7. James McKinley, *Budgetary Control* (New York: Ronald Press, 1922).
8. The minimum wage rate in 1993.
9. McKinley, *Budgetary Control.*
10. "Putting Ratios to Work," *In Business,* December 1988, pp. 14–15.
11. U.S. Small Business Administration, *Ratio Analysis for Small Business,* Small Business Management Series No. 20 (Washington, D.C.: U.S. Government Printing Office, 1977), p. 8.
12. It is unnecessary to use a dollar sign since the manipulation of the control device concerns itself with the relationship between categories and their relative relationships regardless of the denomination involved.

13. Peter Fuhrman, "Drinking Your Profits Is the Best Revenge," *Forbes,* June 25, 1990, pp. 270–72.

14. John J. Curran, "Hard Lessons from the Debt Decade," *Fortune,* June 18, 1990.

15. William P. Barrett, "It's Legal, but Is It Smart?" *Forbes,* June 25, 1990, pp. 126–27.

16. Dean Planeaus, "Factoring Guarantees Cash Flow for Diaper Startup," *Corporate Cashflow Magazine,* August 1991, p. 42.

17. Dana Wechster Linden, "Lies of the Bottom Line," *Forbes,* November 12, 1990, pp. 106ff.

18. *Tax Guide for Small Business,* Department of Treasury, IRS Pub. No. 334 (Washington, D.C.: U.S. Government Printing Office), p. 94.

19. Joe Anthony, "How I Survived a Tax Audit," *Changing Times,* May 1990, pp. 39–44; "The Taxman Cometh," *Inc.,* September 1991, p. 100.

20. John Merwin, "Dumb Like Foxes," *Forbes,* October 24, 1988, pp. 45–46.

21. U.S. Department of the Treasury, Internal Revenue Service, *1992 Forms and Instructions, 1040* (Washington, D.C.: U.S. Government Printing Office, 1992).

14 CONTROLLING ASSETS, RISK AND COMPUTER APPLICATIONS

In this chapter you will learn how the control process enables the business plan to be implemented, how to control quality and cost, how to prevent crime, and how to maintain credit collection in order to protect assets. You will also learn about risk management and how insurance transfers the risk of loss of assets and earnings. Finally, control through the use of computers is presented, including computer basics, software applications, buying the computer system, and training employees to use the computer.

Chapter Learning Objectives

After completing this chapter, you should be able to:

· List and describe the steps in the control process.
· Define and discuss quality and total quality management.
· List and explain six guidelines for controlling quality and six guidelines for controlling cost.
· List and discuss four types of business crime.
· Explain the difference between trade and consumer credit and describe how to age accounts receivables.
· List and explain four types of risk.
· List and describe three types of insurance that transfer risk of loss of assets and four types of insurance that transfer risk of loss of earnings.
· Explain how small businesses use several applications software programs.
· Define the following 15 key terms:

Controlling	Risk management
Control process	Insurance

Standards   Key-person insurance
Quality   Computer hardware
Total quality management   Computer software
Business crime   Microprocessor
Trade credit   Integrated software
Consumer credit

The Interrelationship between Controlling and the Business Plan Components

Controlling is *the process of establishing methods that ensure that the business objectives are achieved.* The primary objective of a small business owner or manager should be to provide a product of high quality at a minimum cost when needed. In fulfilling that responsibility, the owner must make sure plans are carried out and that the firm's assets are protected. And that, as our definition implies, means controlling. The better your skills are at controlling, the greater are your chances of success in business.[1]

Controlling is a function of management; it is a method to ensure that plans in the functional areas of accounting and finance, marketing, production/operations, and human resources are successfully implemented. Business planning and control are inseparable. So, as you develop plans, you should also develop controls for each functional area.

The controls established must also be coordinated as a system within the functional areas to ensure success. Control systems for production, sales, delivery, and accounting must be coordinated to ensure customer satisfaction. Producing more than the firm can sell, late deliveries, and bad debts cause problems.

The Control Process

The **control process** *includes setting objectives; establishing standards, methods, and times for measuring performance; measuring and comparing performance to standards; and reinforcing or correcting.* See Exhibit 14.1 for an illustration of the steps in the control process.

Step 1. Set objectives. The first step in the control process is also a part of planning. In Chapter 6 you learned about setting objectives.

Step 2. Establish standards, methods, and times for measuring performance. Complete **standards** *describe performance levels in the areas of quantity, quality, time, and cost.* Objectives are standards. However, additional standards are needed if objectives are to be achieved. In Chapters 12 and 13 you learned about setting accounting budgets and financial analysis ratios, which are standards. Budgets are usually set up on a monthly basis.

Exhibit 14.1

*Steps in the control
process*

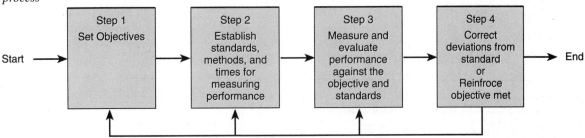

Step 3. Measure and compare performance to standards. Once your budget is formulated it becomes the standard, and at the end of the month you compare how much you planned to sell or spend to how much you actually did.

Step 4. Reinforce or correct. If you are selling or spending at standard you are achieving your objective; therefore, you need take no action. However, if you are underselling or overspending, there is need for corrective action. You may have to go back to prior steps and change objectives or standards.

Types of Controls

There are three types of controls: input, process, and output. At different times budgets represent three types of controls. When the budget is developed, it is an *input control* designed to anticipate and prevent possible problems. As the months go by it becomes a *process control* to measure and evaluate work in progress. At the end of the year the budget becomes an *output control;* it's too late for corrective action, but the prior year's budget serves as the basis for the following year's budget.

Controlling Quality and Cost

A quality product is an asset to the firm, and cost control is needed to make sure assets are not wasted. Quality and cost control have been hot topics in the 1980s and 1990s; just about every week on the front page of *The Wall Street Journal* there are examples of companies' efforts to increase quality and decrease cost. However, quality and cost must be balanced as a system.

Total Quality Management

As global competition intensifies for large and small business, more managers are calling for quality.[2] Quality is the most powerful weapon small businesses have over the large corporation. Surveys show that a high percentage of consumers are willing to pay for quality.[3] At many small firms, such as electronics companies, quality is not an option.[4]

Quality is *the predetermined standard that the product or service should meet.* The quality of Ford's Lincoln Town Car is higher than its Escort model. But both cars meet their respective quality standards. **Total quality management (TQM)** *requires everyone in the organization to continually improve products and services.* The key to TQM is setting standards and continually striving to improve them. People are the heart of TQM because they are responsible for continually increasing quality. However, employees will strive for quality only if the manager or owner leads by example.

Statistical process control is used as a feedback method to statistically maintain consistent quality within narrow limits. Products need to be designed so that they will not fail in the field. Quality is a virtue of design. If the product is designed effectively, there will be few defects. Some recommend striving for zero defects as part of the TQM system. However, customer satisfaction is the primary focus of TQM.

Although formal TQM programs are usually instituted by large companies, small businesses such as Den-Con, an oil-drilling equipment company, and Stevens Point Brewery also rely on TQM principles.[5] Granite Rock Company produces ready-mix concrete, asphalt, road treatments, and recycled road-base materials. It has developed a total quality program including a strong service component as the cornerstone of its overall corporate objective. Its TQM program has been a great success; in fact, in 1992 Granite Rock was awarded the Malcolm Baldrige National Quality Award in the category of small business.[6]

Controlling Quality

Poor quality has a direct effect on costs and profits. Poor-quality products result in loss of customers and legal suits for damages caused by injuries from products.

Causes of Poor Quality

Managers tend to blame poor quality on employees. They say workers don't care about quality and don't take pride in their work. Actually, in most cases poor quality is out of the employees' control and is a result of some combination of the following causes:[7]

Resources.   When management furnishes inferior tools, equipment, materials, or supplies, employees cannot do a quality job.

Management.   Poor planning, unclear standards, and poor communication of expectations and instructions often result in poor quality. Managers frequently fail to enforce quality standards.

Training.   Employees cannot do a quality job unless they are properly taught to do so.

Production/Operations.   If the production/operations systems are inefficient, poor quality will result.

What Managers Can Do to Ensure High Quality

Following the six guidelines below can help produce quality products and services.

1. *Use quality resources and systems.* Have quality resources available, when needed. Periodically check the production/operations system and continually improve it. Granite Rock uses innovative technology to satisfy customer needs.

2. *Set clear standards and train employees.* Studies find that problems often arise from differences in standards of acceptability, both the company's and the customers'.[8] Make sure every employee knows the exact level of quality expected and train them to produce at that level of quality. Granite Rock offers skills training and development because it believes that quality products and exemplary service can be accomplished with highly skilled and motivated people. Each employee sets individual goals toward doing the best job possible.

3. *Talk about and reward quality.* One advantage in being small lies in the fact that there are fewer employees and they know each other. These conditions help the small business in quality awareness, training, and implementation.[9] Slogans and signs help communicate the message. Examples include "Quality is job one" (Ford); "Quality, Service, Cleanliness, and Value" (McDonald's); and "We want to give the best customer service of any company in the world" (IBM). Quality should be a part of employee evaluations.

High-quality performers should be rewarded. Incentive programs such as bonuses, merit pay, and piece-rate pay are a common approach to improving quality.[10] Granite Rock recognizes quality and to help strengthen its quality efforts, uses it as a criterion for promotions.

4. *Enforce standards.* With TQM every employee is a quality control person who enforces the high standards. When quality standards are not met, the employee responsible should be informed. Whenever possible, that employee should be required to take corrective action. This employee should redo the job or apologize to the customer. At Granite Rock employees set their own goals to increase their standards of performance.

5. *Use employee suggestions.* Employees often know their jobs better than managers do and can make valuable suggestions on ways to improve quality. A commonly used technique is *quality circles,* which meet regularly to spot and solve problems in their work area. Granite Rock managers are open to employee suggestions.

6. *Keep records and plan improvements.* Keep a record of performance and communicate it to employees. Compare the current period to previous periods to let employees see their progress, or lack of progress. Develop plans for improvement

in the next period. Granite Rock does this with the individual employee and broader levels as well.

Controlling Cost

One of the major costs that is out of control for business is health care.[11] According to the National Federation of Independent Business, some two-thirds of small businesses offer health insurance. Health care exacts a heavier toll on small business, for they pay nearly 75 percent more per employee for medical benefits than large firms with identical claim expenses.[12] One way to help keep health costs down is to join organizations such as Cleveland, Ohio's Council of Smaller Enterprises to get group rates.[13]

The Relationship between Quality and Cost

Poor quality leads to lost customers and lawsuits. There is also corrective cost for poor quality, such as the cost of repairing a faulty product; handling and shipping faulty products; wasted parts, materials and supplies; and hours of staff time to handle customer complaints. Corrective costs can represent anywhere from 2 to 10 percent of an organization's revenue.[14]

There is a need to balance quality and cost. Poor quality is costly, but giving customers a higher level of quality than they want and are willing to pay for is also costly. As Ken Shibilski, president of the small business Stevens Point Brewery, puts it: "The trick is to cut cost without compromising quality."[15] Because quality and cost are directly related, managers should balance both as they focus on controlling both simultaneously.

What Managers Can Do to Control Cost

Follow these six guidelines:[16]

1. *Emphasize profits, not cost.* Balance price, quality, service, and delivery. When purchasing equipment, materials, or supplies don't simply buy the cheapest available. In the long run it may cost less to use higher-quality materials. Late delivery and poor-quality equipment that breaks down can result in idle employees for a time, with the need for overtime later to catch up. Advertising and sales people are expenses, but if the result is increased sales they more than offset the cost.

2. *Set clear cost standards.* All employees should know production costs and expectations. Train employees in techniques that will minimize waste. To reduce cost, look for drains on financial resources through waste and duplication. Look for cost trends. Change the standards. Be sure to sell the employees on the benefits of cost savings to them and to the firm.

3. *Talk about and reward cost consciousness.* Cost should not be a once-a-year subject when the budget is prepared. Talk about cost and quality on a regular basis. Cost control should be a part of employee evaluations. Reward employees for their successful reduction of cost. Many organizations give prizes or cash rewards.

EXHIBIT 14.2   **Controlling quality and cost**

Quality	Cost
1. Use quality resources and systems.	1. Emphasize profits, not costs.
2. Set clear quality standards.	2. Set clear cost standards.
3. Talk about and reward quality.	3. Talk about and reward cost consciousness.
4. Enforce quality standards.	4. Enforce cost standards.
5. Use employee suggestions.	5. Use employee suggestions.
6. Keep records and plan improvements.	6. Keep records and plan improvements.

4. *Enforce standards.* Employees will not be cost conscious if managers don't enforce standards. Watch out for theft and intentional damage, which occurs when employees are given damaged merchandise or when it is sold to them at minimal cost.

5. *Use employee suggestions.* Employees often know or can develop ways to cut cost. Solicit employees' ideas and reward them for their success.

6. *Keep records and plan improvements.* Keep records and communicate results to employees. Combine quality and cost into one report, and plan for improvements in both areas together.

Exhibit 14.2 summarizes what managers can do to control quality and cost.

Controlling Crime

It is the manager's job to protect the firm's assets from crime. However, businesses lose billions of dollars to crime annually. **Business crime** includes *employee theft, shoplifting, burglary, and robbery.* The U.S. Chamber of Commerce estimates that at least 30 percent of all business failures are caused by costs stemming from employee dishonesty, and small businesses are 35 times more likely to be a victim of crime than large companies.[17]

Employee Theft

The majority of criminal losses to small businesses are due to employee theft, not shoplifting. The Justice Department estimates that 30 percent of all employees are "hard-core" pilferers. Many thefts are nickel-and-dime losses of merchandise, supplies, and cash, but the accumulation over time is staggering.

Selecting honest employees is a good preventive precaution. The owner or manager of the small business sets the example. Failure to establish formal controls and procedures invites theft. Employees having the opportunity to steal, and the perception that the probability of being caught is low, encourage employee theft. Sloppy records make it easy for employees to steal. Proper inventory and cash accounting procedures (discussed in Chapters 9 and 12) should be followed by everyone, including the owner. Have at least two people involved in fiscal transactions.

Shoplifting

Shoplifting involves a customer leaving the business with unpaid-for merchandise. It is the most frequent business crime. About half of all shoplifters are juveniles. Well-trained, alert employees are the best defense against shoplifters. If employees keep a close watch, suspects may leave without stealing. Shoplifters commonly are nervous and spend a lot of time looking around to see who is watching, as they linger in the same area for an extended time. They tend to shy away from store personnel. Shoplifters often use props such as bags, large pocketbooks, and baby carriages. They tend to wear loose, bulky clothing. The store layout should enable the cashier to see the entire store; mirrors also can help. Small expensive items should be locked in display cases, and personnel should be assisting customers at dressing rooms. Mechanical devices such as electronic tags are effective at preventing and catching theft.

Employees should be careful not to make false accusations of theft. You don't want to be sued. When employees catch shoplifters, they should be apprehended outside the store. Approach the shoplifter and say something like, "I believe you have merchandise that you did not pay for. Would you please come with me so that we can straighten things out?" Go back into the store and call the police if you plan to prosecute. If the owner simply lets shoplifters go without prosecution, the thief is not discouraged from stealing and the store can get the reputation of being an easy target.

Burglary and Robbery

Burglary is the unlawful entry into an establishment with the intent to commit a felony. Owners who fail to lock doors and windows, install alarm systems, install proper lighting, and have a safe are leaving their business open to internal and external thieves. Burglaries tend to occur when the business is closed, whereas robberies occur when it is open.

Robbery is the taking of another's property by violence, force, or fear. The manager's first concern should be the safety and protection of employees, customers, and self. Employees should follow robbers' instructions, remain calm, and try to remember their description. Surveillance cameras are effective methods for obtaining accurate descriptions of robbers. Hidden weapons to be used in case of robbery often force robbers to use their weapons. In the large majority of cases of confrontation, it is the business owner who gets killed. Are the assets to be taken worth risking your life over?

Establishing Security

Managers should develop a security system for their business. A security system requires an investment of resources that should be cost-effective. Some experts suggest that a business spend at least 10 percent of its theft losses on security.[18]

Credit Collection

Failure to collect debts results in the loss of the firm's assets. The major objective of selling on credit is to increase profits, but increased sales volume must more than offset the cost of credit. Cost of credit includes customers who do not pay and the administrative cost to keep accounts receivable records. Many businesses have large sums tied up in accounts receivable.

The decision to sell on credit is influenced by: (1) the type of business. Most sales of large durable goods are sold on credit, whereas most sales of perishables are sold for cash. About 95 percent of all manufacturers, 90 percent of all wholesalers, and about 50 percent of all retail and service sales are on credit.[19] (2) Competitors' credit policy. The firm may lose sales to competitors who offer credit, or better credit terms. (3) Income level of customers. The ability and willingness to pay promptly are important. Generally, the higher the income level the less risk of offering credit.

Kinds of Credit

The two broad classes of credit include trade credit and consumer credit. **Trade credit** is *typically extended from one business to another,* such as a manufacturer to a wholesaler or retailer. **Consumer credit** is *typically extended by a retailer to the final customer who buys the product for personal use.* However, some small business owners use consumer credit to buy supplies and equipment for use in their own business.

Trade Credit

Businesses may sell products subject to specified terms of sale, such as 2/10, n/30. This means that the buyer can take a 2 percent discount if the bill is paid within 10 days of the invoice date. But the entire amount is due in 30 days. The small business should keep good records and pay within the discount period. EOM is a trade credit term meaning that the buyer is billed at the end of the month for all credit purchases during that month. The sales terms depend on the kind of product sold and the circumstances. Generally, the longer it takes to sell the product, or what is called the turnover period, the more time buyers are given to pay.

The decision to extend credit and the limit of credit extended to a business should be based on its credit rating. Dun & Bradstreet offers credit ratings stating what kind of business the buyer is in and how it is managed, the buyer's latest income statement and balance sheet, an estimate of the buyer's financial strength, and a record of the buyer's promptness in paying bills.

Consumer Credit

The business can sell to consumers by giving them credit directly or by accepting credit cards. For the very small business the easiest and safest way to offer credit is to accept bank credit cards (Visa and MasterCard) and entertainment credit cards (American Express and Diners Club). Using credit cards sharply reduces the investment in accounts receivable, may eliminate it altogether, and puts the burden of credit management and collection on the credit company, which assumes all credit risks as long as the business follows instructions for approval of credit card purchases. These card companies charge a percentage of total credit card sales for their service. Credit card services are especially valuable to the business with a large number of relatively small accounts. They virtually eliminate the risk of uncollectible accounts. Today even businesses with their own credit programs are accepting credit cards to stay competitive.

For the small business that has the option of offering credit directly to its customer, the cost is often lower than accepting credit cards. When offering credit and setting limits, it is important to do a credit check through a local credit bureau.

Control Techniques

Many factors can affect the amount that a company can expect to collect, including: (1) the age of the accounts, (2) the condition of the local economy, and (3) credit policies.[20] *Aging of accounts* receivable is the technique for keeping track of how old each debt is and thus measuring the quality of the receivables. It helps identify the overdue accounts that demand extra follow-up to receive collection. See Exhibit 14.3 for an example.

Businesses have no control over the condition of the local economy, but they can be sure to run a credit check to minimize bad trade and consumer debts. It is recommended that the credit-collections policy and procedures be written in a manual and followed.[21] It is also important to control the average collection period (discussed in Chapter 13). The longer it takes to get your money, the lower the odds are

EXHIBIT 14.3   **Aging of accounts receivables.**

Age	Amount Owed/Receivables
Not past due	$17,295
1–30 days past due	6,428
31–60 days past due	3,279
61–90 days past due	1,874
More than 90 days past due	941
Total accounts receivable	$29,817

of receiving it. To make the job of controlling accounts receivables easier and more effective, there are a variety of software packages available to the small business.[22] Shop around and find the best package to meet your unique needs.

For the business that is short on cash, or wants to offer its own credit program without the work, the *factoring* company is an option. A business with cash flow problems can sell its accounts receivables to a factoring company, which deducts a percentage of the money for its services. Factors can also be used as the credit-collections and receivables management department of the company. One small business example is American Enviro, makers of biodegradable diapers, which uses Heller Financial as its credit department.[23]

Risk Management

Risk Management Programs

Risk is a condition in which there is a probability of loss. The small business has an objective to make a profit and continue conducting business, but there is a risk of loss and business failure. The risk facing small business has multiplied tenfold in recent years.[24] **Risk management** incorporates *efforts to prevent loss of assets and earnings.*

Risk Management Strategies

Handling risk involves a combination of four types of risk strategies: risk avoidance, risk reduction, risk anticipation, and risk transferring.

Risk avoidance is the practice of shunning risky situations. Many people who would like to be self-employed don't start a business to avoid the risk of loss. Leasing rather than owning is a way to avoid ownership risk. Using the corporate form of ownership is a way to avoid unlimited liability.

Risk reduction is the practice of taking measures to minimize loss. Smoke detectors and sprinkler systems help reduce fire damages without avoiding the fire. Safety programs are designed to prevent accidents. Running a credit check helps reduce bad debt expenses.

Risk anticipation, or self-insurance, is the practice of putting money aside to cover losses that might occur. The loss may not occur, but if it does money is available to help defer it. Self-insurance is more common among large businesses than small ones, but a growing number of small businesses are joining together to self-insure.

Risk transfer or risk spreading is the practice of using insurance to cover losses. The best form of protection against many risks is the proper insurance. A relatively small amount of money is required to insure against great loss.[25] During a specified time period, the insured business pays a premium to an insurance carrier in return for a promise to receive a certain amount of money in the event of loss as specified in the insurance policy contract. Transfer of risk is the most commonly used strategy by small business. Therefore, it will be given greater coverage in the next section.

Developing the Risk Management Program

Effective risk management programs can be developed by following four steps:[26]

1. Identify the risk to which the business will be subjected.
2. Evaluate the probability of the occurrence of each risk that has been identified, along with the cost of insurance coverage, when available, that will protect against this risk.
3. Decide which of the four risk strategies offers the best cost/benefit protection for each risk.
4. Control the risk by implementing the best type strategy for each type.

Insurance

Insurance is *the process of transferring risk to protect against loss of assets and earnings.* A wide variety of insurance policies are available to the small business owner or manager, and there are many ways to classify insurance. Because our definition of risk management and insurance includes efforts to prevent loss of assets and earnings, we will use this classification method.

Insuring against Loss of Assets

Some of the major insurance coverages to protect against loss of assets include property, liability, and crime insurance.

Property Insurance

Property insurance protects the small business from damages or theft of plant, equipment (including vehicles, which may be a separate policy), and inventory assets. It is wise to protect assets against fire and natural disasters such as the flooding in the Midwest during the summer of 1993. While property insurance will pay to replace buildings and contents, it does not cover the payroll and other expenses that must be paid during the period of rebuilding. However, *business interruption insurance* covers lost income and other expenses of recovery. Many of those businesses that were destroyed during the flood that did not have property insurance coverage will go out of business, and those with property insurance but without business interruption insurance will wish they had the coverage.

It is also wise to protect against theft of major assets. Suppose that the only tow truck belonging to a small service station were stolen and that the truck, which brings in a significant part of the firm's revenue, was uninsured. Could the owner replace the asset, or would the business lose the investment in the truck and its earnings as well? For most businesses property insurance is very important.

Many commercial property insurance policies contain a *coinsurance clause* under which the policyholder agrees to maintain insurance equal to some specified percentage of the property value (80 percent is common). In exchange for the promise the policyholder gets a reduced insurance rate. If the manager or owner fails to maintain the percentage, only part of the loss is reimbursed.

Liability Insurance

Liability insurance protects the firm in court cases in which it would be required to pay damages to customers who get hurt on the premises or who are injured by the firm's products. Liability insurance will pay the judgment assessed by the court arising from the lawsuit up to a specified amount set forth in the policy. Many small businesses that have decided to use risk avoidance and reduction in order to save money by not purchasing liability insurance have been hit with lawsuits running into the tens of thousands of dollars, resulting in the loss of their business. Medical doctors purchase very expensive malpractice insurance policies to protect against liability.

Employer's Liability, Workers' Compensation, and Unemployment Insurance

These insurances are required by state law to insure employees. Employer's liability insurance protects the business assets against suits brought by employees who suffer injury. Workers' compensation provides employees with money while they cannot come to work, and unemployment insurance helps to provide pay to people who have lost their jobs. These two types of insurance protect employees rather than employer assets.

Crime Insurance

As was stated earlier, employee theft is the most costly crime. Crime insurance is available to protect against loss of assets through theft and embezzlement by employees. There have been businesses without controls that allowed an employee to steal so much money that they could not pay their bills and were forced out of business. For many small businesses carefully controlled risk avoidance and reduction may be a viable risk management strategy, but check the cost versus the benefit of insurance for the specific business.

Insuring against Loss of Earnings

In this section we focus on protecting the owner against loss of earnings. Every small business owner requires four basic types of insurance to cover loss of earnings: health, disability, life, and pension provisions.[27]

Health Insurance

If the business owner who lacks health insurance is seriously injured or has a medical problem that requires an extended stay in the hospital, paying the bills could be a drain on business profits for years. Medical claims have forced companies to go out of business. Business owners are commonly covered by the same policy as their employees, but they can have additional coverage. Joining health care coalitions, which number more than 100 in the United States, helps small business owners to lower insurance premiums and keep employee medical bills down.[28]

Disability Insurance
If the owner can no longer work, can the business continue to operate and provide the present standard of living to the owner? If not, disability insurance would cover lost earnings up to the amount specified in the policy.

Life Insurance
The death of the owner has caused many small businesses to liquidate because there was no money to pay present debts and estate taxes or to buy out partners. **Key-person insurance** is a *life insurance policy on the owner and/or employees purchased by the company with the company as the sole beneficiary.* Although key-person insurance will not replace the owner or other important managers, sales representatives, and engineers, it provides the business with the funds necessary to find and train their replacements, and to cover the lost profits due to their untimely deaths.

Pensions
When the owner retires, will the business continue to provide an income to maintain the present standard of living? One way to guarantee a set income after retirement is to start a pension plan. Three options include a pension plan, 401(k), or a Keogh plan.

Pensions and annuities are special forms of insurance policies that combine insurance with savings. They are also referred to as whole life policies. The premiums go partly to provide standard insurance coverage and partly into a fund that is invested by the company for the policyholder. At a certain age the policyholder is paid an income. If the policyholder dies before reaching that age, the policy either converts to income for the beneficiary or is paid out as proceeds from the policyholder's life insurance.

Many small business owners have found that it is more economical to have a separate term life insurance policy and a 401(k) or Keogh pension plan. The *401(k)* is often the only, and definitely the best, tax break available to the typical small business owner and its employees. Most small business investment menus include stocks, bonds, and money market mutual funds.[29] The *Keogh plan* is limited to proprietors and partners who own at least 10 percent of the business. Unlike the 401(k), with the Keogh all employees with three years or more of service must be included in the plan. Both plans offer compound interest on money that is sheltered from taxes until retirement, when income is usually lower.

From an administrative point of view, one of the simplest and least expensive retirement plans is the IRA-SEP (Simplified Employee Pensions). SEP's are expanded IRAs which allow employer contributions while maintaining employee ownership. The employee maintains contributions to his or her IRA, but the employer also can contribute directly to the employee's IRA using whatever agent the employee has chosen such as a bank or mutual fund. Government limits of $30,000 or 15 percent of compensation on total contributions cannot be exceeded.

A common mistake of the small business owner is to postpone starting a retirement plan. To benefit from the phenomena of compound interest and the advantage of sheltering money from taxes, as long as the business owner or employee is paying his or her bills at least a small amount should be going into the retirement plan. And as income increases, so should the amount placed in the retirement plan up to the maximum contribution allowed under the existing tax codes.

When selecting a retirement option, talk to financial advisers (banker, stockbroker, insurance agent) to get all the updated details on whole life insurance, the 401(k), Keogh plans, and other options that may be available to your business.

Selecting Insurance

Once you have determined which risk you want to insure against, you need the help of a licensed insurance agent who is qualified to help you design an insurance program tailored to your firm's unique needs. The insurance agent can inform you of the legal insurance requirements for the state(s) in which you conduct business. The agent can also inform you of other types of insurance that can save you money and that are geared to your business, such as *association insurance* packages for your specific industry. Other types of insurance that may be applicable include surety insurance to provide protection for losses that are incurred by customers when a contract is not completed on time or is completed incorrectly, and marine insurance to insure goods in transit. Listen to the advice of agents, but remember that generally they are paid a commission; the more insurance they sell, the more money they make.

There are two major types of agents: direct insurance writers and independent insurance agents. *Direct insurance writers* work for one specific insurance company, whereas *independent insurance agents* work with a variety of insurance companies. For the small business person who does not have a good understanding of the many types of insurance available, it is usually advisable to work with one agent who can design a comprehensive insurance program. Placing all your insurance with one agent is often more cost-effective and convenient.

Controlling with Computers

The biggest advantage of computers is their capacity and speed in processing information.[30] Computers have changed the way we do business while creating opportunities for a small business to use and act on information just as quickly as its larger competitors.[31] Computers increase productivity as they are used for both planning and controlling, and they can be used to aid in determining risk that should be insured. Computers are used to control quality and cost, crime, credit, and cash flow. They can also be used to prepare budgets and financial scenarios, and during the year they help managers stay within the budget. Computers produce information about inventory control, accounts receivable, and accounts payable much faster and more reliably. They are also used to design products and to control production.

Computer Basics

There are three major types of computers: mainframes, minicomputers, and micro-computers, commonly known as personal computers, or PCs. The *PC* is designed for use by one person at a time, but they can be linked together to create a *network* using Novell and Banyan products. Although PCs are used by businesses of all sizes, they are by far the primary type of computers used by small business.

Basic Components of a PC System

The computer system has two major parts: hardware and software. **Computer hardware** is *used for data input, data processing and memory, and output,* whereas **computer software** is *programs of instructions that operate the hardware.* The computer has three parts: (1) input, (2) process, (3) output.

1. A *keyboard* is commonly used to *input* the data sent into the processor. A *modem* can also be used to input data from other computers in remote locations and to transfer data as an output to other computers via telephone lines. While inputting the data, the *mouse* is an optional device that gives commands.

2. The *processor* has two parts. The central processing unit (CPU) is the heart of the computer because it controls the computer's operation. The CPU processes the data, whereas the memory unit (MU) stores the inputted data and software. The most important element of the CPU is the microprocessor. The **microprocessor** is a *chip that determines the speed of data processing.* The MU has both short-term and long-term memory. Short-term memory capability is built into the computer for temporary storage of programs and data. This short-term memory is called random access memory (RAM), or working memory. Long-term memory is used to store programs and data indefinitely. Processing data uses both types of memory.

3. The *output* of the computer is displayed on the *video display terminal (VDT),* commonly called the monitor or screen, and can be copied by the *printer.* For a review of the basic components of the computer system see Exhibit 14.4.

When working on the computer it is important to "save" (store) the data on the hard drive and to make a copy of the work on a floppy disk as a backup in case something should happen to the hard disk. The more important and the harder the data is to reenter into the computer, the more frequently data should be saved. As a general rule, don't end a session without saving the data. Ending a session includes leaving the computer to go on break, to lunch, to do some other type of work, to leave for the day, or when the computing job is done.

EXHIBIT 14.4

Basic components of a hard disk PC system

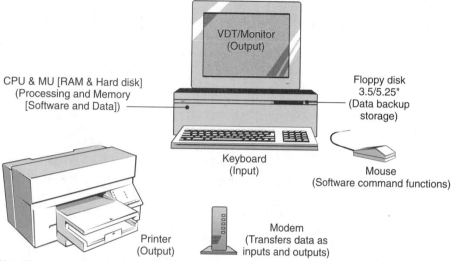

CPU & MU [RAM & Hard disk]
(Processing and Memory
[Software and Data])

VDT/Monitor
(Output)

Floppy disk
3.5/5.25"
(Data backup
storage)

Keyboard
(Input)

Mouse
(Software command functions)

Printer
(Output)

Modem
(Transfers data as
inputs and outputs)

Note: The monitor, printer, modem, and mouse are commonly called peripherals.

Applications Software

There are actually two types of software: systems software and applications software. *Systems software* includes programs that control performance, including input and output processing. They link the hardware devices and the application programs. Systems software, such as the disk operating system (DOS), is usually provided by the computer manufacturer. *Applications software* is programs used to manage particular tasks. Without good applications software programs, the most powerful computers are useless. Application programs can be written by employees or consultants to meet the company's unique needs. However, most small businesses buy preprogrammed packages. Below is a list of commonly owned application software programs used by small business.

Word Processing

Word processing is essentially typing with a computer. Computers have virtually replaced the typewriter for business use. The words go into computer memory rather than on paper, making corrections and adjustments of text much easier. Some other tasks performed by computers include spell checking, thesaurus functions, word wraparound, form letter preparation, pagination, and merge mailing.

A few word processors can also be used for simple electronic (or desktop) publishing of documents, brochures, newsletters, catalogs, reports, and the like. For sophisticated jobs separate software programs are available.

For many small businesses word processing is the first function to be computerized. A variety of word-processing programs are available in a wide price-range, including WordPerfect, Word, WordStar, and Easywriter.

Spreadsheets

Spreadsheets are used for financial planning. All of the business plan accounting functions and financial analysis in Chapters 12 and 13 (budgets, including cash flow and capital equipment, pro forma statements, and financial ratios) can be calculated on an electronic spreadsheet. A spreadsheet is similar to the ledger sheet of an accountant's pad. The user enters data, text, and formulas into the cells or locations (columns and rows) on the spreadsheet. The software performs arithmetic and statistical calculations and financial functions such as present and future value. A major advantage of electronic spreadsheets over handwritten ones is in calculating "what-if" scenarios through cost-volume-profit analysis. For example, you can enter the projected data for a pro forma income statement or sales forecast with either method. But with a computer you can change the revenue and/or expense figures, then push a button and have a new statement in seconds. The output can be produced as a spreadsheet or converted into simple graphics such as line graphs and pie charts. A variety of spreadsheets are available, including Lotus 1-2-3, Quattro Pro, Excel, and PFS:Professional Plan.

When you are developing the business plan, a spreadsheet makes the job much easier, faster, and more accurate over a range of projections such as optimistic, realistic, pessimistic. Some software packages designed specifically for business planning include spreadsheets.

Database Management

Databases are simply electronic files. It's a lot easier and faster to keep a collection of individual records in the computer, and it takes up a lot less space. The user can work on one file at a time or create and work on several files simultaneously. For example, a database can be used when aging accounts receivable. The computer will search all files for customers with account balances up to 30 days past due, 31 to 60 days past due, and so on. The user can also specify only accounts with balances over a set amount such as $100 or $500. A few of the programs available include Q&A, dBase, Alpha Four, and Dayflo.

Accounting

Accounting software programs are commonly used in small business by owners who want general ledger, accounts payable and receivable, inventory control, purchasing, payroll, and financial statement preparation that is much faster and more accurate than manual systems can provide. They are also more effective at controlling crime.

There are two types of accounting programs: modular and integrated. A modular program allows the user to select only one or a few of the accounting functions, whereas an integrated program includes a comprehensive accounting system that usually operates from the transactions entered through the general ledger. Once the user enters the transactions into the general ledger, the program automatically posts them to the appropriate subprograms. Integrated programs can be purchased for as little as $50. Some of the accounting programs include 4-in-1 Basic Accounting, The Accounting Partner 3, Accpac Easy Accounting Series, and Peachtree Complete.

Communications

Computers can be used to communicate with other computers around the world through a modem that links the computer to the telephone line. With the modem the user can link up to large databases like CompuServe, Prodigy, and the Dow-Jones News/Retrieval service.

Telecommunications software enables the user to exchange information with branch offices, sales representatives in the field, or the office next door. It provides automatic telephone dialing and answering, electronic mailbox services (E-mail), and the opportunity to access up-to-date information for decision making (management information systems, or MIS).

Graphics

Graphics programs create, edit, display, and print or "draw" graphic images. Some word-processing programs and spreadsheet offer simple graphics (pie charts, curves, bar graphs), but for the business with sophisticated needs, a graphics program can do the job of a graphic artist's consulting services. Some of the programs include Harvard Graphics, Window Draw, GEM Presentations, and 35mm Express.

Integrated Software

Integrated software is *designed to make the use of multiple programs easier and faster.* There is a trend toward integrated packages that enable users to transfer data from one program to another as they quickly and easily move from word processing, to spreadsheet, to database, and so on. There are three types of integrated software programs: tightly integrated, the integrated series, and the systems integrator.

Tightly integrated packages enable the user to change data in one application and the program automatically updates it in every other application. Although the applications are all in one package, none of them is quite as complete as an individual software program. Some of the tightly integrated programs include Works, Symphony, Framework, and Encore.

Integrated series are related sets of separate programs that allow the user to transport data easily from one program to another. However, moving the data is more difficult than with a tightly integrated package and the data is not updated in other applications. Some of the integrated series include Smart Software, PFS:Family, the Profit Center Series, and the Plan Family.

Systems integrators attempt to combine the advantages of the other two types by allowing the user to store several individual applications programs in the computer's memory and to run them simultaneously. System integrators include DesQview, Concurrent PC-DOS, Top-View, and Microsoft Windows.

Other Programs

In addition to the applications programs discussed, there are also project management software programs designed to help small business managers plan and control the intermediate steps in completing large projects, including introducing new products, entering new markets, and launching businesses. For the manufacturing industry there is computer-aided design and drafting (CADD) and computer-aided manufacturing (CAM), which are commonly used together and called CAD/CAM.[31] A wide variety of programs are also geared to specific industries. For example, retail inventory control programs update inventory records directly from cash register transactions, enabling the user to know which products are selling and when to reorder to avoid under- and overstocked inventory items. Other examples are the "expert system" used by financial planners and tax programs used by accountants.

Buying the Computer System

The small business can use a service bureau to pick up, process, and return the data; use time-sharing of other computers; and lease a computer. With today's low-priced, powerful PCs, however, purchasing is usual the most cost-effective means of computing.

Determining Computer Needs

Small business owners facing the first PC system purchase should spend time reviewing how their business works. It is helpful to look at automation as just another business project. Determine which operations to automate via software. Possible requirements could include processing all orders on the day they are received, generating reports on monthly accounts receivables, and connecting customer information files to the order-entry system.[32] If there aren't any software programs to run your applications, do a cost-benefit analysis of having a computer-programmer consultant develop a program to meet your unique needs.

Buying hardware and software go together in the sense that the hardware must be powerful enough to run all the different software programs you intend to use in order to operate the business. Therefore, it is usually advisable to (1) know what your business system requires, (2) select software to meet requirements, and (3) select hardware. You can determine computer needs with the help of a computer consultant or sales rep experienced in small business computers, but remember that sales reps usually work on commission. Listen to them, but don't overbuy. You can also call What to Buy for Business (800-247-2185), the Office Products Analyst (716-232-5320), and Info-Market Guide (800-866-5206) for help in making computer-purchasing decisions.

Making the Computer System Selection

Sales reps can help you determine business software applications and help make the hardware selection at the same time. When hardware and software are purchased together service-oriented sellers will load the software for you. As with any asset purchase, shop around for the best deal.

When making the selection, focus on profit, not cost. Balance price, quality, service (including maintenance), and dependability (some computer companies have gone out of business). Expandability, adaptability, and compatibility are also important. It may be cheaper to buy a clone through the mail without any local service operation, but it can be very expensive if it breaks down and you have to wait two weeks to get it fixed. For the person who spends a lot of time on the road, a portable laptop or notebook computer may be a wise investment.

IBM and Compaq are considered true computers, but there are many high-quality clones such as Packard-Bell, Gateway, and Dell, just to name a few. IBM compatibles are more commonly used by small business than Apple-compatible machines. But if graphics are a major concern, you may want an Apple computer. The software listed above is for IBM compatibles, but there are also equivalent Apple-compatible programs for most applications. The list of software programs is limited to four, but there are many other programs that are not listed that may do a better job of meeting your business needs.

Remember that when buying the computer hardware, the higher the microprocessor chip number (with MHz), and memory (RAM and hard disk) the more powerful the PC. As a general guide, the least most small businesses should buy is a 486 microprocessor with 50 MHz speed and a 300 megabyte hard disk with 8 megabytes of RAM. These are considered minimums, but some businesses may need more speed and memory. Extra capacity and adaptability is often a good idea for the growing business. Even in stable companies, once managers realize the benefits of computers they often increase software applications.

Most PCs come with a color monitor and mouse but not a printer and modem. The two things to look for in a printer are quality of the print and the speed. If the output is to be seen by target customers, you may want a laser printer. Laser printers don't require computer paper with feeder holes and printer ribbons. This makes it easy to use company stationery for printing. Reconditioned laser cartridges can be purchased to save money. You will need to buy a modem if you want to transmit data to and from your computer to others in remote locations. For the business that wants several PCs at the same location to communicate, look into computer networking using Novell and Banyan products.

Computer Training

Within the computer budget, be sure to include the cost of training. Too many businesses spend thousands of dollars on computer systems without properly training employees to use them. The result is wasted money through underutilization of resources. Computer training should be viewed as an investment, not an expense.

Most employees are not capable of learning to use new software by themselves using only the manual as a teaching tool. If only one or two employees are to be trained, they should be sent to hands-on experience training conducted by experienced teachers. Classes are offered by many computer stores, which have instructors who have been trained and certified by the software maker. Colleges also offer computer seminars and regular classes. If at least five employees are to be trained, it is often cost-effective to have the computer trainer come to your site to conduct the class. Another training method that is often less expensive for the small business is to have a person experienced with the software train other employees. The downside is that many good workers are not good teachers.

In addition to training programs, employees should be given the instruction manual and telephone number of software makers that have trained personnel to answer questions and solve software problems. These specialists give step-by-step instructions over the telephone as customers perform the functions at their own computers. In most cases when the user hangs up, the problem is solved and the employee can perform the function on his or her own in the future. Speakerphones facilitate the process because both hands are free to implement instructions. Many software makers offer this technical assistance free to customers or available for a contracted period; however, if they do not have an 800 number you may run up the long-distance telephone bill.

Summary

The Interrelationship between Controlling and the Business Plan Components

Controlling is *the process of establishing methods to ensure that the business objectives are achieved.* Controlling is a method to ensure that the plans in the functional areas are successfully implemented. As you develop plans for each functional area, you should also develop controls. The **control process** includes *setting objectives; establishing standards, methods, and times for measuring performance; measuring and comparing performance to standards; and reinforcing or correcting.*

Controlling Quality and Cost

Quality is *the predetermined standard that the product or service should meet.* **Total quality management (TQM)** *requires everyone in the organization to continually improve products and services.* The key to TQM is setting standards and continually striving to improve them. Following the six guidelines in Exhibit 14.2 can help TQM. Because there is a need to balance quality and cost, they should be controlled together. Following these six guidelines can help control cost.

Controlling Crime

Business crime includes *employee theft, shoplifting, burglary, and robbery.* Most criminal losses to small businesses stem from employee theft, not shoplifting. Burglary tends to take place when the business is closed, whereas robbery takes place when it is open.

Credit Collection

The decision to sell on credit is influenced by the nature of the business as well as competitor credit policy. There are two broad classes of credit: (1) **Trade credit** is *typically* *extended from one business to another.* (2) **Consumer credit** *is typically extended by a retailer to the final customer who buys use the product for personal use.* The easiest and safest way to offer credit is to accept bank credit cards and entertainment cards. *Aging of accounts receivable* is the technique for keeping track of how old each debt is, and thus it measures the quality of the receivables.

Risk Management

Risk management consists of *efforts to prevent loss of assets and earnings.* Dealing with risk involves a combination of four types of risk management strategies: risk avoidance, risk reduction, risk anticipation or self-insurance, and risk transferring or risk spreading. Effective risk management programs can be developed by following the four-step process listed in the text.

Insurance

Insurance is *the process of transferring risk to protect against loss of assets and earnings.* Three major insurance policies are available to protect against loss of assets: property insurance including business interruption insurance, liability insurance, and crime insurance. Four major insurance policies are available to protect against loss of earnings: health insurance, disability insurance, life insurance, and pension insurance. The 401(k) or Keogh retirement account may supplement or take the place of pension insurance.

Controlling with Computers

The computer system has two major parts: **Computer hardware** is *used for data input, data processing and memory, and output,* whereas **computer software** is *programs of instructions that operate the hardware.* The three parts of computers include: (1) inputs, (2) processing and memory or storage (the **microprocessor** is a *chip that determines the speed of data processing*), and (3) outputs.

Application software are programs to run particular tasks. Popular application software programs include word processing, spreadsheet, database management, accounting, communications, and graphics. **Integrated software** is *designed to make the use of multiple programs easier and faster.*

It is usually advisable to determine software needs before purchasing hardware. When making the selection, focus on profit, not cost. Balance price, quality, service (including maintenance), and dependability. Expandability, adaptability, and compatibility are also important. And be sure to properly train employees to use the computer system to its full capability.

Questions

1. Why are the control function and process so important to the small business owner?
2. Give an example of the role of a specific standard in controlling quality.
3. Why is quality called "a virtue of design"?
4. What can managers do to control quality and cost?
5. What can managers do to help protect the firm's assets from crime?

6. What can managers do to ensure account receivables are collected?

7. What is the advantage to the small business of accepting bank and entertainment credit cards rather than offering its own line of credit?

8. What is the difference between risk management and insurance?

9. What are the four steps in developing a risk management program?

10. How do property, liability, crime, health, disability, life, and pension insurance transfer risk of loss of assets or earnings?

11. What is the difference between direct insurance writers and independent insurance agents?

12. How are computers used to control loss of assets and earnings?

13. What is the difference between the three types of computers and hardware and software?

14. How is data entered into a computer? Produced by a computer?

15. How is data processed and stored by a computer?

16. How can the small business use word-processing, spreadsheet, database management, accounting, communications, and graphics applications software? And what is the advantage of integrated software packages?

17. Is computer training important? Explain.

Application Exercises

When doing these exercises, where applicable, be sure to select a specific business, preferably one where you presently work or previously worked or a business you would like to own someday. If this is not possible, pick a specific organization to which you will refer. Be sure to identify the organization by name. Limit your answers to one or two pages per exercise.

1. Give an example of how a business follows the four steps of the control process. Be specific in stating what is controlled.

2. Give an example of an input, process, and output control.

3. Give an example of the standards and quality requirements for a job you have held.

4. Explain how a business does or does not follow each of the six guidelines to ensure quality and the six guidelines to control cost. What would you do to improve quality and cost control?

5. Give examples of business crime you observed or heard about. What would you do to improve crime control by minimizing these crimes?

6. Give an example of a small business that offers credit. What type of credit is offered? Does it offer its own credit or accept bank, or entertainment cards? What control techniques does it use to collect accounts receivable?

7. Give an example of how a business uses risk avoidance, risk reduction, and risk anticipation, or self-insurance.

8. Identify the types of insurance a company uses to insure against loss of assets (identify the major assets) and loss of earnings. What type of retirement program does the company have?

9. Identify the types of computers and brands a business uses. Be specific about hardware (microprocessor, MHz, RAM, hard disk memory) and software used. Explain how each

software program is used to control specific assets and earnings. Describe how employees are trained to use these computer systems. How would you improve the computer system and utilization?

Application Situations

1. Taylor Inventory and Crime

After graduating from college, Jean Taylor agreed to take over the family business, Taylor Appliances, so her father Ben could take an early retirement. She had only worked as a cashier in the store part-time and weekends during the school year and summers. Taylor Appliances sells a wide variety of smaller appliances—TVs, stereos, telephones, microwave ovens, and so on. The store does not sell large major appliances like refrigerators and stoves.

Taylor has a total of 15 employees, mostly salespeople who also work in the storage room, and a few cashiers. Ben, the owner, was involved in everything, although he primarily handled selling when he was not doing the record keeping, which was his sole responsibility. He really didn't like bookkeeping the way he loved to talk to customers. Ben had a very simple system, including a general ledger, a checkbook, a file for accounts payable and one for accounts receivable. His accounts payable file was also his inventory file. Sales were cash or bank credit card; Ben was not interested in the extra paperwork necessary to offer his own credit. Ben's longtime friend, Carlos, did his taxes, prepared financial statements twice a year, and filled out the necessary government forms for the business.

The business system was simple. Ben ordered the merchandise from manufacturers, which was delivered and put into storage by the sales and storage-room employees. A salesperson would close the sale, fill out a sales receipt, and accompany the customer to the cashier. The salesperson would then instruct the customer to drive around to the back door. While the customer was moving the car, the salesperson would get the merchandise from inventory and help the customer load purchases into the car. Exceptions were smaller items, which the customer could carry out the front door, and the occasional delivery made by the salesperson. Ben liked this system because it gave variety to the job. He felt that no one wants to be stuck in the storage room all day long or standing around the sales floor. His was a small business with the need for generalists, not specialists.

After several requests, Ben finally showed Jean the financial statements and current records. Jean was surprised that profits were not greater. After thinking of a few possible reasons for the low profits, Jean asked Ben, "When was the last time you took a physical inventory?" Ben replied, "I've been too busy to do it. Besides, most of our items are too large for customers to steal anyway." Jean said, "But, what about employees?" To which Ben said, "We're a family. I trust my employees." Jean told her father she'd check into it. That night after closing Jean took the physical inventory and found several thousand dollar's worth of inventory missing. She wondered how long employees had been stealing from her father, and how much he had lost over the past 25 years in business.

Assignment

1. Why do you think this business crime happened, and what type of crime do you suspect?

2. How would you try to find the source of the crime?

3. Which risk management strategy was neglected that lead to crime?

4. Is it possible to recover this inventory loss? If yes, do you think Ben did implement risk management? What makes you think so?

5. How should Jean change the present business system to prevent crime in the future?

6. Should Jean keep the present record-keeping system? If not, what system can she implement? If you recommend computerization, be very specific on what hardware and software to buy.

2. Latoya Flowers

Latoya Green opened a flower shop just over four years ago. Things were tough for the first year, but Latoya proudly tells people that in her second year she made a nice profit. However, in her fourth year she is considering selling the business due to a lawsuit.

Latoya started her corporation with very little money. She had an old van that she gave to the company for flower deliveries. Her insurance policy on the van carried the minimum $10,000/$20,000 per person/per accident coverage for bodily injury. In her first year she rented a shop, and all she had for inventory were flowers; being short of money, she decided to keep costs low by not buying insurance. As her business became profitable, she thought of getting some insurance, but was always too busy to do it. In her third year she bought insurance, but it was really too late.

In her third year of business Latoya was driving her van delivering flowers to the hospital when she ran over a pedestrian, causing serious injury. The pedestrian sued and was awarded a $100,000 judgment. With the $10,000 from the insurance she still needed $90,000 more. She doesn't think the business is worth that much.

Assignment

1. With insurance, did Latoya focus on profits or cost?

2. What type of risk management program would you say Latoya had? Which strategy would you say she used?

3. How could this situation have been avoided? Be specific.

4. Is this a loss of assets, earnings, or both? Explain.

5. Will the pedestrian have to settle for $10,000 or can the person take action against Latoya Flowers to recover the unpaid balance of $90,000?

6. Can Latoya end up losing her business?

7. Can Latoya end up losing her personal assets?

Integrated Case Question—CorLu Foods

Develop a control plan to ensure CorLu's meets its objectives. Discuss quality and cost controls, crime, credit collection, risk management, insurance needs, and computer use for CorLu. (Please refer to the Integrated Case, "CorLu Foods.")

Additional Readings

Braun, Ellen. "How to Select Software for Your Specific Needs." *The Office,* February 1990, p. 64.

"Crime Prevention for Small Business." *Small Business Reporter* 13, no. 1 (1988), p.1.

Diamond, Sam. "You Can Run a Small Business with Personal Finance Software." *Personal Computing,* February 1988, p. 148.

Patterson, Lan. "Industry-Specific Computer Applications." *COSE Up-date,* December 1992, p. 6.

National Federation of Independent Business Foundation. *Small Business Primer.* Washington, D.C., 1988.

"SBA—Being There for Small Business." *Small Business Success* 5 (1992), p. 59.

U.S. Office of Personnel Management. *How to Get Started Implementing Total Quality Management.* Washington, D.C.: U.S. Government Printing Office, June 1991.

Vaughan, Emmett J. *Fundamentals of Risk and Insurance,* 6th ed. New York: Wiley, 1994.

"Ways to Cut Employee Theft." *Nation's Business,* September 1988, p. 15.

"What Price Quality?" *Small Business Reports,* August 1990, p. 7.

Endnotes

1. Robert N. Lussier, *Supervision: A Skill Building Approach,* 2nd ed. (Homewood, Ill.: Richard D. Irwin, 1994), p.103.
2. Randall Schuler, and Drew Harris, "Deming Quality Improvement: Implications for Human Resource Management as Illustrated in a Small Company," *Human Resource Planning* 14, no. 3 (1991), pp. 191–207.
3. "Traps to Avoid as You Seek to Upgrade Service," *Profit-Building Strategies for Business Owners,* October 1992, pp. 4–5.
4. Valerie Rice, and John McCreadie, "Credo at Small Companies: Quality Equals Simplicity; Quality Is Big at Little Companies, Too," *Electronic Business,* October 16, 1989, pp. 136–42.
5. Michael Barrier, "Doing Well What Comes Naturally," *Nation's Business,* September 1992, pp. 25–26.
6. John Kendrick, "Grante Rock Co.," *Quality,* January 1993, p. 31.
7. Lussier, *Supervision,* p. 116.
8. "Traps to Avoid as You Seek to Upgrade Service," pp. 4–5.
9. Karen Benowski, "Small in Size but Not in Stature," *Quality Progress,* November 1992, pp. 23–27.
10. "Traps to Avoid as You Seek to Upgrade Service."
11. Kristin Staroba, "Recasting Health Care," *Association Management,* October 1992, pp. 24–31.
12. Deborah Hairston, "Cutting the High Cost of Health Care," *Black Enterprise,* November 1990, pp. 78–82.
13. James Ellis, "A Small-Business Co-op That Practices Alternative Medicine," *Business Week,* April 19, 1993, p. 117.
14. Lussier, *Supervision,* p. 118.

15. Barrier, "Doing Well What Comes Naturally," pp. 25–26.

16. Lussier, *Supervision,* p. 118.

17. Norman Scarborough, and Thomas Zimmerer, *Effective Small Business Management,* 4th ed. (New York: Macmillian Publishing, 1993), p. 704.

18. Ibid, p. 723.

19. Nicholas Siropolis, *Small Business Management,* 4th ed. (Boston: Houghton Mifflin, 1990), p. 403.

20. Stan Berry, "Get Payment in Full," *Small Business Reports* 15, no. 10 (October 1990), pp. 55–58.

21. Paul Gallaty, "Tailored Tips: Preparing a Policy and Procedure Manual," *Business Credit,* April 1989, pp. 45–46.

22. Larry Schiern, Ron Cavanagh, and Maxine Matta-Rich, "Software Review: Experts Rate Credit Collections Software," *Business Credit,* May 1991, pp. 8–13.

23. Dean Planeaux, "Factoring Guarantees Cash Flow for Diaper Start-Up," *Corporate Cashflow,* August 1991, p. 42.

24. Thomas McDonough, "Risk Management for Small Business," *Security Management,* October 1992, pp. 74–76.

25. William Cohen, "Small-Business Insurance Guide: Protect Yourself," *Success,* March 1990, pp. 33–36.

26. Ibid.

27. Marshall Cranford, "It Takes Straight Talk to Sell to Small-Business Owners," *Life Association News,* January 1991, pp. 109–10.

28. Eileen Davis, "Strength in Numbers," *Small Business Reports* 16, no. 10 (October 1991), pp. 28–38.

29. Jesse Slome, "Your Commercial Clients Are Buying a 401(k): Will They Buy from You?" *Broker World,* August 1990, pp. 34–42.

30. Christine Woolsey, "PC Systems Allow Small Employers to Handle Claims," *Business Insurance,* May 22, 1989, p. 36.

31. Michael Puttre, "Drafting Tools Move off the Drawing Board," *Mechanical Engineering,* June 1991, pp. 60–62.

32. Alan Emerson, "Buying a PC System Means Seeing Software in a New Light," *Office Systems,* August 1991, pp. 10–14.

V GLOBAL BUSINESS

388

15   TAKING THE SMALL BUSINESS GLOBAL

This chapter looks at different issues that are very important if your business becomes active in the international market. It explains the four strategies for going global (exporting, contractual agreements, joint ventures, and establishing international locations) and the six critical areas for global success (global strategy, management team, operations and products, technology and R&D, financing, and marketing). The chapter also looks at the sources of assistance in going global (export-service companies, agents, the Commerce Department, and the SBA), and identifies four sources of financing for going global (U.S. Export-Import Bank, state development agencies, the SBA, and trade finance houses).

Chapter Learning Objectives

After completing this chapter, you should be able to:

· Explain why the small business should go global.
· List and explain four strategies for going global.
· List and describe four common contractual agreements.
· List and discuss six critical areas for global success.
· Describe how export-service companies, agents, the Commerce Department, and the SBA can provide the small business with assistance in going global.
· List and discuss four sources of financing going global.
· Define the following 16 key terms:

International company	Freight forwarders
Going global	Common contractual agreements
European Community (EC)	Licensing
Strategies for going global	Contract manufacturing

Exporting

Export-trading companies

Export-management companies

International distributors

Management contracting

Foreign joint venture

Agent/distributor services

U.S. Export-Import Bank

Why Should the Small Business Go Global?

Peter Drucker was asked, "Apart from the heads of big multinationals, how much should the average CEO worry about globalization? Isn't the domestic market still most companies' bread and butter?" His response was, "The other day, I read a nice quote by a distinguished economist who said that in five years there will be only two kinds of economists—those who think in terms of a world economy and those who are unemployed. The same is true of CEOs, even of small companies. If you don't think globally, you deserve to be unemployed and you will be."[1] Up until the mid-1930s there were practically no national companies except very large ones. But suddenly, an adhesive manufacturer in New England found that there was competition from an adhesive manufacturer in California. The same was true in many industries. A good many companies that did not understand what was happening went under. Even the small ones had to learn to think nationally. Today even the purely domestic company must at least think globally and act locally to keep global competitors from gaining advantage in their home country and to keep from being forced out of business.

The **international company** *conducts business in more than one country.* **Going global** is *the planned process of contracting to do business in foreign countries.* Businesses must become more globally competitive if the United States has any chance of controlling its $600 billion foreign debt. Many domestic companies could profitably become international companies by exporting their products. These companies, which are often small businesses, do not think their products are exportable, but such negative perceptions about exporting are frequently wrong.[2]

Small Businesses Are Going Global

It is actually easier for the small business to operate without much regard for national boundaries than large firms. Most large multinational firms do not have global cultures; it is generally easier for young, small companies to change cultures. Entrepreneurial thinking, with the associated traits of flexibility, innovativeness, and a problem-solving action orientation, are needed for success in the global economy.[3] Small companies can usually change faster than large companies. They are barely visible politically. Smaller companies often score better abroad.[4] They tend to go where the big guys cannot go successfully.[5] Many large businesses are shrinking; some are spinning off parts of their company as smaller businesses to compete more effectively in the global market.[6] Many small businesses are growing by going global at a fast pace. Of 51,000 exporters tracked by a consulting firm, 87 percent employ fewer than 500 people.[7]

International Small Business Examples

Going global is the theme today, even for small businesses.[8] Some examples of small global companies include: Broad Street Books which never intended to be a global company; it just saw market opportunities in Europe for its books and went after them.[9] Rosenbluth Travel specializes in making global travel arrangements for large multinational companies to help them control travel expenses.[10] Pall Corporation went from a small company (sales $7 million) into a thriving midsized company (sales $429 million) through global development in Europe; it is now the world's largest manufacturer of specialty filters.[11] Watching the crumbling of the Berlin Wall on television gave Thomas Bates and William Guthrie the idea to sell *Profit International* business magazine which gives practical advice on how to start and run basic businesses in a market economy in Eastern Europe.[12] John Tschohl saw an opportunity to sell customer service training videos in the free-market countries of the former Soviet Union.[13]

Global Opportunities

Going global offers a much larger target market to the small business. There are approximately 250 million people in the United States, less than 5 percent of the world's population of over 5 billion people. American manufacturers with global operations grow faster and earn more than purely domestic companies.[14] Coca-Cola sees the day coming when as much as 75 percent of its earnings will be from abroad. American companies are not simply going where the most people are. China is the most populated country, with over 1 billion people, but few of its people can afford to buy U.S. goods today. Most global U.S. companies are going to Europe, where the 12 members (United Kingdom, Germany, France, Italy, Spain, Portugal, Belgium, Ireland, Denmark, Greece, Luxembourg, Netherlands) of the European Community (EC) have signed a pact removing trade obstacles and creating a unified European market of 340 million people. Dealing with only one set of trade barriers simplifies international business.[15] The **European Community (EC)** includes *12 unified countries with one set of trade agreements.* Many small businesses are also going to Japan, whose population is over 126 million people.[16] The North American Free Trade Agreement (NAFTA) among the United States, Canada, and Mexico created an arrangement similar to the EC.[17] Entrepreneurs willing to take greater risk for greater returns are going to the other Western European countries, the Pacific Rim (Australia, China, Hong Kong, Taiwan, Singapore, the Philippines, South Korea, Thailand, Indonesia, Malaysia, and Japan), Africa, South America, and the Middle East. See Exhibit 15.1 for a world map. It is argued that trading blocks like the EC rather than individual nations will be the most powerful forces of the future global economy.[18]

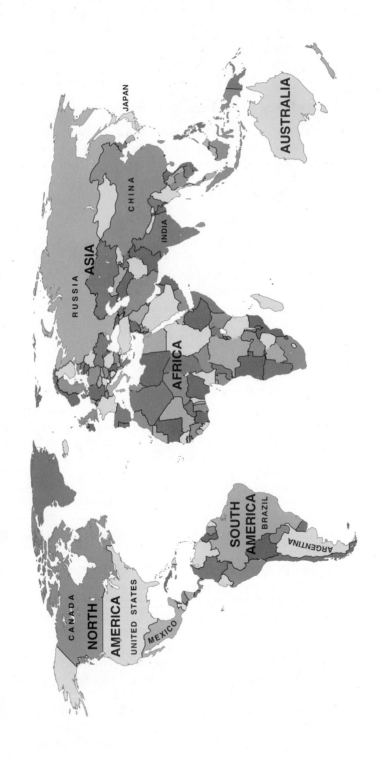

Exhibit 15.1
World map

Strategies for Going Global

The major **strategies for going global** are: *exporting, contractual agreements, joint ventures, and establishing international locations.*

Exporting

Exporting involves *selling goods made in one country to buyers in other countries.* Exporting plays a major role in small businesses that want to attain global stature. Exporting is considered a minimal financial risk approach. The firm finds one or more buyers in one or more foreign countries for its products.[19] Exporting is recommended when the sales potential for the target market is high, the estimated production costs are lower at home, product adaptability requirements are not needed or are simple, import and export restrictions are favorable, raw materials are less costly, the political climate abroad is relatively unstable, and the firm has limited financial resources.[20]

The 12 Most Common Export Mistakes

The 12 most commonly made export mistakes are:[21]

1. Failure to obtain qualified export counseling and to develop a master international marketing plan before starting an export business.
2. Insufficient commitment by top management to overcome the initial difficulties and financial requirements of exporting.
3. Insufficient care in selecting overseas distributors.
4. Chasing orders from around the world instead of establishing a basis for profitable operations and orderly growth.
5. Neglecting export business when the U.S. market booms.
6. Failure to treat international distributors on an equal basis with domestic counterparts.
7. Assuming that a given market technique and product will automatically be successful in all countries.
8. Unwillingness to modify products to meet regulations or cultural preferences of other countries.
9. Failure to print service, sales, and warranty messages in locally understood languages.
10. Failure to consider use of an export management company.
11. Failure to consider licensing or joint-venture agreements.
12. Failure to provide readily available servicing for the product.

Let's look in more detail at how to avoid these mistakes by determining the selection of the target customer or country, shipping the product, and collecting your money.

Selecting the Target Customer or Country

Generally, the more unique the product is (competitive advantage), the greater its acceptance abroad. Small business owners or managers must consider how much time, effort, and money they are willing to invest in exporting. Does the small business owner want to actually perform the marketing function in other countries? Or would the owner prefer to get help?

For the do-it-your-selfer, a good source of information on a variety of countries is published by the Department of Commerce and found in the library. These entities provide a multitude of guides, manuals, books, newsletters, videos, and other resources to help research potential markets. A few high-risk entrepreneurs have traveled to foreign countries and used the countries' business directories and yellow pages, not always called by these names, as a source to make sales calls.

For small business owners who seek help exporting their products, there are two major sources: export-service companies and distributors. The small business that lacks the time or inclination to do all the work itself can hire export-service companies that will to do all the work of taking the small business global through exporting. There are two specific types of export-service companies: (1) **Export-trading companies (ETC)** *buy goods outright, paying below wholesale, and sell them abroad.* Selling to the ETC is like selling to a domestic customer because it takes care of the exporting for the producer. (2) **Export-management companies (EMC)** *perform a variety of export tasks for the client.* An EMC will locate buyers, draft paperwork for shipping and billing, search out financing, ensure that goods meet foreign labeling and testing laws, and display products at trade shows. EMCs tend to specialize by product group or country.

Many small business owners find that foreign distributors offer a low-cost and low-risk way to position products overseas. **International distributors** *purchase the product, provide the sales team, and find the buyers in foreign countries.* They already have established relationships with stores and customers, something that would take U.S. companies years to develop. Broad Street Books used a distributor to go global.[22] Brooktree Corporation, a graphics chip maker, tried to go directly to Japanese companies to do business, but they considered Brooktree too small to acknowledge. So Brooktree found two distributors to successfully introduce its graphic chips to the Japanese market.[23] Unfortunately, too few companies take the time to find the "right" distributor or to check out salient legal and cultural issues. You can use an agent to help you find the right distributor.

The following guidelines are important rules to follow when selecting an international distributor.[24]

1. Evaluate prospective distributors based on their organizational and technical ability to support the business.
2. Get to know and feel comfortable in a working relationship with the prospective distributor before signing an agreement. Have your attorney involved in drawing up the contract, or at least checking a written one to be sure you are protected.

3. Check out cultural differences.
4. Examine local laws in the country.

Shipping

The exporter must ship the goods to the customer. The small business owner can ship the goods or use the services of an international freight forwarder or custom-house agents. A **freight forwarder** *arranges the transportation of products to and from the United States.* The freight forwarder or agent will handle the task of proper packaging, filling out general customs documents, and managing the paperwork.[25]

Collecting Your Money

Collecting foreign accounts can be more complex and take longer than domestic accounts. Financing foreign sales often involves special credit arrangements such as letters of credit and bank drafts. To avoid bad debts select customers carefully and be sure to check credit references. Inform target customers about available financing through American institutions. Be sure the sales contract or purchase agreement specifies the currency payment. Being paid in dollars makes it easier and protects you against currency fluctuations. Cash in advance is the safest way to do business, but don't lose customers who are not willing or able to do business under these terms. You can also purchase transit insurance and credit insurance.

Contractual Agreements

There are a variety of contractual agreements the small business can enter. The most common **types of contractual agreements** include *licensing, franchising, contract manufacturing, and management contracting.* Other forms include reciprocal marketing, swapping of new products and models, and supply agreements. Another growing area of contract agreement is the research and development (R&D) consortium, which is especially helpful to the small business that alone cannot afford to underwrite the high cost of R&D.[26]

Foreign Licensing

Licensing involves *selling for a fee or royalty the rights to use patents, trademarks, copyrights, technology, processes, products, or other rights.* Licensing is a relatively easy way to enter foreign markets with little extra work for extra income. The licensee takes most of the risk by investing money to take the American concept and commercialize it in a foreign country, sending the licenser regular checks based on sales. Disney Studio licenses its famous cartoon characters (e.g., Mickey Mouse) to manufacturers in other countries. Gerber entered the Japanese baby food market this way while still exporting to other countries.

On the down side, the licensing agreement can result in a total loss of product control and profits. Be careful to set up a contract that very clearly specifies what can and cannot be done with the rights. For example, the contract should specify quality requirements so that the American brand is not adversely affected. If quality standards are not met, the contract should be revoked.[27]

Franchising

Franchising, discussed in Chapter 3, is a form of licensing. Franchising is an attractive vehicle for international expansion. American franchisers operate more than 32,000 outlets in foreign countries. Markets with the largest number of franchisers are Canada, Japan, and Europe. Domino's Pizza operates 58 restaurants in Japan, where the top-selling pizza combination is tuna and sweet corn. The favorite in Australia's 34 pizza restaurants is prawns and pineapple.[28]

According to the International Franchise Association (IFA), expansion affords growth and increased revenue, along with the benefits of increased brand recognition and larger market share. However, it also presents problems of increased costs, varying governmental regulations, and cultural differences. The decision to franchise depends on international business trends and the availability of suitable markets, among other factors. The top four factors in achieving success in international franchising are: supporting, recruiting, training, and controlling the activities of the international partner.[29]

Contract Manufacturing

Contract manufacturing involves *turning over the production function to others while retaining the marketing function.* This is an attractive option for the small business that has a good product with high labor cost.[30] With contract marketing the product can be made in a foreign country for less money and sold in the same country and/or exported to other countries. Some American firms have their products made overseas and shipped to the United States for sale. This approach also works well for the firm that is already selling as much as it produces at home so that exporting is not an option. Contract manufacturing is a way to increase revenue without investing more money in plant and equipment. Contract manufacturing is also beneficial where labor relations are difficult, or there are problems getting supplies and "buying" government cooperation. Sears Roebuck used this approach as it opened stores in Latin America and Spain.

Management Contracting

Management contracting involves *providing only management skills; the production facilities are owned by others.* This is a relatively low-risk approach to international marketing because no commitment to fixed facilities is made. This approach is especially attractive in unstable countries, where facilities could be damaged in riots or wars, or whose governments could decide to confiscate the American owners' facilities. If conditions get too bad the managers can leave. Some mines and oil refineries operate this way. Hilton operates hotels all over the world for local owners.

Joint Ventures

Advantages of Joint Ventures

Within a **foreign joint venture** *a domestic firm enters into a partnership with a firm in the target nation.* Although joint ventures usually require a direct investment and result in a loss of control, there are five key advantages to taking on international partners:[31]

1. *Penetrating protected markets.* In countries with high tariffs and ownership limitations restricting access to markets (i.e., India), a company's only choice may be to form a joint venture with a local business.

2. *Lowering cost.* Establishing a business in a foreign country is often too costly for the small business that cannot wait long for the return on investment.[32] The joint venture allows the small firm to do business internationally without an enormous investment of capital,[33] and Europeans favor joint ventures.[34] In many countries the small business can find a manufacturing partner to produce its product at a lower cost than at home.

3. *Sharing the risk and high R&D cost.* Even the large automobile makers need great volume to optimize research and development cost. Therefore, General Motors and Toyota, Ford and Mazda, and Chrysler and Mitsubishi have joint ventures.[35] The major drug companies also have joint ventures.

4. *Gaining access to marketing and distribution channels.* Joint ventures enable the American firm to work with a company overseas that is already familiar with the language and culture and that knows the methods for conducting business.[36] The foreign partner already has established distribution channels to get your product to the customers it knows. Apple Computer says, "We need local partners to do local business."

5. *Gaining access to the partner's know-how.* One of the reasons Chrysler entered into a joint venture with Mitsubishi was to learn its manufacturing methods in order to increase productivity and quality.

Forward-thinking small businesses are taking advantage of these opportunities by working to develop joint ventures.[37] For example, Jim Young entered a joint venture with Hyochi and Akiko Fujisawa, owners of a small Japanese construction-management company, to design, mill, and export log homes to Japan and other countries. The Fujisawas invested $1.3 million to develop Precision Craft Inc., which operates in Meridian, Idaho. The Fujisawas handle all sales and advertising in Japan, while Young and his sales staff manufacture the log homes and develop sales in Mexico, Taiwan, and Europe.[38]

Disadvantages of Joint Ventures

In spite of the five advantages, most joint ventures fail. The average success rate is 43 percent; the average life is 3.5 years.[39] Some of the common problems that lead to failure include improper selection of partners, incompatible management styles, failure to establish common goals, inability to be flexible, and failure to trust one another. A productive joint venture is similar to a marriage, which requires commitment and understanding. The life of the two companies must be joined together to create one company, but all too often, the corporate cultures of the companies clash.[40] A poorly structured joint venture can result in loss of control over product and technology.[41]

Rodney Joffee, owner of American Computer Group, of Chatsworth, California, compiles mailing-list data for mail-order firms. He needed someone to develop computer programs that would enable the firm's clients to better target their mailing lists. But three foreign partners failed to produce useful programs, and Joffee is working with a fourth. When you go overseas you have to be careful. Eastern Computers, in Virginia Beach, Virginia, developed a computer board that created foreign-language characters for producing up to 43 languages and found distributors in Hong Kong and elsewhere. Unfortunately, a counterfeit version of his product grabbed the Chinese market before Eastern could gear up for production.[42]

Finding a Partner

Finding a suitable partner can be a monumental task, and too many Americans jump at the first foreign partner they meet. Approach finding a partner like a marriage: Look carefully to be sure you have found a good match.[43]

Before scouting for a partner, a small business manager should define the characteristics the foreign partner should possess. For instance, a software company may want to join with a computer company, or a pants maker with a shirt manufacturer. Make sure both sides' aims are clear and compatible. Beware of the large corporate conglomerates, which can "gulp you up."[44]

You can get help in searching for a partner from the chambers of commerce located in overseas countries. Based on your defined profile of characteristics, a chamber can provide lists of potential partners. Other sources of assistance include international accounting firms, trade associations, and small-business consultants.

Precautions to take include setting performance standards, auditing results as a means of guarding profits, and maintaining a strong presence. Be sure to fully investigate the prospective partner. As with a domestic partnership, it is important to agree on how the joint venture will be structured. Have a lawyer draw up the contract.[45] However, it is best to keep the structure as simple as possible.[46] And keep the focus on profits.[47]

Establishing International Locations

Establishing your own international locations is the most costly and risky alternative to going global. However, it also has the highest potential for profits. Some businesses believe that reliance on exporting from the United States will not yield adequate market penetration. Plus, export-reliant companies are hostage to currency swings, differences in customers' needs in different markets, and other factors.[48] While large corporations like McDonald's and Coca-Cola have their own

Exhibit 15.2

Global strategies

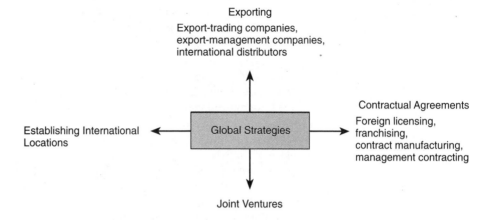

locations in many countries, many small businesses don't have the resources to use this approach to going global.

There are two major strategies for acting independently when establishing international locations: (1) Start the business from scratch. Giro Sport Design Inc., a small business based in Soquel, California, set up its own manufacturing plant in Ireland to sell its bicycle helmets in Europe.[49] (2) Buy existing businesses through mergers and acquisitions. The small software manufacturer, Oracle, first went global by exporting through overseas distributors in Western Europe, Canada, and Australia. As exports grew, Oracle began to buy out its foreign distributors to establish its own offices. Today it has customers in 90 countries.[50]

For a review of the four global strategy options see Exhibit 15.2.

Large versus Small Global Business Strategies

In this section six critical areas for global success are presented, contrasting the large versus small business applications. The development of the small business global strategy is also discussed.

Six Critical Areas for Global Success

The six critical areas for success are: developing global strategy, having a global management team, conducting global operations and products, possessing the technology and R&D, having access to global financing, and developing a plan for global marketing.[51]

Global Strategy

Generally, large international companies have the resources to establish international locations and joint ventures, whereas small international companies with limited resources tend to select contractual agreements and the export global strategies.

Part of the global strategy encompasses the structure of the global venture. The challenge is to balance centralized control at home with the right amount of decentralization of the overseas operation.[52]

Global Management Team

Trying to impose American ideas abroad, without modification, can ultimately lead to failure. Large international companies strive to hire top-level executives from around the world who provide a world view. However, small firms often do not have, and cannot afford to employ, foreign managers.

In place of foreign managers small businesses can use the services of American or foreign consultants and agents. According to Dick Lee, founder and president of Econocorp, which has sold packaging machines in different countries for over 15 years without the help of foreign managers, effective decisions can be made from the domestic office only with the aid of reliable agents.[53] However, it is important to understand other cultures by spending time overseas. Americans will have limited ability in designing products, such as furniture, that will be sold in Europe and Japan if they have never been in European or Japanese homes. The cost of extensive travel may be a negligible part of what is spent on advertising and other expenses.

Global Operations and Products

Many large international companies have operating facilities in all the major countries in which they do business. For small firms this is often not possible. However, the small firm could work to develop joint ventures and/or contract agreements in several countries as part of its global strategy.

Major international firms are striving to develop global products that require little adaptation to local markets. Small firms can also standardize their products. However, the small firm can elect to develop products according to different customer requirements in several countries.[54] Unique global products can be a differential advantage for the small business niche player. While the large company wants to view customers from different countries as being the same, the small firm can cater to cultural differences, such as aesthetic sensibilities, languages, electrical currents, and weights and measures. The small firm can capitalize on its flexibility to meet unique needs that large firms overlook. Dick Lee has developed centralized product design for special production needs. His top concern with overseas products are quality and delivery dates.

Successful global companies introduce products simultaneously on a global basis. Gillette formally introduced its Sensor razor during the 1990 Super Bowl to the United States and to 19 other countries using virtually the same commercial. Companies have learned the hard way that introducing a product in one country, then bringing it to another country, results in loss of product leadership. For example, when an American company introduces a product in the United States, the Japanese, who are watching, quickly copy the product and introduce it in Japan before the American company can do so.

When selecting products to offer overseas the firm has four major options:

1. Sell existing products as is.
2. Adapt existing products to the needs of customers in different countries.
3. Invent new products to attract new foreign customers.
4. Use a combination of these three strategies.[55]

Global Technology and R&D

Less than 50 percent of the world's innovations can legitimately lay claim to being "made in America," down from 80 percent in the 1950s. Large international companies search the world for the latest and best technology. Some countries, including Israel, Ireland, and Canada, offer attractive government R&D subsidies along with ample numbers of well-trained English-speaking researchers who work for attractive wage rates. These sites may be found by contacting foreign commerce departments.

Small firms tend to have small, or no, budget for R&D. With limited research capability it is important to scan the globe for the latest technology and to be able to quickly make it functional. Small American firms can choose to copy the latest technology rather than develop it.

Global Finance

Large international companies search world markets to get the best rates and terms for long-term financing. Generally, small firms will not be able to borrow from one foreign country and invest in another. Before a firm selects a foreign country in which to do business, financing should be considered. Small firms may be able to get loans in Taiwan and Japan at about one-half the U.S. rates. With money tight in the United States, it may be easier to get a loan in a foreign country. Like Jim Young, small businesses might be able to get a foreign partner to invest in the overseas venture. There are also venture capitalists interested in foreign opportunities.

Most small global firms should quote selling prices in the foreign currency, not American dollars. Managers need to be knowledgeable in currency exchange, global purchasing, currency hedging, and management of currency risk exposure to be successful in the global economy.

Global Marketing

Large international companies have the resources to perform all marketing functions on a global basis. For the small business this is not always possible. The small firm that wants to export can use export-service companies and distributors to perform all or some of the marketing functions for them. Contractual agreements for foreign licensing and franchising also provide the small business with foreign marketing help.

Networking is an important marketing tool in foreign sales. One method of networking is to become a member of a local trade center. The world trade center network is a computerized trading and communications database linked to more than

EXHIBIT 15.3

The six critical areas of global success

100 trade centers and their subscribing companies worldwide. Trade shows are also an effective way of networking. These trade shows contain top product offerings within an industry from around the world. Potential buyers come to see the products. Sales transactions and future sales meetings take place at these trade shows. Advertising in international industry publications and direct mail may also lead to global business transactions.[56]

Developing the Small Business Global Strategy

Becoming a successful small global business depends upon the determination and commitment of the entire organization. Management must be committed to spending time in planning and implementation. Preparation often takes six to eight months.

After the commitment has been made to expand globally, the small business manager should develop a master strategy. Don't enter several foreign markets all at once. View each foreign market as a start-up company, take time to get it established, and then move on to another.[57] The strategies should include elements from the six critical areas for success. Exhibit 15.3 reviews the six areas. The starting place is an analysis of the firm's capabilities. Does the firm have products with the potential to go global? If yes, which foreign market(s) will be targeted for penetration? Which of the four global strategies is most appropriate for the firm? Finally, the market entry strategy should be developed, along with appropriate export and transaction procedures.

Sources of Assistance in Going Global

In this section sources of assistance in going global are presented: export-service companies, agents, the Commerce Department, the SBA, and other resources. People to get to know for assistance are also discussed.

Export-Service Companies

A survey revealed that small business owners do not export because they don't know where to start, fear the complexity, or don't think information is easily available.[58] The small business owner that does not have the time or interest to do the work it takes to go global can use the services of the export-trading company or export-management company. The business can start by selling to the ETC, and if the product does well overseas, can change to the EMC to gain control over marketing, distribution, and sales. Over time the work the EMC performs could be done by the small business.

While export-service companies provide valuable services, they do so at a price. The ETC pays prices below wholesale, and the EMC charges 5 to 15 percent of gross sales; most EMCs want a two- or three-year contract.

National Federation of Export Associations (NFEA)

The NFEA's trade group directory lists some 150 export-management and trading companies and the products they handle. The directory price is around $20. For a copy contact the NFEA, 4950 Del Ray Avenue, Suite 302, Bethesda, MD 20814.

Agents

For the small business that plans a global strategy of contractual agreements, joint ventures, or the establishment of international locations, consultants or agents can provide assistance.

Agents represent the principal in dealing with a third party. Agents provide various services, including market investigation and strategic location recommendations, technology support, operations development, help with forming strategic alliances and joint ventures, administration—from employee travel to interviewing—sales and marketing forces, product or service representatives, business planning, sales consulting, and identification of appropriate trade shows.

Small Business Foundation of America

For a fee of $10 to $40 you can also get help finding agents. Call the SBFA (800) 243-7232 or in Washington, D.C. (202) 223-1104.

The U.S. Commerce Department

Programs that can help novices function overseas while utilizing all four global strategies are plentiful. Worthwhile federal help is cheap and abundant, but it can be slow. Ten different agencies provide information. A good place to start is with the Commerce Department.

The Commerce Department has a hot line at (800) 872-8723 that presents the federal export programs, including those listed here. At 68 district offices, trade counselors provide small companies with comprehensive export advice based on personal experience. They have computerized market data on 154 nations and contacts with 67 countries. Small business owners who know the language and who have a marketable product will get free help on everything from picking markets to distribution. Counselors charge for other export aids listed below.

Agent/Distributor Services (ADS)

Agent/Distributor services are *offered by the Commerce Department to locate, screen, and help evaluate agents, distributors, representatives and other foreign partners.* For $125 an ADS search may find you a foreign agent or distributor within two months. An additional $100 will buy a report on the distributor's credit and sales history. Foreign businesses feel more comfortable dealing with a company introduced to them by the government. But it is your responsibility to contact the agent and create the working relationship.

Commercial News USA

The Commerce Department ships *Commercial News USA* to 110,000 international buyers. A $250 ad in this monthly catalog is a fast, inexpensive way to generate leads and build a mailing list of potential distributors. However, you cannot promote an entire product line or target specific markets. Ads are restricted to one product and a photo, price, and phone number. You will need to screen the responses to select an agent or distributor by yourself.

Catalog and Video Shows

To show off full product lines, firms can pay $100 to $300 to have their catalogs or demonstration videos displayed at "catalog shows" held at U.S. embassies and consulates. The Commerce Department advertises each show to potential distributors and passes on the names of interested parties.

Trade Shows

Small exporters find trade shows the best way to assess competition and meet target customers on the spot. The Commerce Department sponsors dozens of trade shows abroad, with fees averaging around $4,000, plus travel expenses. It also has the Commerce Foreign Buyers Programs, which brings overseas buyers to the United States. Signing up is free, but success is a long shot.

Matchmaker Missions

Matchmaker missions are cosponsored by the Commerce Department and the Small Business Administration (SBA). Missions enable first-time exporters in specific fields like medicine or electronics to attend dozens of prearranged individual meetings with potential customers overseas. Fees run from $1,200 to $2,400 (the SBA may pay up to $750) plus travel expenses.

Market Reports

The Commerce Department's *National Trade Data Bank* details foreign demand for specific goods like cellular phones or circuit boards. The monthly publication is available free or at a nominal charge at district offices and some 400 federal depository libraries. Firms can also subscribe for $360 a year or $35 dollars for any month.

Other Publications
Business America is a magazine for small exporters covering legislation and strategies. Issues come out every two weeks for $49 a year. The Department of Commerce also offers *The World Is Your Market, A Basic Guide to Exporting,* and *Overseas Business Reports.* To order, call (202) 783-3238.

The Small Business Administration

Consulting
The SBA funds 700 small-business-development centers offering export counseling. The services of the Corps of Retired Executives and Active Corps of Executives can provide valuable assistance.

Seminars
The SBA offers seminars on different international business topics at reasonable prices.

Export Legal Assistance Network
The SBA offers the export legal assistance network, with the Commerce Department and the Federal Bar Association, to help new exporters arrange a free consultation with a trade attorney to discuss the legal aspects of entering world markets. Call (202) 778-3080.

Other Resources

Export Opportunity Hotline
The Small Business Foundation of America offers this free hotline staffed by specialists who know about federal and state exporting programs and seminars. For a fee of $10 to $40 you can also get help finding trade leads, agents, and market data. Call (800) 243-7232 or in Washington, D.C. (202) 223-1104.

Network
The World Trade Centers Association offer Network. Buy-and-sell requests for hundreds of products are listed in this database. Nonmembers can scan entries via fax. Call fax number (900) 329-4982. To become a member costs approximately $250 or so and $40 to run a two-week listing that is distributed to 75 nations. To join call (800) 937-8886.

Overseas Private Investment Corp.
OPIC offers financing, insurance, and consulting to U.S. firms that will establish international locations in developing nations. For information call (800) 424-6742.

Insurance

Exporters shipping to nations in turmoil might want export insurance, which guarantees payment for goods even if war or bankruptcy scuttles the deal. For an explanation of available policies, call the Foreign Credit Insurance Association at (212) 306-5084.

Freight Forwarders

The exporter who is looking for a customs broker or freight forwarder can get a copy of the *National Customs Brokers and Freight Forwarders Association Directory* by calling (212) 432-0050.

Publications

Exportise: An International Trade Source Book for Small Company Executives is a book with an invaluable A-to-Z exporting reference section. It is available from the Small Business Foundation of America; call (202) 223-1103. Other publications include: *Exporting from Start to Finance* and *Import/Export: How to Get Started in International Trade,* both from Liberty Hall Press; call (800) 822-8158. Other publications include:

> *The Arthur Young International Business Guide,* John Wiley (212) 850-6000.
>
> *Inside Washington: The International Business Executive's Guide to Government Resources,* Venture Marketing Corp. (800) 288-2582.
>
> *Expanding into Exports,* Price Waterhouse.
>
> *North American International Business,* (800) 274-8187.
>
> *Export Today,* (212) 563-2772.

People to Get to Know

According to the University of West Florida Small Business Institute, it's not so much what you know as whom you know. Identify and make yourself known to the following people:[59]

1. Members of the U.S. Department of Commerce, International Trade Administration, United States and foreign Commercial Services, and trade specialists.
2. The state international trade representative who serves your location.
3. United States Customs and Excise senior local officer.
4. One or more freight forwarders, who can handle rail, ship, and air merchandise movements.
5. One or more attorneys who deal with international business and one who can handle property rights (i.e., protection of patents and inventions outside the United States).
6. One or more bankers who handle international transactions such as letters of credit or wire transfers.

7. Visit your nearest World Trade Council or equivalent. See if your local chamber of commerce has an international trade section, and cultivate both.

Sources of Financing Going Global

In addition to the sources of financing discussed in Chapter 11, the small business can try the U.S. Export-Import Bank, state development agencies, the Small Business Administration, and trade finance houses.

The U.S. Export-Import Bank

American businesses looking for U.S. loans to go global should consider the Eximbank. The **U.S. Export-Import Bank** *is run by the government to spur export financing.* To encourage small businesses to sell overseas, Eximbank maintains a special office to provide information on the availability and use of export credit, insurance, guarantees, and direct and intermediary loans extended to finance the sale of goods and services abroad. The bank offers briefing programs available to the small business community. The program includes group briefing and individual discussions held both within the bank and around the country. Businesses new to exporting are not likely to get a loan to build inventory without a third-party guarantee. To qualify you have to show an excellent credit history, pledge your home as collateral, and pay annual fees besides the interest on the loan. And all businesses will need foreign orders in hand to get the loan.

State Development Agencies

Some states have special finance programs to encourage international trade. For information on any available programs in your state contact the National Association of State Development Agencies at (202) 898-1302.

Small Business Administration

The SBA has an Export Revolving Line of Credit guaranteed loan program. For details contact the nearest SBA office.

Trade Finance Houses

If these other sources do not lend you the money, you can try a small but growing number of trade finance houses like Bristol Trade Finance Inc. in Dallas, Texas, or U.S. World Trade Corp. in Portland, Oregon, which loan up to 100 percent of the cost of making foreign orders. The cost is high, with interest rates of up to 18 percent or a profit cut of up to one-third. Though expensive, this route enables firms to export without selling off part of the business to raise the needed cash.

Like starting a domestic business, taking the small business global is risky, but the rewards can be great. For the small business that wants to be successful in our present global environment, the obstacles for going global should be overcome.

Summary

Why Should the Small Business Go Global?

Business today competes in a global economy, and many small companies successfully compete globally. Even the domestic small firm may compete against foreign competition. The **international company** *conducts business in more than one country.* **Going global** is *the planned process of contracting to do business in foreign countries.* There are global opportunities in the EC and other parts of the world. The **European Community (EC)** includes *12 unified countries with one set of trade agreements.*

Strategies for Going Global

The major **strategies for going global** are: *exporting, contractual agreements, joint ventures, and establishing international locations.*

1. **Exporting** involves *the selling of goods made in one country to buyers in other countries.* Exporting is a minimal-financial-risk approach to going global. There are two specific types of export-service companies the small business can use to go global. **Export-trading companies (ETC)** *buy goods outright, paying below wholesale, and sell them abroad;* **export-management companies (EMC)** perform *a variety of export tasks for the client.* **International distributors** *purchase the product, provide the sales team, and find the buyers in foreign countries.* A **freight forwarder** *arranges the transportation of products to and from the United States.* Financing foreign sales often involves special credit arrangements such as letters of credit and bank drafts.

2. The most common **types of contractual agreements** include *licensing, franchising, contract manufacturing, and management contracting.* **Licensing** *involves* selling for a fee or royalty the rights to use patents, trademarks, copyrights, technology, processes, products, or other rights. Franchising is a form of licensing. **Contract manufacturing** involves *turning over the production function to others while retaining the marketing function.* **Management contracting** *involves* providing only management skills; the production facilities are owned by others.

3. Within a **foreign joint venture** *a domestic firm enters into a partnership with a firm in the target nation.* Joint ventures usually require a direct investment and result in a loss of control. There are five key advantages to taking on international partners: penetrating protected markets, lowering cost, sharing the risk and high R&D cost, gaining access to marketing and distribution channels, and gaining access to the partner's know-how. Because over 50 percent of joint ventures fail, a careful match must be made between partners.

4. Establishing international locations is the most costly and risky alternative to going global. But it also has the highest potential for profits. However, many small businesses don't have the resources to use this approach to going global.

Large versus Small Global Business Strategies

The six critical areas for success are: global strategy, a global management team, global operations and products, technology and R&D, global financing, and global marketing. The master strategy to going global should include elements from the six critical areas for success.

Sources of Assistance in Going Global

The small business owner who does not have the time or interest in doing the work it takes to go global can use the services of the export-trading company or export-management company.

For the small business that plans a global strategy of contractual agreements, joint ventures, or the establishment of international locations, agents can provide assistance.

Commerce Department trade counselors provide small companies with comprehensive export advice on everything from picking markets to distribution. **Agent/Distributor services** are *offered by the Commerce Department to locate, screen, and help evaluate agents, distributors, representatives, and other foreign partners.* Other sources of assistance from the Commerce Department include: *Commercial News USA,* catalog and video shows, trade shows, matchmaker missions, market reports, *Business America, The World Is Your Market, A Basic Guide to Exporting,* and *Overseas Business Reports.*

Through the SBA, the services of the Corps of Retired Executives and Active Corps of Executives, seminars, and the export legal assistance network can provide valuable assistance in going global.

Other resources include: Export Opportunity Hotline, Network, the Overseas Private Investment Corp., the Foreign Credit Insurance Association, and a variety of publications.

There are also a variety of people the small business manager should get to know when doing business internationally.

Sources of Financing Going Global

The **U.S. Export-Import Bank** is *run by the government to spur export financing.* Some of the state development agencies offer aid in going global. The SBA has an Export Revolving Line of Credit guaranteed loan program. Trade finance houses are another source of expensive capital.

Questions

1. Why should the small business go global?
2. Why would a small business want to do business in the EC?
3. List the major advantages and disadvantages of each of the four strategies for going global.
4. What is the difference between an export-trade company, export-management company, and international distributor?
5. Why would a small business want to use the services of a freight forwarder?
6. What is the difference between licensing and franchising?
7. How do large versus small businesses differ in global strategies most often selected, their global management teams, their global operations and products, global technology and R&D, global financing, and global marketing?
8. Should the small business enter several foreign markets all at once? Explain your answer.
9. What is the difference between an agent and agent/distributor services?
10. What services does the Commerce Department offer to the small business?

11. Who are some of the key people the small business manager should get to know when operating on a world-wide scale?

12. Typically, when would a small business owner seek out a trade finance house?

Application Exercises

When doing these exercises, where applicable, be sure to select a specific business, preferably one where you presently work or previously worked or a business you would like to own someday. If this is not possible, pick a specific organization to which you will refer. Be sure to identify the organization by name. Limit your answer to one or two pages per exercise.

1. Identify a small business exporter.
   (a) Give the name and products of the firm and the countries to which it exports these products.
   (b) Does the firm use an export-trading company, export-management company, or international distributor? Give the export assistance company name and functions it performs for the small business.
   (c) How did the small business owner find this source of assistance?
   (d) Does the firm use a freight forwarder or custom-house agent? If yes, identify the company and the functions it performs for the small business.
   (e) Describe the collection procedures the small business uses.
   (f) Describe some of the positive and negative experiences the small business has had in exporting.

2. Identify small businesses that use contractual agreements for licensing, franchising, contract manufacturing, and/or management contracting.
   (a) Give the name and products of the firm and the countries in which it has contractual agreements.
   (b) How did the small business owner find this source of contractual agreement?
   (c) Give details of the contract agreement.
   (d) Describe some of the positive and negative experiences the small business has had in contractual agreements.

3. Identify a small business that is a partner in a joint venture.
   (a) Give the name and products of the joint venture and the country of the foreign partner.
   (b) In which countries does the joint venture do business?
   (c) How did the small business owner find its partner?
   (d) Describe the joint venture agreement.
   (e) Which of the five key advantages to taking on international partners has the small firm experienced?
   (f) Describe some of the positive and negative experiences the small business has had with its partner.
   (g) Is this the firm's first partner?

4. Identify a small business that has established one or more international locations.
   (a) Give the name and products of the firm and the countries in which it does business.
   (c) How did the small business owner or manager find and select the location?

    (d) Did the firm start a foreign establishment from scratch or buy an existing business? Why did it use this strategy?

    (e) What percentage of its profits come from overseas?

5. Applications 1–4 are examples of the four strategies for going global. Taking each of these firms, identify the degree to which they have global management teams, global operations and products, global technology and R&D, global finance, and global marketing.

6. Taking each of the firms from applications 1–4, identify the sources of assistance not already identified that they used in going global.

7. Taking each of the firms from applications 1–4, identify the sources of financing they used in going global.

Application Situations

1. Natural Beauty Cosmetics

Jean and Tom Wentworth started to manufacture women's cosmetics with all-natural ingredients four years ago. The first two years' sales were slow and the Wentworths were just getting by. But in the third year sales increased by 50 percent after Jean and Tom attended a Foreign Buyers Program in a nearby city. The Wentworths never planned to sell their cosmetics overseas, but sales in America were slow and they had heard about the Foreign Buyers Program through the local chamber of commerce, so they decided to attend. They heard that the percentage of businesses actually finding a foreign deal were slim, but they felt they had nothing to lose by trying. After all, attendance was free; Uncle Sam was sponsoring the program.

As fate would have it, Pierre Loiselle liked their products and asked them if he could sell them in France. Jean and Tom could not believe it. All they had to do was to produce their present line of cosmetics and send them to Pierre. He would, in turn, sell them to stores in France. After all, Tom said, "We have plenty of extra production capacity. What a great way to use it while increasing profits!"

Sales and profits in years three and four were about the same. Manufacturing was running at over 90 percent of capacity. In year five a very reputable American distributor that had earlier turned down carrying Natural Beauty Cosmetics approached the Wentworths with an offer to sell their cosmetics. This distributor estimated that it could sell slightly more cosmetics per year than the French distributor.

Jean and Tom were wondering what to do. They did not want to turn down the new distributor, who was originally their first choice. Shipping costs to France ate into the profits. Since their contract expired soon, they could drop Pierre and sell the goods to the new distributor; but they were happy with their arrangement with Pierre. With a new distributor they were confident they could raise more money. They knew they would like to increase their revenue, but neither Jean or Tom wanted to manage an expanded production plant. They were not sure what to do.

Assignment

    1. Is Natural Beauty Cosmetics an international company? Why or why not?

    2. Which of the four strategies for going global did the Wentworths use?

3. Which source of assistance for going global identified in the case did Jean and Tom use?

4. Which other source, not stated in the case, did Jean and Tom probably use in conducting international business?

5. List other alternatives that Jean and Tom can implement to increase revenue without dropping Pierre or increasing production in their plant while taking on the new distributor.

6. What plan of action would you recommend to Jean and Tom?

7. Based on your answer to question 6, what sources of assistance are available to Jean and Tom in implementing the plan?

2. Trancom Inc.

Bill Rucker founded Trancom Inc. in Forth Worth, Texas.[60] Bill operates a highly specialized junk yard. He buys used diesel engines and parts and resells them to remanufacturers. Some of the parts include old crankshafts, cylinder blocks, steering boxes, and diesel injectors. One day Bill got a long-distance phone call from Leon Will in Australia. Apparently Leon got a copy of an ad Bill placed in a local magazine. Leon asked Bill for some used Ford steering boxes. Bill said he did not have any in stock but that he would try to get them for him. Bill called someone he knew who had 100 steering boxes and wanted $5 apiece for them. Bill called Leon back and said, "I'll sell you 100 of them for $25 apiece." Leon said, "Sold." Bill and Leon went on to conduct more business.

Bill realized that foreigners generally are not as well off as Americans, and they tend to rebuild engines over and over again rather than buy new ones. So using an industrial directory of truck dealers, Bill went to large rebuilders and distributors of diesel engines in Australia and England to establish buyers for his parts.

Even though Bill had solid letters of credit, he was denied credit from several banks. He ended up going to Vijay Fozdar and Fred Waldkoetter, two entrepreneurs who had launched Bristol International Ltd., which specializes in financing foreign sales. They started their business realizing that few banks have the international capability to help small companies. Bill asked for $50,000 to ship engines to Australia. Bristol approved the deal and released the funds that same day before any paper had been signed. With a source of financing, Bill went on to develop a global business. Bill says that if he can go global, anyone can.

Assignment

1. Is Trancom Inc. an international company? Why or why not?

2. Which of the four strategies for going global did Bill use?

3. Which source of assistance for going global identified in the case did Bill use?

4. Which source of assistance for going global, not listed in the case, did Bill probably use in conducting international business?

5. Would you recommend any type of contract agreements, a foreign joint venture, and/or establishing international locations to Bill as a way to increase business? If yes, specify which type. Explain your answer.

6. What source of financing is Bristol?

Integrated Case Question—CorLu Foods

Would you recommend CorLu go global? Explain your answer. Regardless of your answer—Which of the four major global strategies for going global would be most appropriate for CorLu? How do the six critical areas of global success apply? (Please refer to the Integrated Case, "CorLu Foods.")

Additional Readings

See the section "Sources of Assistance in Going Global" in the chapter for additional readings.

Endnotes

1. Peter Drucker, "The New World According to Drucker," *Business Month,* May 1989, p. 50.
2. Keith Denton, and Peter Richardson, "Globally Competitive: It's a Matter of the Right Attitude," *Business Forum,* Spring 1992, pp. 22–25.
3. Kumar Chittipeddi, and Tammy Wallett, "Entrepreneurship and Competitive Strategy for the 1990's," *Journal of Small Business Management* 29, no. 1 (January 1991), pp. 94–98.
4. William Holstein, "Going Global," *Business Week,* October 20, 1989, pp. 9–18.
5. Rosalind Resnick, "Corporate Strategy: Going Where the Big Guys Aren't," *International Business,* March 1992, pp. 52–56.
6. John Case, "Back to the Future," *Inc.,* October 1989, pp. 33–34.
7. Julie Lopez, "Going Global," *The Wall Street Journal,* October 16, 1992, p. R20.
8. Ibid.
9. Ibid.
10. Joan Feldman, "Marketing: Going Global," *Air Transport World,* April 1991, pp. 66–72.
11. Maurice Hardy, "Going Global: One Company's Road to International Markets," *Journal of Business Strategy* 10, no. 6 (November/December 1989), pp. 24–27.
12. Dyan Machan, "Educating Ivan," *Forbes,* January 6, 1992, pp. 72–77.
13. Mark Stevens, "Big Russian Market for Small U.S. Businesses," *Small Business Reports,* September 1990, pp. 24–27.
14. Earl Anderson, "Going Global Pays Off for U.S. Chemical Firms," *Chemical & Engineering News,* December 16, 1991, pp. 10–11.
15. Andre Metzer, "Europe 1992: Opportunities Await Small Businesses," *Transportation & Distribution,* February 1989, pp. 26–29.
16. Christopher Chipello, "Small U.S. Companies Take the Plunge into Japan's Market," *The Wall Street Journal,* July 7, 1992, p. B1.

17. Joann Lublin, "NAFTA Has Recruiters Expanding in Mexico," *The Wall Street Journal,* March 12, 1993, p. B1.
18. Preston Townley, "Going Global in the 1990's: The Case for Trading Blocks," *Vital Speeches,* July 15, 1990, pp. 589–93.
19. Joel Corman, Robert Lussier, and Robert Baeder, "Global Strategies for the Future: Large vs. Small Business," *Journal of Business Strategies* 8, no. 2 (Fall 1991), pp. 86–93.
20. R. J. Mockler, "Strategic Planning for Multinational Operations: The Decision Making Process Involved," *Business Research Institute,* August 1990, no. WP90s-4.
21. *A Basic Guide to Exporting* (Washington, D.C.: U.S. Department of Commerce, 1986), pp. 85–86.
22. Julie Lopez, "Going Global," *The Wall Street Journal,* October 16, 1992, p. R20.
23. Valerie Rice, "Breaking into Japan—Small U.S. Companies Find Success in a Demanding Market," *Electronic Business,* November 27, 1989, pp. 60–62.
24. Richard Lucash, James Geisman, and William Contente, "Choosing an Overseas Distributor," *Small Business Reports,* August 1991, pp. 68–71.
25. Ray Firstel, "Going Global," *Successful Meetings,* October 1991, pp. 68–72, 78–82.
26. John Lorinc, "Alliances: Going Global Made Simple," *Canadian Business,* November 1990, pp. 126–37.
27. Lopez, "Going Global."
28. Monica Jo William, "Rewriting the Export Rules," *Fortune,* April 23, 1990, p. 90.
29. Frank Go, and Julia Christensen, "Going Global," *Cornell Hotel & Restaurant Administration Quarterly,* November 1989, pp. 72–79.
30. William Holstein, "Little Companies, Big Exports," *Business Week,* April 13, 1992, pp. 70–72.
31. Joseph Pattison, "Global Joint Ventures," *Overseas Business,* Winter 1990, pp. 25–29.
32. Alfred Haggerty, "Going Global: Is the Cost Too High?" *National Underwriter,* August 13, 1990, pp. 3, 26.
33. "Working with a Partner," *D&B Reports,* March/April 1989, pp. 62–63.
34. Haggerty, "Going Global: Is the Cost Too High?"
35. Ken Gooding, "Going Global to Stay Ahead," *Business-London,* September 1990, pp. 14–15.
36. Corman, Lussier, and Baeder, "Global Strategies for the Future: Large vs. Small Business."
37. Joseph Duncan, "Big Global Opportunities for Small Business," *D&B Reports,* July/August 1990, p. 8.
38. Thomas Menzel, "Going Global From Scratch," *World Trade,* January 1993, pp. 46–50.
39. Pattison, "Global Joint Ventures."
40. Gooding, "Going Global to Stay Ahead."
41. "Working with a Partner."
42. Barbara Marsh, "Casual Business Links Often End in Divorce," *The Wall Street Journal,* June 25, 1993, p. B1.
43. Lopez, "Going Global."
44. Ibid.
45. Ibid.
46. Gooding, "Going Global to Stay Ahead."

47. Emily Plishner, "Valspar Plan Calls for Going Global," *Chemical Week,* April 15, 1992, p. 21.
48. Hardy, "Going Global: One Company's Road to International Markets."
49. Lopez, "Going Global."
50. William, "Rewriting the Export Rules."
51. Corman, Lussier, Baeder, "Global Strategies for the Future: Large vs. Small Business."
52. Linda Runyan, "Global IS Strategies," *Datamation,* December 1, 1989, pp. 71–78.
53. Corman, Lussier, and Baeder, "Global Strategies for the Future: Large vs. Small Business."
54. Denton and Richardson, "Globally Competitive: It's a Matter of the Right Attitude."
55. Peng Chan, and Robert Justis, "Developing a Global Business Strategy Vision for the Next Decade and Beyond," *Journal of Management Development* 10, no. 2 (1991), pp. 38–45.
56. Kurt Wiedenhaupt, "Taking the Grief Out of Going Global," *Business Month,* February 1990, pp. 72–73.
57. Lopez, "Going Global."
58. Lisa Moore, "Selling Abroad," *U.S. News & World Report,* March 2, 1992, pp. 64–67.
59. The University of West Florida Small Business Institute, *The International SBI,* paper presented at the Small Business Institute Directors Association, January 1993.
60. Stephen Soloman, "The Accidental Trader," *Inc.,* March 1990, pp. 84–89.

VI   THE BUSINESS PLAN

The following format presents a simplified approach for developing a business plan. In many instances, a business is complex enough, however, to warrant a business plan such as the one that is prepared by working through the CorLu Case. If this is the situation, refer to the chapters in the text for an in-depth treatment of each of the functional areas of a business.

HOW TO DEVELOP A BUSINESS PLAN

I. Introduction

A. The Business Plan

The business plan is probably the most useful and important document you, as a present or prospective small business owner, will ever put together. It is a written statement setting forth the business's mission and objectives, its operational and financial details, its ownership and management structure, and how it hopes to achieve its objectives.

B. The Purpose of a Business Plan

A well-developed and well-presented business plan can be a "treasure map"—or at least a pathway to a satisfactory profit. There are at least five reasons for preparing a business plan, which include the following:

1. It provides a blueprint, or plan, to follow in developing and operating the business. It helps keep your creativity on target and helps you concentrate on taking the actions that are needed to achieve your goals and objectives.
2. It can serve as a powerful money-raising tool.
3. It can be an effective communication tool for attracting and dealing with personnel, suppliers, customers, providers of capital, and others. It helps them understand your goals and operations.
4. It can help you develop as a manager, because it provides practice in studying competitive conditions, promotional opportunities, and situations that can be advantageous to your business. Thus, it can help you operate your business more effectively.
5. It provides an effective basis for controlling operations so you can see if your actions are following your plans.

In summary, the plan performs three important functions: (1) being an effective communication tool to convey ideas, research findings, and proposed plans to others, especially financiers; (2) serving as a blueprint for organizing and managing the new venture; and (3) providing a measuring device, or yardstick, by which to gauge progress and evaluate needed changes.

C. Contents of a Business Plan

Regardless of the specific format used, an effective plan *should include at least* the following:

1. Cover sheet.
2. Executive summary.
3. Table of contents.

4. History of the (proposed) business.
5. Description of the business.
6. Description of the market.
7. Description of the product(s).
8. Ownership and management structure.
9. Objectives and goals.
10. Financial analysis.
11. Appendixes.

II. Preparing a Business Plan

You should start by considering your business's background, origins, philosophy, mission, and objectives. Then, you should determine the means for fulfilling the mission and obtaining the objectives. A sound approach is to (1) determine where the business is at present (if an ongoing business) or what is needed to get the business going, (2) decide where you would like the business to be at some point in the future, and (3) determine how to get there; in other words, determine the best strategies for accomplishing the objectives in order to achieve your mission.

The following is one feasible approach you can use in preparing a business plan:

1. Survey consumer demands for your product(s) and decide how to satisfy those demands.
2. Ask questions that cover everything from your firm's target market to its long-run competitive prospects.
3. Establish a long-range strategic plan for the entire business and its various parts.
4. Develop short-term detailed plans for every aspect of the business, involving the owner(s), managers, and key employees, if feasible.
5. Plan for every facet of the business's structure, including finances, operations, sales, distribution, personnel, and general and administrative activities.
6. Prepare a business plan that will use your time and that of your personnel most effectively.

III. Using This Business Plan Format

This format is a detailed, practical, how-to approach to researching and preparing an actual business plan. It is designed so that you can answer the questions that are asked or find the information that is called for, record it in the spaces provided, and prepare the final plan.

A. Sources of Information

There are several possible sources of information you can use in preparing this workbook. First, we have included a case study of an actual business (the name has been disguised) that contains most of the information—CorLu Foods—that you will need to complete the plan. A second source is a business with which you trade, the business of a friend or relative, or some other business that will be willing to provide the information.

Finally, you may want to come up with a possible business to start on your own. In that case, you would start from scratch, gathering the information you need to complete the plan.

B. Completing the Business Plan

The business plan should be completed essentially in two stages. The first stage is to gather the information beginning with Item 4, History of the Business, and going through Item 11, Appendixes.

C. Appendixes

In the appendixes (beginning on a separate sheet of paper at the end of your plan) you can include pertinent information about yourself and your business that is not included elsewhere in the plan. Some possible details to include are (1) narrative history of firm; (2) organizational structure (if not done in Item 8), including management structure, organization chart(s), and résumés of key people; (3) major assumptions you have made in preparing the plan; (4) brochures or other published information describing the product(s) and services you provide; (5) letters of recommendation or endorsement; (6) historical financial information, for the past three years (if not done in Item 10); (7) details of objectives and goals; and (8) catalog sheets, photographs, or technical information.

CorLu Foods

Introduction

The CorLu case* has been developed so that students, using a common base, can answer questions specific to each chapter and, at the completion of the text, can craft a complete business plan.

---

* The name of the company has been changed at the owner's request and to protect confidentiality.

CorLu Foods

As a result of the breakup of the Soviet Union and the destruction of the Berlin Wall, the perceived need for massive defense industries and foreign commitments diminished. Having worked in the defense industry for many years, but anticipating the oncoming corporate reengineering and downsizing, both Melvin Coren and Jeanne Lu decided that it might be a good idea to go into business for themselves. Both Melvin and Jeanne had been involved in defense communication and had worked comfortably together for years. In fact, both shared a hobby of gourmet cooking and food preparation involving natural and healthy foods. Two years earlier, Marianne Coren, Melvin's wife, opened a small retail store selling health foods and natural supplements. As the store was now in its second year and reasonably successful, Melvin decided to open a second store in a different location in which he and Jeanne could share ownership and management when their jobs were phased out. They would learn what they could from the Marianne's store and, building upon its experiences, they believed they would be successful almost immediately. Both figured that their accountant would be able to provide advice and financial controls, when necessary. Incorporation papers were drawn up and filed for CorLu Company, Inc.

Location

Coren's of Providence

The successful Rhode Island operation is located in a strip shopping mall close to downtown Providence. It is next door to a Giant Market and 10 other convenience and specialty operations.

Giant is by far the major retailer on the strip. With the close proximity of Brown University and the traffic generated by Giant's popularity, the shopping center is one of Providence's most successful.

Proposed Location: Burlington, Massachusetts

The proposed location in Burlington is also a strip center consisting primarily of specialty stores and convenience stores. The major difference between Providence and this location is that there is no major "name" store on the strip. The strip is said to do well, as it is conveniently located off Route 3A, a heavily traveled road. The two owners chose the location that would be close to home (with the intention of taking over the store when either was let go by their current employer).

About the Business

The Providence store primarily consisted of retailing health foods and related products. The store itself was 2,500 square feet, including a spacious back room that was used for storage and a small office. In addition, the front store consisted of two freezers for frozen foods such as fish and other foods requiring refrigeration. Other products included health food cookbooks and cooking paraphernalia, which generated a sizable portion of the retail sales.

Regarded as a burden was the company's wholesale food operation. Chris, the store manager, considered the wholesale business to be an interruption and not very profitable because of its low profit margin. The customers of the wholesale operation were a select number of food restaurants in and around the greater Providence area that were popular with the university students who were becoming increasingly aware of the benefits of natural food; the health food market, according to Marianne, Melvin, and Jeanne, could only continue to grow.

The third generator of sales was the small take-out lunch operation that Coren's conducted. A special deal was worked out so that one of the wholesale customers provided Coren's with hot foods and simple dishes for its popular take-out lunch operation in return for "special considerations" on the wholesale end. This proved to be a very lucrative arrangement, as Coren's did not have to worry about food preparation and the restaurant was assured a daily bulk sale. The only preparation required by Coren's was to fill the final luncheon plate from heated chafing dishes.

This operation was conveniently integrated into the daily routine of the store's personnel and required no additional space or people. The gross margin on the luncheons was approximately 50 percent. Sales of luncheons averaged $5,000 per month. Costs of paper plates and utensils were approximately 2 percent of the sales.

CorLu's: Burlington, Massachusetts

The Burlington store was not scheduled to open with a luncheon service or a wholesaling business, since neither operation was likely to be significant given the store's location. Both Melvin and Jeanne were satisfied with opening simply as a retail store. They believed that the wholesaling and luncheons did not compensate the organization for the "aggravation required to run it."

Receiving/Distribution

The company owned a van that made seven to nine trips to New York per month to pick up the grocery order placed by the store manager one week earlier. The driver was a full-time employee who also helped with stocking shelves. Other employees include two cashiers and a store manager who earned a salary of $225 per week plus commissions. The owners were committed to growth and agreed not to draw salaries until the new store was operating profitably.

While the preceding information seemed to promise a successful operation, both Melvin and Jeanne realized that further research was necessary to ensure success. They both were convinced that the store could show a handsome profit without the additional two departments.

The following information was provided for their analysis by their accountant, Bailey Golden.

COREN'S OF PROVIDENCE
Balance Sheet
December 31, 1995

Current Assets

Cash	$ 28,473
Inventory	45,285
Prepaid expenses	2,000
Receivables	14,598
Total current assets	$ 90,506

Equipment and Improvements

Equipment	14,963
Furniture	12,730
Leasehold improvements (sign included)	11,401
Less accumulated depreciation	21,000
Total assets	$108,450

Liabilities and Equity

Accounts payable	$ 33,810
Accrued expenses	2,539
Income tax	6,013
Total current liabilities	$ 45,362

Long-Term Liabilities

Common Stock, no par, authorized 300 shares issued and outstanding, 100 shares	5,000
Retained earnings	61,088
Total liabilities and equity	$108,450

COREN'S OF PROVIDENCE
Income Statement
December 31, 1995

Retail sales	$114,694
Retail cost of goods	33,097
Retail gross margin	81,547
Wholesale sales	84,000
Wholesale cost of goods	71,400
Wholesale gross margin	12,600
Hot food sales	65,062
Hot food cost of goods	32,531
Hot food gross margin	32,531
Total sales	$236,706
Total cost of goods	137,838
Total gross margin	125,868

Selling Expenses

In-freight	7,712
Store supplies	4,798
Net payroll	23,872
FICA	3,994
FWT (all taxes)	1,698
RIWT	324
FUTA	928
R.I. unemployment	1,285
TDS	660
State sales tax	4,868
Gas	652
Telephone	1,184
Advertising	60
Registration/license	100
Utensils	149
Casual labor	975
Maintenance repair	50
Auto maintenance	4,512
Truck rental	1,336
Pest control	90
Rubbish removal	484
Total selling expenses	$ 59,735

(*continued*)

COREN'S OF PROVIDENCE
Income Statement
December 31, 1995
(Concluded)

General Administrative

Rent	$ 11,000
Petty cash	2,326
Common area	759
Security	295
Property tax	911
City tax	350
Electric	5,124
Store insurance	1,540
Auto insurance	1,911
Interest	1,698
Travel	2,088
Cleaning	1,458
Accounting	800
Estimated intercompany exchange	4,000
Data processing	678
Total general administrative expenses	34,138
Miscellaneous expenses	458
Total expenses	$ 94,311
Net income	$ 31,537

COREN'S OF PROVIDENCE
Pro Forma Income Statement
Year Ending December 31, 1995

Retail sales	$138,955
Retail cost of goods sold	40,297
Retail gross margin	$ 98,658
Wholesale sales	$103,217
Wholesale cost of goods sold	87,729
Wholesale gross margin	15,482
Hot food sales	80,984
Hot food cost of goods sold	40,492
Hot food gross margin	40,492
Total sales	$323,150
Total cost of goods	168,518
Total gross margin	154,632
Total expenses	108,854
(plus advertising)	7,986
	$116,826
Net profit	$ 37,806

Total sales and expenses have been increased by 15.4 percent as compared to the actual increase in January, February, and March of 1994. New advertising expense has been included in this statement.

CORLU'S OF BURLINGTON
Pro Forma Balance Sheet
May 1, 1995

Current Assets

Cash	$ 5,000
Inventory	40,000
Total current assets	$45,000

Equipment and Improvements

Equipment	19,500
Office furniture	1,500
Leasehold improvements	14,000
Total equipment and improvement	35,000
Less depreciation*	0
Total assets	$80,000

Liabilities and Equity

Current liabilities

Current portion long-term debt	0
Accrued expenses	0
Total current liabilities	0
Long-term debt	40,000
Paid-in capital	40,000
	$80,000

*No depreciation as of this date (May 2), for the store has not legally started operations.

CORLU'S OF BURLINGTON
Pro Forma Income Statement
May 21, 1995

Retail sales (1)	$114,761
Retail cost of goods	33,096
Retail gross margin	81,547
Wholesale sales (2)	0
Hot food sales (3)	0
Total sales	114,761
Total cost of goods sold	33,092
Total gross margin	$ 81,547

Selling Expenses

Supplies expense	$ 3,500
FICA	
FWT	
FUTA	
Mass. unemployment TDI	9,950
Taxes (prop., income)	3,000
Advertising and design	3,000
Truck	7,000
Office expense	7,000
Telephone	600
Registration/license	1,500
Buying expense	500
Payroll	35,000
Total selling expenses	$66,050

General and Administrative Expenses

Rent	$ 20,900
Bank interest	12,000
Insurance	500
Automobile insurance	1,000
Legal	1,000
Accounting	500
Rubbish removal	800
Utilities	7,000
Automobile	1,000
New subscriptions; donations	500
Total general administrative	466,700
Total expense	112,750
Net profit (loss)	$(−21,203)

(1) Retail sales: (114,761) same figures as retail sales in Providence; comparing market areas, this figure may be high.
(2) Wholesale: No wholesale operation has been developed in Burlington.
(3) Hot Foods Sales: No hot food operation has been developed because of zoning regulations against cooking in the store.

Before deciding where to locate the Massachusetts store, Melvin and Jeanne assembled the following demographic information.

I. General Statement

1.	Town	Burlington
2.	County	Middlesex
3.	Location	Northeastern Massachusetts, bordered by Bedford on the west, Billerica on the northwest, Wilmington on the northeast, Woburn on the southeast and south, and Lexington on the south. It is about 14 miles from Boston, 13 miles from Lowell, 41 miles from Fitchburg, and 224 miles from New York City.

4.	Population	1970	3,250
		1975	5,225
		1980	12,852
		1985	19,473
		1990	21,980
5.	Land area		11.84 square miles
6.	Density	1970	274 persons per square mile
		1975	441 persons per square mile
		1980	1,085 persons per square mile
		1985	1,645 persons per square mile
		1990	1,856 persons per square mile

7.	Climate	Normal temperature in January—26.7°F Normal temperature in July—73.6°F Normal annual precipitation—43.34 inches
8.	Elevation at town hall	Approximately 220 feet above mean sea level.
9.	Topographical characteristics	Terrain is uneven and diversified by conspicuous hills rising to an elevation of about 200 feet. Soil is a mixture of moist but somewhat rough and stony types, and moist soils of good texture.
10.	Plates	U.S.G.S. Topographic Lexington, Wilmington
11.	Aerial survey photos	Aerial survey photos for this municipality are available. For further information contact: Planning Assistance Section, Mass. Department of Community Affairs, 141 Milk St., Boston, MA

B. 1. Incorporated as a town: February 20, 1799
C. 1. Type of government: Town meeting
   2. Special districts: 7th Massachusetts Congressional District
                                   6th Councillor District
                                   23rd Middlesex State Representative
                                   District

   Statistical area   Boston Standard Metropolitan
                                   Massachusetts Bay Transportation
                                   Authority

II. Population—U.S. Census: 1990

A–1 During the decade 1980 to 1990, the population of Burlington increased by 9,128, or 71 percent. Since the excess of births over deaths was 4,082, the net in-migration during this period was 5,046.

B–1 Number of People—Ratio to 1955

Year	Number	Burlington (%)	Boston SMSA* (%)
1960	2,275	132.1	101.9
1965	2,656	154.2	106.7
1970	2,250	188.7	111.2
1975	5,225	303.4	113.1
1980	12,852	746.3	119.5
1985	19,743	1,130.8	120.0
1990	21,980	1,276.5	126.8

* Standard Metropolitan Statistical Area.

B–2 Age Composition

Age	Number	Percent of Burlington	Total Boston SMSA
1–5	4,822,482	11.3	7.9
5–14	6,542	29.8	18.6
15–19	1,797	8.2	9.1
20–64	10,470	47.6	53.1
65 and over	689	3.1	11.3
Under 18	292	46.8	31.9
21 and over	10,972	49.9	62.5
Median age		21.0	29.0

B–3 Racial Data

	Number	Percent of Burlington	Total Boston SMSA
White	21,908	98.8	94.5
Black	141	0.6	4.6
Other	131	0.6	0.9
Foreign stock	6,549	29.8	35.4
Foreign born	1,244	5.79	0.9

Of the 6,459 persons of foreign stock, 31.7 percent were from Canada, 24.9 Italy, 11.0 Ireland, 6.0 United Kingdom, 3.6 Germany, and 2.9 Poland.

B–4 Education (Persons 25 years old and over)

	Burlington	Boston
Median number of school years completed	12.5	12.4
Completing < 5 grades	.9	3.6
Completing high school	42.8	36.8
Completing college	15.4	15.8

B–5 Occupation

Of the 12,523 persons 16 years old and over in Burlington, 8,240, or 65.8 percent, were in the civilian labor force. Of these, 66.7 percent were males and 33.3 percent females.

		Percent of Total in	
Group	Number	Burlington	Boston
Professional, Technical, Kindred	1,722	22.1	20.0
Managers, prop. and office	863	10.8	9.0
Clerical	1,391	17.4	22.9
Sales	752	9.4	7.7
Craftsmen	1,289	16.1	11.6
Foremen, operatives	993	12.4	12.8
Private household workers	5	0.1	0.7
Service	741	9.3	11.9
Laborers	194	2.4	3.4

B–6 Politics, Party Affiliation, 1990

Total registered voters	9,975	
Registered Democrats		41.90%
Registered Republicans		9.9
Unenrolled voters		49.1

B–7 Incomes of Families and Unrelated Individuals

	Burlington	Boston
Incomes < $3,000	2.8	6.1
From $3,000–$5,900	4.9	10.8
From $6,000–$9,999	16.9	23.2
$10,000—$14,000	40.2	29.8
$15,000 and over	35.2	30.1
Median income	$12,897	$8,742
Per capita income	$3,197	$3,713

III. Housing—U.S. Census: 1990

B–1 Of the 5,423 housing units in Burlington, 5,237 were occupied; and 157, or 2.9 percent, were vacant and available for occupancy. Of the occupied units 93.9 percent were owner-occupied and 8.1 percent were rented. Of the Boston Metropolitan areas, 896,273 housing units (50.4 percent) were owner-occupied, 45.5 percent tenant-occupied and 2.3 percent were vacant and available for occupancy.

B–1 Type of Structure

		Percent of Total in	
	Number	Burlington	Boston SMSA
Unit	5,127	94.7%	43.7%
2 Units	34	0.6	18.4
3 to 4 Units	17	0.3	16.3
4 or more Units	237	4.4	21.4
Moble home or trailer		0	0.0%/0.2%

B–2 New Dwelling Units*

Year	Number
1980–1984	1,455
1985–1990	1,686
1991	512

*From building permits issued

B–3 Age

Year Built	Units	Percent
1965–March 1970	833	15.4%
1960–1964	1,516	28.0
1959–1959	2,248	41.5
1940–1949	121	2.2
1939 or earlier	697	12.9

B–4 Persons per Unit

Persons	Unit	Burlington	Boston SMSA
1 person	226	4.3	19.9%
2 persons	855	16.3	28.2
3 persons	845	16.1	16.5
4 persons	1,188	22.7	14.6
5 persons	947	18.1	9.9
6 persons or more	1,176	22.5	10.9
Median persons/unit			4.1%/2.6%

B–5 Value of One-Dwelling-Unit-Structure

		Percent of	
	Number	Burlington	Boston SMSA
Under $10,000	52	1.1%	2.7%
$10,000–$19,900	1,241	25.6	29.0
$20,000–$24,900	1,776	36.7	24.4
$25,000 or more	1,774	36.6	43.9
Median value	$23,200		$23,800

B–6 Monthly Rents Plus Utilities and Heat

	Percent of	
	Burlington	*Boston SMSA*
Under $60	0.0%	3.9%
$60–$79	16.7	8.2
$80–$99	3.0	10.8
$100–$149	25.6	41.9
$150 and over	54.8	35.2
Median rent	$172	$133

IV. Economic Base

A. Historic Trends

Burlington was originally a portion of Woburn but incorporated as a separate town in 1799. Agriculture was the major economic activity throughout most of the town's history. However, some small manufacturing plants have operated at various times. Only one of these firms was in operation in 1936, engaged in curing hams. The strategic location of the town is borne out by its location on the Old Boston–Concord stage route, a situation that enlivened the village.

B. Present Economy

1. General   Burlington has undergone a considerable change in its economic base in recent years. In 1991, 440 firms reporting to the Massachusetts Division of Employment Security employed an average of 14,344 persons with a total annual payroll of $131,218,313. The three industry groups contributing most to the economy of the town in order of their importance as employers were the service industry, wholesale and retail trade, and manufacturing.

2. Manufacturing   In 1991, 61 firms reported to the Division of Employment Security that they employed an average of 3,644 persons and had an annual payroll of $34,933,567. The following firms employed 2,509 or more persons: High Voltage Engineering Corp., particle accelerators; Houghton Mifflin Co., book warehouse; Microwave Associates Inc., electronic components; Raytheon Co., consumer electronics; Inforex, Inc., computer systems equipment; Itek Corp., business machines; RCA Corp., airborne electronics systems; and United-Carr Division of TRW Inc., fasteners, electro-mechanical assemblies, switches.

3. Trade   In 1991, 53 wholesale firms reported an average of 950 employees and had an annual payroll of $8,489.054; 97 retail firms reported an average of 3,080 employees and had an annual payroll of $9,580,348.

The 1987 U.S. Census of Business reported the following retail trade data on Burlington and the State of Massachusetts:

	Burlington	State
Establishments	89	46,849
Sales	$20,674,000	$9,166,844,000
Per capita sales	$1,062	$1,761
Paid employees in workweek nearest March 12	740	308,553

Classification of business	Estab.	Sales ($000)	% of Total	Estab.	Sales ($000)	% of Total
Building materials, hardware farm equipment dealers	5	$ 417	2.0	1,797	$ 385,715	4.2
General merchandise group	2	(D)	—	1,913	1,309,348	14.3
Food stores	11	(D)	—	7,228	2,127,904	23.2
Automotive dealers	5	306	1.5	2,359	1,403,454	15.3
Gasoline service stations	12	2,770	12.4	4,318	545,326	6.0
Apparel, accessories stores	3	(D)	—	2,146	568,125	6.2
Furniture, home furnishings, equipment stores	6	168	0.8	2,750	459,518	5.0
Eating and drinking places	15	1,636	7.9	9,078	777,110	8.5
Drug, proprietary stores	4	880	4.3	1,973	294,364	3.2
Misc. retail stores	18	1,393	6.7	10,063	1,031,131	11.2
Nonstore retailers	8	186	0.9	2,224	264,844	2.9

(D) Withheld to avoid disclosure

4. Class of Worker The 1990 U.S. Census of Population, which reported information on the basis of residence rather than place of employment, showed that there were 6,084 private wage and salary workers, 918 government workers, 278 self-employed, and 0 unpaid family workers living in Burlington.

VI. Employment and Payrolls as Reported to the Division of Employment Security: Burlington

A. All Industry

Industry	Number of Firms	Annual Payroll	Average Employees	Distribution by Employees
1. Agriculture & Mining	6	$ 895,906	103	0.7%
2. Construction	70	11,997,221	980	6.8
3. Manufacturing	61	34,933,567	2,644	25.4
4. Trans., Comm. & Utilities	11	850,877	114	0.8
5. Wholesale & Retail Trade	150	18,069,402	4,030	28.1
6. Finance, Ins. & Real Estate	26	1,659,874	212	1.5
7. Service Ind.	116	62,811,466	5,261	36.7

B. Manufacturing

Group	Number of Firms	1990 Annual Payroll	Average 1990 Employees
1. Ordnance and accessories	n/a	n/a	n/a
2. Food and kindred products	n/a	n/a	n/a
3. Tobacco manufacturing	n/a	n/a	n/a
4. Textile mill products			
5. Apparel and other finished goods	1		
6. Lumber and wood	1		
7. Furniture and fixtures			
8. Paper and allied products			
9. Printing, publishing, and allied	6	$ 3,396,633	465
10. Chemicals and allied	1		
11. Production of petroleum and coal			
12. Rubber products	2		
13. Leather and leather products			
14. Stone, clay, and glass products	2		
15. Primary metal industries	3	132,427	12
16. Fabricated metal products	4	671,036	68
17. Machinery (ex. electrical)	17	7,091,627	652
18. Electrical machinery	16	13,639,145	1,414
19. Transportation equipment			
20. Professional, scientific, and controlling instruments	8	7,334,115	696
21. Miscellaneous manufacturing industry	7	2,668,584	337

*Firms included in miscellaneous manufacturing

Recognizing that financial analysis requires benchmarks, data from a leading publisher of business information provided the following ratio information for comparable retail food stores.

APPENDIX 1 **Retail Trade Food Stores**
Comparing Providence to the Industry Averages: Providence

	Coren's	*Industry*
1. Cost of operations	0.52	77.8
2. Compensation of officers	—	4.0
3. Repairs	1.7	0.3
4. Bad debts	—	0.1
5. Rent	4.6	1.7
6. Tax (excluding federal)	3.06	1.4
7. Interest	0.7	0.2
8. Depreciation	—	0.7
9. Advertising	0.25	0.5
10. Pension and other benefits	—	0.3
11. Other expenses	29	12.0
12. Net profit before tax	13.32	1.1
13. Current ratio	2.136	2.5
14. Quick ratio	1.06	0.9
15. Net sales to net working capital	5.477	21.9
16. Net sales to net worth	3.99	16.8
17. Inventory turnover	5.82	19.1
18. Total liabilities to net worth	0.64	0.9
19. Current liabilities to net worth	0.64	52.2
20. Inventory to current assets	0.50	57.9
21. Net income to net worth	47.7	27.2
22. Returned earnings to net income	193.7	40

Breakeven for the Stores

	Providence	Percent		Burlington	Percent
Total sales (1990)	263,706				
Cost of goods sold (1990)	−137,838	0.52			
*(1) Gross profit margin	125,868	0.48	(3) Retail gross profit margin of Providence store		0.29
(2) Fixed costs	94,331	0.36	(4) 112,750		

Breakeven formula (Providence):

$$x - \text{Cost of goods sold } (x) - \text{Total fixed costs} = 0$$
$$- 0.48x - 96,120 = 0$$
$$52x = 94,331$$
$$x = 181,405$$

Breakeven formula (Burlington):

$$x - \text{cogs } (x) - \text{Fixed Costs} = 0$$
$$x - 0.29 \, (x) = 112,750$$
$$0.71x = 112,750$$
$$x = 158,802$$

*(1) Gross margin is amount items marked up for profit. 48% for Providence with the combined margin of retail and wholesale.
(2) Fixed cost—figures from 1989 expense sheet.
(3) Store has not opened; figure derived from gross profit margin of Providence retail operation.
(4) Fixed costs for Burlington supplied by manager.

Breakdown Customers Surveyed—Providence Store

Date	Men	Women	White	Oriental	Indian	Black
2/19	17	30	37	3	0	7
3/3	54	80	95	22	5	12
3/6	30	38	35	17	6	10
3/19	28	36	41	12	3	6
4/5	8	13	14	5	1	1
4/9	21	29	42	4	0	4
	184	267	305	78	21	47
	41%	59%	68%	17%	5%	10%

Population—Providence, RI—167, 724
Sample Size—451

Customers' Residence and Distance from Store

I. Providence, RI Trade Area			II. Burlington, Mass. Trade Area		
By Mile	*Cumulative*	*Number of Miles*	*By Mile*	*Cumulative*	*Number of Miles*
1. 23/73 = 31%	—	1 mile	1. 12/51 = 23%	—	1 mile
2. 11/73 = 15%	34/73 = 47%	2 miles	2. 7/51 = 14%	19/51 = 37%	2 miles
3. 9/73 = 12%	43/73 = 59%	3 miles	3. 7/51 = 14%	26/51 = 51%	3 miles
4. 6/73 = 8%	49/73 = 67%	4 miles	4. 25/51 = 49%	49%	Outside 3 miles
5. 24/73 = 33%	33%	Outside 4 miles